Poetic Desire and Literary Thievery

How do we define plagiarism in literature? In this wide-ranging and innovative study, Muhsin J. al-Musawi examines debates surrounding literary authenticity across Arabic and Islamic culture over seven centuries. Al-Musawi argues that intertextual borrowing was driven by personal desire alongside the competitive economy of the Abbasid Islamic Empire. Here, accusations of plagiarism had wide-ranging consequences, as competition among poets and writers grew fierce, while philologists and critics served as public arbiters over controversies of alleged poetic thefts. Taking in an extensive remit of Arabic sources, from Persian writers to the poets of Andalusia and Morocco, al-Musawi extends his argument all the way to Ibrāhīm ʿAbd al-Qādir al-Māzinī's writing in Egypt and the Iraqi poet Nāzik al-Malāʾikah's work in the twentieth century to present "theft" as a necessary condition of creative production in Arabic literature. As a result, this study sheds light on a vast yet understudied aspect of the Arabic literary tradition, while raising important questions surrounding the rising challenge of artificial intelligence in matters of academic integrity.

Muhsin J. al-Musawi is Professor of Arabic and Comparative Studies at Columbia University. He is the editor of the *Journal of Arabic Literature* and the recipient of numerous awards including the 2002 Owais Award in Literary Criticism, the 2018 Kuwait Prize in Arabic Language and Literature, and the 2022 King Faisal International Prize for Arabic Literature in English. Recent publications include *The Arabian Nights in Contemporary World Cultures* (Cambridge, 2021), which won the Sheikh Zayed Book Award.

Poetic Desire and Literary Thievery

Economies of Intertextuality in Arabic Literature

Muhsin J. al-Musawi
Columbia University

CAMBRIDGE
UNIVERSITY PRESS

CAMBRIDGE
UNIVERSITY PRESS

Shaftesbury Road, Cambridge CB2 8EA, United Kingdom

One Liberty Plaza, 20th Floor, New York, NY 10006, USA

477 Williamstown Road, Port Melbourne, VIC 3207, Australia

314–321, 3rd Floor, Plot 3, Splendor Forum, Jasola District Centre, New Delhi – 110025, India

103 Penang Road, #05–06/07, Visioncrest Commercial, Singapore 238467

Cambridge University Press is part of Cambridge University Press & Assessment, a department of the University of Cambridge.

We share the University's mission to contribute to society through the pursuit of education, learning and research at the highest international levels of excellence.

www.cambridge.org
Information on this title: www.cambridge.org/9781009584579

DOI: 10.1017/9781009584548

When citing this work, please include a reference to the DOI 10.1017/9781009584548

First published 2026

Cover image: Hanoos Hanoos, *Twilight Lines* 2025

A catalogue record for this publication is available from the British Library

Library of Congress Cataloging-in-Publication Data
Names: Mūsawī, Muḥsin Jāsim author
Title: Poetic desire and literary thievery : economies of intertextuality in Arabic literature / Muhsin J. al-Musawi.
Description: Cambridge ; New York, NY : Cambridge University Press, 2026. | Includes bibliographical references and index.
Identifiers: LCCN 2025018936 | ISBN 9781009584579 hardback | ISBN 9781009584562 paperback | ISBN 9781009584548 ebook
Subjects: LCSH: Arabic literature – History and criticism | Plagiarism in literature | Intertextuality | LCGFT: Literary criticism
Classification: LCC PJ7519.P54 M87 2026 | DDC 892.7/09–dc23/eng/20250514
LC record available at https://lccn.loc.gov/2025018936

ISBN 978-1-009-58457-9 Hardback
ISBN 978-1-009-58456-2 Paperback

Contents

List of Figures *page* viii
Preface: Inceptions
The Battle for Words: The Underlying Economies of Desire ix
Acknowledgments xxiv

1 Canons, Thefts, and Palimpsests in the Arabic Literary Tradition 1
Transtextuality, Intertextuality, and Plagiarism? 5
Terminological Tabulation 7
Self-Arrogation under Twentieth-Century Scrutiny 10
Intertextual Narrative: Novels? 14
Intertextual Terrains: Old and New 16
Canonization and Intertextuality 17
Originality Claims and Plural Ancestry 21
The Colonial Encounter and Global South Intertexts 24
What to Reclaim from Poetic Ancestry? 27
The Canon: Dissemination and Deflection 30
Between Patching Texts and Postcapitalist Pilfering 35

2 Thresholds: Dependency and Thievery in the *Adab* Marketplace 41
Reconstituting a Literary Domain 51
The Epistemic Turn 53
Theft Allegations 57
Terms, Borders, and Horizons 61
Private and Public Properties 63
Al-ʿAskarī's Foundational Input 66
Slicing Ancestors 69
Craft in an Intertextual Space 74

3 Grounding Arabic Literary History and Literary Theory 76
Theoretical Beginnings 79
Authentication Processes 81
Diverted Theory? 86
Textual Navigations 91
Prosification and Versification 95

Reporters, Transmitters-Narrators, and Forgery 98
The Rise of Disciplines: Poetics and Criticism 101
Competitive Marketplace 105
The Centrality of a Term 108
Twentieth-Century Neo-Classicists 112

4 A Genealogy for Poetic Property: Rights, Infringements, and Arbitration 118
Cultural Diversity 119
Ḥirfat al-Adab: Obsession with Literary Pursuits 119
Booksellers, Functionaries, and Poets: Defining Plagiarism 122
Al-Āmidī: Modalities for Arbitration 124
The Fight for Distinction: Poetic Naturalness or Newness? 125
Al-Qāḍī al-Jurjānī's Mediational Stance: Its Significance for Later Criticism 128
Prioritizing Terminologies: The Slackening of a Pejorative *Saraq* 129
Tabulation: The Effort to Systemize Textual Trading 131
Al-Ḥātimī's Pioneering Manual 134
Tabulation as an Invigorating Theoretical Dynamic 140
The Consolidation of the Term *Nuqqād* (Critics) 142
Discourse on Discourse (*Kalām ʿalā Kalam*) as Justification for Fluidity 147
Placing *Saraq* in Innovation and Invention 148
Opening the Gate: No Creditors and Debtors 149
The Shift to Unique Poetic Application 153
Further Epistemological Shifts: Ibn al-Athīr's Divisions 156

5 Disputed Poetic Territories: Proponents and Interlocutors 158
Rules for Debates 159
Terms for Nonpartial Discussion 160
Exponents, Proponents, and Detractors 167
Disparities in a Cultural Market 170
Politics of Allegations 172
A Tournament for Competitors 174
The Embittered Critical Response: al-Ḥātimī 175
Undermining Strategies 178
The Knights of Poetry 180
The Problematic Position of Ibn ʿAbbād 183
The Disconcerting Fame 186
Tabulation for a Purpose 189
The Discursive Tenth Century 192

6 The Waning Economies of Textual Theft: The Andalusian Shift 198
Thievery Terminology between Ibn Rashīq and Ibn Sharaf 199
Exploding the Geographies of the Center and Periphery 201
Ibn Shuhayd's Contrapuntal Critique 204
Ibn Bassām's Treasury and *Sariqāt* Lexicon 208
The Slender Andalusian *Saraq* Lexicon 219
The Other Side of Spatial Poetics 230

Conclusion: A Sense of Unending 238

Appendix A: Adab 244

Etymology 244

Use and Evolution of the Term 244

Relevant Articles and Contributions 247

Appendix B: The Perfect Muwashshaḥ 249

Al-Aʿmā al-Tuṭīlī 250

Bibliography 251

Index 269

Figures

0.1 The nostalgic prelude initiator: Ibn Khidhām or Ḥumām (also the other Imru' al-Qays) *page* xii
0.2 *Ighārah* (friendly or intimidating raiding) xv
1.1 *Taqsīm* (balanced poetic distribution) 7
2.1 Divisions of *adab* 43
2.2 *Ijtilāb* as practiced by Jarīr 55
2.3 Classification of theft 60
2.4 Ibn Aydamir's recognition of predecessors 64
2.5 Thematic lack 68
3.1 *Naql* (thematic transposition) 95
3.2 Improving *akhdh* as adding value 104
4.1 Discursive space as interfused textuality 135
4.2 Reprehensible practices 139
4.3 Equivalence in poetic value between the originator and follower (*takāfu'*) 141
4.4 *Al-Majdūd* (fame gained by the follower at the expense of the creator) 142
4.5 *Iṣṭirāf* (to include another's verses) 146
5.1 Differentiating the craft of poetry from the craft of criticism 167
5.2 *Istilḥāq* and *ijtilāb*: unacknowledged acquisition as *saraq* in Abū 'Amrū b. al-'Alā''s view 186
5.3 Blaming al-Mutanabbī for *khal'* (invading a verse with a new rhyme) 187
6.1 Poetic openings resonating with endings 203
6.2 Permissible infringements 226

Preface: Inceptions

The Battle for Words: The Underlying Economies of Desire

Taking something from one man and making it worse is plagiarism.
George A. Moore

This book argues the case of borrowing – or what the pre-Islamic and later Arab literati placed under theft – as a matter of desire whereby every poet or writer is compelled by a desire for another's poetic property. At the bottom of this irresistible desire for the other is competition, a search for distinction that stamps the human quest. With the increasing attention to property rights under the postcapitalist economy, prominent critics like Roland Barthes drew the association between literary theft, legality, and common practices. Barthes argues: "To rob a man of his language in the very name of language: this is the first step in all legal murders."[1] Hence, the aptness of the use of *Economies* in the subtitle. Whether in whole or in part, this seeming encroachment on another's intellectual property turned into an enormous literary movement with ramifications that touch every side of life and enlist the participation and discussion not only of the literati but also of patrons and attendees of renowned *majālis* (social assemblies). The variations on *saraq* or theft are many, and their connotations or complications touch social, political, and economic lifestyles. Accusations and debates multiplied, and philologists and critics stepped in to tabulate, explain, and classify echoes, raids, and corresponding poetic renderings under acceptable and reprehensible thefts. As an outcome of this activity for several centuries, a lexicon has been growing ever since that impels us as readers to look at it anew in view of the rising challenge of artificial intelligence in matters of authorship, research, and academic integrity. Thus, this enormous body of earlier and recent scholarship, which the present study analyzes and

[1] Roland Barthes, *Mythologies* (London: Paladin Grafton Books, 1973), 52.

interrogates, is timely to demonstrate the perennial human concerns that time recommences, unsettles, or polishes every now and then.

In a neat remark on poetic circulation, imitation, emulation, and redirected repetition, Gian Biagio Conte argues what sounds like the Abbasid polymath al-Jāḥiẓ's (d. 255/868) surmise that introduces Chapter 5.[2] Conte concludes: "Once the word has issued from the living voice of the poet's personal invention and has entered the code of poetic tradition, it has the responsibility of imposing the emblematic *quality* of poetry upon its new host discourse."[3] What was once, in the eighth century, a battleground among poets, critics, and grammarians has become a given, as many Abbasid and medieval Arab critics tried to say. The summation is the locus of this study, and it might sound like another argument for intertextuality as an ultimate negotiatory space. Their contributions, especially in defining Arabic discursivity, amount to the same conclusion drawn by twentieth-century structuralists and semioticians. Their search for proper and articulate rules, then, was behind the large corpus of *sariqāt* (thefts), which, ironically, are qualified not only as proper and improper but also as refined or uncouth. Many conclude that verbal space and written script provide a shared and common lexicon, open to all, as the illustrious grammarian Abū ʿAlī al-Fārisī (d. 377/987) argues.[4] Furthermore, the celebrated critic al-Qāḍī al-Jurjānī (d. 392/1001) goes so far as to speak of refined theft (*laṭīf al-saraq*),[5] while concluding that there are only precursors and successors in the discursive space, or *kalām*, that propels further exploration of *adab* at large(see Figure 2.1), a point which he offers as a better conclusion to the heated argument on poetic ownership. Before following up his further explication, we may need to keep in mind that the claim for priority as in Abū Ṭayyib al-Mutanabbī's famed verse as a precursor provoked the anger and rebuttal of several critics and poets who exerted an effort to debunk the claim.[6] To recapitulate, al-Qāḍī al-Jurjānī argues, in line with Abū Bishr al-Āmidī (d. 370/980),[7] that actual theft takes place when a unique invented meaning or expression is taken over by another without due

[2] Full name: Abū ʿUthmān ʿAmr b. Baḥr al-Jāḥiẓ. Throughout, full names will be listed in the notes.

[3] Gian Biagio Conte, *The Rhetoric of Imitation: Genre and Poetic Memory in Virgil and Other Latin Poets*, trans. Charles Segal (Ithaca, NY: Cornell University Press, 1986), 70.

[4] Quoted in Abū ʿAlī al-Ḥātimī, *Ḥilyat al-muḥāḍarah*, ed. Jaʿfar al-Katānī [or al-Kattānī] (Baghdad: Dār al-Rashīd, 1979), 2:28.

[5] al-Qāḍī ʿAlī b. ʿAbd al-ʿAzīz al-Jurjānī, *al-Wasāṭah bayna al-Mutanabbī wa-khuṣumih*, ed. Muḥammad Abū al-Faḍl Ibrāhīm and ʿAlī Bajāwī (Cairo: ʿĪsā al-Bābī al-Ḥalabī, 1966), 206.

[6] Notably early to mid-tenth-century critics were behind a campaign against the poet, trying to refute his being a precursor.

[7] Full name: Abū al-Qāsim al-Ḥasan b. Bishr al-Āmidī.

acknowledgment.[8] In other words, al-Qāḍī al-Jurjānī situates the argument in a navigational textual space that also initiates conventions, motifs, and codes. Hence, the recourse to anciency regarding the application of certain conventions sustains a tradition without negating possibilities of contrafaction, refraction, and transformation. The most visible case in pre-Islamic poetry is the nostalgic prelude, halting at the campsite of a departed tribe, and along with it is the poet's beloved. Imaginary in most cases, the recurrent naming of women in these preludes happened to be the mainstay of a tradition before successors switched to other motifs and preludes to debunk an ancient, now obsolete, lifestyle.

The nostalgic prelude, and especially in Imru' al-Qays's popular opening, has become the mainstay in a poetics of ruination, separation, nostalgia, and a struggle for some social or communal reintegration. This is what the late Jaroslav Stetkevych shows in his masterpiece, *The Zephyrs of Najd*,[9] where he considers the poet's opening as the "*Locus classicus* of pre-Islamic *nasīb* toponymy": "Halt, let us weep, you two and I, as we remember beloved and campsite."[10]

Regardless of the precursor Ibn Khidhām or Ibn Ḥumām al-Kalbī[11] (see Figure 0.1), to whom Imru' al-Qays gives credit for an earlier prelude of nostalgia,[12] the ultimate credit goes to him for inviting every other poet to emulate, *yaḥdhū*, his opening. Latin poets seem to be aware of the need for a striking opening, and the ancient tradition of pre-Islamic poetry confirms a postulation that the opening is "a mark of the relation that it must necessarily maintain with the *quality* itself of the literary action it is initiating."[13] Thus, the pre-Islamic/Islamic poet Labīd (d. 41/661) thinks of Imru' al-Qays as the pioneering discoverer of new poetic territories.[14] A tradition is initiated, and the question of imaginative poetics, a tradition, assumes more traction and purchase than even the real and experienced. The initiation and subsequent application of the prelude's opening lines, with some contextual and verbal variations, set a convention in motion. But

[8] Abū al-Ḥasan al-Qāḍī ʿAlī b. ʿAbd al-Azīz al-Jurjānī, *al-Wasāṭah bayna al-Mutanabbī wa-khuṣūmih* (Cairo: ʿĪsā al-Bābī al-Ḥalabī, 1900), 210; *al-Wasāṭah* (1966), 181, 185–86, 191–92.

[9] Jaroslav Stetkevych, *The Zephyrs of Najd: The Poetics of Nostalgia in the Classical Arabic Nasīb* (Chicago: University of Chicago Press, 1994).

[10] Ibid., 110.

[11] On the authority of Ibn al-Kalbī, Ibn Aydamir spells the name as Ibn Ḥumām, whose first name is also Imru' al-Qays, and full name Imru' al-Qays b. Ḥumām al-Kalbī. See Muḥammad Ibn Aydamur [or Aydamir as he had his written name, 1:491] al-Mustaʿṣimī, *al-Durr al-farīd wa-bayt al-qaṣīd*, ed. Kāmil Salmān al-Jabūrī (Beirut: Dār al-Kutub al-ʿIlmiyyah, 2015), 1:401–2. Al-Ḥātimī mentions him as Ibn Ḥadhām in *Ḥilyat al-muḥāḍarah*, 2:30.

[12] Stetkevych, *Zephyrs of Najd*, 54. [13] Conte, *Rhetoric of Imitation*, 76.

[14] Full name: Labīd b. Rabīʿah (Abū ʿAqīl). See further Chapter 3.

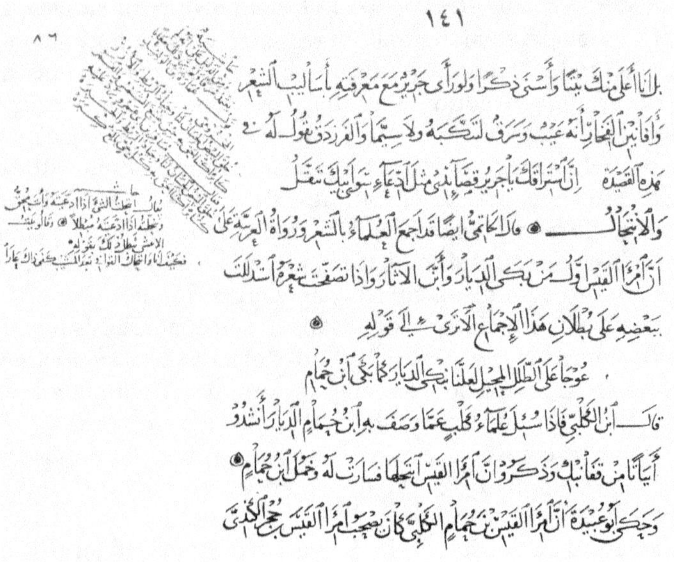
١٤١

بالنا أعلى منك بيتا وأسنى ذكرا ولو رأى جرير مع معرفته بأساليب الشعر
وأفانين الفخار أنه عيب وسرق لتركه ولاسيما والفرزدق يقول له في
هذه القصيدة إن استراقك يا جرير قصائدي مثل ادعاء سوى أبيك تنقل
والانتحال . وقال الحاتمي أيضا قد أجمع العلماء بالشعر ورواة العربية على
أن امرأ القيس أول من بكى الديار وأبن الآثار وإذا تصفحت شعره استدللت
ببعضه على بطلان هذا الإجماع الأترى في قوله
عوجا على الطلل المحيل لعلنا نبكي الديار كما بكى ابن حمام
قال ابن الكلبي فإذا سئل علماء كلب عمن وصف به ابن حمام الديار أنشدوا
وحكى أبو عبيدة أن امرأ القيس بن حمام الكلبي كان يصحب امرأ القيس بن حجر الكندي

Figure 0.1 The nostalgic prelude initiator: Ibn Khidhām or Ḥumām (also the other Imru' al-Qays)

had some philologists' and critics' strictures been applied, the same preludial openings could have supplied more *saraq* terms for the stringent group that provoked al-Qāḍī al-Jurjānī's criticism.[15]

The awareness of and engagement with pre-Islamic poetry and subsequent poetic traditions happened to be a vital component of the modernist traditions, as the poetry of the late Palestinian poet Maḥmūd Darwīsh (d. 2008) shows. After all, his mythopoeia is this canvas of an intertextual space where there is also reconciliation with poets like the pre-Islamic poet Ṭarafah b. al-ʿAbd, whose opening line for his ode's prelude functions as a motto and title for Darwīsh, whose poetic map poignantly redraws places confiscated and stolen by settlers. Thus, in his poem "Ka-washm al-yad fī muʿallaqat al-shāʿir al-jāhilī" (Like a Hand Tattoo in the Pre-Islamic Poet's Ode) the double says: "Those our relics, like a hand tattoo / in the Jahili poet's ode, they pass through us / and we through them."[16] His choice of Ṭarafah b. al-ʿAbd's opening two lines needs to be read against his "Khilāf

[15] In another print, al-Qāḍī ʿAlī b. ʿAbd al-ʿAzīz al-Jurjānī, *al-Wasāṭah bayna al-Mutanabbī wa-khuṣumah*, ed. Muḥammad Abū al-Faḍl Ibrāhīm and ʿAlī Bajāwī (Ṣaydā: al-Maktabah al-ʿAṣriyyah, 2006), 11–12, 18, 57, 157–58, 161, 181.

[16] See Muhsin J. al-Musawi, *Arabic Disclosures: The Postcolonial Autobiographical Atlas* (Notre Dame, IN: University of Notre Dame Press, 2022), 362.

ghayr lughawī ma'a Imru' al-Qays" (A Nonlinguistic Dispute with Imru' al-Qays), where the iconic pre-Islamic poet Imru' al-Qays is sliced in two: the corporal one and the poetry.[17] As Jaroslav Stetkevych argues, "Ṭarafah's … abrupt change from the abandoned encampment of Khawlah to the distant perspective of a caravan that, like ships at sea, disappears in dune-crested desert sands" signals a scene of departure of the "beloved and her entourage."[18] The shift from campsite to departure enables Darwīsh to move from lamentation to identitarian spatial politics.

Variations and fluctuations in a convention function as dynamic, not a detraction. As further proved by Darwīsh's mythopoeia and its intertextual matrixes, the late modernist poet Badr Shākir al-Sayyāb (d. 1964) would not be the last in his recourse to the nostalgic prelude to address Iraq and its south as the charming beloved that struggles for liberation from the shackles of British occupation.[19] Our contemporary novelists also intrude in this territory, and we find the narrator in the Lebanese novelist Elias Khouri's *Majma' al-asrār* (The Complex of Secrets) contrafacting Imru' al-Qays's prelude because "the longing of our master Adam for the past is a blend of reality and vision, that being the essence of a longing for ruins and campsites in ancient Arabic poetry. The very first to halt and ask others to do so, to weep and ask the rest to do so, was Adam, then Imru' al-Qays."[20] Adam is voiceless, however, whereas the poet left us his ode. The literary engagement with the first line of a poem, as the actual title and motif that runs throughout a text or recitation, initiates terms like *ḥadhw* and *muḥādhāt* ("following," "imitating"; noun: "imitation," or thematic approximation). Since the eighth century, these terms have become part and parcel of the terminological compendium whose purpose was to measure, define, and classify borrowing and to distinguish thereby not only the discernible theft from the subtle but also *al-saraq al-ṣaḥīḥ* (actual theft) from the common and shared script.[21] Al-Āmidī's *al-Muwāzanah* is focused on this distinction for reasons which Chapters 4 and 5 tend to explain. The effort undergoes further systematization in conjunction with the governance of the carefully ruled urban centers.

The increasing sense of property rights and the availability of manuals and books on rules, as required by a rising empire, need to be addressed as a major mechanism that involves many areas, ranging from land tax to the surge in the studies of *sariqāt* (thefts) as a blanket term for suspected borrowing. Caught between "the code of poetic tradition" and the

[17] See further Chapter 2. [18] Stetkevych, *Zephyrs of Najd*, 20.
[19] Terri DeYoung, "A New Reading of Badr Shākir al-Sayyāb's 'Hymn of the Rain,'" *Journal of Arabic Literature* 24 (1993): 39–40.
[20] Elias Khouri (Ilyās Khūrī), *Majma' al-asrār* (Beirut: Dār al-Ādāb, 1994), 44.
[21] See al-Jurjānī, *al-Wasāṭah* (2006), 161–62, 165, 177–79.

availability of wording and meaning in a shared cultural script, on the one hand, and the claim for property rights, on the other, poets, critics, and philologists in general should have suffered an anxiety and a sense of responsibility with respect to an expanding textual and spoken landscape, where the discussion exerted an impact on everyone, including patrons.

Cases of bias or venom notwithstanding, the presence of the philologist as arbiter could not be ignored. Gradually the counter contention of literary critics, as being the more informed in literary analysis, minimized the grammarians' intervention.[22] The circulation of a verse in pre-Islamic times, but especially under the Umayyads and the Abbasids later, could have incited others to emulate, refract, deflect, or contrafact it; to slice part of a meaning or wording; or even to force the owner to give it up, either peacefully or under threat. The case leads to the borrowing of the term *ighārah* (raid, forcing the less famed to give up a verse or more) from the lexicon of tribal wars (see Figure 0.2). Hence, the mounting accumulation of terminology, and a *saraq* lexicon has been passing through further revisions and additions ever since. In the end, a verse or part of it permeating the poetic tradition as a "code," imposing an emblematic "quality" on the poetic process, is, in its availability as part of the shared script, "already stored" in memories of poets and readers.[23] Allusions and similarities are an ultimate outcome that can generate joy, but also retort, as in the reported case of al-Mutanabbī's improvisation in Sayf al-Dawlah al-Ḥamdānī's assembly,[24] where the latter's cousin, the warrior and poet Abū Firās al-Ḥamdānī (d. 357/968), interrupted the poet's recitation every now and then, referencing echoes and allusions as thefts. Although the poet's celebrated fluency, magisterial performance, and mastery of poetry could have raised envy, venom, and frustration among the court's audience, Abū Firās's spontaneous referencing and retort might have been as effective in a divided assembly. Thus, in the same poem, when the poet reaches the verse "for the horsemen know me, and the night, and the desert, and the sword and lance, and the paper and pen,"[25] Abū Firās retorts, "What have you left for the prince?"[26] As we will notice in Chapter 5, Abū Firās harps on the

[22] Al-Qāḍī al-Jurjānī affirms the role of the knowledgeable in discursive analysis, *jahābithat al-kalām*, and literary critics to distinguish theft from common usage and classify types of thieveries. See *al-Wasāṭah* (2006), 161, 165, 177–78.

[23] Conte, *Rhetoric of Imitation*, 35.

[24] Full name: ʿAlī b. Abū al-Hayjāʾ ʿAbdallāh b. Ḥamdān Sayf al-Dawlah (r. 333–56/945–67). His emirate was a powerful, warlike frontier, and his court was known for its galaxy of poets, critics, and grammarians.

[25] A. J. Arberry, ed., *Poems of al-Mutanabbī* (Cambridge: Cambridge University Press, 1967), 72–73. The original says "horses," but as the wording connotes horsemanship, Arberry prefers the connotative sense.

[26] A detailed reference to this is in Chapter 5.

١٣٥

والإغارة ﴿ هي أن يسمع الشاعر المفلق والفحل المتقدم الأبيات الرائعة
تندر لشاعر آخر في عصره قد باينت مذاهبه في أمثالها من شعره وتكون
بمذهب ذلك الشاعر المغير أليق وبكلامه أعلق فيغير عليها مصافحة
وينتحلها مكافحة ويستنزل شاعرها عنها قوة وقهرا ويغتصبها بفضل القدرة
عنوة وقسرا فيسلمها قائلها إليه اعتمادا للسلامة ونكولا عن حربه وعجزا عن
مساجلته بمثله وهذه كانت شاكلة الفرزدق فيما استمرت له الإغارة
عليه من شعر جميل وغيره فإنه أغار وجماعة من شعراء عصره على قطع من
أشعارهم واستضافها إلى شعره وجرت في أساليب كلامه وشاكلت منظومها
بأرجح نظامه فسلموها إليه راغبين وصفحوا عنها لأمره طائعين ﴿
أخبرنا علي بن أبي غسان عن محمد بن سلام عن أبي يحيى الضبي قال قال ذو الرمة

Figure 0.2 *Ighārah* (friendly or intimidating raiding)

prince's possible anger at the poet laureate, especially upon his being accused of committing thefts to obtain rewards. The reported allusions at the base of the cousin's retort could be no more than a shared script, for, as Conte argues, as if in resonance with classical Arabic critics, "imitatio and aemulatio" were common in classical tradition, as part of "a poetic langue, a system of literary conventions, motifs, ideas, and expressions, with its laws and constraints." Moreover, poetic allusions "will occur as a literary act if a sympathetic vibration can be set up between the poet's and the reader's memories when these are directed to a source already stored in both."[27]

The battle for words is not a passing matter, and accusations of theft could damage the economies of reciprocal trading of a poem for a reward – but they could emanate from an unfulfilled desire to be on par with a poet or to possess that specific talent. Moreover, "the poetic overrides the communicative function, so that the arbitrary nature of the linguistic sign disappears to become fully motivated by the internal system of the poetic word."[28] Abū Firās could not be alien to a poetic tradition, "to a poetic *setting* rather than to individual *lines*,"[29] nor unaware of the writings of Ibn Abī Ṭāhir Ṭayfūr (d. 280/893) or those

[27] Conte, *Rhetoric of Imitation*, 37, 35, respectively. [28] Ibid., 75. [29] Ibid., 35.

of his own early contemporaries like Ibn Ṭabāṭabā al-ʿAlawī (d. 322/934) that negate the emphasis on meanings or expressions that are part of a tradition. However, his main purpose is to shame the poet laureate and antagonize him, with the ultimate goal of forcing him to depart. Even so, there is something in Abū Firās's strategy of shaming that is worth looking at, and that makes it more serious than sundry rebuttals by Ibn Khālawayh (d. 370/980) and others.[30] There is first the issue of royalty, as the ruler assumes all the iconic symbolism and its attending rituals usually associated with political power beyond the corporal presence. Thus, to claim to possess all symbols and icons of power and knowledge, as in al-Mutanabbī's verse, is a transgressive act, an excessive violation of limits, which Abū Firās highlights: "What have you left for the prince?" There is an incitement to action, not only because of "the king's two bodies," as in Ernst H. Kantorowicz's analysis that enforces the subjects' submission,[31] but also because the poet should be reduced to an ordinary size, a desperate subject in search of rewards. The accusation of thievery is intended not only to humiliate the poet but also to deprive him of rewards. In other words, the implications of the accusation rest on a deliberate effort to rescind a reciprocal prestation: a poem for a reward. Although Mauss's classic reading of gift exchange applies to archaic dealings, its theoretical thread is ahistorical, for "to give something is to give a part of oneself."[32] If, according to Abū Firās, the poet's gift amounts to nothing, there is no exchange contract. As argued by Suzanne P. Stetkevych, "The exchange of poem and prize ... [is] a ritual, a contractual one that establishes a bond of fidelity and clientage between the two."[33] Nevertheless, although the prince could have been unhappy with the poet's self-boast, he was too smart and knowledgeable to be duped by his cousin's accusations. In all cases, we have here a unique case whereby there are no borderlines between literary and financial transactions, as the desire for money is as powerful as the desire for magisterial verse.

Even so, the case of this encounter between al-Mutanabbī and his admirers, on the one hand, and Abū Firās and his group, on the other, serves as a nexus for several concerns of this book. The shaming strategy followed by strong poets' detractors varies according to the motivations

[30] Full name: Abū ʿAbdallāh al-Ḥusayn b. Aḥmad b. Ḥamdān.

[31] Ernst H. Kantorowitz, *The King's Two Bodies: A Study in Medieval Political Theology* (Princeton, NJ: Princeton University Press, 1957).

[32] Marcel Mauss, *The Gift: Forms and Functions of Exchange in Archaic Societies*, trans. Ian Gunnison (New York: Norton, 1967), 10.

[33] Suzanne P. Stetkevych, *The Poetics of Islamic Legitimacy: Myth, Gender, and Ceremony in the Classical Arabic Ode* (Bloomington, IN: Indiana University Press, 2002), 277.

behind each. Even without these detractors, poets since pre-Islamic times have thought of the arrogation of others' poetry or its like as disgraceful (*ʿār*), as the pre-Islamic al-ʿAshā Maymūn b. Qays (d. 625 CE) declares in an often-quoted verse.[34] Indeed, as Tarek El-Ariss shows, to scandalize, *faḍḥ*, is a powerful defaming or undermining tactic.[35]

This book provides some cases that relate to shaming strategies, but it primarily centers on ongoing disputations among poets and contenders. It also draws readers even more closely to the discussion of the theft/borrowing lexicon. Throughout the analysis of these two directions, there are the axial forces that cut across debates and terminology: economies and desire. Economies relate not only to gifts and contractual transactions – that is, poems for rewards – but also to the surplus value that is an ongoing process in an ongoing transaction. If the next host of a certain expression or meaning brings something better than the first producer, the first laborer or poet, this host is very much like the capitalist who draws a surplus value from a product at the expense of the laborer, the producer whose basal poem, for better or worse, undergoes further manipulation. On the other hand, at the root of poetic borrowing or theft is a desire to produce poems, and secure rewards and prestige. Motivated as such by, or simply emanating from, absorption of a discursive tradition, desire functions as a propelling dynamic. In Thomas Nagel's reading of desire, "The claim that a desire underlines every act is true only if desires are taken to include motivated as well as unmotivated desires"; adding: "and it is true only in the sense that *whatever* may be the motivation for someone's intentional pursuit of a goal, it becomes in virtue of his pursuit *ipso facto* appropriate to ascribe to him a desire for that goal."[36] Whether it is the search for distinction or an exercise of talent and erudition that may stand behind a production, the marketability of the latter situates it in economies of desire whereby poets, critics, philologists, and readers become participants, or even shareholders. The emerging commodity invites, if not enforces, this involvement, and calls therefore for regulation. Hence the birth and application of terms denoting or connoting such transactions in poetic property.

[34] For more, see Ibn Sallām (d. 231/845) in *Ṭabaqāt fuḥūl al-shuʿarāʾ*, ed. Shaykh Muḥammad Suwayd (Beirut: Dār Iḥyāʾ al-ʿUlūm, 1998), 36. For specific references, see Aḥmad Muḥammad Maʿtūq, "Al-Sharīf al-Murtaḍā's Contribution to the Theory of Plagiarism in Arabic Poetry" (PhD diss., University of Pennsylvania, 1987), 24. The poet says:

فكيف أنا وانتحال القوافي   بعد المشيب كفى بذلك عارا

How could I self-arrogate verses at such an advanced age!
That alone would be disgrace enough!

[35] Tarek El-Ariss, *Leaks, Hacks, and Scandals: Arab Culture in the Digital Age* (Princeton, NJ: Princeton University Press, 2019), 3, 22, 28, 33.

[36] Thomas Nagel, *The Possibility of Altruism* (Oxford: Oxford University Press, 1970), 29.

Terms have continued to appear such as *ighārah* (forcing the less known to surrender or give up a verse), *ihtidām* (partial takeover), *ilmām* (thematic inversion), and *naql* (thematic transposition). There are many others that address variations, denoting, for example, patching from multiple verses (*talfīq*), procuring poetic support (*ijtilāb*), self-arrogation of another's verse (*intiḥāl*), plunder (*salb*), flaying a verse (*salkh*), arrogating a poem to another (*inḥāl*), insertion of another's verse in one's poem (*istilḥāq*), and many other terms. A more recurrent term that sounds less offensive but is no less indicative of partial manipulation is *akhdh*. Along with these axial forces of desire and economy, poetry becomes a domain of creativity where a struggle for excellence is in motion. The poem is also a site of textual tension where the poet fights for the right placement of expressions and themes.

Harold Bloom's anxiety of influence works only as a partial nod in a process that functions economically and psychologically. Thus, according to Lacan, for example, desire operates in the following manner: "The object of man's desire ... is essentially an object desired by someone else."[37] If we apply the saying, minus its further accentuations, the desire for another person's verse is the reason behind the invasion in full or in part of another's property and marauding the available script. Although Arab classical and postclassical philologists and literary critics limit the discussion of this activity to citations of examples from poetry – comparisons between one verse and another, the application of terms, and instances of the struggle for excellence – the terms themselves speak up of, and lead readers to, a corpus, a verbal capital, where distinction is credited to the host poem if it improves on the basal or source poem thematically and verbally. In Gérard Genette's (d. 2018) terms, the hypertext renders the basal or the source – the hypotext – a "literature in the second degree."[38] In the Arabic literary tradition, however, credit remains the right of the precursor's text if the successor fails to surpass it in value. To improve on the expression or poetic meaning of an original amounts to an increase in value, which is the core of the intertextual or *saraq* discussion and thereby functions as the driving force in literary market economies.

Chapter 1, "Canons, Thefts, and Palimpsests in the Arabic Literary Tradition," explores the navigational space addressed and utilized by poets and novelists who are bent on an appealing production that can earn them the right to be considered new hosts of precursors' themes and expressions and thus to be thought of as writers of distinctive merit. While

[37] J. Lacan, "Some Reflection on the Ego," *International Journal of Psycho-Analysis* 34 (1953): 11–17.

[38] Gérard Genette, *Palimpsests: Literature in the Second Degree*, trans. Channa Newman and Claude Doubinsky (Lincoln: University of Nebraska Press, 1997), 5.

philologists and literary critics are on the watch to uncover infringements, the new intertext is often an elaboration of multiple textual engagements driven by a desire for something desired by another. Applied to a cultural field, and to poetry or novels in particular, this principle means that there are works that set a standard for the host who would like to own or surpass them. Simultaneously, a struggle with a strong ancestor or contemporary creates a combative arena where players devise innovations and inventions that strive to escape the strict applications of the canon. This chapter introduces the major tenth-century critics and their perspective on language and its transformation from the uncouth to the refined, as shown in poetry and poetics, where a grounding for a large intertext rests on precursors' texts that serve now as palimpsests, an almost unrecognized basal source. Twentieth-century structuralists and semioticians are also present in this chapter so as to enable readers to compare classical and twentieth-century perspectives. The chapter discusses cases, old and new, ancient and modern, to demonstrate how cultural dynamism is always given impetus and traction by this navigation. As the chapter is introductory, it goes over cases like the early twentieth-century *dīwān* controversy that brought the issues of absorption, emulation, memory, borrowing, and thefts anew to the attention of the growing twentieth-century intelligentsia.

Hence, it prepares for Chapter 2, "Thresholds: Dependency and Thievery in the *Adab* Marketplace." While there is a dependency on some ancestry, there is also an effort to go beyond ancestors in terms of style and poetic meaning or thought in concomitance with transformations that enforce new lifestyles and new ways of expression and thinking, a point which al-Qāḍī al-Jurjānī recognized. The understanding of *adab* as a combined effort of learning, cultivation of merits, and refinement, along with the contributions of critics to understand the field as an entangled discursive space, minimize the random application of *saraq*, theft, and initiate a counter understanding of production whereby inventiveness stands out as a challenge to conservative philology.[39] The consolidation of literary criticism with a terminological arsenal in order to define theft, borrowing, and shared script was not an isolated occurrence. It was part of a mounting production, a library of books on expressions, *alfāẓ*, and poetic meanings, *maʿānī*. It is also in line with the rising wave of poetic inventiveness and newness as a literary endeavor to escape the ordeal of apparent dearth and depletion of expressions. Even if there is no such thing, the mere sense of discursive exhaustibility that early tenth-century critics highlight suggests not only a relative search for independence from an overwhelming

[39] See Appendix A.

pre-Islamic poetic tradition but also an anxiety to be on par with or even surpass that tradition. Thus, more than one thesaurus is available in the cultural market. Even so, some critics who are more inclined to naturalness in poetry, not to craft and affectedness, speak of commendable poets as the ones who sustain this naturalness. Nevertheless, a gradual shift to specific intertextual terminology and parlance, like *iḥtidhā'* and *iqtidā'* (emulating and in the steps of . . .), takes over at the expense of the stark usage of *saraq*. Thus, this part of the book prepares for Chapter 3, "Grounding Arabic Literary History and Literary Theory."

This chapter is crucial to the argument of the book, as it looks upon eighth-century activity in transmission, authorship, and mentoring as being basic to a theoretical and historical grounding. Along with al-Farāhīdī's significant study of prosody and musicology, Ibn Sallām provides a subtle reading of poetry as a combination of craft, perceptive subtlety, and informativeness, qualities that were taken for granted by the learned and knowledgeable. Moreover, Ibn Sallām reiterates that, for pre-Islamic society, poetry was the public register, anchor, and resource of the Arabs' knowledge. Thus, in line with his prominent mentors, his *Ṭabaqāt al-shu'arā'* (Ranks of Champion Poets) emphasizes the role of meticulous transmitters and philologists who were then bent on filtering and authenticating transmission in order to uncover forgeries. His attention to forgeries would soon become not only exciting material for new generations of critics and philologists but also a basis for a tenth-century backlash aimed at ninth-century scholars who showed excessiveness in the random application of theft. Ibn Sallām's notes on untrustworthy transmitters would become the mainstay of the accusatory discourse of late nineteenth- and early twentieth-century Orientalists like Margoliouth – who, however, overlooked Ibn Sallām – and, among Arab scholars, Ṭāhā Ḥusayn. Lyall's response to Margoliouth's blanket negation of ancient poetry as forgery modeled on the Qur'ān builds on logic and vast knowledge to demonstrate that forgery requires prior models which should have existed in pre-Islamic times. Even if we assume there were unscrupulous transmitters, there should have been others like al-Mufaḍḍal al-Ḍabbī (d. 171/780) whose anthology of pre-Islamic poets Lyall translated and annotated. Ibn Sallām's brief accounts and conclusions traverse history and theory, and especially as the illustrious authorities whom he documents and records form a genealogy of a cultural tree that connects neatly with pivotal controversies, not only between advocates of anciency or modernity but also between grammarians and literary critics. The outcome of these debates finds its summation in a critical arsenal where Ibn Sallām's *saraq* terminologies and their approximations remain central. Thus, rather than a rupture, a deviation from an almost finished literary theory, the borrowing lexicon functions as a driving force, an energizer, in a literary marketplace that twentieth-century critics and poets expand.

Chapter 4, "A Genealogy for Poetic Property: Rights, Infringements, and Arbitration," takes the argument laid out in Chapter 3 further. It certainly builds on Ibn Sallām's application of several terms that have become part and parcel of the mounting intertextual lexicon. At the root of these terms, the cases that invite their application, there is a desire to possess what could be another person's property. The chapter draws attention to the increasing reference to the literary vocation, *ḥirfat al-adab*, which is misfortune for Abū Manṣūr al-Thaʿālibī (d. 429/1038) and, centuries later, for the poet ʿAbd al-Wahhāb al-Bayātī (d. 1999). More pivotal are the self-institutionalized philologists and critics, the experts, who act as arbiters and speak therefore for the public regarding what is happening in the literary market. These cultural market inspectors set the terms for discussions. Even if they act as advocates for one poet against another, they usually have recourse to a justification that, in the case of al-Āmidī, for example, blames al-Buḥturī for taking over, *akhadha*, too many verses from Abū Tammām's poetry; this blame is only a stepping stone to the process of accusing the latter of invading the poetry of obscure poets or leaning on his fecund memory and readings in order to buttress his own poetry, which is excessive in its inventiveness. Thus, the main point in this presumably balanced argument, which is the title of his book, *al-Muwāzanah*, is that al-Āmidī sides with al-Buḥturī because of his naturalness and application of the canon. In such a heated cultural climate, and given the need to supervise the literary market, a terminological lexicon appeared in the form of instructive manuals that would soon become the subject of further detraction or redirection. Thus, while ʿAbd al-Qāhir al-Jurjānī (d. 471/1078) emphasizes *muḥādhāt*, close following, others assess the outcome in terms of value: If the new production outshines the basal source, credit goes to the new host. In literary marketing economies function as the generative force.

Chapter 5, "Disputed Poetic Territories: Proponents and Interlocutors," foregrounds the case of disputation and debates about borrowing, theft, and intertextuality, demonstrating how that case generates not only further terminologies, adding to the already large lexicon, but also worldviews like al-Jāḥiẓ's that encapsulate what would become a late twentieth-century intertextuality as theorized by semioticians and structuralists. Al-Jāḥiẓ succinctly argues that a certain appealing saying would undergo or suffer use and modification over time until no one could claim it, although everyone regards it as its new host's property. Thus, when al-Āmidī, and later al-Qāḍī al-Jurjānī, argue that theft applies only to unique inventions, the property of a specific person, disputation was to calm down, but not to disappear. The shift in discussion centered on invention and, by implication, away from *ʿamūd al-shiʿr* (the standardized poetry canon). While previous debates relate to Abū Tammām and his detractors' critique of the presumed excessive stylistic contrivance found in *badīʿ* (inventiveness in meaning, figuration, and expression), the discursive tenth-century debates shift more toward al-Mutanabbī, as the strongest poet who was bound to gather his defenders and detractors, a two-camp situation, carefully studied by al-Qāḍī al-Jurjānī in his *al-Wasāṭah*, where he provides a concise terminology that is to feed generations of critics like Ibn Rashīq (d. 456/1064),[40] whose short chapter on thievery undermines al-Ḥātimī's significant albeit convoluted lexicon.[41] Ibn Rashīq shifts attention to al-Mutanabbī, as the most expressive and popular poet, a point which even the poet's detractors recognize in their web of theft accusations. Al-Ḥātimī's effort to denigrate the poet and his popularity exposed this writer as opinionated, venomous, and unreasonably aggressive. Even so, detractors – and they are many – failed to damage a poet whose lapses are minimal in comparison with his magnificent achievement. Critics such as the influential Ibn al-Athīr lead the discussion of thievery toward intertextuality as a discursive space, a point that the Andalusian Ḥāzim al-Qarṭājannī (d. 684/1386) almost brings to a neat formulation consisting of four categories: invention, shared property, and either a deserved hosting (*istiḥqāq*) that adds to poetic meaning and expression or an undeserved hosting that causes a decline in value, *inḥiṭāṭ*. This surmise underlines the economies of desire as matters of value, not ethics.

Chapter 6, "The Waning Economies of Textual Theft: The Andalusian Shift," takes the conversation to Andalusia. Over time, an effort intended to highlight and boost the significant contributions of Andalusians to philosophy, science, and cultural and literary studies has grown into books, treatises, and compendiums. The effort was bound to minimize the presence of theft or its neighboring terms. Even their commentaries on the poetry of Abū Tammām, al-Buḥturī, and al-Mutanabbī tend to water down such issues, in line with a general cultural preference for discursive refinement and elegance.[42] Nevertheless, Ibn Bassām – and despite his strong advocacy of Andalusian contributions – provides some terms in his rich compilation or treasury, *al-Dhakhīrah*, that center on *akhdh*, not only from poets of the eastern flank but also from other Andalusians.[43] His *al-Dhakhīrah* provides significant contributions to the study of poetry and culture in general, and his approach to thievery shows a departure from al-Ḥātimī and his ilk and an

[40] Full name: Abū ʿAlī al-Ḥasan al-Qayrawānī.
[41] Full name: Abū ʿAlī Muḥammad b. al-Ḥasan b. al-Muẓaffar al-Ḥātimī (d. 388/998).
[42] Full names of these illustrious poets: Ḥabīb b. Aws al-Ṭāʾī Abū Tammām (d. 269/845); Abū ʿUbādah al-Buḥturī (d. 284/897); Aḥmad b. al-Ḥusayn al-Mutanabbī (d. 354/965).
[43] Full name: Abū al-Ḥasan ʿAlī b. Bassām al-Shantarīnī (d. 542/1147).

affinity with Ibn Rashīq. Even his application of *ihtidām*, partial use of another's verse, in relation to Ibn Zaydūn, sounds like a deft swerve away from harsher terms. The same applies to Ibn al-Iflīlī, whose *Sharḥ* (commentary) on al-Mutanabbī's poetry falls within this line of reading. Even when Ibn Bassām quotes others who use harsh terms, he shows no inclination to depart from Ibn ʿAbd Rabbihi's preference for "borrowing" as an inclusive term. While there are cultural issues, such as the Andalusian milieu, that inform such an attitude, the initiation and flowering of the strophic *muwashshaḥāt* with their romance dialect *kharjah* (exit) demonstrate that insertions – and regardless of their *saraq* implications in the eastern flank – are only a dynamic in a shared script. Andalusian poets even resort to eastern poetry to rewrite it and fit it into their *muwashshaḥāt*, demonstrating again a discursivity that knows no limits. It is this discursivity that draws to it twentieth-century poets and novelists who preserve a rapport with an undying culture that resists closure.

Upon looking at the names of philologists, grammarians, and critics and their engagements with so many poets from ancient, pre-Islamic, and Islamic times, and assessing the enormous number of books on thefts or on literary discussion and analysis, alongside monographs on meanings and expressions, we are in the presence of a vast textual universe. Rather than being a divergence from a mainstream literary theory, this growth and its theoretical thrust endow the scene with an activity that otherwise might not be there, as the Conclusion suggests. Nowadays, when artificial intelligence, albeit with its very rigid capacity to theorize, is a tool for plagiarism, its lack of the economies of desire that propel *sariqāt* and its adjacent terminologies will deter it from actual participation in the dynamics of literary life, the poetry that involves and evokes feeling and emotions. Even so, artificial intelligence and the open possibilities of infringement on intellectual property pose a challenge to scholarship.

Acknowledgments

As readers can tell from the enormous body of terminologies, figures, names of poets, critics, linguists, grammarians, and philologists, and navigations between classical, medieval, and modem periods, the present project is a life-long occupation that started in Baghdad and accompanied me wherever I settled. The reason behind this uneasy occupation is a latent feeling that the underlying centuries-long motivation and hence dynamic for the enormous body of material on the so-called theft, and its variables, is competitiveness for distinction, a point with which the tenth-century literary critic and poet al-Qāḍī al-Jurjānī begins his poetic mediations. A compelling desire to be as distinguished as the strongest forebears, or even to beat them, or improve on other poets' verse functions as the generator that sets literary history and theory in motion, a point that the production of seven centuries demonstrates. Poets strive to be at the forefront, and a majority were known for robust memory, vast erudition, and mastery of language that outsmarts grammarians and linguists. Hence, a magisterial presence like al-Mutanabbī never settles for less than being first; and he often calls on his fecundity and erudition to dispute contending critics or grammarians and prove they are not better arbiters. His analogy of clothier (critic) and weaver (poet) is a mainstay in the battle for poetic supremacy.

I called on colleagues and friends like Roger Allen, Geert Jan van Gelder, Suzanne P. Stetkevych, Bilal Orfali, Tarek El-Ariss, and Stefan Sperl to read parts or all of the manuscript. As usual they offered a lot of help, which I am grateful for. Both Bilal Orfali and Roger Allen went through the web of names and transliterations in an arduous chase of irregularities. With his serenity and watchfulness, Geert Jan van Gelder read Chapters 2 and 3 very carefully and made many suggestions. With his insightfulness, Tarek El-Ariss stressed the underlying desire that runs through the argument of the book. An early proposed title, "Economies of Borrowing and Theft in Arabic Literary Tradition," gave way to this new title. After submitting the manuscript, I came across a title that is focused on libidinal desires, but I share with its title "economies of desire." While this edited book has a different direction and deals with the Victorian *fin de siècle*, its title's partial wording only testifies to the argument of my book that coincidental correspondence occurs regardless of culture, space, and time.

On the other hand, the enormous transliteration can be daunting, and the fear of slips accompanies such journeying. Terminologies do not always present stable meanings, as these vary according to use and application, or according to each critic's perspective. Interpretations of terms and applications abound according to their usage and place. Due to formatting needs, the verse of the second hemstitch is placed under the first in some cases instead of having both in one line.

Throughout this journey, I benefited from the keen eye of Bob Banning and his skillful detection of inconsistency or irregularity. My former student Omar Alhmashi helped in the compilation of the Index and Bibliography, while my work-study assistant Madeline Victoria Sprute has been always available to help in library errands, formatting, tagged indexing, preparing material, and securing permissions, and so on. I would like to thank our librarian, Peter Magierski, for putting me in touch with the Turkish bookseller Rifat Bali who secured permission to use images from Ibn Aydamir's manuscript al-*Durr al-farīd*, al-Fatih Collection, 3761, available at Istanbul Bölge Müdürlügü Süleymaniye Yazma Eser Kütüphanesi Müdürlügü. Thanks also go to Dr. Gesine Yildiz, Institut für Geschichte der Arabisch-Islamischen Wissenschaften Westendstrasse (Frankfurt am Main), for using the high-resolution copy of Ibn Aydamir's *al-Durr al-farīd*. I express appreciation to the Schoff Fund at the University Seminars at Columbia University for their help in publication. The ideas presented here have benefited from discussions in the University Seminar on Arabic Studies.

Profuse gratitude goes to Cambridge University Press Commissioning Editor Maria Marsh, who has always been a great support for rigorous scholarship and criticism; and I thank Natasha Burton, who showed sincere support to see the project materialize. Gratitude goes also to the production team at the Press, especially Jodie Mardell-Lines, and Muhammad Ridwaan for copyediting. The figures received the artistic attention of our MPhil journalist and photographer, Joscelyn Shawn Ganjhara Jurish, and my former student Gabriel Spratt. The front cover image is courtesy of the Iraqi Spanish painter Hanoos Hanoos. As usual my family has been always supportive, especially my son Adnan, whose technical expertise and AI specialization came to my rescue whenever the manuscript got garbled for one reason or another. My wife, Bahera, took care of the Arabic citations. My apologies in advance if the reader comes across slips.

1 Canons, Thefts, and Palimpsests in the Arabic Literary Tradition

And fame in time to come canonizes us.

William Shakespeare, *Troilus and Cressida*

The purpose of this introductory chapter is to explain and problematize the reasons behind my use in this book of a phrase like "intertextual" (and/or "transtextual") as an inclusive term that cuts across time and space. It purports to replace, or modify for good, the term *sariqāt* (roughly: plagiarisms or thieveries), which has been used extensively, but not always pejoratively, in the classical and postclassical (i.e., medieval) Arabic traditions. As argued throughout the book, Arab classicists and post-classicists often reference cases that twentieth-century structuralists, semioticians, and deconstructionists consider in terms of textual fluidity. The purpose of this chapter is therefore to prepare readers for the following five chapters that are focused on poetry and its long history of exchange, disputation, accusation, and/or mere textual transactions, while giving a nod to other discursive or performative practices. The issue of plagiarism has received attention in other cultures, which often concludes, in W. A. Heidel's words regarding the Greeks, that "there was neither a legal nor a clear moral recognition among the Greeks of rights of property in literary matters and since above all anything published was considered as thereby made *publici juris*, there really was no plagiarism."[1] Nevertheless, the issue has over time assumed a stupendous presence in the powerful Arabic poetic tradition, a presence that has ever since been inviting the participation of renowned philologists and critics. As an introductory chapter to this legacy, the focus here is primarily on current

[1] See, for example, Edward Stemplinger, *Das Plagiat in der griechischen Literatur* (Leipzig: B. G. Teubner, 1912). W. A. Heidel's review of the book is worth looking at as he draws conclusions based on the book's third section, where the author studies sources and issues of authorship and practices, followed by "verbatim quotations, (3) free rendering, (4) unconscious borrowing." W. A. Heidel, review of *Das Plagiat in der griechischen Literatur*, by Edward Stemplinger, *Classical Philology* 8, no. 3 (1913): 252. Although more concerned with the truthfulness of historical narrative, Hermann Peter's book is relevant. See Hermann Peter, *Wahrheit und Kunst Geschichtschreibung und Plagiat im klassischen Altertum* (Leipzig: B. G. Teubner, 1911).

issues. It aims to place the discussion in the context of cultural history as a dialectic of continuity and rupture. Throughout, transactional activity in its multiple forms is perceived in economic terms, simply because the issue of inventiveness or originality and imitation or stark thievery centers on the protection of intellectual property or its confiscation. As will be shown in due course, every act of gift or debt takes place within a transactional activity. If the process is condoned as a given in contemporary culture, its classical and postclassical occurrence used to invite a different response, one that ranges from condemnation to approval, depending on a layered politics that could call for mediation and arbitration, as the titles of some tenth-century books indicate.[2]

The implications involved in these seemly transactions or blunt appropriations invite further analysis whenever we place them in the framework of structuralist or poststructuralist poetics. When we address a verse or narrative making use of another without due acknowledgment or visible allusion, the primary text or the original material turns into an undertext and thereby loses its primacy. It becomes what Gérard Genette terms literature "in the second degree."[3] In Genette's phrasing the preexistent text upon which a contemporaneous or succeeding text is grafted is a *hypotext*, whereas the grafted one is a *hypertext*.[4] If we apply this same mode of reading to the raging controversy over poetic property in the classical Arabic tradition, for example, pre-Islamic poetry is very much in the position of a hypotext that roughly feeds ensuing poetries or provokes difference. Later, in early Abbasid times, there were specific cases that called for arbitration, a point that will receive further discussion in Chapters 3 and 4. As examples of current idioms and how they relate to classical Arabic idiomacy, we can argue that Abū Tammām's (d. 232/845) poetry could have served as hypotext for some of al-Buḥturī's (d. 284/897) poems. In other words, twentieth-century structuralists and semioticians have provided literary theory with a new terminological arsenal that might help in rephrasing what once sounded pejorative and accusatory phrasing. Nevertheless, current terms and applications within intertextual or transtextual spaces are not free from debt and credit transactions; nor are they beyond the scope of surplus value, as the pretext, or preexisting text, feeds the ensuing grafted one to the maximal benefit of the latter. The beneficiary is the grafted text, while the hypotext or preexistent text is literature in the second degree order, an indelible trace of a palimpsest. Intertextuality has its own logic of power, as it is an

[2] See nn. 16 and 80.

[3] Gérard Genette, *Palimpsests: Literature in the Second Degree*, trans. Channa Newman and Claude Doubinsky (Lincoln: University of Nebraska Press, 1997).

[4] Ibid., 5.

inevitable discursive practice whereby texts borrow from each other to the advantage of an emerging one that is no more than a skillful and creative reordering of others. In other words, the practice is a "definitional co-option and seizure as much as it is by reciprocity and mutuality."[5]

Whether we are addressing quotes, commentaries, unacknowledged or acknowledged borrowings, or free textual negotiation and navigation, we are in the domain of what Kristeva defines as intertextuality, a relational engagement that was not lost on Arab classicists in their enormous effort to define the scope and limits of textual or performative correspondence among poems. To explain further how structuralists and poststructuralists approach this issue as a significant shift in understanding poetics, Genette quotes Michael Riffaterre: "Intertextuality is ... the mechanism specific to literary reading. It alone, in fact, produces significance, while linear reading, common to literary and nonliterary texts, produces only Meaning."[6] In a further citation from Riffaterre, "The intertext ... is the perception, by the reader, of the relationship between a work and others that have either preceded or followed it."[7] In differentiating between intertext and intertextuality, Riffaterre argues: "An intertext is a corpus of texts, textual fragments, or textlike segments of the sociolect that shares a lexicon and, to a lesser extent, a syntax with the text we are reading (directly or indirectly) in the form of synonyms or, even conversely, in the form of antonyms."[8] He sets intertextuality in opposition because, as he argues, it "refers to an operation of the reader's mind, but it is an obligatory one, necessary to any textual decoding."[9] Looking upon these as too broad and simultaneously restrictive as "semantic-semiotic microstructures,"[10] Genette coins transtextuality, whereby preexisting or undertexts function as palimpsests upon which others are grafted. He explains: "The subject of poetics is transtextuality, or the textual transcendence of the text, which I have already defined roughly as 'all that sets the text in a relationship, whether obvious or concealed, with other texts.'"[11] Genette's intervention is free from Lacanian stipulations regarding desire; that is, the incompatibility between cause of desire as an unobtainable object, "the *objet petit a*," and the subject's

[5] Jacob R. Berman, *American Arabesque: Arabs, Islam, and the 19th-Century Imaginary* (New York: New York University Press, 2012), 51. For an intelligent application of this argument, see Rym Chakraoui, "Arabic Narrative in American Voices," *Journal of Arabic Literature* 55 (2024): 253–85.

[6] Genette, *Palimpsests*, 2. [7] Ibid.

[8] Michael Riffaterre, "Intertextual Representation: On Mimesis as Interpretive Discourse," *Critical Inquiry* 11, no. 1 (1984): 141–62.

[9] Ibid., 142. [10] Genette, *Palimpsests*, 2. [11] Ibid., 1.

undeterminability. Genette's economies of grafting are purely formalist. Nevertheless, the shift from the blunt use of "plagiarism" to relationality in defining this textual transcendence signifies a radical epistemic transformation in the age of mass communication and social media. While we need current phrasing to bring Arab classicists' and post-classicists' terminologies into ongoing conversations, we have to remember that critical poetics works adequately in a relational contextual climate, which was not overlooked by tenth-century Arab philologists and critics. It should not be surprising, therefore, that some current formulations sound at times like a slick rephrasing of antecedent parlance. Thus, Jonathan Culler's "discursive space of culture" or Roland Barthes's "infinite text"[12] recall for this chapter a ninth-century Baghdadi critical insight of Arabic discursive space, which Ibn Abī Ṭāhir Ṭayfūr (d. 280/893) emphasizes in his book as what he calls textual thieveries (see Figure 4.1).[13] Nevertheless, Julia Kristeva's effort to systematize intertextuality along two axial patterns sets the stage for further discussions that rarely depart from formalistic or semiotic readings where the issue of ethics remains an unwanted outsider. Her horizontal axis is centered on the author and her/his potential readers; whereas the vertical is more or less the dialogue of the present text with current or past texts, a notion which further discussions tend to amplify.[14] In summing up Genette's *Palimpsests*, Gerald Prince, for example, states in his brief introductory note to the book, "any writing is rewriting; and literature is always in the second degree. Now though all literary texts are hypertextual, some are more hypertextual than others, more massively and explicitly palimpsestuous."[15] Looking back in search of continuities and ruptures in cultural formative movements, one cannot help but agreeing with a common proverbial saying attributed to the Prophet's cousin, the fourth caliph, Imam ʿAlī (d. 40/661): "If speech could not be repeated, it would have long been exhausted."[16]

[12] Jonathan Culler, *The Pursuit of Signs: Semiotics, Literature, Deconstruction* (Ithaca, NY: Cornell University Press, 2002), 103; Roland Barthes, *The Pleasure of the Text* (New York: Hill and Wang, 1975), 36. For a survey of different approaches to the reader-oriented text, see Linda H. Hutcheon, "Literary Borrowing . . . and Stealing: Plagiarism, Sources, Influences, and Intertexts," *ESC: English Studies in Canada* 12, no. 2 (1986): 229–39.

[13] Quoted in al-Ḥātimī, *Ḥilyat al-muḥāḍarah*, 2:28.

[14] Julia Kristeva, *Sēmeiōtikē* (Paris: Seuil, 1969), 145. [15] Genette, *Palimpsests*, ix.

[16] Quoted in Abū Hilāl al-ʿAskarī, *Kitāb al-ṣināʿatayn: al-kitābah wa-l-shiʿr*, ed. ʿAlī Muḥammad al-Bajāwī and Muḥammad Abū al-Faḍl Ibrāhīm (Beirut: al-Maktabah al-ʿAṣriyyah, 1998), 196. See Gustave E. von Grunebaum, "The Concept of Plagiarism in Arabic Literary Theory," *Journal of Near Eastern Studies* 3, no. 4 (1944): 234–53 (in reference to Abū Hilāl's proposed conceptualizations, at 237).

Repetition is bound to occur in *ma'nā* (poetic meaning) and *lafẓ* (wording and expression), a point which mid-twentieth-century critics, semioticians, and structuralists approach with a different terminological arsenal.

Transtextuality, Intertextuality, and Plagiarism?

Although widely used in classical texts, the term *sariqāt* (plagiarisms) underwent qualifications through six centuries of debate that present it akin to what modernist critics, especially structuralists, call intertextuality, but with a body of classifications that demonstrates a highly developed literary and cultural sense.[17] Visible and deliberate acts of literary thievery were easily traced and condemned. On the other hand, although the term intertextuality is a seemingly recent coinage usually associated with Julia Kristeva and Roland Barthes, as will be shown in due time, its thematic existence goes deep into tradition under several rubrics and applications. Nowhere is this application more visible than in the discussions of *saraq* (plagiarism) as a literary term that was commonplace during a long period in Arabic literary production. Thus, regarding Arabic literary production, ancient and modern, intertextuality recalls a similar classical and premodern understanding of textual engagements as manifestations of textual navigation, subordination, anxiety, empowerment, competitiveness, and supremacy. As argued in Chapters 3–5, the Arab classicists of the ninth–tenth centuries speak of discursive influx, interfusion, textual entanglement as a given, a point which also helps initiate a tendency to tabulate the script and define what is virgin or unique in usage, expression, or meaning. Even so, and as mentioned earlier, known classicists from among ninth-century Baghdadi philologists and critics like Ibn Abī Ṭāhir Ṭayfūr admit that Arabic discourse and speech presents an interfused space,[18] a point that will receive more attention in due course. Poets and

[17] An adequate synthesis of what theorists and critics argued over six centuries is by Muḥammad b. Sayf al-Dīn Ibn Aydamur (or Aydamir, d. 710/1310), *Kitāb al-durr al-farīd wa-bayt al-qaṣīd*, ed. Fu'ād Sazkīn (Frankfurt: Ma'had Tārīkh al-'Ulūm al-'Arabiyyah wa-l-Islāmiyyah fī Iṭār Jāmi'at Frānkfūrt, 1988), vol. 1. This is a facsimile edition of Fātiḥ Collection, vols. 1 and 2, facsimile reprint of MS [1294]; vols. 3 and 4, facsimile reprint of MS 2301, Ahmet III Collection, Topkapı Sarayı Library, Istanbul, 705/1305. As for recent editions, this one is used: Ibn Aydamir, *al-Durr al-farīd* (2015), 1:338–76.

[18] Quoted in al-Ḥātimī, *Ḥilyat al-muḥāḍarah*, 2:28. Ibn Rashīq repeats what was commonly held among a class of philologists that the pre-Islamic poet 'Antarah b. Shaddād's rhetorical question about poetic repetition only stresses the rarity of originality. Abdelfattah Kilito adds, there is no discourse except in repetition. See *L'Auteur et ses doubles: Essai sur la culture arabe classique* (Paris: Éditions du Seuil, 1985); trans. Michael Cooperson as *The Author and His Doubles: Essays on Classical Arabic Culture* (Syracuse, NY: Syracuse University Press, 2001). The Arabic version is translated from the French

philologists offer an expansive terminological map to come to terms with acts of hospitality, for example, that resist common terminological applications of *saraq* (also: textual infringement). Poets often practice free textual and recitational transactions in a seemingly fluid market space.

The hospitable act, as much as that of forceful violation of another's property, alerts us to the existence of a vast textual space that invites an explorative and archaeological research beyond stock commonalities with respect to the so-called *sariqāt*. Even within the rising tendency in the ninth–tenth centuries for lexicographic organization and tabulation, there is a spatial-temporal malleability that allows navigation between the extremes of elasticity and rigidity, as will be shown in Chapters 4 and 5. Such a term as *ighārah* (roughly, raid; often forcing the less known to surrender a verse), for example, is differentially applied to a forced takeover from a living poet, or as a confiscation of a verse from a dead poet. In both cases, there is a desire for the other that redefines these as acts of love. The poet invades another's verse out of preference for the verse, and a desire to possess it, and indeed to reclaim it as one's own. An overpowering desire might not stop at partial confiscation or re-management of thematic and lexical patterns; it could even invade a unique balanced distribution, *taqsīm*, as noted by Ibn Aydamir (see Figure 1.1). The intricate side of *taqsīm* is its rare application especially in matters of borrowing or theft. Al-Ḥātimī, as quoted by Ibn Aydamir, thinks of the pre-Islamic al-Asʿar al-Juʿfī as unique in this practice, followed by the poet ʿUmar b. Abī Rabīʿah (d. 93/712). According to Ibn Aydamir's synthesis of early authorities, "I am aware of nobody who stole this *taqsīm* other than al-Khārakī [Aḥmad b. Isḥāq]," who was al-Jāḥiẓ's junior contemporary. The desire for the other is paramount here, and its textual or recitational locus notwithstanding is a perverted love. The intertextual discursive script turns into an available and inviting space.

While terminological manuals and studies or listings of poets' presumed thefts began to multiply early in the ninth century, there were instances of gratuitous gifts that come under the term *murāfadah* (yielding a verse to another; or offering poetic support, i.e., coming poetically to one's rescue), which complicate the issue of gifts and reciprocity, and problematize poetic hospitality.[19] These acts contribute to a basic understanding of a shared discursive script, which is in turn a process of substitution. Thus, even when targeting a towering name or defending his case, there is a discreet interest in being on par or in association with him. Indeed, this inclination draws the attention of modernists like

by ʿAbd al-Salām Benʿabd al-ʿĀlī, *al-Kitābah wa-l-tanāsukh* (Beirut: al-Tanwīr, 1985), 19. The Arabic version is used. The author references Borges's saying that all works are by one author, anonymous and outside time (ibid., 8); Genette, *Palimpsests*, 9.

[19] Ibn Rashīq uses this in *al-ʿUmdah* (Beirut: al-Maktabah al-ʿAṣriyyah, 2001), 2:270–71.

Figure 1.1 *Taqsīm* (balanced poetic distribution)

Gérard Genette, for example, who speaks of posthumous dedications to big names "to produce an intellectual lineage without consulting the precursor whose patronage he is bestowing upon himself in this way."[20] The whole plagiarism corpus that comprises the controversies around big names like Abū Tammām, al-Buḥturī, and al-Mutanabbī, for example, can be looked upon as an aspiration to be associated with them, or in their company, as contenders or advocates. Thus, a competitive space of love and grudge emerged, and was centered on the so-called *saraq* (infringement or stealing).

Terminological Tabulation

Each pertinent term applied to poetic transactions presents a loaded case. Especially in acts of prestation, when a gift sounds smooth, the question of reciprocity raises further complications that at times go beyond Marcel

[20] Gérard Genette, *Paratexts: Thresholds of Interpretation*, trans. Jane E. Lewin (Cambridge: Cambridge University Press, 1997), 132, quoted in Muhsin J. al-Musawi, *Arabic Poetry: Trajectories of Modernity and Tradition* (London: Routledge, 2006), 138.

Mauss's pioneering reflections.[21] To Mauss, prestation is a structuring element, for "through gifts a social and economic hierarchy is established."[22] Along this line, and centuries before Mauss, we have verses that suggest as much. Indeed, al-Rāghib al-Iṣfahānī (d. 502/1108) cites a quote that speaks of giving acts in terms of social and economic exchange:

I noticed people engaged in gift giving / As sale at a marketplace: take from me and give back.[23]

Does *murāfadah* (free poetic gift to another), for example, imply some obligation? Presumably, it is a gift, but, as Jacques Derrida argues, "For there to be a gift, there must be no reciprocity, return, exchange, counter-gift, or debt."[24] On the other hand, Emerson has something with which to define poetic gifts: "Rings and jewels are not gifts, but apologies for gifts. The only gift is a portion of thyself. Thou must bleed for me. Therefore, the poet brings his poem; the shepherd, his lamb; the farmer, corn; the miner, a gem; the sailor, coral and shells."[25] An anonymous poet of tenth-century Baghdad says:

A property gift perishes
whereas a poetic one lasts.[26]

Other instances like *iṣṭirāf* (intentional appropriation of a verse),[27] for example, raise different questions: Does this act necessitate a grudge? On the other side of this transaction, *iṣṭirāf* as a deliberate appropriation of an inviting verse looks upon the verse as a fetish inciting an uncontrollable appetite. Should this be taken as a common practice, or a substitution, which for Harold Bloom is a positive attitude: "The strength of any poet is in his skill and inventiveness at substitution"?[28] What about the emergence of terms applicable to variations on intertextual trading like *istilḥāq* (to fit into one's verse), which means in the end that it can be the successor's property as long as it serves the latter's poetic interest?

21 Marcel Mauss, *The Gift: The Form and Reason for Exchange in Archaic Societies*, trans. W. D. Halls (London: Routledge, 1990). Another edition is also used.

22 Quoted in Alan D. Schrift, "Introduction: Why Gift," in *The Logic of the Gift: Toward an Ethic of Generosity*, ed. Alan D. Schrift (London: Routledge, 1997), 5.

23 Sāmī al-Dahhān, ed., *Kitāb al-tuḥaf wa-l-hadāyā* (Cairo: Dār al-Maʿārif, 1956), 230, quoted in al-Musawi, *Arabic Poetry*, 131.

24 Jacques Derrida, *Given Time: I. Counterfeit Money* (Chicago: University of Chicago Press, 1994), 12.

25 Ralph Waldo Emerson, "Gift," in *The Logic of the Gift*, 26.

26 al-Dahhān, *Kitāb al-tuḥaf*, 156, quoted in al-Musawi, *Arabic Poetry*, 132.

27 On these terms, see Grunebaum, "Concept of Plagiarism," 239.

28 Harold Bloom, "The Internalization of Quest-Romance," in *Romanticism and Consciousness: Essays in Criticism*, ed. Harold Bloom (New York: W. W. Norton, 1970), 6.

While there are many cases of ceding a verse to another poet, as explained in Chapters 3 and 4, there are cases of blunt rejection of similar appeals in the ninth century.[29] The Abbasid poet Khālid b. Yazīd al-Kātib (d. 269/883) rejected the celebrated poet ʿAlī b. al-Jahm's (d. 249/863) plea to cede a verse to him.[30] Does this rejection destabilize a normative practice of hospitality? How did both poets respond to this situation? What are the motivations behind al-Kātib's unwillingness to cede a verse despite his gentility and refinement as exemplified in his poetry? Does the poet reject parting with a property that belongs to him, like his flesh? Nothing on record suggests al-Kātib's inhospitable disposition. On the other hand, and if we keep up with the deconstructionists, al-Kātib might have thought it appropriate to stay outside these credit/debit transactions. As noted earlier, Derrida for one suggests: "For there to be a gift, there must be no reciprocity, return, exchange, countergift, or debt."[31]

Even so, there is in the forementioned case a breach of hospitability, whereby the gift, a verse in this case, assumes great significance; or, as Derrida suggests elsewhere, "An act of hospitability can only be poetic."[32] There are several readings offered by poets and theorists in the twentieth century that attempt to grapple with the complexity of literary and cultural transactions. There is first an application of "gift" that can serve poetic transactions, especially if we take "gift" "at once as value and the – priceless – origin of all value."[33] Moreover, if Mauss's reading is "oriented by an ethics and politics that tend to valorize the generosity of the giving-being,"[34] deconstructionists like Derrida find in Paul Valéry a source not only for problematizing the issue of gift but also bringing into the discussion the specific referentiality of poetry. Derrida also builds on Mallarmé's prioritization of a poetic gift, to ask: "Why must one begin with a poem when one speaks of the gift? And why does the gift always appear to be the *gift of the poem*, the *don du poème* as Mallarmé says?"[35] The question is not rhetorical, because, as argued here, the gift of a poem, or any piece of writing, entails "the marking of a trace."[36] Taking a lead from Franz Boas, Derrida suggests that

> the gift would always be the gift of a writing, a memory, a poem, or a narrative, in any case, the legacy of a text; and writing would not be the formal auxiliary, the

[29] Full name: Abū al-Haytham Khālid b. Yazīd al-Kātib. See Grunebaum, "Concept of Plagiarism," 235n4.
[30] Ibid. [31] Derrida, *Given Time*, 12.
[32] Jacques Derrida, *Of Hospitability: Anne Dufourmantelle Invites Jacques Derrida to Respond*, trans. Rachel Bowlby (Stanford: Stanford University Press, 2000), 2.
[33] Quote in Derrida, *Given Time*, 44, from Paul Valery, *Oeuvres complés* (Paris: Bibliotheque de la Pléïade, 1960), 2:1077–58.
[34] Derrida, *Given Time*, 44. [35] Ibid., 40. [36] Ibid.

external archive of the gift, as Boas suggests here, but "something" that is tied to the very act of the gift, act in the sense both of the archive and the performative operation.[37]

Even more inviting for further exploration is the restitution: if the Baghdadi poet al-Ḥusayn al-Ḍaḥḥāk (or al-Khalīʿ, d. 250/864) ceded a verse to Abū Nuwās (d. 198/813), did he expect credit? According to the related anecdote, the former asks the latter jokingly if this is *muṣālaṭah*, that is, poetic theft.[38] Although said in jest, the wording raises the implication of forthright seizure or borrowing. Would there be future reciprocity or credit? In presenting Mauss's reading, Derrida suggests that Mauss's argument includes "making credit" into "a demand, an *interest of the thing itself*."[39] Nevertheless, there is no straightforward transaction whenever rewards are expected. Especially when we read panegyrics where an exchange is expected, a poem for reward, the panegyrist might suffer the scrutiny of others, who could strive to debase the gift and its poet out of a grudge. The label of thievery is available for the purpose, as will be shown in due course. Thus, the decried "cold economic reason" is bound to suffer interrogation in this literary market where terms and applications and actors multiply.[40] These and other terms and their implications invite problematization to justify the enormous corpus that was subsumed under plagiarism. Although qualified every now and then under commendable or reprehensible practice, the term *saraq* (plagiarism) carries negative connotations, and requires therefore reorientation as transtextuality or intertextuality.

Self-Arrogation under Twentieth-Century Scrutiny

Thus, what once fell under the rubric of plagiarism has a shared register, parlance, and postulates with current intertextual practices. They both address textual tapestries and matrices whereby threads are woven in an intricate manner. Over time, words, meanings, motifs, and thence theorizations form a constellation. Worth adding, however, is the fact that the twentieth century onward is also the scene not only of a renewal of *saraq* accusations, and the notorious rift among the Dīwān group in Egypt,[41] especially between ʿAbd al-Raḥmān Shukrī (1886–1958) and Ibrāhīm ʿAbd al-Qādir al-Māzinī (1889–1949), but also of a sweeping metafiction

[37] Ibid., 44.
[38] Quoted from Ibn Rashīq's *al-ʿUmdah* and al-Bāqillānī's *Iʿjāz al-Qurʾān* in Grunebaum, "Concept of Plagiarism," 235. See further in Chapters 3–5.
[39] Derrida, *Given Time*, 42. [40] Ibid.
[41] For more on this group or school, see A. M. K. al-Zubaidi, "The Dīwān School," *Journal of Arabic Literature* 1 (1970): 36–48, esp. 41–42.

that is self-reflective and also intertextual. Shukrī's knowledge of English literature led him to read echoes in al-Māzinī's poetry, hence accusing him of thematic borrowings and duplications. In 1917, Shukrī poses as a custodian of a literary scene, an arbiter of taste, and an advocate of literary ethics. He justifies his position as a gatekeeper and a bulwark against "chaos in arts and sciences," as "every man of letters is a guard of literature." Moreover, he has to dissociate his name from that of al-Māzinī after a long and intimate friendship.[42] Apart from claiming thematic traces and similarities traceable in al-Māzinī's poetry and some prose writings, he suggests that al-Māzinī relies heavily on Palgrave's *Golden Treasury of Songs and Lyrics* (1861). Shukrī uses terms that are part of the *sariqāt* lexicon, like *saraq*, *intiḥāl* (arrogating others' verses to oneself; i.e., claiming another's verse), and *akhdh* (seizing part of either expression or meaning from others' verses). Although well-versed in English Romantic literature, he started the criticism of his colleague in the second decade of the twentieth century when an English lexicon of textual and relational terms was still thin, in comparison with a very sophisticated classical and postclassical Arabic literary tradition. Aristotelian in focus, the European literary scene was still then unable to dig deep into Romanticism, a point which drew the attention of mid-twentieth-century critics and others since. Thus, Shukrī reverts to an available Arabic lexicon. Immersed in Romanticism, like the other members of the Dīwān group, al-Māzinī and ʿAbbās Maḥmūd al-ʿAqqād (1889–1964), he was bound to trace echoes and images from the Romantics in al-Māzinī's writings. The debate is important to this chapter, not only because of the complexity of the relationship with European cultures, especially the British and French colonial powers, which had their own literary curriculum imposed on the colonized through teaching colleges,[43] but also because al-Māzinī's poems that focus on the vocation of poetry and the character of the poet convey a correspondence with Percy Shelley's poems, and that of the German Romantics, especially Heinrich Heine, whose poetry was popular in England. Whether in his report on al-Māzinī's response to these accusations, or in al-Māzinī's own published response four years later, al-Māzinī reiterates that meanings and expressions might well become enmeshed in one's memory to spill thereafter into

[42] ʿAbd al-Raḥmān Shukrī, *al-Muqtaṭaf*, January 1917, 28, 87. Especially in the introduction to the fifth volume of his *Dīwān*; see the 1961 edition of *al-Maʿārik* cited (520–21). This piece and the rest of accusations and response are found in Aḥmad Anwar al-Jindī, *al-Maʿārik al-adabiyyah* (Cairo: Anjilo-Miṣriyyah, 1982); or under the title *al-Maʿārik al-adabiyyah fī al-shiʿr wa-l-thaqāfah wa-l-lughah wa-l-qawmiyyah al-ʿArabiyyah* (Cairo: Maṭbaʿat al-Risālah, 1961). See also nn. 44 and 45.

[43] See Muhsin J. al-Musawi, *Islam on the Street* (Lanham, MD: Rowman and Littlefield, 2009), 32. See also J. Brugman, *An Introduction to the History of Modern Arabic Literature in Egypt* (Leiden: Brill, 1984).

one's writing. The literary battle among the major figures of the first Arabic poetic movement in the twentieth century that claims renewal and deviation from some classical norms created a sensational climate that involved many contributors. Although started publicly in 1917, al-Māzinī's response in the first two parts of the Dīwān school's journal, *al-Dīwān*, was more or less an attack on Shukrī; but specific responses to plagiarism accusations appeared much later.[44] More important are his explanations in 1931 and 1934 of the irresistible identification with readings. This overwhelming desire for cherished writings coupled with claims to absent-mindedness alarmed Shukrī and other contemporaries. His responses include something that is central to the argument of this chapter, that is, the substitution of plagiarism with intertextuality. Followed by other articles and apologies, the extract on plagiarism argues as follows:

> I didn't feel bad due to his accusations of stealing because it is my disposition not to deliberately rob (*saṭw*) others or raid (*lamm ughir*; n. *ighārah*) a poet, but meanings get enmeshed as I read, and they slip into writing when absent-minded or unwary as I have a weak memory and prone to forgetfulness.[45]

Does this justification entail a wider possibility, namely, that reading with pleasure and affectionate engagement entails unguarded textual permeation? Discriminatory memory is obviously absent, but there is so much love for some writings and lyrics that they settle in one's language to generate thereby a polyphonic text that is no more than shreds and bits from several other texts. This resonates with al-Māzinī's explanation of how Mikhail Petrovich Artsybashev's *Sanin* was so captivating as a reading that he translated it from an English version,[46] and found himself identifying with its protagonist, Sanin, to become one with him. In al-Māzinī's pseudo-autobiography *Ibrāhīm al-kātib* (*Ibrāhīm* the Writer, 1931), there are many passages that recur in his own serialized translation from an English version of *Sanin* in 1922.[47] In justifying verbatim duplication, al-Māzinī does not deny the allegations of "the illustrious critic" from Aleppo: "The allegation was undoubtedly well founded. I could see how the illustrious critic had reached his conclusion. It is clear that four or five pages were borrowed

[44] *al-Dīwān*, pt. 1 (January 1921): 57–73, pt. 2 (February 1921): 177–90. A third print is also used.

[45] *al-Balāgh*, May 20, 1934, also September 1, 1934. The documented controversy appears in al-Jindī, *al-Maʿārik al-adabiyyah* (1961), 520–36 (above quote, 529). The online copy is also used: al-Maktabah al-Shāmilah (1983), ch. 2, 547–58 (above quote, 556). Al-Jindī mentioned the controversy also appeared in the journal *al-Risālah* (August 1937).

[46] For an excellent reading of this case in terms of cultural malleability, over-writing, and intertextuality, see Maria Elena Paniconi, "Reframing the Politics of Aesthetic Appropriation in the Late-Nahḍah Novel: The Case of 'Plagiarism' in Ibrāhīm al-Māzinī's *Ibrāhīm al-kātib*," *Journal of Arabic Literature* 50, no. 1 (2019): 56–80.

[47] Ibid., 57. Paniconi's translations are used.

from *Ibn al-ṭabīʿah* [i.e., *Sanin*] and placed in my novel, four or five pages that flowed from my pen while I believed they were my own words."[48] These pages "had remained embedded in my mind."[49] Furthermore, the issue of memory is raised as problematic, because "our memory is not a tidy and well-organized storehouse, it is more like a wavy sea where things float and sink against our will."[50] In his introduction to the first edition of *Ibrāhīm al-kātib* (1931), the author explains a genesis of narrative that could have started even earlier than 1925–26, which he specified as actual dates for authorship. It could have become the hypertext whereas *Sanin* is a hypotext, literature "in the second degree," a palimpsest, even though visible traces remain there as he admits. Paniconi draws on Sir Hamilton Gibb's 1933 article, "Studies in Contemporary Arabic Literature," where the scholar takes it for granted that al-Māzinī resorts to "free adaptation of episodes and methods from well-known books."[51] This free handling and reading can be read as a counter engagement, a writing back, or even a mélange. Self-identification with Sanin is an extreme and unbridled desire for the other. In al-Māzinī's witty self-analysis, he writes: "Fortunately, my head is like a sieve whose holes are too large to retain anything. In other words, my memory is always tricking me and I never know what I have done."[52] While it is true that al-Māzinī was working then in a context of malleable duality of translation and/as authorship, his tendency to identify with his readings brings us to the pleasure that Barthes explores. Al-Māzinī presents himself as the case of an author willingly molded in texts. Even so, and with an albeit feeble memory, the case raises questions of self-conscious textual absorption.

Does the proclaimed frail memory also generate the capacity for learning by heart and rehearsing passages, expressions, and images? Does self-identification with Sanin legitimate personal ownership of a specific piece? Does his translation of *Sanin*, and his affinity with lyrics by the English Romantics or Heine, pose a hard case for twentieth-century theorizations by Kristeva, Riffaterre, and Genette? Riffaterre redirects the conversation about subtexts and intertexts as one of a reader-oriented completion, not reduction:[53]

> The term [intertextuality] indeed refers to an operation of the reader's mind, but it is an obligatory one, necessary to any textual decoding. Intertextuality necessarily complements our experience of textuality. It is the perception that our reading of the text cannot be complete or satisfactory without going through the

[48] Ibid., 65. [49] Ibid., 66. [50] Ibid.
[51] Ibid., 58, quoted in H. A. R. Gibb, "Studies in Contemporary Arabic Literature," *Bulletin of the School of Oriental Studies* 7, no. 1 (1933): 20.
[52] Ibid. [53] See Riffaterre, "Intertextual Representation," 142–43.

intertext, that the text does not signify unless as a function of complementary or contradictory intertextual homologue.

Al-Māzinī poses as a reader who suffers no qualms as author: He is inadvertently implicated in self-identification, driven, as it were, by a latent desire that is an extreme case of love. Does the case require the use of the well-developed terminological *saraq* lexicon partly used by Shukrī, and al-Māzinī? Or does it sound in line with the grand philologist and grammarian Abū ʿAlī al-Fārisī's (d. 377/987) espousal of discursive malleability; and later with Ibn Rashīq's (d. 456/1063–64 or 463/1071) disposition to dismiss the thievery discussion on the ground of inevitable textual indebtedness?[54] Similar or even harder complications arise as other discursive or performative practices gain momentum over time, especially with the rise of the middle classes, the expansion of the publishing industry, mass media communication, and also the unfolding of wider prospects of intercultural and across-cultural influx in the wake of the Bandung Conference (West Jafa, Indonesia) in 1955, and the ultimate rise of the nonaligned movement. New prospects for cultural exchange were now open.

Intertextual Narrative: Novels?

Poetry and essays are not the only domains that demonstrate the complexity brought about and problematized in an uneven colonial encounter. The stupendous growth in novelistic production raises more questions and may redirect the conversation about theft and borrowing even more toward intertextuality in its intricate webs. Thus, this chapter also explores several Arabic novels of the third millennium as examples of this textual engagement not only with Arabic literary tradition but also with texts from outside the Euro-American orbit. Such a substantial and visible textual appropriation invites this critical intervention, something that, in turn, is bound in dialogue with contemporary literary forays that reflect on texts as tissues of quotations.

Shared features in the third millennium novelistic tradition include reliance on Qurʾānic verses, the inclusion of earlier classical Arabic texts, and, more often, a nod to the literary production of the Global South.[55] The drift

[54] See further in Chapters 3 and 4. See also al-Ḥātimī, *Ḥilyat al-muḥāḍarah*, 2:28; Zakī al-Dīn Abū Muḥammad ʿAbd al-ʿAẓīm b. ʿAbd al-Wāḥid b. Ẓāfir b. ʿAbdallāh al-Miṣrī al-ʿAdwānī (d. 654/1256), better known as Ibn Abī al-Iṣbaʿ, *Taḥrīr al-taḥbīr fī ṣināʿat al-shiʿr wa-l-nathr*, ed. Ḥafnī Muḥammad Sharaf (Cairo: Lajnat Iḥyāʾal-Turāth, n.p.), 1:418; Abū ʿAlī al-Ḥasan Ibn Rashīq al-Qayrawānī, *al-ʿUmdah*, ed. Muḥammad Muḥyī al-Dīn ʿAbd al-Ḥamīd (Beirut: Dār al-Jīl, 1981), 2:289; *al-ʿUmdah* (2001), 2:289.

[55] Muhsin J. al-Musawi, "The Prize-Winning Arabic Novel," *The Middle East in London* 15, no. 1 (2018–19): 16–17.

of the argument is to demonstrate that narrative proper is no less susceptible to dialogue with texts than poetry in relation to both a memorized and cherished tradition, and a poetic script where towering figures leave an indelible stamp. Semioticians and structuralists are no less involved in these narrative textual forays, as the writings of Barthes, Genette, and Riffaterre demonstrate. Readings in other cultural scripts entail some relational dependence that is also distinctive of postcapitalist economies whereby almost every practice bears the stamp of a commodified culture. The rich memorizing practices of poetic *ruwāt* (transmitters) and the concomitant narration of classical and even medieval times gave way to a sweeping reliance on spectacle, including its virtual manifestations. Like the human self, no text can claim immunity, as contamination is the primary feature of contemporary culture. Thus, "transtextual" or "intertextual space" is more than a mere placing of a word, image, or an idea and a line here and there; it weaves its threads in an intricate manner whereby words, meanings, motifs, and thence theorizations form an assemblage.

Arab classicists and medievalists (i.e., twelfth–seventeenth centuries) addressed a large corpus of intertextual use or misuse under the rubric of plagiarism,[56] while modernists have delved into it headlong as being part of their property, regardless of what the early Nahḍah generation stood for.[57] Hence, this interlaced excursion denies the need for specific periodization and classification and addresses the matter of borrowing and the production of texts as a fabric of quotations. In the end, this undertaking may also serve as a preliminary engagement with my own lifetime interest in whatever comes under such rubrics as intertextual space and plagiarism. While casual reproduction, imitativeness, or even a hurried pastiche or parody, and superfluous practices in contemporary narrative and poetry can be dismissed as tangential and negligible, the more noticeable novels demonstrate their writers' readings and interests and display in a nutshell a cultural register, a library shelf, one that also conveys an impression of the formative powers involved in cultural production. Such narratives are often self-conscious, in that their authors reflect on their own personal record while at the same time crafting a narrative or poetics

[56] For a short theoretical framework, see Muhsin J. al-Musawi, *The Medieval Islamic Republic of Letters: Arabic Knowledge Construction* (Notre Dame, IN: University of Notre Dame Press, 2015), 121–24, 127–30, 188–89.

[57] For the Nahḍah's attitude with respect to authentication and originality, see al-Musawi, *Islam on the Street*; Tarek El-Ariss, *Trials of Arab Modernity: Literary Affects and the New Political* (New York: Fordham University Press, 2013); Brugman, *Modern Arabic Literature in Egypt*. See also Roger Allen, "The End of the *Nahḍah*?," in *Arabic Literature in a Posthuman World*, ed. Stephan Guth and Teresa Pepe (Wiesbaden: Harrassowitz Verlag, 2019), 3–12. See Paniconi, "Reframing Politics," for a brief survey of translation studies by Rebecca C. Johnson, Samah Salim, and others.

of some aesthetic concern. Although often trapped in prize-winning competitions,[58] these novels also crave ancestral belonging, a lineage of one sort or another. In those interstices that often carve out a substantive ancestry in their conversation with a precursor's life story or oeuvre, the classical Arabic tradition looms large.

Intertextual Terrains: Old and New

These intertexts may also be taking advantage of worldwide transactional practices in an overwhelming postcapitalist global economy. Like current solicitation of celebrities in satellite TV shows and media, a classical or postclassical craving for lineage and ancestry will often involve conspicuous or overt raids on prominent precursors' legacy and, particularly, on the Qur'ān as a foundational or constitutive text. A large intertextual space, one that makes extensive use of sedimentary texts, appears to be the most distinctive feature of current novel writing in Arabic. Texts often emerge as intersectional sites that correspond to Roland Barthes's tissue of quotations,[59] or Bakhtin's and Julia Kristeva's notion of dialogic space.[60] In these conversational matrices there are reminders and traces of ancient and modern textual practices. There is also a nod to postcolonial intertextual and revisionist forays, as practiced, for example, by the Dominican-born British author Jean Rhys in *Wide Sargasso Sea* (1966), or by Aimé Césaire in *A Tempest* (1969). While subtextual implications abound, there remains a systematic application of other novels, poetries, and theoretical explorations.

[58] On the bestseller, see Roger Allen, "Fiction and Publics: The Emergence of the 'Arabic Best-Seller,'" in "The State of the Art in the Middle East," special issue, *Middle East Journal* (2009): 8–12; expanded in Roger Allen, "Fiction and Publics: The Emergence of the Arabic 'Best-Seller,'" in *Desire, Pleasure and the Taboo: New Voices and Freedom of Expression in Contemporary Arabic Literature*, ed. Sobhi Boustani, Isabella Camera D'Afflitto, Rasheed El-Enany, and William Granara (Pisa: Fabrizio Serra Editore, 2014), 103–11.

[59] Roland Barthes argues that "the text is a tissue of quotations drawn from the innumerable centres of culture." Roland Barthes, "The Death of the Author," in *Image – Music – Text*, trans. Stephen Heath (New York: Hill and Wang, 1977), 146.

[60] For Bakhtin, there is a differentiation between immanence and the dialogic principle. He argues that "such a maximal proximity of the creator's position to the material is immanent in the very genre" and that, for the novel, the "issue of authorship . . . is a formal and generic concern as well." See M. M. Bakhtin, "Forms of Time and of the Chronotope in the Novel: Notes towards a Historical Poetics," in *The Dialogic Imagination: Four Essays*, trans. Caryl Emerson and Michael Holquist (Austin: University of Texas Press, 1994), 161. But there is also "heteroglossia," which can be traced in "speeches of characters, narrators, and inserted genres." See "Discourse in the Novel," in *Dialogic Imagination*, 263. For Julia Kristeva, see "Word, Dialogue and Novel," in *The Kristeva Reader*, ed. Toril Moi (London: Blackwell, 1986).

There are multiple potential purposes behind this noticeable weave of quotes, texts, and wording. Apart from expediency, there are interrogations of nostalgia and memory, a critique of collective stupor, rewriting of precursors' poetry or theory, and an urge for fertilization and replenishment. When taken together, these raise further questions about our understanding of stabilities that come under the rubric of canon formation. To quote Jean-François Lyotard in *The Postmodern Condition*,[61] "invention is always born of dissension," a point which the Arabic *badīʿ* (inventiveness; euphonical embellishment; also anomaly) tradition has abundantly exemplified.[62] Even so, these new literary productions also reprise the discussion of the resilient trace, not in a campsite this time, but in lands that suffer occupation and violent mutilation. Moreover, they also search for meaning outside the Arabic corpus.

Canonization and Intertextuality

My concern with modernist intertextual tendencies is focused on a dynamic of continuity and disruption. This dynamic decenters the sovereignty of the subject as it navigates among texts that reflect on each other through several appropriating or invading strategies which are subsumed under the classical Arabic rubric of plagiarism. I argue that "plagiarism" is an inclusive term like intertextuality, one that can provide directions for the study of the canon.[63] Albeit the tendency here and elsewhere to discredit it and replace it with intertextuality, it appears in this book as a rubric used by Arab classicists. As a term, it should serve as a means of studying Arabic literary theory, and not only through the enormous corpus of *wasāṭah* (philological mediations among poets) but also through a rich intertextual space, both ancient and modern.[64] Variations on borrowing, whether direct and visible or discreet and repressed, operate within a space that poststructuralists approach as being dialogic or intertextual. Also, and as part of this lively climate of poetics, what is raided or contrafacted should have been invoked as an

[61] Jean-François Lyotard, *The Postmodern Condition: A Report on Knowledge*, trans. Geoff Bennington and Brian Massumi (Minneapolis: University of Minnesota Press, 1984), xxv.

[62] In Qurʾān 46:9, "Say: I am not singular or anomalous (*bidʿan*) from among the messengers."

[63] An important contribution is Roger Allen, "Transforming the Canons," in *New Geographies: Texts and Contexts in Modern Arabic Literature*, ed. Roger Allen, Gonzalo Fernández Parrilla, Francisco M. Rodríguez Sierra, and Tetz Rooke (Madrid: UAM Ediciones, 2018), 15–26.

[64] For preparatory readings, see Grunebaum, "Concept of Plagiarism"; Seeger A. Bonebakker, "Ancient Arabic Poetry and Plagiarism: A Terminological Labyrinth," *Quaderni di Studi Arabi* 15 (1997): 65–92.

exemplary model. The act of reproduction, improvement, or slippage is only a variation on this pattern. Mutation within seeming stability initiates inventiveness as a process. In other words, the canon retains a variable sustainability in the process of negotiation, revision, destabilization, and negation. Being a consortium of formulas, themes, preludial motifs, and names, it is the shared property of writers, readers, and grammarians. Bearing in mind the use of "canon" as a broad term for educators, philologists, media experts, and arbiters of taste, the grammarians "take upon themselves the power to set up and impose norms," and hence "to consecrate and codify a particular use of language by rationalizing it and 'giving reason' to it."[65] Pierre Bourdieu's articulation resonates with a classical Arabic philological articulation of "*ʿamūd al-shiʿr,*" the standardized canon, or the standard model in poetry as set by the ancient poets, a point which is the concern of Chapter 2. Standardization becomes an issue in urban poetry and poetics, as the ancients rarely suffered the qualms of anxiety in a common climate of shared tradition. Newly emerging anxieties, especially in relation or reaction to *badīʿ* (inventiveness and innovation) that swept the urban scene, drove well-established scholars to draw attention to the canon, especially when applied to *badīʿ* practitioners. Deviations from the common practice of writing and ancient poetics were bound to occur in rapidly transformed milieus. Ancient parlance and preludial openings underwent interrogation and change. Moderate or excessive inventiveness in wording and structure were not easily condoned. Thus, ninth- and tenth-century philologists showed an unease with the practice that is *bidʿah* (hence the noun *badīʿ*, as deviation from the normative).[66] Both al-Buḥturī and Abū Tammām are often drawn upon to make a point with respect to the former's restrained use of inventiveness versus the presumed excessiveness of the latter, a case that will be studied further in Chapters 3 and 4. This same urban endeavor applies to the role of scholars in the field of intertextual space or plagiarism.

In dialogic engagements with Qurʾānic narratives, for example, modernist poets and novelists recall the story of Joseph and his brothers for several reasons. Thematically, it provides allegory for a paradigmatic betrayal that prompts Maḥmūd Darwīsh's heart-wrenching lamentation

[65] Pierre Bourdieu, *Language and Symbolic Power*, trans. Gino Raymond and Matthew Adamson, 7th ed. (Cambridge, MA: Harvard University Press, 2003), 59.

[66] See ʿAlī Aḥmad Saʿīd (Adūnīs), *al-Thābit wa-l-mutaḥawwil: baḥth fī al-ibdāʿ wa-l-ittibāʿ ʿinda al-ʿArab* (1973; Beirut: Dār al-Sāqī, 8th print, 2002), 2:160–61; Suzanne P. Stetkevych, "Toward a Redefinition of *Badīʿ* Poetry," *Journal of Arabic Literature* 12 (1981): 1–29. For the recurrence of the term *ittibāʿ* and its spelling, see Muḥammad Muṣṭafā al-Zabīdī, *Tāj al-ʿarūs* (Beirut: Dār Ṣādir, 2011), 2:17.

in "Anā Yūsuf yā Abī" (I Am Joseph, O Father).[67] The implied treachery of Arab rulers regarding Palestine endows the poem with significant political overtones.[68] The same Qurʾānic story provides the Moroccan poet and novelist Muḥammad al-Achʿarī (Mohammed Achaari) in his *al-Qaws wa-l-farāshah* (The Arch and the Butterfly) with a paradoxical analogy, involving a meeting with a blind father who can feel from afar the approaching steps of his son Yūsuf.[69] From the Qurʾān he borrows the collapse of sight, smell, and hearing: *Innī la-ajidu rīḥa Yūsuf* (Verily, I can see [feel] Joseph's scent).[70] Like the Qurʾānic father, Achaari's al-Firsiwi is privileged with the gift of synesthesia that finds its expression in dense figurative language, something that makes him speak of himself as a "great mosaic." With multiple reflections on blindness, ancient and modern, in the writer's mind, the father's blindness turns him into a tableau, or, even better, a mosaic of knowledge and quotes, an exemplary human nod to textual space. Moreover, visions and dreams in the same Qurʾānic story of Joseph prompt another Moroccan, Abdelfattah Kilito, to take Potiphar's order to Joseph to interpret dreams and visions as the title for a fictitious autobiography, *Anbiʾūnī bi-l-ruʾyā* (Inform Me of This Vision [or Dream]).[71] This command to interpret dreams sets the action in the Qurʾānic story. This same Qurʾānic narrative found its way earlier into a strong precursor's poetry: Abū Tammām, for one, uses the brothers' plea for succor in a relatively joyful request for patronage.[72] The extensive use of the Qurʾān for thematic, metaphorical, and broad stylistic purposes is noticeable in the structure of an enormous epistemological shift in knowledge construction. Linguistic sedimentation through

[67] Maḥmūd Darwīsh, *Ward aqall* (Beirut: Dār al-ʿAwdah, 1986).

[68] In his poem "I Am Joseph, O Father," Darwīsh writes:

> I am Joseph, O father.
> O father, my brothers do not love me or want me among them.
> They assault me and throw stones and words at me.
> They want me to die so they can eulogize me.

[69] Muḥammad al-Achʿarī, *al-Qaws wa-l-farāshah, riwāyah* (Beirut: al-Markaz al-Thaqāfī al-ʿArabī, 2013); trans. Aida Bamia as Mohammed Achaari, *The Arch and the Butterfly* (Doha: Bloomsbury Qatar Foundation Publishing, 2015).

[70] al-Achʿarī, *al-Qaws wa-l-farāshah*, 53.

[71] Abdelfattah Kilito, *Anbiʾūnī bi-l-ruʾyā* (Beirut: Dār al-Ādāb, 2010).

[72] On this, see Muhsin J. al-Musawi, "Pre-modern Belletristic Prose," in *The Cambridge History of Arabic Literature*, vol. 6, *Arabic Literature in the Post-classical Period*, ed. Roger Allen and D. S. Richards (Cambridge: Cambridge University Press, 2006), 99–133. See also ʿAlī b. Muḥammad al-Ḥamūd, *Athar al-Qurʾān al-karīm fī shiʿr Abī Tammām* (Damascus: Dār al-Fikr, 2018); ʿAbd al-Khāliq ʿĪsā, "Intertexuality in Abū Tammām's Poems," *Al-Azhar* 14, no. 2 (2012): 431–46, www.alazhar.edu.ps/journal123/human_Sciences.asp?typeno=0. The reference is to Abū Bakr al-Ṣūlī, *Akhbār Abī Tammām* (Beirut: al-Tijāriyyah, n.d.), 211–13; al-Thaʿālibī, *al-Kināyah wa-l-taʿrīḍ* (Beirut: Dār Ṣaʿb, n.d.), 22.

ḥall al-manẓūm and *naẓm al-manthūr* – or as al-Thaʿālibī (d. 429/1039) terms it in his *Nathr al-naẓm wa-ḥall al-ʿiqd* (Prosification of Poetry and the Untying of the Knot) in the late classical period,[73] or in Ḍiyāʾ al-Dīn b. al-Athīr's (d. 637/1239) *Washī al-marqūm fī ḥall al-manẓūm* (The Embroidered Tapestry in Prosification) – was an enterprise of both prosification and versification that went hand in hand with philological scholarship in its untiring effort to study textual malleability and fluid practices. Whether rewriting prose in a poetic form or turning prose into poetry, the practice was among strategies used to escape specific strictures on cultural production. As will be shown in due course, tenth-century critics look upon the practice as a commendable one in a highly competitive space. More so than before, statecraft requires writers for its chancery who are capable of persuasion and intimidation, and who should show a mastery in moving back and forth between poetry and prose.[74] The outcome was another understanding of intellectual property.[75] Early philological strictures with respect to plagiarism had begun to break down in the face of a series of itemizations, gradations, and categories that allowed medieval (postclassical) literati to navigate their way freely in a vast empire of texts and anecdotes.[76] With this legacy in mind, it is difficult to look upon modern intertextualities as abnormalities.

Almost every modernist feels some sense of engagement with ancestors and precursors. More often than not, these textual instances amount to partial raids, misreadings, and multiple transactions that are larger and more problematic than *overt* literary *sariqāt* or thefts.[77] To recapitulate, if modernity and its postulates confront us with vast intertextual spaces, the volatile literary tradition in Arabic started its negotiations, navigations, and textual and performative transactions with the rise of poetry as a neatly defined *dīwān* (verse collection), genre, and practice. With the rise of empire, it also witnessed the canonization of *tarassul* (epistolary writing) with the notable contribution of ʿAbd al-Ḥamīd al-Kātib (d. 132/749). This other lengthy process reached a peak in Ibn Munjib al-Ṣayrafī's (d. 542/1147) specific use of the term *qānūn* in the title of his *Qānūn dīwān al-rasāʾil* (The Canon [Standards] for the Chancery). Before him, Abū Naṣr al-

[73] Full name: ʿAbd al-Malik b. Muḥammad al-Thaʿālibī.

[74] Muhsin J. al-Musawi, "Vindicating a Profession or a Personal Career? Al-Qalqashandī's *Maqāmah* in Context," *Review of Mamluk Studies* 7 (2003): 111–35.

[75] The term *sariqah* (theft) was already in use in pre-Islamic poetry and was studied soon after. For example, Muḥammad b. ʿAbdallāh (d. 123/741), Ibn Kunāsah, had authored *Sariqāt al-Kumayt min al-Qurʾān wa-ghayrih* (The Plagiarisms of al-Kumayt from the Qurʾān and Other Sources).

[76] For more, see al-Musawi, *Republic of Letters*.

[77] For a detailed reading, see al-Musawi, *Arabic Poetry*, esp. the chapters on tradition and dedications.

Fārābī (d. 339/950) was credited with the invention of the musical instrument *al-qānūn* as central to music as the heart is to the body. Ibn Sīnā (d. 427/1037) had used the word as an inclusive term for comprehensive and definitive knowledge. His *al-Qānūn fī al-ṭibb* (The Canon of Medicine) reflects a tendency to have knowledge tabulated, systematized, and made available to wider readerships, as indicated by the rise of compendia, lexicons, and compilations of every sort. While disrupting canonization, these compendia make use of canonical works; but in this vast textual empire canonical standards begin to lose their exceptional presence. Selections from these new types of compilation appear alongside a variety of popular arts. One of the most visible signs of these shifts can be seen in the writings of Muḥammad al-Nawājī, whose *Ḥalbat al-kumayt* (The Racecourse of the Bay – i.e., the arena of deep red wine)[78] and erotic poetry appeared alongside his devastating exposé of the alleged plagiarisms committed by his mentor, Ibn Ḥijjah al-Ḥamawī (d. 837/1433).[79] The canonized *ʿamūd al-shiʿr* (standardized poetics) was to undergo challenges,[80] not only because of the rise and growth of popular poetries, the *seven arts* that received a good deal of attention in the postclassical period,[81] but also because the raging discussion of theft and borrowing and the ultimate epistemological turn to malleable practices forced standardization to relent.

Originality Claims and Plural Ancestry

As is usual in these epistemological shifts, nothing could be clear-cut. The claim to originality, authenticity, precedence, and uniqueness continued to appear in writers' and poets' prefaces, but these seem of minimal significance in relation to the daunting presence of constellations that bring all names, big and small, under one cover. While claims to originality and inventiveness (*al-badīʿ al-mukhtaraʿ*)[82] as central to a critical corpus on plagiarism make a shy appearance here and there, a marketplace culture takes over, one that diversifies reception and entails further multiplication of terms. In a word, a turn to a wider readership replaces a dominating classical conversation among the elite and

[78] Full name: Ibn Ḥasan b. ʿAlī b. ʿUthmān (d. 859/1455).

[79] See further al-Musawi, *Republic of Letters*, 126, 276–77, 282–84.

[80] An earlier application of the term in reference to al-Buḥturī occurs in Abū al-Qāsim al-Ḥasan b. Bishr al-Āmidī, *al-Muwāzanah bayna shiʿr Abī Tammām wa-l-Buḥturī*, ed. Aḥmad Ṣaqr, 2 vols. (Cairo: Dār al-Maʿārif, 1972); and also applied by al-Qāḍī al-Jurjānī, *al-Wasāṭah* (1966). A detailed standardization is by ʿAlī Aḥmad b. Muḥammad B. al-Ḥasan al-Marzūqī (d. 421/1030) in his *Sharḥ dīwān al-ḥamāsah*. See further in Chapters 2 and 3.

[81] For a reading of these, see al-Musawi, *Republic of Letters*, 199–200, 384, 406.

[82] The phrase occurs in al-Jurjānī, *al-Wasāṭah* (1966), 186.

privileged.[83] The compendia served then, as today, the needs for miscellaneous merchandise among large audiences. Notwithstanding the disconnect of many modernists with the medieval corpus in particular,[84] there is a multifaceted tradition that finds its venues in modernist and postmodernist writings and invigorates a body of poetry and fiction.[85]

In other words, the act of recalling this tradition empowers descendants without necessarily limiting their poetics. But rather than being solely Arab, this ancestry is plural, and Latin American and Portuguese in particular. While explicit reference to ancestors or contemporaries grants the third-millennium Arabic novel and its embedded poetries a rite of passage to other shores, there are also invisible linkages to unacknowledged texts. The Cuban José Lezama Lima's *Paradiso* is the unacknowledged textual ghost in Achaari's *The Arch and the Butterfly*. Its repression raises questions of contamination or borrowing, especially since the Cuban writer's work sets a standard in both style and method. Even if we assume that this intertextual or sedimentary practice is prompted by expediency in order to produce a work modeled on a strong precursor in a relatively short time, this matter of convenience also provokes the anxieties of literary production, marketability, affiliation, and fame.[86]

Arabic novels of the third millennium often underline what Harold Bloom has already theorized as a literary tradition in his *Western Canon* (1994). Notwithstanding Bloom's dispute with "resenters" and their politicization of literature,[87] his significant insights into canonization are worth considering. There is always anxiety in texts that are engaged with the writings and images of forebears and precursors: "A canon is an *achieved anxiety*, just as any strong literary work is its author's achieved anxiety."[88] Even when there is rejection, as is the case with the famed Iraqi poet ʿAbd al-Wahhāb al-Bayātī's (d. 1999) avowed denunciation of T. S. Eliot's vision,[89] itself a case similar to Hart Crane's in Bloom's

[83] See al-Musawi, *Republic of Letters*, 51, 111, 130–31, 172, 251, 259.

[84] See further Thomas Bauer, "Literarische Anthologien der Mamliikenzeit," in *Die Mamliiken: Studien zu ihrer Geschichte und Kultur*, ed. S. Conermann and A. Pistor-Hatam (Hamburg: EB-Verlag, 2003), 71–122; Thomas Bauer, "In Search of 'Post-classical Literature': A Review Article," *Mamluk Studies Review* 11, no. 2 (2007): 137–67; Bauer, "Mamluk Literature: Misunderstandings and New Approaches," *Mamluk Studies Review* 9, no. 2 (2005): 105–32. See also al-Musawi, *Republic of Letters*.

[85] See further al-Musawi, *Arabic Disclosures*.

[86] See al-Musawi, "Prize-Winning Arabic Novel," 16–17; al-Musawi, "The Medieval Turn in Modern Arabic Narrative," in *The Oxford Handbook of Arab Novelistic Traditions*, ed. Wail Hassan (Oxford: Oxford University Press, 2017), 67–88.

[87] Harold Bloom, *The Western Canon: The Books and School of the Ages* (New York: Riverhead Books, 1995), 483–84.

[88] Ibid., 492. [89] See al-Musawi, *Arabic Poetry*, 220.

critique,[90] there is still contamination in style, not only in idioms but also in the mythical method and the "heap of broken images."[91] "Great styles are sufficient for canonicity because they possess the power of contamination, and contamination is the pragmatic test for canon formation."[92] At an early stage in Arabic criticism, a neat summation by ʿAbd al-Raḥmān al-Hamadhānī (d. 327/939) stipulates, "People get prioritized and given precedence for word order, composition, and poetic weave."[93] His classification builds on that of other authorities. He says:

سمعت ما قيل: إن من أخذ معنى بلفظه كان له سارقا، ومن أخذه ببعض لفظه كان له سالخا، ومن أخذه فكساه لفظا من عنده أجود من لفظه كان هو أولى به ممن تقدمه

I heard it said that someone who takes over poetic meaning [i.e., theme] with all its wording is a plagiarist, but someone else who takes it with partial wording is like a person who peels off [flays] things. Anyone who clothes a meaning with better wording has the right to it as his own.

The summation, to be found, for example, in al-Hamadhānī's manual for learners, *al-Alfāẓ al-kitābiyyah* (Scriptable Expressions), is important, especially as ʿAbd al-Qāhir al-Jurjānī (d. 471/1078) refers to it as a manual with which the youth of the Islamic world are familiar.[94] Improvement in wording and expression negates ethical or other claims of ownership. Hence, since expression and wording were crucial to Arabic theories of plagiarism, they were and still are the domain for appropriation, raid, and theft.[95] In reporting the authority of those knowledgeable in poetry (*man adraktuhu min ahl al-ʿilm bi-l-shiʿr*), al-Āmidī (d. 370/980) places a similar emphasis on style.[96] As for the semantic side of poetry, it is

90 Bloom, *Western Canon*, 488.
91 T.S. Eliot, "The Burial of the Dead," in *The Waste Land* (New York: Boni and Liveright, 1922), 11.
92 Bloom, *Western Canon*, 488.
93 ʿAbd al-Raḥmān b. ʿĪsā al-Hamadhānī, *Kitāb al-alfāẓ al-kitābiyyah*, ed. Father Luwīs Shaykhū (Beirut: Maṭbaʿat al-Ābāʾ al-Yasūʿiyyīn, 1911), viii–ix. Also Muḥsin J. al-Mūsawī, "al-Tarjīʿāt: naẓariyyat al-tafāʿul fī al-shiʿr al-ʿArabī," *ʿAlāmāt* 6, no. 24 (1997): 58; the quote in this latter article references the collected theoretical texts *Nuṣūṣ al-naẓariyyah al-naqdiyyah*, ed. Jamīl Saʿīd and Dāwūd Sallūm, where it is mistakenly attributed to Qudāmah b. Jaʿfar (d. 337/948).
94 See also n. 38 in Chapter 3 on ʿAbd al-Qāhir's reference.
95 See al-Āmidī, *al-Muwāzanah*. He relies on "those whom I have met from among scholars of poetry, and whom I have outlived." He explains *sariqah* as being confined to "the invented new which distinguishes a poet, not the common meanings which are common in people's ways of exemplary sayings and conversations." See al-Mūsawī, "al-Tarjīʿāt," 58. See also Abū Bakr al-Ṣūlī, *The Life and Times of Abū Tammām*, trans. Beatrice Gruendler (New York: New York University Press, 2018). A general survey of the theory of plagiarism in Arabic with focus on al-Sharīf al-Murtaḍā (d. 436/1044) is by Maʿtūq, "Al-Sharīf al-Murtaḍā's Contribution." A general chapter on the topic is in Amjad Trabulsi, *La critique poétique des Arabes, jusqu'au Ve siècle de l'Hégire* (Damascus: l'Institut Français de Damas, 1956).
96 Full name: Abū al-Qāsim al-Ḥasan b. Bishr. He says: "those whom I have outlived. . . ."

often played down as consisting of shared motifs in a public domain. It is reported that the renowned philologist and critic Abū ʿAmrū b. al-ʿAlāʾ (d. 154/770) speaks of these motifs as follows:

تلك عقول رجال توافت على ألسنتها

These were concurrent thoughts in people's speech.

It is this stylistic contamination that is turned to the advantage of newly produced Arabic novels and poems, a contamination that can at times get out of hand when it amounts to textual invasion, raid, or *ighārah*. In narratives, this dependency is broader than style, in that writers may find both matter and manner to assist in the design of a new novel. In both cases, reliance on an established, canonical text provides one way of connecting with a tradition of strong precursors and canons, and thus of mainstreaming the current work. Although classical Arabic theories of plagiarism were dominated by a formalist reading of style, enunciation, and wording, they nevertheless leave some space for thematic intertextualities. In two works that have not reached us, but are referenced by late contemporaries, the tenth-century philologist Abū al-Ḍiyāʾ Bishr b. Yaḥyā al-Naṣībī came up with a significant departure from common stylistic preoccupations, one that proposes an alternative negotiatory line in his *Sariqāt al-Buḥturī min Abī Tammām* (al-Buḥturī's Plagiarisms from Abī Tammam) and *Kitāb al-sariqāt al-kabīr* (The Grand Book of Plagiarisms),[97] where emphasis is laid on themes and ideas as relevant to societal change. Therefore, we can speak of three directions in the study of *sariqāt*: the formalist, the thematic, and the mediatory. As long as there are categories for *laṭīf al-saraq* (subtle or fine plagiarism), we have to assume that plagiarism is not to be regarded as equivalent to theft, a point which the introduction to the present chapter purports to emphasize. Instead, it may be viewed as another name for intertextuality. This is precisely the domain where modern and postmodern Arabic production begs for the broader contexts of classical/medieval Arabic tradition and world literature.

The Colonial Encounter and Global South Intertexts

That said, this still cannot be a straightforward transaction: The implied reader will often be the common public, a group that is not necessarily aware of a specific intertextual practice. The other point is the shift in this intertextualizing enterprise from the European/

[97] See Maʿtūq, "Al-Sharīf al-Murtaḍā's Contribution," 66.

American tradition to Latin American and Portuguese poetry and novels; a shift that signifies not only a disconnect with Arabic Nahḍah narratives of encounter as exemplified in Tawfīq al-Ḥakīm's *ʿUṣfūr min al-sharq* (1938; A Sparrow from the East; translated and published in English as *The Bird of the East*) and Yaḥyā Ḥaqqī's *Qindīl Umm Hāshim* (1944; The Lamp of Umm Hāshim or The Saint's Lamp),[98] for example. The shift also entails a new wave of resistance to the surging imperial encroachment, its imposition of neoliberalism, and the New World Order, with its deliberate destruction of ancient sites and cities in order to open up space for its colossal glass megamall structures. Thus, Hugo Friedrich describes the outcome as the "attempt of the modern soul, trapped in a technologized, imperialistic commercial era, to preserve its own freedom."[99] The drive for freedom is so compelling as to incite early in the 1950s the retention of preludial practices, which both critics and poets endorse. We may cite, as an example, the Moroccan poet Muḥammad Bennīs's (b. 1948) self-styled "lineage to the pre-Islamic poet Imruʾ al-Qays":

> He is the ʿArabiyyah, Arabic language, in a canticle state, face to face with absence-death, as he halts to weep over a deserted campsite, alone in the desert, which I cherish inside my study room. From this canticle, I derive my filiations as an Arab, and to it I listen whenever I detect a *qaṣīdah* or its opposite.[100]

This shows even in practice in the poetry of the Iraqi poet and pioneer of modernist Arabic poetry Badr Shākir al-Sayyāb (d. 1964), as exemplified in his popular poem "Canticle of the Rain."[101]

Thus, and in response to new situations, new production struggles to engage with multidimensional conditions in order to appeal to an emerging readership. The market, as well as the anticipated award and other prospects of publicity, are no less powerful in deciding the future of a book in its multiple formats. The widespread use of intertexts and subtexts – such as Mary Shelley's outstanding *Frankenstein* in Aḥmad Saʿdāwī's

[98] See further Roger Allen, *The Arabic Novel: An Historical and Critical Introduction* (Syracuse, NY: Syracuse University Press, 1995); Muhsin J. al-Musawi, *The Postcolonial Arabic Novel* (Leiden: Brill, 2003), 191–94; al-Musawi, *Islam on the Street*, 46–58, 185–95.

[99] Jonathan Culler, "On the Negativity of Modern Poetry: Friedrich, Baudelaire, and the Critical Tradition," in *Languages of the Unsayable: The Play of Negativity in Literature and Literary Theory*, ed. Sanford Budick and Wolfgang Iser (New York: Columbia University Press, 1989), 198.

[100] Muḥammad Bennīs, *al-Aʿmāl al-shiʿriyyah*, 2 vols. (Casablanca: Dār Tubqāl, 2002), 1:9.

[101] See Terri DeYoung, "A New Reading of Badr Shākir al-Sayyāb's 'Hymn of the Rain,'" *Journal of Arabic Literature* 24 (1993): 39–40nn1–2.

Farānkashtāyn fī baghdād (2014; Frankenstein in Baghdad),[102] the canonical Fernando Pessoa's heteronyms in *The Tobacco Shop* in Ali Bader's *Ḥāris al-tubgh* (2008; The Tobacco Keeper),[103] S. Yizhar's (Smilansky) *Khirbet Khizeh* (1949) and the poetry of Waḍḍāḥ of Yemen in Elias Khouri's *Awlād al-ghītū: ismī Ādam* (2016; Children of the Ghetto: My Name Is Adam),[104] and Rajāʾ ʿĀlim's *Ṭawq al-ḥamām* (2010; The Dove's Necklace) – attests to this reliance on strong precursors.[105] ʿĀlim's *Dove's Necklace* needs Ibn Ḥazm's (d. 1064) monumental treatise of the same title to juxtapose the sublime view of love with mundane practices in decrepit Meccan quarters and streets. In *The Arch and the Butterfly* Mohammed Achaari plays with intertextuality even more broadly. He engages with several texts, including the Nobel Prize winner José Saramago's *Blindness* and *The Gospel according to Jesus Christ*, along with the poetry of Hölderlin, Guillermo Cabrera Infante's *Three Trapped Tigers*,[106] and a fictitious Hans Roeder's *Elegies*. Lineages are redrawn, and a new map of authorship, along with new textual genealogies, is established. Ali Bader is almost the pioneer in an acknowledged patterning of his *Tobacco Keeper* on the heteronyms of disappearance in Pessoa's (d. 1935) *The Tobacco Shop*. The issues of multiple identity and imagined communities are raised not only to expose a certain fluidity in the history of ideas but also to cater to recent sociological and metahistorical readings – such as Benedict Anderson's *Imagined Communities* – that destabilize totalities. This conversation with other forms and methods from outside Arabic's multiple canons may receive substantiation in Rajāʾ ʿĀlim's *The Dove's Necklace* or in Achaari's framing of blindness in terms of recognition and misrecognition as conveyed by Joseph's story in the Qurʾān, and yet the overwhelming cultural presence of a Global South is conspicuous.

[102] Aḥmad Saʿdāwī, *Farānkashtāyn fī baghdād* (Beirut: Dār al-Jamal, 2014); trans. Jonathan Wright as Ahmed Saadawi, *Frankenstein in Baghdad: A Novel* (New York: Penguin, 2018).

[103] ʿAlī Bader, *Ḥāris al-tubgh* (Beirut: MADN, 2008); trans. Amira Nowaira as Ali Bader, *The Tobacco Keeper* (Doha: Bloomsbury, 2011). In 1914, Fernando Pessoa has as alter egos, or heteronyms, Alberto Caeiro, Ricardo Reis, and Álvaro de Campos.

[104] Elias Khouri, *Awlād al-ghītū: ismī Ādam* (Beirut: Dār al-Ādāb, 2016); trans. Humphrey Davies as *Children of the Ghetto: My Name Is Adam* (New York: Archipelago Books, 2019).

[105] Rajāʾ ʿĀlim, *Ṭawq al-ḥamām* (Casablanca: al-Markaz al-Thaqāfī al-ʿArabī, 2010); trans. Katharine Halls and Adam Talib as Raja Alem, *The Dove's Necklace: A Novel* (London: Overlook Press, 2016).

[106] Guillermo Cabrera Infante, *Three Trapped Tigers*, trans. Suzanne Jill Levine and Donald Gardner (1967; New York: Harper and Row, 1971).

What to Reclaim from Poetic Ancestry?

The case becomes even more complicated when we recall that poetic ancestors can be reclaimed and engaged with in order to address situations that need to be given more visibility. As patronage is out of the question, textual ancestry turns out to be a quest for some kind of anchor and, along with it, an assured identity in an otherwise bleak situation. This is the space into which Maḥmūd Darwīsh steps, and, along with him and from beyond poetic frontiers, Elias Khouri in his *Awlād al-ghītū*. There is no negativism in either author's writing; and their sense of the power of the ancient canon, especially the pre-Islamic nostalgic prelude, is invigorating. It is so to such an extent that, even under siege and bombardment and appalled and angered by trendy talk among intellectuals, Darwīsh allows a stream of consciousness to take over, impelling him to call for an intervention from informed criticism:

> At this juncture, we cry out for help from criticism. We call upon it to regain faith in its power and usefulness. We call upon it to enter the lists [*sic*: scene], now open for spoils. We call upon it to set down norms, the absence of which has opened the field for the ignorant and the counter-revolutionary to foist themselves off as moderns.[107]

A plea to "set down the norms" is no random cry; under bombardment and bloody siege, the ongoing theoretical skirting commonly encountered among Lebanese and Arab dilettantes and practitioners sounds not only out of place but also irresponsible, if not blatantly cruel. It also brings us to the issue of scriptoria, for Darwīsh's engagement with precursors often touches on land and scriptoria, erasure and resilience. A palimpsest is there, one that struggles to retain his village of Birwah, and his house, horse, carob tree, and neighbors. This palimpsest holds to a reference to be found in "The Birwah Prelude,"[108] which invokes a hemistich from Abū al-ʿAlāʾ al-Maʿarrī (d. 449/1057), alerting readers that they need to tread lightly where mass graves tell the story of occupation. This engagement with the canonical prelude structures the threshold and style in several poems that recall Imruʾ al-Qays and the *Muʿallaqāt* tradition, in which poets make reference to the durable trace.[109]

Both Darwīsh and Khouri provide a threshold leading to this exploration of canons, keys, and palimpsests. Khouri keeps on rereading or even

[107] Maḥmūd Darwīsh, "Dhākirah li-l-nisyān," *Al-Karmel* 21–22 (1986): 4–96; trans. Ibrahim Muhawi as Mahmoud Darwish, *Memory for Forgetfulness: August, Beirut, 1982* (Berkeley: University of California Press, 1995), 139.

[108] Muhsin J. al-Musawi, *Arabic Literature for the Classroom: Teaching Methods, Theories, Themes and Texts* (London: Routledge, 2017), 189–209.

[109] See Stetkevych, *Zephyrs of Najd.*

misreading the canon – for example, in *Majmaʿ al-asrār* (Complex of Secrets)[110] or in *Awlād al-ghītū*. The canon requires reinvention in order to continue. Constructed over time in competitive circumstances, including tournaments and marketplaces, it acquires a lasting legitimacy that also invites dissension. Not all people can come up with ʿAbd al-Malik al-Aṣmaʿī's (d. 216/831) retort to a poet who dared to use the word *saqaṭ* (fall) in the presence of the caliph – namely, "Asqaṭa Allāh ʿaynak" (God extract [make to fall] your eye!). In certain places, such as the caliph's court, language gets sanitized. In his take on postmodernist transgressions, Lyotard argues: "An institution differs from a conversation in that it always requires supplementary constraints for statements to be declared admissible within its bounds."[111] He adds: "The constraints function to filter discursive potentials, interrupting possible connections in the communication networks: there are things that should not be said."[112] Dissent in form and matter involves the literary market in a process of obliterating norms or building up others, for "boundaries only stabilize when they cease to be stakes in the game."[113]

In other words, mutation is the dynamic that sustains a changing presence. The prelude has to suffer Abū Nuwās's sneer in order to pass through the process of change before finally reaching Badr Shākir al-Sayyāb's (d. 1964) celebratory opening in "Canticle of the Rain."[114] Its early formulaic and institutive pattern and association with campsites and departures has to undergo transformation or give way to other variations on openings or intersections. Modernist narratives and poems are often a fabric of textual relations. As argued, Khouri summons the poetry of the Sufi master al-Junayd of Baghdad (d. 296–98/908–10) in one novel and that of the poet Waḍḍāḥ al-Yaman (d. 89/708) in another in order to present multiple canons and registers. Darwīsh enlists the pre-Islamic ode on his side, not to weep over loss, but to project a postcolonial reading of occupation. Darwīsh's debate with the iconoclast poet Imruʾ al-Qays focuses on the latter's misreading of competing empires and emperors: It is "Khilāf ghayr lughawī maʿa Imruʾ al-Qays" (A Nonlinguistic Dispute with Imruʾ al-Qays), who is recalled to be disputed, not for his poetics, but rather for being duped by the powerful Caesar. In "A Nonlinguistic Dispute with Imruʾ al-Qays," Darwīsh asks:

> What have you done to us, and to yourself? So go the way of
> Caesar, behind the smoke that towers black over

---

[110] Elias Khouri, *Majmaʿ al-asrār* (Beirut: Dār al-Ādāb, 1994).
[111] Lyotard, *Postmodern Condition*, 17.   [112] Ibid.   [113] Ibid.
[114] See DeYoung, "A New Reading."

time. Go the way of Caesar
alone, alone, alone
and leave us your language.[115]

An exchange takes place between a scroll and land; in both a palimpsest persists. In De Quincey's early definition, "A palimpsest, then, is a membrane or roll cleansed of its manuscript by reiterated successions."[116] In an exchange of land and scroll, Palestinian villages are erased to establish settlements for Europeans. To Darwīsh, Imruʾ al-Qays's poetry retains a pre-ruination language of the departing tribe, the fresh ʿArabiyyah with a compelling energy and life. If there is any figuration in these recalls, it is meant as a stepping trope in the formative constellation of a preoccupation record. In a letter to his fellow Palestinian poet and friend Samīḥ al-Qāsim, Darwīsh describes the remains of his village as follows: "When I performed the first pilgrimage ritual to my original village, al-Birwah, I found only the carob tree and the abandoned church, and a cowhand who spoke neither clear Arabic nor broken Hebrew."[117] He adds:

I remember the house's courtyard with a mulberry tree at its center, which pulled the houses together to form a home, my grandfather's home. We left everything as it was: the horse, sheep, bull, open doors, hot dinner, the adhan [call to prayer] of suppertime, and the lone radio – perhaps it has stayed on until now to broadcast the news of our victories. We went down into the valley that swerves and leads to the southeast, opening to a wellspring in a meadow that led us to the village of Shaʿb – this is where my mother's relatives live and where her family members were arriving from the village of Damun, which fell to the occupation.[118]

115 Maḥmūd Darwīsh, *Limādhā tarakta al-ḥiṣān waḥidan* (Beirut: Riad al-Rayyes, 1995); trans. Jeffrey Sacks as Mahmoud Darwish, *Why Did You Leave the Horse Alone?* (Brooklyn: Archipelago Books, 2006), 180–84.

116 Thomas De Quincey, "The Palimpsest of the Human Brain," was part of the four short essays to conclude *Suspiria de Profundis*, pt. 1. See David Masson, ed., *The Collected Writings of Thomas De Quincey*, 14 vols. (Edinburgh: Adam Charles Black, 1889–90), 13:340.

117 For a translation and commentary of the "Birwah Prelude," see Muhsin J. al-Musawi, "Teaching the Modernist Arabic Poem in Translation," in *Arabic Literature for the Classroom*, 197–98, 203–4. For more on Darwīsh, see his *Why Have You Left the Horse Alone?*, 171–88. Dated June 3, 1986, the abovementioned letter is in Maḥmūd Darwīsh, *al-Rasāʾil* (Haifa: Arabesque Publishing House, 1989). The letter also adds: "There, after a few days, the farmers from the nearby villages gathered, those who sold their wives' gold, to buy French-made rifles to liberate al-Birwah. They liberated it early in the evening. They drank the occupier's hot tea and slept the first night of victory. The next day, the 'salvation army' took it over without interruption, then the Jews re-occupied it and destroyed it to the last stone. And now we wait on the heights of the homeland, we wait for the return." See Lucian Dieterman, "The Destroyed Villages of the Nakba: Mahmoud Darwish on Visiting al-Birwah after 1948," Jerusalem Fund, May 18, 2015, https://tinyurl.com/33zt28wa.

118 Dieterman, "The Destroyed Villages of the Nakba."

However, Imruʾ al-Qays is brought back not as a crutch, prop, ploy, or artifice, but as a text to be claimed and invigorated. The first to weep and beg his companions to weep was not Imruʾ al-Qays, writes Khouri in *The Children of the Ghetto*, and before that in *Complex of Secrets*. Adam, not Imruʾ al-Qays, is the first to cry over loss. Weeping is a sublimation of love and passion. It is expressive and suggestive, but it is also the reclamation of a trace that is endangered by wind and time. In Darwīsh's poetry, as in Khouri's novels, the trace of the pre-Islamic ode swerves away from its nostalgic prelude to grow as the metaphor for enforced deportation, exodus, and erasure,[119] something that is captured by no less than the eyewitness Israeli officer in Smilansky's *Khirbet Khizeh* so as to become a sedimentary text for another text by Khouri, one that redraws the scene in Lod in 1947–48. Khouri draws on Imruʾ al-Qays and borrows the trace and prelude in order to reclaim another poet, Waḍḍāḥ al-Yaman, whose death in silence resembles the same silence imposed on the scene that Smilansky exposes in *Khirbet Khizeh*,[120] itself a text that also suffered its own silence until it was translated in 2008. In Darwīsh and Khouri there is an *achieved anxiety*; it is so because forebears are present to bear witness to the colossal effort aimed at erasing every trace in that scroll, as both written document and land.

The Canon: Dissemination and Deflection

The canon undergoes deflection, reflection, appropriation, and assimilation, even as new writers are assimilated in turn so as to become part of that canon. Both Khouri and Darwīsh need more than dedications to establish that lineage.[121] In the partial documentary *The Children of the Ghetto*, Khouri also recalls the story of the Palestinian poet Rāshid Ḥusayn (d. 1977), whose death and the partly burnt remains of his writings in New York bear witness to the other side of the Palestinian diaspora, the loneliness and loss in a heartless world. Darwīsh's other poems rewrite pre-Islamic and modern poets and place their poetics and sites in the context of current loss, not only in order to vindicate

[119] Darwīsh explained the exodus and the massive obliteration of Palestinian villages in his poetry and prose. His "Birwah Prelude" is among his last poems on this. Khouri relates the horror of forced evacuation of Lodd in his novel.

[120] Khouri's novel relates the story of his death as ordered by the Umayyad caliph after rumors were circulated that his wife was infatuated with that extremely handsome poet. For more, see A. Arazi, "Waḍḍāḥ al-Yaman," in *Encyclopedia of Islam*, ed. P. Bearman, Th. Bianquis, C. E. Bosworth, E. van Donzel, and W. P. Heinrichs, 2nd ed. (Leiden: Brill, 2012), http://dx.doi.org/10.1163/1573-3912_islam_SIM_7798.

[121] See Muhsin J. al-Musawi, "Dedications as Poetic Intersections," *Journal of Arabic Literature* 31, no. 1 (2000): 1–37.

continuity but also – and more importantly – to attest to "these fragments I have shored against my ruins,"[122] to collapse and coalesce sites of loss in a dense, multilayered, and resilient script of belonging.

Is this literary effort ephemeral in the face of stupendous monopolization and mobilization of media, military, and economic powers against the dispossessed? Not for Darwīsh and Khouri. Darwīsh writes in recognition of poetic ancestors, "For here, where we are, is the tent for wandering meanings and words gone astray and the orphaned light, scattered and banished from the center."[123] However, this search is not random. "There is a role for literature, and severing the relationship between the text and those for whom it is transformed into power is the very alienation of letters which the prophets of the final defeat of everything are now extolling."[124] Excavation takes place in this space, coalescing genealogy and cultural trees,[125] and retaining, as it should, power for the word in moments of fresh encounter with absence and loss. In its affiliation with Imru᾽ al-Qays and his companions, the poem sustains immortality and permanence. Darwīsh's poetry and prose provide substantial itineraries in the realm of canon formation. Preludial sites are now reinstated in the face of an onslaught of the temporal that depends on mythical silhouettes in the establishment of yet another variation on the rhetoric of empire:

> My poems circulate not just images and metaphors, but also actual landscapes, villages, fields. That is, they make a place. They thus give to one absent from a geography – one who nonetheless dwells presently in its image – the ability to take up residence in a poem as if he were standing on the actual ground. A poet cannot ask for greater satisfaction than seeing people use his verses (*buyūt shiʿriyyah*) as actual dwellings (*buyūt ḥaqīqiyyah*). In this respect, the Arabic language has a beautiful and rare homonym between the line of

[122] Eliot, *Waste Land*, part 5, "What the Thunder Said":

I sat upon the shore
Fishing, with the arid plain behind me
Shall I at least set my lands in order?
London Bridge is falling down falling down falling down
Poi s'ascose nel foco che gli affina
Quando fiam uti chelidon – O swallow swallow
Le Prince d'Aquitaine à la tour abolie
These fragments I have shored against my ruins
Why then Ile fit you. Hieronymo's mad againe.
Datta. Dayadhvam. Damyata.
Shantih shantih shantih

[123] Darwish, *Memory for Forgetfulness*, 11.

[124] Ibid., 139.

[125] See more on trees in Franco Moretti, *Graphs, Maps, Trees: Abstract Models for Literary History* (London: Verso, 2005).

poetry and actual homes. One and the other are called *bayt* as if humans could inhabit this dwelling.[126]

Working in two seemingly separate generic fields, Darwīsh and Khouri problematize the canonical nexus: The genealogical father is recalled not only to fit into current situations of loss and dispossession but also and primarily to undergo revision and interrogation. A normative instance is affectionately recalled, but that norm sets in motion other thematic and poetic patterns which convey, but also seethe with, anxiety, not because of the "influence" complex, but primarily because the present moment engenders new dynamics: loss, estrangement, and alienation. Being shocked and astounded by an enormous loss, the poet or writer can no longer take Imruʾ al-Qays's weeping literally. Loss now assumes major proportions because the stakes are high. Darwīsh recreates the encounter with settlers in his "Birwah Prelude," in order to free the reader or listener from the complacency, placidity, and stupor that have dulled language. The persona's monologues, recalling a village that was once his, are juxtaposed with a Western journalist's celebration of an infrastructure on top of the ruins of Birwah that duplicates urban centers in America and Europe. Poetry here exposes the enduring heartlessness of public opinion. In his *The Children of the Ghetto* Khouri goes back to his *Majmaʿ al-asrār* (Complex of Secrets); a metafictional narrative emerges in conjunction with other sedimentary texts. The thematic locus is strangeness, alienation, and estrangement. But these are existential concerns, in that they are linked to a human estrangement from the divine, to the curse that befell Adam. Adam is reborn in the character of Ibrahim Nassar in Khouri's *Complex of Secrets*, in Marquez's Santiago, and in the Palestinian Adam of *The Children of the Ghetto*. Both texts, *Complex of Secrets* and *The Children of the Ghetto*, explore the poetics of metafiction, its self-reflexivity, theoretical experimentations, and transgeneric forays. The author cannot hide for long; here and there a leak emerges, one that presents him not as in the anxious metapoetics of ancient poets, classical and postclassical, but through actual or symbolic cultural presence. If pre-Islamic and Islamic poets argue that poetry is a demanding and straining craft that operates in conjunction with individual talents,[127] modernists are professionals and craftsmen with a clear mission in mind.

[126] Simone Bitton, dir., *Mahmoud Darwich. Et la terre comme la langue* (Paris: Point du Jour International, 1997). Translation from Hassanaly Ladha, "Allegories of Ruin: Architecture and Knowledge in Early Arabic Poetry," *Journal of Arabic Literature* 50, no. 2 (2019): 115.

[127] See al-Mūsawī, "al-Tarjīʿāt."

Does this imply the sedimentation of a canon? Or otherwise? Is this partial use of Marquez's *Chronicle of a Death Foretold* an intertext or pretext to make a Lebanese version of the story of the Arab stranger Santiago, Jacob, Nassar? Or does naming invoke destinies? Khouri writes: "The names of protagonists are the problematic of the modern novel, because modernity entails individuality, and the individual has to have a name to be."[128] But names are also signs of estrangement and alienation. This is the thematic thread that connects *Complex of Secrets* and *The Children of the Ghetto*. All these names of individuals dying as strangers in their own lands or as émigrés lead to the first, to Adam: "Our master Adam, peace upon him, is the first stranger" (*Majmaʿ al-asrār*, 41). Also: "Adam is the first poet and the first human, his language is the first, the language of paradise, fire, earth and heaven, then follows the curse in the Tower of Babel that tears language apart" (42). Khouri plays even further on this thread and borrows several pages from the grand Sufi master Abū al-Qāsim al-Junayd of Baghdad, with respect to Adam's weeping and nostalgia. In the comment that follows there is a rewriting of the canon that continues to celebrate Imruʾ al-Qays as beginning. Treading between jest, humor, and an unstable personality, the narrator adds: "The longing of our master Adam for the past is a blend of reality and vision, that being the essence of a longing for ruins and campsites in ancient Arabic poetry. The very first to halt and ask others to do so, to weep and ask the rest to do so, was Adam, then Imru' al-Qays" (44). The Palestinian Adam has this genealogy behind him. Exchanging roles with the author, he eventually comes up with processes of embedding, intertextuality, narrative raids, parody, and contrafaction to argue that the canon is a diversified, unstable formation. Such is the case as long as it is rooted in nostalgia and estrangement. Are these postmodernist artifices and techniques operating in tandem with canonicity? Even Harold Bloom, the vigorous upholder of the "Western canon," does not raise this as a problem in his consideration of Latin American poets and novelists, especially Borges, Neruda, Alejo Carpentier, and the Portuguese Fernando Pessoa.[129]

Achaari picks up on this line of argument in his *The Arch and the Butterfly*, drawing on Hölderlin and presenting al-Firsiwi the father as poet, archaeologist, blind tourist guide, and master in resurrecting the hidden, the lost, and the erased. In comparing his role with his son, the writer of novels, his monologue runs as follows: "He's unconcerned with what will happen in the centuries to come because he lives in the present, in restaurants, bars and airports and sleeps with an assortment of

[128] Khouri, *Majmaʿ al-asrār*, 36. Further citations are in the text.
[129] Bloom, *Western Canon*, 417–30.

women."[130] As for al-Firsiwi, his self-reflection runs as follows: "This furious blind man spends his days chasing Hercules, Antaeus, Bacchus, Orpheus, Hylas, Venus, Medusa, Ariadne, Juba, and Ptolemy."[131] This archaeological analogy takes us away from the Arabic canon and places us at the intersection that books like al-Khwārizmī's *Mafātīḥ al-ʿulūm* (Keys to the Sciences) address. Compiled in 975–97, this work divides knowledge construction first in terms of indigenous sciences such as jurisprudence, theology or scholastic philosophy, language, and its philological domains like grammar. The last category includes prosody, poetry, and also history and secretarial functions. In his second category he places nonindigenous or foreign knowledge like philosophy, logic, medicine, arithmetic, geometry, astronomy, music, mechanics, and alchemy.[132] This classification overlooks intercultural and political dynamics that offer other genealogies of knowledge. However, for the present argument, its significance derives from similar retentions in the contemporary cultural spectrum that disconnect from strict applications of a canon.

The other underlying texts in Achaari's novel, including the father's reclamation of the biblical and Qurʾānic father in the story of Joseph, disturb this dichotomy between the humanities and sciences and situate the narrative in a Global South terrain. They dispute a centric canon and advocate instead a universal ethic that is a trademark in cultural dynamism, both ancient and modern. The father in Achaari's novel encapsulates the comparison in temporal terms so as to assign permanence to ancient relics and hence to his archaeological vocation: "Youssef works on fleeting stories and novels that wilt as soon as they are picked up. I, on the other hand, work on eternity."[133] Bloom's "universalism" and Frank Kermode's notion of canons as "instruments of survival built to be time-proof, not reason-proof" can be placed alongside al-Firsiwi's stipulations.[134] In the same vein and like poets such as al-Mutanabbī who also claim eternal poetic fame, al-Firsiwi professes another talent, that of a poet whose two poems, avowedly inserted into a collection composed by an obscure but fictional Hans Roeder, are spoken of as the best in the collection. They are taken to be the core of Roeder's poetry. Upon being told so, al-Firsiwi comments: "Then I've screwed Hans Roeder with those two poems!"[135] Youssef's father in *The Arch and the Butterfly* is presented as an archetypal

[130] Achaari, *Arch and the Butterfly*, 176. [131] Ibid.
[132] See "The Arab World," in "History of Encyclopedias," *Britannica*, www.britannica.com/topic/encyclopaedia/History-of-encyclopaedias#ref307723.
[133] Achaari, *Arch and the Butterfly*, 176.
[134] Frank Kermode, *Forms of Attention* (Chicago: Chicago University Press, 1985), quoted in Bloom, *Western Canon*, 3.
[135] Achaari, *Arch and the Butterfly*, 213.

figure whose presence may antagonize others, especially the son, but manages nevertheless to sustain continuity and permanence.

Regardless of the fictitiousness of this episode, the narrative should alert us to canon formation in relation to significant developments in Arabic cultural production over the ages. Along with a recourse to intertextuality, textual sedimentation, embedding, plot borrowing, and appropriation of narrative blocks, images, or structure, there are other techniques (and also foibles) in the establishment of literary or cultural phenomena. Conditions of possibility, such as cultural fluidity, virtual space, and global exchange, allow an amount of freedom that at times can verge on transgression, raids, and even theft.

Between Patching Texts and Postcapitalist Pilfering

Shifts, detours, deflections of the canonized works, and light or dense textual embeddings over time should alert us to the complexity of what has been passingly touched on under *saraq*. The recourse to structuralist and poststructuralist theories and applications that introduce the discussion of this chapter probably demonstrates the increasing need for further problematization of transtexuality or intertextuality in relation to such a rich tradition like pre-Islamic, classical and postclassical discussion of textual or performative navigations, their centrality to cultural and, specifically, literary life. Between deference to tradition and continuity, on the one hand, and a turn toward an open cultural economy, on the other, we confront a series of issues and challenges that invite theorization. The dialectic of fame and canonicity that Bloom traces in a Shakespearean axiom is only one dynamic in this cultural economy: "And fame in time to come canonizes us." If Bloom considers the retention of ancestors a post-Renaissance phenomenon, probably in tandem with an empowering imperial conquest, then the same can apply to other cultural economies. The case is even more so in Arabic during the heyday of cultural efflorescence. *Sariqāt*, as a broad theoretical term used for comparisons, contrafactions, mediations, and also differential levels of borrowings and raids, only takes shape in times of cultural and economic expansion, such as the lengthy Abbasid period. More than a defense of authorial or textual sovereignty, it is a sustained effort to tabulate, systematize, and also codify transactions in an otherwise free cultural market. With Shihāb al-Dīn al-Nuwayrī's (d. 733/1333) *Nihāyat al-arab fī funūn al-adab* (The Ultimate Ambition in the Arts of Erudition), and other massive compilations, intertextual space opens up to accommodate the thoughts and writings of others. He argues, "I have followed the traces of those excellent ones before me, pursuing their path and connecting my rope to theirs. So, if there should be any complaint, the dishonor is upon them and not me."[136] The underlying stipulation here is one of deference and subordination to antecedent authority that minimizes the issue of borrowing or raid. With its unacknowledged borrowings, the compilation legitimizes its presence as a repository of erudition and knowledge. His "arts of erudition," *funūn al-adab*, functions as an inclusive term for a compendious production. *Adab* is applied as an inclusive term, an acquisition of knowledge and admirable ethics, carefully articulated by the great philologist Ismāʿīl b. Ḥammād al-Jawharī (d. 393/1002) in his lexicon, *al-Ṣiḥāḥ fī al-lughah*. There he defines it succinctly as *adab al-nafs wa-l-dars* (self-refinement and erudition). Otherwise, how is one to rationalize the massive medieval cultural movement that involved prominent names all over the Arab-Islamic world, as shown and documented in *The Medieval Islamic Republic: The Arabic Construction of Knowledge*? A substantial theory for intertextuality and cultural competitiveness is laid down, one that resonates in part with modernists' explorations in poetry, poetics, and narrative. As system, it is in the mind of Darwīsh in his "Nonlinguistic Dispute with Imruʾ al-Qays." His dispute is with misconceived politics. Modernists quote from ancestors and versify or prosify their output. Their raids are often acknowledged in an otherwise navigational production in an age of global variability.

Is it possible to draw an analogy between the ancestors' age of "expansion," and the free global market economy? Do acknowledged readings and misreadings of the ancestral archive provide feasible means for the exploration of canon formation in an otherwise reifying commodity transaction? Is the "raid" in the gradations of *sariqāt* another name for pilfering in a postcapitalist economy? The war machine that erases cultures and people also invests in a myth of ancestry and origin. And more than ever before, cultures have to regain power against an onslaught that erases while calling on an imaginary scriptorium.

At this juncture, the Abbasid critic al-Qāḍī al-Jurjānī (d. 392/1001) can offer a theoretical framework for literary and poetic transaction that is worthy of our attention.[137] He underlines urban expansion and migration to towns as factors in a fundamental transformation that prompted a dominant literary taste and *ẓarf* (refinement). People chose from language what is "soft and easy," to such an extent that they "allowed slang and idiolect." He concludes that, in the end, *intasakhat al-sunnah* (the canon was displaced).[138] He justified this turn against servile reclamations

[136] Shihāb al-Dīn al-Nuwayrī, *Nihāyat al-arab fī funūn al-adab*, ed. and trans. Elias Muhanna as *The Ultimate Ambition in the Arts of Erudition* (New York: Penguin, 2016), 2.

[137] See Suzanne P. Stetkevych, *Abū Tammām and the Poetics of the ʿAbbāsid Age* (Leiden: Brill, 1991): on al-Qāḍī al-Jurjānī's *Wasāṭah*, see 90–104; on *sariqah*, 101–4.

[138] See al-Mūsawī, "al-Tarjīʿāt," 55.

of ancients as being a lexical departure from uncouth expression and usage to a lighter and sweeter one. Whatever follows in literary traditions presents variations on this structural transformation. As I have argued elsewhere, even the substantial theorization of and for *sariqāt* should be seen in terms of mobility and transformation.[139] Several directions are noticeable in cultural production, especially its theory. Lexical refinement and softness are an outcome of urban expansion, but they are also a motivation for further social mobility. Abū Nuwās's poetry was so popular among social margins, as Muhalhil b. Yamūt b. al-Muzarraʿ (d. 304/916) argues,[140] that his phenomenal success incited versifiers and practitioners to raid the poetry of others and assign it to him.[141] Moreover, trading poetry was a fashion and, along with it, the growth of a transactional market vocabulary. Thus, in one poem, al-Sarī al-Raffāʾ (d. 362/972–73) spoke of the Khālidiyyān Brothers (Abū Bakr Muḥammad [d. 380/990] and Abū ʿUthmān Saʿīd [d. 371/981]),[142] the anthologists and poets who were his countrymen, as traders. He labels their compilations as commodities, and their role as no more than traders in verse who return loaded with looted rarities of poetry like merchants scurrying with their merchandise.[143] In a postmodernist vein that nevertheless resonates with mercantile society economies, and the Abbasid economy in particular, Lyotard argues that knowledge construction is as follows: "Knowledge is and will be produced in order to be sold, it is and will be consumed in order to be valorized in a new production: in both cases, the goal is exchange."[144] In this cultural market, trading in poetry as merchandise opens the door for exchange, borrowing, partial theft, and plagiarism. Nowhere is this clearer than in the medieval (i.e., postclassical) period when ʿUmar b. al-Wardī (d. 749/1349) declares:

> I steal of meanings whatever I can
> and if I can surpass the ancients, I praise my feat
> But if I am on equal footing with the ancients
> it is still to my credit to be so.
> . . .
> A dirham issued under my name is more to my taste
> than somebody else's dinar.[145]

139 Ibid., 55–61.
140 Muhalhil b. Yamūt Ibn al-Muzarraʿ, *Sariqāt Abī Nuwās*, ed. Muḥammad Muṣṭafā Haddārah (Cairo: Dār al-Fikr al-ʿArabī, 1957).
141 al-Mūsawī, "al-Tarjīʿāt," 60–61.
142 Full name: al-Sarī b. Aḥmad b. al-Sarī al-Raffāʾ.
143 al-Mūsawī, "al-Tarjīʿāt," 67. For a recent contribution, see Erez Naaman, "An Outline of a Plagiarism Controversy from the Abbasid Era: Al-Sarī l-Raffāʾ vs. the Khālidī Brothers," *Journal of Arabic Literature* 54, nos. 1–2 (2023): 51–72.
144 Lyotard, *Postmodern Condition*, 4.
145 Quoted in al-Musawi, *Republic of Letters*, 130.

From the ninth century onward, a significant corpus engages with *sariqāt*. Manuals and commentaries or critical insights appeared to monitor, cope with, and codify a massive production. Especially between the ninth and twelfth centuries, critics appeared as both arbiters of taste and cultural market inspectors. The phenomenon necessarily questions stabilities. To claim ancestry, the modernist poet or novelist has to accept this process as one entailing change in terms of affiliation, not only because theories of plagiarism have already disturbed wholesale endorsement of names and poems but also because ancestors like Imru᾽ al-Qays make no claim to absolute sovereignty, as shown in their metapoetics. Furthermore, a differential schema sets the politics of a person apart from the production. On the other hand, there are strong ancestors who often speak of poetry as craft, and their art as craftsmanship, and they used to spend some time in producing an ode. Recited, practiced, and performed, poetry turns into a contending commodity. Its practice in salons or gatherings entails a desire for marketability; hence competition and hierarchy prevail. In this marketplace, the poet as anthologist assumes the right to tamper with selections, as Abū Tammān did in his compilation of the *Ḥamāsah*.[146] In this vast field, one that also has its compilers in prose, there emerged the need for regulation. Every critic of note had to participate in this theoretical and critical effort, using different labels like *wasāṭah* (mediation) or *muwāzanah* (parity, equity, and comparability: evaluative comparison and contrast) or, like Ibn Wakīʿ (d. 393/1003), creating a treatise entitled *al-Munṣif fī al-sāriq wa-l-masrūq minhu* (The Equitable Stand between the Plagiarist and the One Plagiarized).[147] Al-Ḥātimī's (d. 388/998)[148] theoretical classification of plagiarism in *Ḥilyat al-muḥāḍarah* (The Ornament of Discourse) is worth mentioning here, because he opens the door for figurative multiplication. In such raging controversies and the prominence of textual battling, *sariqah* becomes a fetish, a searched-for commodity in a marketplace where the exchange of accusations and rebuttals tend to be rampant, and only a handful of contributors retain balance and composure alongside scholarly serenity. Under the *sariqāt* rubric, one can observe the extensive use of language, preludes, and images. Even the *badīʿiyyāt* genre offers mantle odes openings that are variations on preludial plagiarism.[149] These long poems, with their rhetorical apparatus, can be seen as part of a substantial

146 On Abū Tammām's selection and manipulation, see Stetkevych, *Abū Tammām*, 257–81.

147 al-Ḥasan b. ʿAlī Ibn Wakīʿ, *Kitāb al-munṣif li-l-sāriq wa-l-masrūq minhu*, ed. ʿUmar Khalīfah b. Idrīs (Benghazi: Qār Yūnis University, 1994).

148 Full name: Abū ʿAlī Muḥammad b. al-Ḥasan al-Ḥātimī.

149 Suzanne P. Stetkevych, "From Text to Talisman: Al-Būṣīrī's 'Qaṣīdat al-Burdah' (Mantle Ode) and the Supplicatory Ode," *Journal of Arabic Literature* 37, no. 2 (2006): 145–89; Stetkevych, "From Jāhiliyya to Badīʿiyyah: Orality, Literacy, and the

multiplication of theoretical practice that unites poets, critics, grammarians, rhetors, and philologists in a single theoretical constellation which the culture market inspector labels as *sariqāt.* Al-Ḥātimī's early attempt in his *al-Risālah al-mūḍiḥah* to downplay al-Mutanabbī's verse of wisdom as being Greek-inspired is less popular than al-Mutanabbī's own sayings. What resonates well in theory is the latter's phrase *al-shiʿr jādah wa-rubbamā waqaʿa al-ḥāfir ʿalā mawḍiʿ al-ḥāfir* (poetry is a trail, and a hoof may tread on the space of another).[150] Poets fare freely in a fluid literary market and linguistic malleability. The possibility of a foreign presence in Arabic poetry is thus dismissed.

If we are to accept the premise that theoretical multiplication in the field of exchange, mediation, comparison, and theft is evidence of a thriving cultural phenomenon, does this resonate with the tendency to diversify sources among Arab modernists and also to reinvent tradition in order to meet pressing cultural, political, and economic needs? Similar questions were raised alongside poetic and narrative experimentations. The early twentieth-century rift between Ibrāhīm ʿAbd al-Qādir al-Māzinī (d. 1949) and ʿAbd al-Raḥmān Shukrī (d. 1958), discussed, and others over the former's alleged plagiarisms is only one notorious case,[151] whereas the 1950s–60s witnessed more heated discussions and accusations.[152] In all these controversies, the relationship with other cultures, texts, authors, and the process of acculturation are paramount. Although often generated because of partisan politics, these controversies relate to a relative lack of touch with the classical Arabic tradition on the part of some modern Arab critics and/or to their unfamiliarity with intertextualizing strategies as theorized by poets and critics elsewhere. ʿAlī Aḥmad Saʿīd (Adūnis) appealed to *wasāṭah* (mediation) to explain the impact of Rimbaud, Baudelaire, Macramé, and Andre Breton to justify a "new" understanding of his classical Arab forebears.[153] The poetess

Transformations of Rhetoric in Arabic Poetry," *Oral Tradition* 25 (2010): 211–30. See also al-Musawi, *Republic of Letters*, 39–42, 120–21, 148–50, 161–65.

150 There are multiple references, but see Ibn Abī al-Iṣbaʿ, *Taḥrīr al-taḥbīr*, 1:418; Ibn Rashīq, *al-ʿUmdah*, ed. Muḥammad Muḥyī al-Dīn ʿAbd al-Ḥamīd (Beirut: Dār al-Jīl, 4th print, 1972), 2:289; *al-ʿUmdah* (2001), 2:289. Ibn Aydamir places this alongside *muwāradah* (i.e., coincidental similarity) and *ishtirāk* (sharing) expression and meaning. See Ibn Aydamir, *al-Durr al-farīd* (2015), 1:257.

151 For brief notes on these accusations, see Julie Scott Meisami and Paul Starkey, eds., *Encyclopedia of Arabic Literature* (London: Routledge, 1998), 2:521; Brugman, *Modern Arabic Literature in Egypt*, 143; al-Musawi, *Islam on the Street*, xiv. For a detailed reading of one case, see Paniconi, "Reframing Politics."

152 See Muḥyī al-Dīn Ismāʿīl's attacks on ʿAbd al-Wahhāb al-Bayātī in Muḥsin J. al-Mūsawī, "Marjiʿiyyāt naqd al-shiʿr al-ʿArabī al-ḥadīth fī al-khamsīnāt," *Fuṣūl* 15, no. 3 (1996): 54, 36–37, 50, respectively.

153 Ibid.

Nāzik al-Malāʾikah (d. 2007), a free verse movement pioneer, accused Jabrā Ibrāhīm Jabrā (d. 1994) of plagiarism not only because he used her terms for the free verse movement without due acknowledgment, but also because he allegedly misapplied them.[154] The formidable critic Iḥsān ʿAbbās (d. 2003) came to the rescue of many by explaining poets' resort to *talfīq* (patching) as a widely practiced style among poets, ancient and modern,[155] and, as ʿAbbās notes, "it is part of a form, not a raid on others' property."[156] Especially when the practice means making use of multiple verses to create a new one, *talfīq* becomes an art form, highly lauded by Ibn Rashīq when applying it to al-Mutanabbī.[157]

No matter how much new waves in literary production manage to recall the past and its theoretical regulation, codification, and diversification of assets, their ancestral retentions and conversation with other cultures, especially from Asia, Africa, and Latin America, are still acts of refurbishment, something that the American novelist John Barth once advocated in order to revitalize a European-American culture, which he saw as suffering from exhaustion.[158] As Borges notes in his "Kafka and His Precursors," "Each writer creates his precursors."[159] Borges even "began to favor the view that canonical literature is more than continuity, [it] is indeed one vast poem and story composed by many hands through the ages."[160] In more than one sense, the engagement of modernists with precursors and texts testifies to this inclusive perspective. Its specificity derives from particular situations that involve thematic and stylistic appropriations. In this undertaking there is also an underlying awareness of a vast theory of plagiarism (currently: intertextuality) that, despite the starkness of the term, presents continuity as a struggle for renewal and inventiveness. In its makeup and outcome, the tendency resonates with economies of desire, either as an impulse to merge into another text, reclaim it, downplay it, or work in its shadow, as Chapter 2 argues. Desire functions strongly in the field of "creative" writing, and in the arts in general, very much like its operation in the marketplace, as a driving force, especially relentless in the politics of a postcapitalist economy as propelled by the ferocious greed for others' resources.

[154] Ibid., 36–37.

[155] On *talfīq*, or patching, see al-Ḥātimī, *Ḥilyat al-muḥāḍarah*, 2:90; Abū ʿAlī al-Ḥasan Ibn Rashīq al-Qayrawānī, *Qurāḍat al-dhahab fī naqd ashʿār al-ʿArab*, ed. al-Shādhlī bū Yayā (Tunis: al-Sharikah al-Tūnisiyyah li-l-Tawzīʿ, 1972), 106.

[156] Quoted in al-Mūsawī, "Marjiʿiyyāt," 50. [157] See further Chapters 4 and 5.

[158] John Barth, "Literature of Exhaustion," *The Atlantic Monthly*, August 1967, 29–35; Barth, "The Literature of Replenishment," *The Atlantic Monthly*, January 1980, 65–71.

[159] Jorge Luis Borges, "Kafka and His Precursors," 1951, *in Labyrinths* (New York: New Directions, 1964), quoted in Bloom, *Western Canon*, 437.

[160] Ibid.

2 Thresholds

Dependency and Thievery in the Adab *Marketplace*

> Art is either plagiarism or revolution. Individuality of expression is the beginning and the end of all art.
>
> Johann Wolfgang von Goethe (1749–1832)

The twentieth-century obsession with *adab*, its early adoption and use, categories, semantic spread, and afterlife as a literary frontier, has not developed in a vacuum. The vast activity that takes the form of books, anthologies, table-talks, biographical dictionaries, and lexicographic inventories is only witness to a very active civilization. However, what is missing in the conversation about this active culture is the compelling presence of thievery, *sariqāt*, which has long been at the center of controversial discussions, literary confrontations, accusations, rebuttals, and mediations.[1] An alarming sensitivity to authenticity and originality has a double function, derailing or incitive, a case that other cultures treat lightly. The famed Russian musician Igor Stravinsky remarked once that he and T. S. Eliot were different from James Joyce and others, in the sense they refit "old ships." He adds: "We did not pretend to have invented new conveyors or new means of travel, for the true job of the artist is to refit old ships. He can say again, in his way, only what others have already said before him."[2]

This cursory but significant reflection on reprocessing was already discussed in ninth-century Baghdad, but its ramifications took a wide range in a thriving and competitive culture. Thus, the accusations of theft in the field of *adab*, and especially poetry, multiplied and invited the participation of prominent names. Although its shades, fluctuations, varieties, and terms have been central to *adab* as a field of knowledge, edification, and

[1] "Liṣṣ al-qarīḍ" was also used by al-Buḥturī, Ibn al-Ḥājib, Ibn al-Rūmī, and many others. Hence, the literary or poetic term "*luṣūṣiyyah*" is relevant. See further Ibn Wakīʿ, *Kitāb al-munṣif.* See also Manfred Ullmann, *Wörterbuch der klassischen arabischen Sprache* (Wiesbaden: Harrassowitz, 1970), 643. The motto is a quote from Stravinsky, in Sonallah Ibrahim, *Yawmiyyat al-wāḥāt*, ed. and trans. Robyn Creswell, *That Smell and Notes from Prison* (New York: New Directions Publishing, 2013), 88.

[2] Igor Stravinsky, *Refitting Old Ships*, GES House of Culture. Also in his *Autobiography* (New York: W. W. Norton, 1962).

refinement, it is rare to come across it as relevant to current *adab* discussions. One encounters recognition of this issue as "the most important part of ancient Arabic criticism," as the late Palestinian-Iraqi critic Hind Ḥusayn Ṭāhā argues;[3] or as another Arab scholar has it, "the *sariqāt* theory is a critical diving in the depth of creative production, as much as it is its interlocutor, and an interrogation of its originality."[4] However, this is not followed up theoretically. The late Wolfhart Heinrichs lamented that, even in classical poetics, the increasing *sariqāt* (thievery) terminology has not been collected in a neat corpus of literary criticism: "At first sight, these terms appear to be very suitable for a study of the history of Arabic poetry, at least in the field of *maʿānī*, but they have never been put into use for this purpose."[5] A twentieth-century shift to *adab* as a literary domain still suffers from a failure to put things together when trying to establish a workable framework for a literary history or literary theory.[6] While single studies on several aspects, trends, and even literary theory and metacriticism[7] and poets have been accumulating in the last forty years or so, a viable working system that can accommodate the fervent discussion of plagiarism is not easy to find.

Even the discussions of *adab* that make good use of current theory often betray a lamentable lacuna. Nallino's early contribution and some Arabists' responses to it happened to be pivotal to an ongoing conversation with respect to this field, as aptly defined by Abū al-Naṣr Ismāʿīl b. Ḥammad al-Jawharī, a point that is already emphasized. No less important is Ibn Aydamir's significant synthesis of a legacy of *adab* as a basically philological or literary endeavor with poetry at its center and critical correctness as its guide.[8] Equally stimulating to further discussion is the subsequent turn of *adab* to literariness.[9] The turn relates to the rise

[3] Hind Ḥusayn Ṭāhā, *al-Naẓariyyah al-naqdiyyah ʿinda al-ʿArab* (Baghdad: Dār al-Rashīd, 1981), 187.

[4] ʿIṣām Bin Shallāl, *Naqd al-naqd wa-tajalliyātih fī al-turāth al-naqdī wa-l-balāghī* (Algiers: Editions Ḍifaf, 2021), 192.

[5] Wolfhart Heinrichs, "Literary Theory: The Problem of Its Efficiency," in *Arabic Poetry: Theory & Development*, ed. G. E. von Grunebaum (Wiesbaden: Harrassowitz, 1973), 56.

[6] See Appendix A.

[7] See ʿAbduh ʿAbd al-ʿAzīz Qalqīlah, *Naqd al-naqd fī al-turāth al-ʿArabī* (Cairo: Maktabat al-Anjilū al-Miṣriyyah, 1975); Muḥammad al-Daghmūmī, *Naqd al-naqd* (Rabat: College of Arts Publications, 1999). There are several books in Arabic on matters of poetics and literary theory; but in English, see Huda J. Fakhreddine, *Metapoetics in the Arabic Tradition* (Leiden: Brill, 2015); Lara Harb, *Arabic Poetics: Aesthetic Experience in Classical Arabic Literature* (Cambridge: Cambridge University Press, 2020). See also Wen-Ching Ouyang, *Literary Criticism in Medieval Arabic-Islamic Culture: The Making of a Tradition* (Edinburgh: Edinburgh University Press, 1997).

[8] See the author's introduction, Ibn Aydamir, *al-Durr al-farīd* (2015), 303–37.

[9] For a review of Nallino's *adab*, see Salah Nantij, "Le concept d'adab est-il dérivé du mot daʾb? Retour sur une hypothèse ancienne de Vollers et Nallino," *Journal of Arabic Literature*

١٠٠

كفقدان ذي السلاح الشجاعة والنجدة وفقدان صاحب الطبع الأدب
كفقدان ذي النجدة السلاح والعدة ولا يحصل لأحدهما دون الآخر
ومتى أحاط الأديب بطرف من الأدب وتعدّى به الطبع عن إظهاره
كان والعاري من الأدب والعطل من المعرفة في نظم القوافي سواء

ويتلوهما أقسام الأدب

فمن ذلك النحو الذي هو قوام اللسان وميزان البيان
ورونق الإشارة وزينة النطق والعبارة والفاصل بين الوصل والقطع
والفارق بين التسكين والنصب والخفض والرفع ومميز المبني
من المنصرف وذوات الياء من ذوات الألف ومهذب اللفظ
بالإعراب ومسدد القول بالصواب

٦٥

Figure 2.1 Divisions of *adab*

of disciplines in Europe by the end of the eighteenth century, the compartmentalization of knowledge, and its tabulation in order to meet the needs of empires for texts and languages that would reach and control the hearts and minds of the colonized, even at the height of brutality and exploitation. Colonial educational systems were soon to impose their curricula in the colonies.[10] Thus, Thomas b. Macaulay's notorious maxim of 1835 that went into effect sums up the colonial turn to education, "a single shelf of a good European library is worth the whole native literature of India and Arabia."[11] Before the turn to literariness, *adab* is more or less an inclusive *adab al-nafs wa-l-dars*, as it had appeared in refined *kalām*. Indeed, in his *Kitāb sariqāt al-shuʿarāʾ* (The Book of Poets'

50 (2019): 342–68. For a short bibliographic index, see the two issues of *Journal of Arabic Literature* on *adab*: "*Adab* Criticism & Theory," special issue, *Journal of Arabic Literature* 50, nos. 3–4 (2019). More writings are forthcoming, among them Lara Harb, *Mimesis and Adab*; Sarah R. Bin Tyeer, *The Well-Tempered Reader. The Legitimization of Adab in the Arabic Literary Tradition.* See also Appendix A.

10 See al-Musawi, *Republic of Letters*, 182–83. For more on *adab* and transformation, see Appendix A. See also Benedict Anderson's significant intervention with respect to Macaulay's imperial indoctrination in the colonies: *Imagined Communities*, rev. ed. (London: Verso, 1983), 90–91. See also Edward Said, *Orientalism* (New York: Random House, 1978), 152, 340n66.

11 Anderson, *Imagined Communities*, 91.

Thefts), Ibn Abī Ṭāhir Ṭayfūr (d. 280/893), for example, suggests that "*kalām al-ʿArab*," which Bonebakker translates as the "literature of the Arabs," has been the common shared source for poets, writers, and orators. Vast and rich, this shared legacy that functions as an intertext, Genette's hypotext, militates against strict claims of originality and uniqueness; for, as Ibn Ṭayfūr argues, *kalām al-ʿArab* is "*multabis baʿḍuhu bi-baʿḍ*" (fused, welded, and interfused), and posterity implies ancestry[12] – an issue that paradoxically generates a struggle for excellence and distinction. This is not a mere passing remark, as it falls within the context of a heated discussion involving inventiveness, innovation, imitation, and appropriation. Abū ʿAlī al-Ḥātimī also reports that Ibn Ṭayfūr concludes that even a poet with a natural talent for rhetoric and poetry is susceptible to having his speech depend on others, even if that person is meticulously guarding his lexical store of meanings and expressions.[13] The well-known philologist and grammarian Abū ʿAlī al-Fārisī (d. 377/987) goes so far as to say, "Speech (*al-kalām*) is open to all, and so is the circulation of expressions."[14] Many later scholars argue for varieties of poetic or prosaic echoes and borrowings against wholesale repudiations. Thus al-Qāḍī al-Jurjānī (d. 392/1001) concludes that conversations that focus on a pejorative use of the term *saraq* may even end up with an inference that "*al-kalām kulluhu sariqah*" (all speech is plagiarism).[15] The celebrated poet Abū Tammām (d. 231/845), for one, was known in his time as a very well-read poet, a compiler of multiple anthologies of poetry, as enumerated by Abū al-Qāsim al-Āmidī (d. 370/980 or 371/981) in his *Muwāzanah*.[16] It is justifiable therefore to state that his poetry could not escape his massive readings and learning. This point of strength was redirected against him by the latter prominent philologist and critic. Thus, while al-Āmidī argues against Ibn Ṭayfūr's sweeping application of thievery terms, he qualifies that judgment because "the plagiarisms that lie concealed in his [Abū Tammām's] poetry outnumber the ones that are evident, despite their multitude."[17] Both the objection to Ibn Ṭayfūr's confusion of common and shared expressions and meanings with thievery proper and the

[12] Quoted from al-Ḥātimī, *Ḥilyat al-muḥāḍarah*, 2:28, and Ibn Aydamir, *al-Durr al-farīd*, in Bonebakker, "Ancient Arabic Poetry and Plagiarism," 81.

[13] Quoted in al-Ḥātimī, *Ḥilyat al-muḥāḍarah*, 2:28.

[14] Quoted in al-Ḥātimī, *Ḥilyat al-muḥāḍarah*, 2:29, without mentioning Abū ʿAlī al-Fārisī by name, resorting instead to "*wa-qad zaʿama qawmun mimman yuḥsin al-ṣināʿah*" (some people who are learned in this domain claim . . .).

[15] al-Jurjānī, *al-Wasāṭah* (1900), 210.

[16] al-Āmidī, *al-Muwāzanah*, 1:429; also quoted in Stetkevych, *Abū Tammām*, 46.

[17] See Stetkevych, *Abū Tammām*, 53. She italicizes the sentence (not followed here) to underscore both the hesitant judgment and the problematics involved in the available large terrain of *adab*.

implication of invisible thieveries stand for al-Āmidī's method in his otherwise significant book that claims to balance and compare two poets, al-Buḥturī (d. 284/898) and Abū Tammām, through the unearthing of echoes and borrowings, in order to demonstrate the naturalness of one, al-Buḥturī, and the artificiality of the other – that is, Abū Tammām.[18] In the end, whatever al-Āmidī assigns to al-Buḥturī derives from the former's standards of "*al-shuʿarāʾ al-muḥsinīn*" (commendable poets).[19] The term is stretched further and further at every turn of the argument, for the target poet, as cited from Muḥammad b. Dāwūd al-Jarrāḥ's (d. 296/908–9) quotes from antecedent authorities, "strives for *badīʿ* [inventiveness, or euphonic and also semantic embellishment] to end up with the impossible."[20] To substantiate his point of view and also to uncover invisible plagiarisms, al-Āmidī resorts to a number of authorities, like Abū ʿAlī Muḥammad b. al-ʿAlāʾ al-Sijistānī, whom he claims to have heard saying of Abū Tammām: "He has no uniquely invented *maʿānī* [poetic meanings] other than three."[21] Al-Āmidī adds that expressions and motifs borrowed or plagiarized from recent contemporaries, early Islamic poets, and the ancients abound, but instead of "an innovation, he blunders," because he writes "against what the Arabs enunciate."[22] As if this is not enough, al-Āmidī resorts to the Kufic grammarian, philologist, genealogist, and traditionalist of tribal poetry Ibn al-Aʿrābī (d. 231/845),[23] quite often despite his proclaimed resistance to grammarians' emphasis on *lafẓ* (expression),[24] for the latter with his stringent ancient role models stipulates respecting a line by the target poet: "I haven't found in the poetry of the Arabs anything that resembles it [Abū Tammām's poetry] excepting a verse by ʿĀmir b. Ṣaʿṣaʿah."[25] The irony that underlines this statement suggests that, for better or worse, the poet is an innovator. It is worth mentioning, and in line with the comparatist approach between current theorizations and classical Arabic ones, that the cultural script undergoes its changes and fluctuations as conditions of possibility allow or require. The objection as raised by al-Āmidī rests on a preference for a stable canon, a set of conventions that should be impregnable to violations and transgressions.

[18] Full name: al-Walīd b. ʿUbayd Allāh b. Yaḥyā Abū ʿUbādah al-Buḥturī.

[19] al-Āmidī, *al-Muwāzanah*, 1:135.

[20] Ibid., 2:134, 218. The chain that Muḥammad b. Dāwūd al-Jarrāḥ reports in his *al-Waraqah* relates that Muḥammad b. al-Qāsim b. Mihrawayh transmits from his father, who also concludes: "The first to corrupt poetry was Muslim b. al-Walīd, and Abū Tammām followed him, as he adopted his *badīʿ* trend and got lost there." Ibid., 1:135. Al-Marzubānī's chain of reporters ends with Ḥudhayfah b. Muḥammad al-Ṭāʾī al-Kūfī, "and he was one of the learned, saying . . ." See al-Marzubānī, *al-Muwashshaḥ*, ed. Muḥammad Ḥusayn Shams al-Dīn (Beirut: Dār al-Kutub al-ʿIlmiyyah, 1995), 343–44.

[21] al-Āmidī, *al-Muwāzanah*, 1:133. [22] Ibid., 143.

[23] Full name: Abū ʿAbdallāh Muḥammad b. Ziyād b. al-Aʿrābī.

[24] al-Āmidī, *al-Muwāzanah*, 1:49. [25] Ibid., 180.

Conversely, current theories highlight the "modification in the principle of exclusion and the principle of the possibility of choices," which Michel Foucault deems necessary in any "new discursive constellation."[26] It is this constellation with its prescribed canons and revisionist practices in a large field of knowledge with poetry at its center for being, in Ibn Sallām's panoramic review,[27] the register of the Arabs, that invites us to place the argument of this and the next chapter (see Chapter 3) in the domain of *adab* (see Figure 2.1). Al-Āmidī's nuanced, albeit partisan, reading of poetry in his *al-Muwāzanah* should be argued in this context.

While crediting Abū Tammām – on the authority of Muḥammad b. al-ʿAlāʾ al-Sijistānī – with only three invented meanings, al-Āmidī conversely resorts to Muḥammad b. Dāwūd al-Jarrāḥ, who reports that Ibn Ṭayfūr cited a hundred verses stolen by al-Buḥturī from Abū Tammām.[28] A seemingly balanced critique emerges that can well set the ground for accepting al-Āmidī's otherwise harsh criticism of the target poet. Is al-Āmidī fair and impartial in his *al-Muwāzanah* in this assessment of both poets? His book might invite such an approval, but the underlying loyalty to *ʿamūd al-shiʿr* (the acceptable or standardized canon of poetry), something that he wholeheartedly assigns to al-Buḥturī, suggests the impossibility of such fairness.[29] It is a comparative reading that derives its strength from a fecund memory and wide acquaintance with poetry – ancient, early Islamic, and modern; it celebrates naturalness against craft, the recognized canons of poetry as applied by the ancients against what he deems mere virtuosity, artificiality, and pomposity.[30] In other words, it is meant to celebrate al-Buḥturī, while critiquing his possible pitfalls. One can argue that al-Āmidī's use of plagiarism as the crux of a raging dispute is tipped toward the ancients despite his wide range of reference to modernists' poetry. In fact, he repeatedly argues, "You have to be familiar with what the imams of the science of poetry have agreed on, their consensus respecting prioritization of some poets to others."[31] The quotes from and references to these authorities show them to be the upholders of the canonized tradition.

One way of looking at the direction of al-Āmidī's approach to *sariqāt* is to draw attention to the minimal space that he gives to philologists or critics who blamed Abū Tammām, like Ibn Ṭayfūr and Abū al-ʿAbbās Aḥmad al-Quṭrabbulī (nicknamed al-Farīd, or al-ʿUzayr), because he

[26] Michel Foucault, *The Archaeology of Knowledge*, trans. A. M. Sheridan Smith (New York: Pantheon Books, 1972), 67.

[27] Ibn Sallām, *Ṭabaqāt al-shuʿarāʾ* (1998), 22. [28] al-Āmidī, *al-Muwāzanah*, 1:291.

[29] Ibid., 5–6. [30] Ibid. [31] Ibid., 395.

finds them confusing shared meanings with *sariqāt* or simply multiplying accusations without enough evidence, for al-Quṭrabbulī "does not provide evidence."[32] Taking as a start a sweeping designation of the target poet as "*kathīr al-saraq*" (an excessive plagiarist),[33] al-Āmidī objects to some detractors and indictors, including al-Quṭrabbulī, who provide an excuse for an elaboration of what they think are Abū Tammām's plagiarisms or incorrect diction and meanings.[34] Apparently, he does this in order to pave the way for his relative espousal of al-Buḥturī. Thus, he provides multiple comparisons to show that most of Abū Tammām's poetry consists of duplications of contemporaries and ancients and to illustrate the poet's failed effort to create something ingenious out of their poetry: "*Yurīdu an yabtadiʿ fa-yaqaʿu fī al-khaṭaʾ*" (He makes mistakes while trying to be innovative/original).[35] Having now established a pseudo fairness by way of rejecting the input of two writers, al-Āmidī can devote forty-six pages to dislodging Abū al-Ḍiyāʾ Bishr b. Yaḥyā's (al-Naṣībī) criticism of al-Buḥturī and his proclaimed list of thefts from Abū Tammām.[36]

Even if we take into account al-Āmidī's preference for *ʿamūd al-shiʿr*, as exemplified by the ancients,[37] and his resistance to strenuous poetics followed and applied by his early contemporaries like Ibn Ṭabāṭabā (d. 322/934) in his *ʿIyār al-shiʿr* (The Standard of Poetry) and Qudāmah b. Jaʿfar in his *Naqd al-shiʿr* (Evaluation of Poetry),[38] his misdirected conclusions lack the serenity of his later contemporary al-Qāḍī al-Jurjānī, who, in other ways, often echoes al-Āmidī in both method and conclusions. The effort to "balance" arguments for and against both poets suffers whenever al-Āmidī's critique of the wholesale application of the term *saraq* succumbs to his own personal preference for the acceptable canons of poetry, a point that is aggravated by inadequate poetic analysis,[39] as noticed by both critics and polyglots.[40] The positive side of this enormous effort derives, however, from his marshaling of the names

[32] Ibid., 135–36. [33] Ibid., 133. [34] Ibid., 135–38.

[35] He cites al-Quṭrabbulī; ibid., 135–36. [36] Ibid., 110–29, 135–36, 304–50.

[37] For his use of the term to indicate the ancients' model, see ibid., 6.

[38] Al-Āmidī authored an epistle addressed to Ibn al-ʿAmīd (d. 360/970): *Tabyīn ghalaṭ Qudāmah b. Jaʿfar fī naqd al-shiʿr*. See al-Āmidī, *al-Muwāzanah*, 2:368–69, also Aḥmad Ṣaqr's n. 1 on p. 369. Another book is under the title *Fī iṣlāḥ mā fī ʿiyār al-shiʿr li-Ibn Ṭabāṭabā*. See further Abū Faraj Muḥammad b. Isḥāq al-Nadīm, *The Fihrist: A 10th-Century AD Survey of Islamic Culture*, ed. and trans. Bayard Dodge (1970; New York: Columbia University Press, 1988); Abū ʿAbdallāh al-Rūmī Yāqūt al-Ḥamawī, *Muʿjam al-udabāʾ* (Cairo: Dār al-Maʾmūn, n.d.), 8:75. Another edition is also used (see n. 97). See also Iḥsān ʿAbbās, *Tārīkh al-naqd al-adabī ʿinda al-ʿArab* (Amman: al-Shurūq, 2006), 142–43.

[39] ʿAbbās, *Tārīkh al-naqd al-adabī*, 149.

[40] For ʿAbbās's citation from Yāqūt's quotes, see ibid., 15–151.

of a large number of poets, philologists, and critics. Al-Āmidī portrays the literary scene as an enormous cultural marketspace with recognizable creditors, debtors, and middlemen, dealing with an available merchandise. As the reason behind this effort, plagiarism stands out not only as dynamic for such a consortium but also as the space that enforces and spreads its demands on participants. It calls on all to define an understanding of the field and its demands, a situation that brings into the discussion a terminological "labyrinth" (in Bonebakker's words). Al-Āmidī reiterates his conviction that poetry is a domain solely reserved for the knowledgeable.[41]

These conclusions fit more easily in either the ancient-modernist controversy or the prejudice that al-Qāḍī al-Jurjānī noticed among philologists, grammarians, and rhetors who were prone to one model or another.[42] Although often welded with multiple positions, the grammarians' lack of acquaintance with literary analysis and applicable models presents them in al-Āmidī's documentations as rigid traditionalists.[43] Hence, the applicants of *ʿamūd al-shiʿr* in poetry in emulation of the ancients run the risk of thievery more than the modernists, because the latter tend to invent, a point that is clearly evident in the poetry of Bashshār b. Burd (d. 168/784), Muslim b. al-Walīd (d. 208/823), and down to Abū Tammām. However, while attempting to map out a cultural scene where some trends lose momentum over time, a point that Ibn Qutaybah (d. 276/889) had recognized a long time ago,[44] we have to keep in mind that the battle over *ʿamūd al-shiʿr* has never abated all the way down to mid-twentieth-century writings, as shown in the sociologist ʿAlī al-Wardī's *Usṭūrat al-adab al-rafīʿ* (The Myth of Elite [or Highbrow] Literature).[45]

Moreover, even when some benefit might emerge when philologists or critics strive to target a towering figure, the endeavor loses validation the moment the reader becomes aware that it is a paid-for enterprise in this competitive marketplace. While we may agree, as readers, that al-Ḥātimī,[46] Abū al-ʿAbbās al-Nāmī (d. 399/1009), Abū Saʿd Muḥammad b. Aḥmad al-ʿAmīdī (d. 433/1041), and Abū Muḥammad b. Wakīʿ (d. 393/1003) have

[41] al-Āmidī, *al-Muwāzanah*, 2:388–89, 394–95, 496.
[42] al-Jurjānī, *al-Wasāṭah* (1966), 411.
[43] Jamāl al-Dīn al-Qifṭī, *Inbāʾ al-ruwāt ʿalā anbāʾ al-nuḥāt*, ed. Muḥammad Abū al-Faḍl Ibrāhīm (Beirut: al-ʿAṣriyyah, 2003), 1:323.
[44] See Abū Muḥammad ʿAbdallāh b. Muslim Ibn Qutaybah, *al-Shiʿr wa-l-shuʿarāʾ*, ed. Aḥmad Muḥammad Shākir (Cairo: Dār al-Ḥadīth, 2001), 1:63.
[45] For more, see al-Musawi, *Arabic Poetry*, 12.
[46] On other issues relating to poetics, see Geert Jan van Gelder, "The Poet as a Body-Builder: On a Passage from al-Ḥātimī's *Ḥilyat al-Muḥāḍara*," *Journal of Arabic Literature* 13 (1982): 58–65.

provided us with some significant suggestions and critical terms, the fact that they were either commissioned or driven by malice relegates their opinions to the large sensational margin of literary gossip.[47] Even so, their writings receive attention as colorful interventions or, in Ibn Wakīʿ's case, as vilifications. The case is just as bitter in al-Ḥātimī's (d. 388/998) *al-Risālah al-mūḍiḥah fī dhikr sariqāt al-Mutanabbī wa-sāqiṭ shiʿrih* (The Explanatory Epistle in Pointing Out al-Mutanabbī's Plagiarisms and Low Verse).[48] The latter's venom, which his subsequent apology cannot mitigate,[49] was released at a time when criticism was to witness a systematic application of terms. He was not alone, as will be clear in Chapter 5. Part of the discussion of creditors and debtors in a vibrant literary marketplace involves not only jealousy, venom, and lack of a "hospitable" accommodation but also the interposition of literary patrons against one towering figure or another. In other words, there are several reasons as to why *sariqāt* received enormous attention in a competitive space. If we leave aside the economies of competitiveness, the accusation of *saraq* is the most available strategy for undermining a growing poetic status and fame.[50]

One can go as far as to suggest that in some cases we come across readings predating modernist criticism that argue also for an intertextual space, as practiced by Roland Barthes, Julia Kristeva, and Pierre Macherey.[51] No text stands alone; every text is in conversation with other texts and enunciations. On the positive side, al-Āmidī, for example, finds an association between the poet's (Abū Tammām) wide range of reading, ultimate prodigious memory, and studious effort to compete with other poets, an association that should have implied a subtle diffusion in his poetry. In other words, this could have been credited to the poet's significant contribution to a lively literary milieu, and thence to a theoretical base for that enormous detective pursuit of similarities and echoes that is pejoratively termed "plagiarism." Moreover, the underlying

47 See further Chapter 4.

48 Muḥammad b. al-Ḥasan al-Ḥātimī, *al-Risālah al-mūḍiḥah fī dhikr sariqāt al-Mutanabbī wa-sāqiṭ shiʿrihi*, ed. Muḥammad Yūsuf Najm (Beirut: Dār Ṣādir li-l-Ṭibāʿah wa-l-Nashr, 1965).

49 See ʿUmar Khalīfah b. Idrīs's quotes from al-Ḥātimī's *al-Risālah al-mūḍiḥah* and comments on the underlying venom al-Ḥātimī was expressing, even when claiming otherwise, in Ibn Wakīʿ, *Kitāb al-munṣif*, 1:41–42.

50 For a succinct summary of al-Nadīm's list and comments on the *saraq* phenomenon, see ʿAbd al-Ḥakīm al-Anīs, "Bayān Muḥammad b. Isḥāq al-Nadīm li-l-sariqāt al-ʿilmiyyah wa-l-adabiyya," Alukah.net, September 26, 2015, https://tinyurl.com/mrxuhcp9.

51 See Chapter 1. For Pierre Macherey, see *A Theory of Literary Production*, trans. Geoffrey Wall (London: Routledge, 1978), 53: a "book never arrives unaccompanied: it is a figure against a background of other formations, depending on them rather than contrasting with them." See also al-Musawi, *Islam on the Street*, xiv.

recognition of repetitive (i.e., common) images and *ma'ānī* (poetic ideas and meanings) entails a counter-emphasis on expressions as a field for innovation. Alongside the reference in the Qur'ān (18:109) to the infinity of God's words in comparison to the finitude of human lexis, and hence its inevitable repetitiveness, there is, as was noted in Chapter 1, Imam 'Alī b. Abī Ṭālib's (d. 40/661) saying: "If speech could not be repeated, it would have long been exhausted."[52] From the times of 'Antara b. Shaddād (d. 608 CE) down to the era of Abū Tammām, poets complain about the exhaustibility of expressions and meanings.[53] Instead of inviting surrender and resignation, this finitude incites poets and writers to master the field of Arabic, be acquainted with poetry and poetics, and share tacit rules and codes governing literary production. Ibn Rashīq's summary of the celebrated birth of poets, as well as Ibn Qutaybah's (d. 279/828) sketch of the ode, tells us much about a competitive space confirmed by established literary conventions, tribal celebrations of poets, poetry competitions, and other attending ceremonial activities. These present the domain as one that is politically and culturally charged.[54]

These two issues – repetitiveness as a given but also as a driving force for innovation and inventiveness, and the role of memory in the ultimate permeation of one's poetic text and matrix – should have been considered in the search for a formative base to a poetic theory. That base should have gained currency in such a competitive field as another constellation of poetry collections, anthologies, and varieties of criticism. However, the matter is not resolved here, especially because prominent critics, rhetors, and grammarians, anonymous producers of such an encyclopedic work as Ikhwān al-Ṣafā''s (The Pure Brethren),[55] anthologists, and poets all present the tenth century as being one of a thriving and lively culture. Even al-Āmidī's allusion to Abū Tammām's indiscernible "plagiarisms" must be seen as applicable to the poetry of all other poets, major and minor alike.[56] If so, the allegation of plagiarism and its application show misplacement and misdirection. After all, *kalām al-'Arab* is "*multabis*

[52] Quoted in al-'Askarī, *Kitāb al-ṣinā'atayn*, 196.

[53] Bonebakker, "Ancient Arabic Poetry and Plagiarism," 82–83.

[54] See Ibn Qutaybah, *al-Shi'r wa-l-shu'arā'* (2001), 1:63, 74–75; Ibn Rashīq, *al-'Umdah* (2001), 1:10–11, 12–21, 2:305–6; Reynold A. Nicholson, *A Literary History of the Arabs* (1907; repr., Cambridge: Cambridge University Press, 1956), 77–79. See also al-Musawi, *Arabic Poetry*, 238.

[55] For identification of the members of the group, see al-Musawi, *Republic of Letters*, 63–67, esp. 339n5.

[56] Ibn Qutaybah has already drawn attention to cases of indiscernible borrowing. See *al-Shi'r wa-l-shu'arā'*, ed. Aḥmad Muḥammad Shākir (Cairo: Dār al-Ma'ārif, 1982), 1:134, 1:134 (2001). See al-Qāḍī al-Jurjānī's significant note on discursive fluidity and the strained search for newness in *al-Wasāṭah* (1966), 214–15. See further in Chapter 4.

ba'ḍuhu bi-ba'ḍ" (fused, welded, and interfused), a point that, as mentioned earlier, is well taken by the renowned linguist and grammarian Abū 'Alī al-Fārisī. Even so, there are other thorny issues that drove a sober-minded critic like al-Qāḍī al-Jurjānī to conclude his chapter on plagiarisms with an apologetic statement, one that almost dismisses the term and its application. He concludes:

> For this reason, I forbid myself – and do not think it proper for anyone else – to pass the judgment of plagiarism against a poet . . . but rather, I say that so-and-so said such-and-such and so-and-so had said it before him and said such-and-such. Thus, I avail myself of the virtue of truthfulness and preserve myself from rushing headlong into rash judgments.[57]

Reconstituting a Literary Domain

Notwithstanding the seeming pejorative tone of the term *saraq* (theft), its mention and analysis in the Arabic tradition never diminishes its massive presence and significance in literary production. The amount of effort spent classifying its varieties and applications demonstrates its presence as a vital element, a dynamic, in the makeup of a powerful tradition. Moreover, the fact that the allegation of *saraq* leaves no poet untouched, from al-Kumayt b. Zayd (d. 126/744) to Abū al-Ṭayyib al-Mutanabbī (d. 354/965), Taqī al-Dīn b. Ḥijjah (d. 837/1366), and Shams al-Dīn al-Nawājī (d. 859/1455), down to modern times, involving Ibrāhīm 'Abd al-Qādir al-Māzinī and even Adūnīs, should alert us to its significance beyond pejorative connotations.[58] To come to grips with this massive presence of commentaries, debates, classification, and tabulation, and claim it as a vital and generative cultural principle, we have to review it from different angles. Furthermore, its pervasive presence brings us even closer to what has been a belated reading of the essence of writings and speech as intertextual or transtextual spaces.

There is first the nature of poetics as shown in poetries or relevant philological inquiries. Second, there is the early effort to transcribe and document poetry in the shadow of rising doubts concerning transmission, fabrication, and *intiḥāl*, as followed up in modern times by David Samuel Margoliouth (d. 1940) and Ṭāhā Ḥusayn (d. 1973) based on early references and disputes. Third, there is the progression of theoretical explorations before and soon after Ibn Sallām's classifications of ranks and merits among poets. Fourth, there is the lingual dimension, in relation

57 Stetkevych's translation, *Abū Tammām*, 103. See al-Jurjānī, *al-Wasāṭah* (1966), 215.

58 On accusations leveled against Adūnīs, see al-Mūsawī's response in "Marji'iyyāt."

not only to Persian, Indic, or Greek poetries, for example, but also to *fuṣḥā* and *ʿāmmiyyah*. Fifth, there is the hegemonic presence of ancient poetry as a referential framework, which is central not only to *ʿamūd al-shiʿr* as the canonized poetic standard but also to Arabic standards of *aṣālah* (originality) in relation to the massive growth of philological input from scholars of non-Arab descent. Ancient poetry became a last defense in a dynamic cultural transformation that accompanied the rise of the Islamic empire. As the undisputed source of eloquence, and hence of an Arab stock, it is always available to be recalled and referenced, defended, and held high, especially in relation to *sariqāt*. Even when a sober-minded critic like Ibn Qutaybah has to confront the celebration or assessment of ancients and moderns solely on the basis of their times and affiliation, he still believes that genres and modes established by ancient tradition remain the standard to be applied and followed: "for the splendid and illustrious poet is the one who follows these styles."[59] He adds: "It is not permissible for a later poet to deviate and depart from the ancients' modality."[60] There is already an issue between *itbāʿ* (following; or in the steps of ...) or *iḥtidhāʾ* (emulation) and creation. Thus, al-Ḥasan b. Hānī's (Abū Nuwās, d. 198/813) rebuke is addressed to his *fadm* (dull-witted) contemporaries for trying to emulate the ancients.[61] The raging discussion on what constitutes *sariqah* proper, with respect to wording and expression or poetic meaning – and especially the newly invented one – does not occur in a vacuum. In the mid-ninth century the whole field of poetics was on fire, and several philologists felt the urge to dig deep into this realm of synonyms and expressions. While that enormous effort throughout the late eighth century and onward might have been part and parcel of the needs of empire to codify and standardize Arabic, it was certainly no less relevant to a competitive literary marketplace in which allegations of theft were rampant, downplaying the distinction conferred on this or that poet. Thievery and inventiveness were, as they always are, means to boost or degrade a poet; they directly relate to social, cultural, and symbolic capital, and hence they play on matters of reception or denial. The whole movement is not only a marker of a thriving culture

[59] Ibn Qutaybah, *al-Shiʿr wa-l-shuʿarāʾ* (2001), 1:75. [60] Ibid., 76.

[61] See n. 66 in Chapter 3, but also Jaroslav Stetkevych's significant contribution to the theory of Arabic poetry in *Zephyrs of Najd*, number 33, pp. 17, 208:

> Talk of effete ruins is an affair for the dull
> Your epithets must fit the daughter of the vine!

In another version of the *dīwān*, and also in some critics' account: the verse reads:

> To address ruins is the rhetoric of anciency.

but also an invigorating one. Without going into the maze of what comes first – thievery accusations in relation to expressions and poetic ideas, or lexical activity – the significant contributions to the corpus of synonyms are no passing matter. They are so because several books devoted their attention to the issue not only of poetic meanings but also synonyms. ʿAbd al-Raḥmān al-Hamadhānī's *al-Alfāẓ al-kitābiyyah* stands out as a significant landmark for its erudition, neatness, and hence popularity among the youth, as attested to by the renowned rhetor and critic ʿAbd al-Qāhir al-Jurjānī (d. 471/1078).[62]

The Epistemic Turn

A thriving culture that turned into a competitive space involved philologists, poets, critics, and littérateurs in corresponding activities. If *maʿānī* and *alfāẓ* were the trade of the day in the fierce poetic competition, philologists were strong participants to reckon with as their contributions demonstrate. Very prominent among these works are Yaʿqūb b. Isḥāq b. al-Sikkīt's (d. 244/858) *Kitāb tahdhīb al-alfāẓ* (The Book of Cultivating Expressions);[63] Muḥammad b. Khalaf b. al-Marzubān's (d. 330/920) *Kitāb al-alfāẓ: al-kitābah wa-al-taʿbīr* (The Book of Wording: Writing and Expression); and ʿAbd al-Raḥmān al-Hamadhānī's (d. 320/933) *al-Alfāẓ al-kitābiyyah* (Written Words), which was referenced earlier. Before them, an enormous written production in this territory shows more concern with not only the systematization of Arabic that laid the ground for further detection of echoes, similarities, and thefts[64] but also the increasing preference for poets known for a fecund memory of poetry and cultural tradition. Ibn Sallām (d. 231/846), ʿAbd al-Malik al-Aṣmaʿī (d. 216/831), Yūnus b. Ḥabīb (d. 182/798), Abū ʿAlī Diʿbil al-Khuzāʿī (d. 246/835),[65] and others regarded this as a criterion for the prioritization of poets and littérateurs. While echoing al-Jāḥiẓ, al-Āmidī sums up this endeavor and expertise as *ṣināʿah* (craft) like any profession that requires knowledge. His enumeration of professions is important for this discussion of the marketplace.[66] If other professions have their set of values, familiarity, and expertise, poetry is no less so. It is no longer an

[62] See n. 67; also nn. 94 and 95 in Chapter 1. See further Chapter 3.
[63] Abū Yūsuf Yaʿqūb Ibn al-Sikkīt, *Kanz al-ḥuffāẓ fī Kitāb tahdhīb al-alfāẓ*, annot. Abū Zakarīyā Yaḥyā b. ʿAlī al-Khaṭīb al-Tibrīzī, ed. Luwīs Shīkhū al-Yasūʿī (Beirut: al-Maṭbaʿah al-Kāthūlīkiyyah li-l-Ābāʾ al-Yasūʿiyyīn, 1895).
[64] For a survey, see Ṣabāḥ Kzārah, "Fī al-muʿjamiyyah al-ʿArabiyyah," *Majallat Majmaʿ al-Lughah al-ʿArabiyyah bi-Dimashq* 78, no. 4 (2003): 965–88.
[65] al-Āmidī, *al-Muwāzanah*, 1:22–23, 395.
[66] See Abū ʿUthmān ʿAmr b. Baḥr al-Jāḥiẓ, *al-Bayān wa-l-tabyīn*, ed. Ḥasan al-Sandūbī (UK: Hindāwī, 2017), 157–59; al-Āmidī, *al-Muwāzanah*, 1:394.

unpoliced domain, for philologists felt bound to step in to direct this production or at least to demonstrate its expanding horizons. Ibn Durayd's (d. 321/933) mentor, Abū ʿUthmān Saʿīd b. Hārūn al-Ushnāndānī (d. 256/870), who has his *Kitāb maʿānī al-shiʿr* (Poetic Meanings), was not the only one in a field that happened to gain power in time, as we understand from many erudite scholars and philologists or literary critics like Ibn Sallām and Ibn Qutaybah. These books prepare the ground for a more tabulated tenth-century production. Al-Āmidī resorts to many of those renowned in the science of poetry to bolster the argument that Abū Tammām's poetry is more akin to oration and prose than to poetry.[67] This tenth-century production should direct our attention to multiple meanings that in the end underscore a method that looks on plagiarism of meaning as a practice in synonyms. Ibn al-Marzubān's book is concerned with idioms and their approximate synonyms or departures, while al-Hamadhānī's offers multiple meanings to select expressions in a book that ʿAbd al-Qāhir al-Jurjānī (d. 471/1078) references in relation to issues of *akhdh* and *sariqah*. There al-Hamadhānī affirms that "a person who takes a bare meaning and dresses it in his own expression has the right to it."[68] While many *saraq* terminologies fit under this rubric, *ijtilāb* as an open plea for poetic support was practiced by prominent poets like Jarīr and al-Farazdaq, as in Figure 2.2.

As if it were not enough to side with al-Jāḥiẓ's conclusion that meanings and ideas are available for all regardless of ethnicity or race, thesaurus-like books offer an enormous supportive canvas of poetic meanings and expressions that could serve as a source for poets and scribes. Otherwise, weak poets or even prominent ones might let a poem slide into some malpractice, as shown succinctly in Ibn Aydamir's list of reprehensive practices (see Figure 4.2), with *salkh* among them. *Salkh* (flaying) is after all a practice involving the replacement of an original wording by a synonymous another, a practice that ʿAbd al-Qāhir al-Jurjānī singles out as a denigrated recourse, and not *iḥtidhāʾ*.[69] No less significant is the increasing navigation among different cultures and languages that displays an invigoratingly heterogeneous activity. The noticeable participation of several writers, critics, poets, philologists, and polymaths who inhale from multiple ethnic backgrounds presents a case that over an extended period generated a compelling movement to

[67] al-Āmidī, *al-Muwāzanah*, 1:19.

[68] ʿAbd al-Qāhir al-Jurjānī, *Dalāʾil al-iʿjāz fī ʿilm al-maʿānī* (Beirut: al-Maktabah al-ʿAṣriyyah, 2002), 436. He comments: "This is a well-known saying that is read by youth in the first pages of ʿAbd al-Raḥmān's book."

[69] Ibid., 431. For the root, origin, conjugation, and subsequent shift to poetics of *iḥtidhāʾ* in relation to the ongoing plagiarism conversation, see ibid., 428–29. See further Chapter 3.

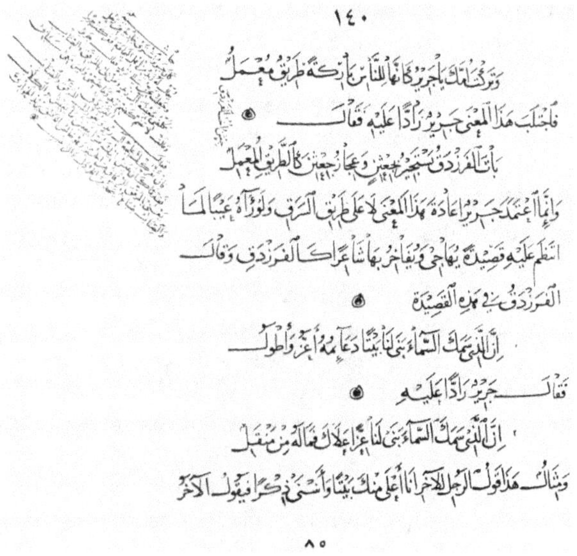
١٤٠
فاجتلب هذا المعنى جرير رادا عليه فقال
بان الفرزدق يتجر بجعثن وعجان جعثن كالطريق المعمل
وانما اعتمد جرير اعادة هذا المعنى لا على طريق السرق ولو رآه عيبا لما
انظم عليه قصيدة يهاجي ويفاخر بها شاعرا كالفرزدق وقال
الفرزدق في هذه القصيدة
ان الذي سمك السماء بنى لنا بيتا دعائمه اعز واطول
فقال جرير رادا عليه
ان الذي سمك السماء بنى لنا عزا علاك فما له من منقل
ومثال هذا قول الرجل الآخر انا اعلى منك بيتا واسنى ذكرا فيقول الآخر
٨٥

Figure 2.2 *Ijtilāb* as practiced by Jarīr

codify and organize knowledge. Reports, debates, and an enormous treasury of anecdotes work hand in hand with biographical records and encyclopedias of littérateurs. Whenever there is a rich cultural tide with distinctive features and concerns, we speak of an epistemological turn. But, to recapitulate, and in relation to current theoretical explorations in such cultural transformations, do we have the right to speak of epistemic change that carries the turn further? In Michel Foucault's popular theorem, an episteme is "a total set of relations that unite, at a given period, the discursive practices that give rise to epistemological figures, sciences, and possibly formalized systems."[70] Even a cursory survey of these components in the vibrant tenth century can tell us as much.

The mere fact that there were then many authored books, treatises, chapters, or debates focusing on a phenomenal rise not only in lexicographic activity but also in the domain of interrelations speaks of a vibrant literary market. While the most visible signs of this vibrancy and vigor relate to detective tracing that collapses imitation, borrowing, reflection, and refraction, and also to straightforward raids on others' poetries, there is also a never-ending referentiality that culminates in the matrix of quotes from named authors that distinguishes writings by

[70] Foucault, *Archaeology of Knowledge*, 191.

al-Āmidī and al-Qāḍī al-Jurjānī, and later by Ṣafī al-Dīn al-Ḥillī (d. 752/1349), Taqī al-Dīn b. Ḥijjah (d. 837/1434), Ibn Aybak al-Ṣafadī (d. 764/1363), and certainly Yāqūt (d. 626/1229), Ibn Khallikān (d. 681/1282), and dozens of others. When we reach the twentieth century, writers and poets people their novels and poetry with names, as in Jabrā Ibrāhīm Jabrā's (d. 1994) novels and essays – a trend that is exemplified by the poet Saʿdī Yūsuf (d. 2021), whose split persona plays openly with its masks in poems like "America, America," and "Thulāthiyyat al-ṣabāḥ" (The Morning Trilogy). His welcome intruders are not *zuwwār al-fajr* (Dawn Visitors – i.e., security officers) but Walt Whitman, Lorca, Baudelaire, and unannounced others.[71] Are these references, allusions, borrowings, intrusions, passing intertextualities, or woven matrices? Do they function as catalysts, or settlers in one's memory that colonized it and imposed their presence on expression and poetic meanings? The poet Ḥamīd Saʿīd dives headlong into readings of translated novels that evolve as the matter of his *Dīwān*: *Ulāʾika aṣḥābī* (Those Are My Companions).[72] The difference between different stages in a twentieth-century scene and scenes from earlier periods is a matter of power dialectic. A waning culture might find itself immersed in borrowing. Colonized cultures usually suffer an enormous contamination, a point that did not escape the attention of Ibn Manẓūr (d. 711/1311), for example, in the preface to his voluminous lexicon, *Lisān al-ʿArab*. With the fall of the center in Baghdad, and the waning of other centers in the Arab east and west looming, philologists and grammarians found themselves involved in translation from Turkish and Persian, whereby translation stood out as a visible sign of dependency.[73] Athīr Muḥammad Abū Ḥayyān of Granada (d. 745/1344) came up with a basic grammar for the Turkish language; a facilitating manual for the interested readers of Turkish that was thriving on the ruins of a divided Mamluk dynasty. Cultural dependency is an outcome of this power dialectic. Ibn Manẓūr had other instances in mind, and he bemoaned dependency upon perceiving an activity in contending cultures that was lacking in Arabic.[74] The same dialectic is applicable to the arena of poetry, as strong poets impose poetic modalities on the scene while they may use their power to invade other poets. Lacking that antecedent authority, many early twentieth-century poets show an enormous reliance on European poetry, French, British, and somehow Russian, for example, not only because of an

[71] See Saʿdī Yūsuf, *al-Aʿmāl al-kāmilah* (Damascus: Dār al-Madā, 1995), 2:410–14.
[72] Ḥamīd Saʿīd, *Dīwān: ulāʾika aṣḥābī* (Amman: Mirsāl, 2018).
[73] See al-Musawi, *Republic of Letters*, 54. [74] Ibid., 68, 211–12.

imposed colonial educational system, but also because some, like al-Māzinī, found themselves trapped in identification with their poets. Mid-twentieth-century Arab poets may offer a different image, as they are poised between self and persona, ego and mask. This tension distinguishes an anxiety undergone by the modern Arab subject that suffers a wound, a split with no healing in sight. It is so, not for lack of imagination, but rather because of a trepidation that emanates from interconnections worldwide, and from a situation at home, its distrust of poets and fear of their defiance. This is not what Harold Bloom traced solely in English and French poetry. What increasingly distinguishes twentieth-century European cultures is already distinctive of dynamic cultures, for no culture has a claim to profusion without this interaction and interrelation that Pierre Bourdieu, in line with his own sociological pursuits, assigns to twentieth-century European culture: "Silent and hidden references to other artists, present or past, affirm, in and by games of distinction, a complicity ... that is precisely the interrelations and the interactions of which the work is just a silent trace. Never has the structure of the field been as present in each act of production."[75] The last surmise might be stretched a bit, as it asserts what is already a given in the tenth-century Arab script when all critics assert this interdependency among texts. There is, however, the struggle for prominence and distinction when knowledge consortiums during the Abbasid period in particular witnessed a stupendous growth. Moreover, the rising number of functionaries, grammarians, poets, linguists, scribes, scientists, and polymaths also entailed a competitive search for prominence, not only in poetry but also in prose that was to witness a striding movement forward.

Theft Allegations

If the matter of interrelations adopts so many appellations and justifications, can we ever justify the mounting allegations of theft especially leveled at prominent figures? Although I intend to deal with this at length in Chapter 4, it suffices here to view the case as a two-track movement: an awareness of a vast corpus of literary traditions that invites comparisons while taking multiple directions, and a search for terms to market accusations or to account for echoes, duplications, reiterations, or plain thefts. Sustained over long periods, such an activity, one that generated book-length studies, chapters, and interventions, cannot be dismissed as

[75] Pierre Bourdieu, *The Rules of Art: Genesis and Structure of the Literary Field*, trans. Susan Emanuel (Stanford, CA: Stanford University Press, 1996), 161.

marginal issues to specific controversies. It derives its initiation and impetus from competitiveness. Very pertinent in this respect is the opening line of al-Qāḍī al-Jurjānī's *al-Wasāṭah*, where he unequivocally argues that the ambition of literati to join the lofty ranks of poets and writers invokes and generates competitiveness.[76] He adds that such competitiveness is the motivating factor behind jealousy and venom. The poet is bound to resort to every means possible in order to achieve and accumulate further cultural and symbolic capital, but the poet or prose writer or orator has to be a good *rāwiyah* (with eidetic memory, memorizer, and transmitter of tradition), a kind of custodian with a rich available material in store, a point which al-Qāḍī al-Jurjānī also underscores: "The *muḥdath*'s [often the Abbasid period modernist, i.e., innovator] need for memorization and knowledge and thence communication [of poetry] is more pressing" (*ḥājatu al-muḥdath ilā al-riwāyah amass*).[77] Such knowledge functions as an inciting dynamic in a cultural environment from which poets and writers inhale, but it also involves memory in intentional or unintentional dependency. In the absence of clear-cut definitions of *saraq*, thievery is a given practice, but its pejorative connotations must demand some examination, a process which literary critics were to undertake. Instances of poets lamenting the raid on their poetry illustrate the rife struggle to surpass one another – a point that will be discussed in Chapter 5. On the other hand, poets often found themselves under attack by critics and philologists, who were themselves not necessarily devoid of their own malice or allegiance to another poet, group, or literary trend. Indeed, al-Marzubānī's title *al-Muwashshaḥ fī ma'ākhidh al-'ulamā' 'alā al-shu'arā'* (The Adorned on the Faults Leveled by the Learned against Poets) reflects the enormous body of critical assessments that gather together both the fair and prejudicial. Furthermore, since pre-Islamic times the mere denial of theft only attests to its presence as a practice aimed at augmenting a poetic reputation. Al-'Ashā Maymūn b. Qays (d. 625 CE), for example, denies accusations of thievery, *intiḥāl al-qawāfī* (arrogating verses to oneself), equating the act with disgrace.[78] Contrafactional poetry and poetic feuds, especially feuds around the two warring camps of Jarīr (d. 110/728) and al-Farazdaq (d. 110/728),[79] entailed the use of literary appropriation or raids as one way of accumulating competitive cultural capital. Poets were, as they are now, to vie for a better position in a demanding space.

76 al-Jurjānī, *al-Wasāṭah* (1966), 1: "al-tafāḍul … dā'iyat al-tanāfus; wa-l-tanāfus sabab al-taḥāsud."

77 Ibid., 15–16.

78 See Ma'tūq, "Al-Sharīf al-Murtaḍā's Contribution," 25.

79 Full name: Abū Firās Hammām b. Ghālib (also known as Abū Ḥarzah).

An open conversational field is bound to emerge, and the search for literary innovation and inventiveness was to prompt not only serious learning by heart of rich poetic and literary traditions but also a diligent search for rare expressions. In his early and important contribution to the twentieth-century study of plagiarism, Gustave E. von Grunebaum has a different take: He suggests that poetic conventions with their "small number of motives" entail repetitiveness and limit inventiveness.[80] In other words, Grunebaum argues that, in order to escape conventional constraints, poets find thievery inevitable, a point that Ibn Ṭabāṭabā al-ʿAlawī (d. 322/934) stressed: "The ordeal faced by our contemporary poets is harder than what confronted predecessors, because they were preceded in every innovative meaning and eloquent expression."[81] While both approaches opt to explain or justify some practices that come under the blanket term *sariqah* (theft), they also predicate on a vast field of commentaries, accusations, rebuttals, refutations, corrections, and justifications and on a mounting effort to place this issue at the heart of cultural dynamics. On the other hand, this available vast space of poetry, poetics, oratory, letter writing, and narratives offers a gateway to textual marauding that is manifested in a parlance which philologists continue to expand under the rubric of *sariqāt*, updating an already large thievery (intertextuality) lexicon with further classifications and differentiations, as shown in Figure 2.3. Classifications of the term *saraq* under commendable and reprehensible thefts alert us to consider it as a discursive domain, an intertextual space with positive and negative properties.

The theoretical framework for this corpus is important for any reading of *adab*, not only because of its immediate association or concomitance with all *adab* concerns and practices, but also because the discussions around it concerning originality, borrowing, and imitation offer a sketch of literary history and theory. In these conversations, there is always reference to an ongoing passion for publicity, visibility, and mastery. Alongside the steady effort to improve one's poetic acumen and thence claim mastery, every other literary effort, be it poetic or in prose, is driven by a latent or conspicuous sense of competitiveness, which implies a struggle with predecessors or contemporaries. In Arabic, as probably in other languages, this competitive search for prominence is what makes literary history. Harold Bloom is not far off this understanding when he argues, "Strong poets make that history by misreading one another, so as

[80] Grunebaum, "Concept of Plagiarism," 234.
[81] Ibn Ṭabāṭabā al-ʿAlawī, *ʿIyār al-shiʿr*, ed. Ṭāhā al-Ḥājirī and Muḥammad Zaghlūl Salām (Cairo: al-Maktabah al-Tijāriyyah, 1956), 8–9.

Figure 2.3 Classification of theft

to clear imaginative space for themselves."[82] Elsewhere, he offers six terms to account for the transaction between predecessors and successors. In these revisionary terms or ratios, Bloom thinks of the struggle among strong poets, ancestors and successors, as a multisided one. The ephebe tries a "clinamen," to depart from the predecessor, a departure that is a trace of anxiety. If the successor works hard to demonstrate a completion or finalization of a precedent's work, then it is "tessera." His other terms also have their equivalence in Arabic.[83] His term "misreading" is merely a gentle way to deal with issues that some Arab philologists classify broadly under the terms *akhdh* (partial seizing of either meaning or expression) or *laṭīf al-saraq* (subtle thievery) and a number of other terms that are less harsh.[84] Indeed, al-Muẓaffar

[82] Harold Bloom, "A Meditation upon Priority and a Synopsis," in *The Anxiety of Influence* (New York: Oxford University Press, 1973), 5.

[83] Bloom also cites other instances of denial of influence that fall under "kenosis." On the other hand, anxiety could be so mounting that the successor fights back predecessors, vilifying or "demonizing" them. Anxiety could take the form of renunciation, an attempt to claim freedom from influence, where "askesis" is a method of purification. The last category, "Apophrades," is a dedicatory act, a paying homage to the precursor. Harold Bloom, *The Anxiety of Influence: A Theory of Poetry*, 2nd ed. (Oxford: Oxford University Press, 1997), 91.

[84] al-Jurjānī, *al-Wasāṭah*, 206 (1966), 179 (2006).

b. al-Faḍl al-ʿAlawī (d. 656/1258) is quite explicit in arguing that the term *tawārud* (exact thematic or wording correspondence) implies "haughtiness to mention thievery, and arrogance to be stigmatized."[85]

Terms, Borders, and Horizons

Even acts of recognition or refutation that resist specific labels within the daunting itinerary of poetic and prose thievery form a relevant index in this competitive space, one that is often collapsed under the term *saraq* (plagiarism), although with significant qualifications and reservations from renowned philologists and litterateurs.[86] While justifiable in terms of the need for a tight corpus of theory, the lament pronounced by scholars around this accumulation of terminology and the relative lack of systematization down to the first half of the tenth century overlooks processes of ongoing formations. In these processes, a literary scene is in motion, whereby poetry is a recognizable *ṣanʿah* (craft), and the poet is a talented artificer who is either responding to a cultural milieu or inviting response. Upholders of the canons of prosody left us massive negative criticism of inventors and innovators, especially around the modernists. Al-Āmidī's *Muwāzanah* is only one of these compilations. As noticed by scholars, Abū al-Muẓaffar al-Ḥātimī (d. 388/998) justified his effort in *Ḥilyat al-muḥāḍarah* to list predecessors' terminology, multiply it, and tabulate idioms under the concept of their indispensability to the *adīb*.[87]

Like any other literary concern, the issue of *saraq* is not a straightforward preoccupation with intellectual property. It is known among critics that al-Zubayr b. Bakkār b. ʿAbdallāh (d. 256/870) wrote *Ighārat Kuthayyir ʿalā al-shuʿarāʾ* (Kuthayyir's Raid on Poets) because the poet lampooned Ibn Bakkār's tribe and because Kuthayyir ʿAzzah (d. 105/723) was on the side of the Prophet's cousin and family.[88] On the other hand, an authority on ancient poetry such as al-Aṣmaʿī could not restrain his vilification of al-Farazdaq because the latter lampooned the former's tribe, Bāhilah.[89]

[85] al-Muẓaffar b. al-Faḍl al-ʿAlawī, *Naḍrat al-ighrīḍ fī nuṣrat al-qarīḍ*, ed. Nuhā ʿĀrif Ḥasan (Damascus: Majmaʿ al-Lughah al-ʿArabiyyah bi-Dimashq, 1976), 222.

[86] See, for example, al-Qāḍī al-Jurjānī's reservations in *al-Wasāṭāh* (1966), 3, 10, 15–17, 208–9, 214, 411.

[87] Bonebakker, "Ancient Arabic Poetry and Plagiarism," 66. See also Thomas Bauer, *Altarabische: Dichtkunst eine Untersuchung ihrer Struktur und Entwicklung am Beispiel der Onagerepisode* (Wiesbaden: Harrassowitz Verlag, 1992), 1, 80–87.

[88] Jamīl Saʿīd and Dāʾūd Sallūm, eds., *Nuṣūṣ al-naẓariyyah al-naqdiyyah* (Baghdad: Dār al-Shuʾūn al-Thaqāfiyyah al-ʿĀmmah, 1986), 24.

[89] ʿAbd al-Malik b. Qurayb al-Aṣmaʿī, *Fuḥūlat al-shuʿarāʾ* (Beirut: Dār al-Kitāb al-Jadīd, 1980), 19. On al-Aṣmaʿī's prejudicial stance, see Abū ʿAbdallāh b. Muḥammad b. ʿUmrān b. Mūsā al-Marzubānī, *al-Muwashshaḥ fī maʾākhidh al-ʿulamāʾ ʿalā al-shuʿarāʾ*, ed. Muḥammad ʿAlī al-Bajāwī (Cairo: Dār al-Fikr al-ʿArabī, 1965), 141.

Although there are ups and downs, tributaries, and eddies in this literary movement toward codification, a common understanding began to take shape by the end of the ninth century. A swerve or shift toward *saraq* as being applicable only to expressions and very rare meanings or invented ones was to gain currency in line with noticeable critical attention being paid not only to *badīʿ* (the art of expressive inventiveness; euphonical embellishment)[90] but also to mannerism, stylization, embellishment, and verbosity as a pragmatic application intended to achieve a musical impact on listeners who were not necessarily versed in the language.[91] If *badīʿ*, especially at the hands of Muslim b. al-Walīd and the rest of the *muḥdathūn* (innovators) poets, is transgressive of the normative, an innovative stance in relation to customary use, then a post-tenth-century elitist prose, often associated with al-Qāḍī al-Fāḍil ʿAbd al-Raḥīm al-Baysānī (d. 596/1199), is only an outgrowth called for by the expanding republic of letters.[92] On the other hand, an apologetic reading of recurrence and repetition in *maʿānī* (poetic ideas or meanings), which often finds enough justification in al-Jāḥiẓ's early note (d. 255/868) in this respect,[93] gains greater support as is illustrated by the stupendous rise in lexical activity. While seemingly unrelated, multiple writings and reflections on *maʿānī* were central to a climate that witnessed heated discussions on what constitutes, and therefore counts as, *saraq*. This activity often deals with multiplicity in meanings, as shown in a contemporaneous work by Isḥāq b. al-Sikkīt (d. 244/858), who also authored a book on thievery, to be followed by others, especially ʿAbd al-Raḥmān al-Hamadhānī's (d. 325/937) *al-Alfāẓ al-kitābiyyah* and Abū Hilāl al-ʿAskarī's (d. 395/1005) *Dīwān al-maʿānī* (The Book of Poetic Motifs).[94] I take ʿAbd al-Raḥmān al-Hamadhānī's short preface to his significant thesaurus of equivalent meanings as being not only a gateway to the mounting search for poetic meanings that depart in wording from an original, and hence from accusation of theft or infringement on a property, but also as an effort to provide us with a cultural marketplace where there were also dabblers and mediocre exponents. He focuses on

[90] Al-Qāḍī al-Jurjānī offers the most acclaimed argument in this respect in *al-Wasāṭah* (1966), 183–217, 178–79.

[91] For more on the implications of belletristic prose, which bewildered scholars and led them to associate the phenomenal recourse to verbosity with decline, see al-Musawi, "Pre-modern Belletristic Prose."

[92] al-Musawi, *Republic of Letters*, 53–55, 83–84, 114–15.

[93] See Abū Hilāl al-ʿAskarī's rephrasing of al-Jāḥiẓ's *Kitāb al-ḥayawān*, ed. ʿAbd al-Salām Hārūn (Cairo: al-Khānjī, 1948), 3:131, in *Kitāb al-ṣināʿatayn*, 196. See further Ṭāhā, *al-Naẓariyyah al-naqdiyyah*, 177.

[94] Abū Hilāl al-ʿAskarī, *Dīwān al-maʿānī*, ed. Aḥmad Salīm Ghānim (Beirut: Dār al-Gharb al-Islāmī, 2003). Fuat Sezgin lists sixty books dealing with this topic in his monumental *Geschichte des Arabischen Schrifttums*, vol. 2 (Leiden: Brill, 1996), 58–60.

the seeming divide between ancients and modernists, blaming some dabblers for claiming linguistic efficiency. He shows how certain contemporaries who suffer from deficiency in wording and poetic meanings strive to capture strange vocabulary and eccentric expression, that being one way to achieve linguistic distinction at the expense of the common people.[95] "They fail to change a meaning with a new wording because of their lexical deficiency."[96] While not strictly literary, this lexicographical and linguistic treatment of thorny or difficult expressions was a significant element in a domain focused on *alfāẓ* and *maʿānī*. Moreover, the whole discussion of recurrence and the ultimate use of an available vast textual space cannot be seen apart from social, political, and theological transformations that are evident in a dynamic culture. Poetry was not the only literary domain that attracted interest and keen competition, for the epistolary art, as well as varieties of narrative, were as palpable.[97]

Private and Public Properties

In his *Muwāzanah*, al-Āmidī is unequivocal in criticizing the celebrated Abū al-Ḍiyāʾ Bishr b. Yaḥyā (al-Naṣībī) for regarding shared meanings or their corresponding themes and echoes as *sariqāt*.[98] With early contemporary critics' opinions on this matter in mind, he argues, "Theft (*sariqah*) is only in the innovative expression belonging to a specific poet, not in the meanings shared among people that are common in their customs, proverbial sayings, and conversations."[99] Philologists and critics have taken cognizance of recurrent poetic meanings and sources or available ideas and expressions under *ittisāʿ fī al-maʿnā* (elaboration or expansion), or *mushtarak ʿāmm al-sharikah* (*ishtirāk*; a shared and common property),[100]

95 ʿAbd al-Raḥman b. ʿĪsā al-Hamadhānī, *Kitāb al-alfāẓ al-kitābiyyah*, ed. Father Luwīs Shaykhū (Beirut: Maṭbaʿat al-Ābāʾal-Yasūʿiyyīn, 1911), vi–vii.

96 Ibid., vii.

97 Muhsin J. al-Musawi, "Abbasid Popular Narrative: The Formation of Readership and Cultural Production," *Journal of Arabic Literature* 38, no. 3 (2007): 261–92.

98 Mentioned by Abū ʿAbdallāh al-Rūmī Yāqūt al-Ḥamawī, *Muʿjam al-udabāʾ aw irshād al-arīb ilā maʿrifat al-adīb* (Beirut: Dār al-Kutub al-ʿIlmiyyah, 1991), 2:329. Al-Nadīm mentions some of his books, such as *Sariqāt al-Buḥturī ʿan Abī Tammām*, *Kitāb al-jawāhir*, *Kitāb al-adab*, and *Kitāb al-sariqāt al-kabīr* (unfinished).

99 al-Āmidī, *al-Muwāzanah*, 1:291, 325: إن السرقة إنما هي في البديع المخترع الذي يختص به الشاعر، لا في المعاني المشتركة بين الناس التي هي جارية في عاداتهم ومستعملة في أمثالهم ومحاوراتهم

The idea is widely espoused in the last decades of the tenth century. See also al-Jurjānī, *al-Wasāṭah* (1966), 192–93.

100 See al-Jurjānī, *al-Wasāṭah* (1966), 185.

Figure 2.4 Ibn Aydamir's recognition of predecessors

but the medieval period was to witness a liberal understanding that finds no separation between *lafẓ* (expression) and *maʿnā*; for, as Ibn al-Athīr argues, "Meaning is expression, and *lafẓ* is the adornment of meaning."[101] Ibn al-Athīr's surmise cannot be seen outside the larger activity of the medieval period with its significant distribution of the assets of the classical period (seventh–twelfth centuries) and its compendiums and careful recognition of predecessors. Thus, Ibn Aydamir admits that his voluminous al-*Durr al-farīd* gathers, condenses, and synthesizes precursors' material (see Figure 2.4). There was then even a better receptivity to generous terms that raised discussion early in the ninth century. Ninth-century philologists allowed space for some terms that poets like Jarīr speak of in terms of a shared muse.[102] They speak of *muwāradah* (coincidental correspondence) and its variations. Abū ʿAmrū b. al-ʿAlāʾ's (d. 155/771) response to al-Aṣmaʿī's (d. 216/831)[103] query has become

[101] Ibn al-Athīr, *al-Jāmiʿ al-kabīr fī ṣināʿat al-manẓūm min al-kalām wa-l-manthūr*, ed. Muṣṭafā Jawād and Jamīl Saʿīd (Baghdad: Maṭbaʿat al-Majmaʿ al-ʿIrāqī, 1956), 21.
[102] See al-Ḥātimī, *Ḥilyat al-muḥāḍarah*, 2:47.
[103] Full name: ʿAbd al-Malik b. Qurayb al-Aṣmaʿī.

proverbial and authoritative: "Those are minds of men that meet by chance on their tongues" (*tilka ʿuqūl rijāl tawāfat ʿalā alsinatihā*).[104]

As poets and writers work in a wide textual space, reflections, wording, images, and tropes compose a medium that philological arbiters try hard to define, tabulate, and differentiate. On many occasions, poets or prose writers try their hand in literary space itself and come up with comments and rejoinders. Although Ibn Ṭayfūr speaks of poets' thefts, his articulation of fluidity in *kalām al-ʿArab* implies a free zone with no custodians or proprietors. This is why we come across such recurrent terms as *mushtarak ʿāmm al-sharikah* (shared)[105] or *muwāradah* (coincidental correspondence), *istilḥāq* (to fit into one's verse), *iṣṭirāf* (intentional appropriation of an appealing verse) (see Figure 4.6), or *murāfadah* – that is, a willing yielding of a verse to another, as in the reported case involving Ḥusayn al-Ḍaḥḥāk's (or al-Khalīʿ, d. 250/864) act of conceding a verse to Abū Nuwās (d. 197/813). Alongside compromising terms like the ones cited earlier, there is an inventory of terms concerning objectionable borrowing, a point that will be discussed in Chapter 4. Moreover, there are issues of a problematic nature that relate to strong poets who rob others of their verse or force them to abnegate a verse, simply because the strong poet finds the verse more to his taste. Al-Qāḍī al-Jurjānī repeats some well-known examples, as will be explained in Chapter 4. On some occasions, the less famous poet resists yielding a poetic property.[106] A counter action is no less compelling when fame provokes the less-known poet to pilfer the strong poet's production by recourse to *ihtidām* (raid with partial change), theft, or *salkh* (flaying). This feature was not lost on tenth-century littérateurs like Abū al-Faraj al-Iṣfahānī, who mentions it as an auxiliary dynamic in a poetic marketplace involving creditors and debtors.[107]

The mythopoeic space around Imruʾ al-Qays, Abū Tammām, al-Mutanabbī, and – for Nahḍah literati – Abū al-ʿAlāʾ al-Maʿarrī offers an invitation, if not an incitement, to invade, challenge, or contrafact.

[104] See Chapter 1; but for more quotes from al-Ḥātimī and Ibn Aydamir, see Bonebakker, "Ancient Arabic Poetry," 87. See also al-Rāghib al-Iṣfahānī, *Muḥāḍarāt al-udabāʾ*, 4 vols. in 2 (Beirut: Maktabat al-Ḥayāt, n.d.), 1:86. For a reading of Ibn Aydamir's style, see G. Jan van Gelder, "Arabic Poetics and Stylistics according to the Introduction of *al-Durr al-Farīd*, by Ibn Aydamir," *Zeitschrift der Deutschen Morgenländischen Gesellschaft* 146 (1996): 381–414. See also Ibn Aydamir, *al-Durr al-farīd* (2015), 1:491.

[105] al-Jurjānī, *al-Wasāṭah* (1966), 185.

[106] In a note that references H. Pêrès, von Grunebaum cites how Khālid al-Kātib (d. 269/882) refuses ʿAlī b. al-Jahm's (d. 249/863) request to cede a verse. See Grunebaum, "Concept of Plagiarism," 235n4. Al-Qāḍī al-Jurjānī's chapter on *al-sariqāt* covers these issues in *al-Wasāṭah* (1966), 183–208.

[107] Abū al-Faraj al-Iṣfahānī, *al-Aghānī*, ed. ʿAbd al-Sattār Farrāj (Beirut: Dār al-Thaqāfah, 1955–61), 16:303.

Among twentieth-century modernists the same is applicable to poetics associated with Badr Shākir al-Sayyāb. If such space is difficult to use or abuse because of its towering owner, you must either displace the owner or else characterize that presence as undesirable. ʿAbd al-Wahhāb al-Bayātī (d. 1999) disparages the panegyrist in al-Mutanabbī, but keeps his poetry. He does the same with T. S. Eliot.[108] A tendency for displacement, bifurcation, and slicing is so recurrent and conspicuous that it has overshadowed other tendencies or subsumed them.

Overall, lesser-known poets, essayists, and versifiers from among the common people suffer in these transactions. A case in point are the poetries of the common people during the Amīn-Maʾmūn war (195–97/811–13), which could have been a source for the poetry of prominent names.[109] More visible are cases that gave birth to specific terminologies like *salb* (plunder), *akhdh* (partial appropriation or possession), and *ghaṣb* (willful seizure). These terms were already in use before the advent of the Umayyads and Abbasids. Especially so in the case of the ones associated with tribal raids and conquests, which could have been applied and easily transposed to the domain of intellectual and poetic property. Ibn Qutaybah's specific mention of subtle *akhdh* or *sariqah* (borrowing or theft)[110] predates al-Āmidī's insinuation that Abū Tammām's poetry is implicated in indiscernible plagiarisms. That accusation should encompass the whole poetic corpus, since it is a shared lexical domain where wording and meaning overshadow each other's space and enunciation while leaving no small margin for inventiveness and distinction. The mere battling over one case or another testifies to both anxiety, on the one hand, and vanity and venom, on the other.

Al-ʿAskarī's Foundational Input

Moreover, it has been common to exercise eclectic navigation through the available merchandise in a thriving literary market. What is seemingly surprising to gentle sensibilities may have been ordinary practice in a domain of growing demands on the literati. Poets, scholars, and critics duplicate ideas and expressions. Critics and philologists might echo with each other, and, as often happens in literary history and theory, ancestral authority offers the foundational work for posterity. Such are the works of Ibn Sallām al-Jumaḥī, Abū ʿAmrū b. al-ʿAlāʾ, al-Aṣmaʿī, Ibn Qutaybah,

108 See al-Musawi, *Arabic Poetry*, 47, 220.

109 Ibrāhīm al-Karwī, *Ṭabaqāt mujtamaʿ Baghdād fī al-ʿaṣr al-ʿAbbāsī al-awwal* (Baghdad: Shabāb al-Jāmiʿah, 1989); Badrī Muḥammad Fahd, *al-ʿĀmmah bi-Baghdād fī al-qarn al-khāmis al-hijrī* (Baghdad: Maṭbaʿat al-Irshād, 1967).

110 Ibn Qutaybah, *al-Shiʿr wa-l-shuʿarāʾ* (2001), 1:134.

Ibn Ṭayfūr, and al-Jāḥiẓ. Acknowledgment of a source was rare, not because of loose ethical standards regarding cultural property, but primarily because their foundational sayings were soon to become common property.[111] However, in cases that require mediational or balancing efforts, the claiming of names on one's side or discrediting others from the opposition are a visible marker of the tenth-century marketplace. Moreover, as memory can be fickle, there is also a substantial archive of evasive phrases such as "I heard some say" that constitute the stock-in-trade of a literary market. A blind general term intended to reference an unidentified authority is also available as a way to shore up support. In arguing in defense of his views on *sariqāt*, al-Āmidī is not alone in saying that "scholars of poetry who were still alive in my time did not see thievery in meanings as the greatest mishap among poets, especially poets of later generations, simply because this is a domain that nobody before or after could have avoided."[112] We often end up with a prominent name like Abū Hilāl al-ʿAskarī organizing or using examples and elaborations to repeat what is already in circulation.[113] There is, however, some reservation with respect to this conclusion, which von Grunebaum endorses. Al-ʿAskarī offers a very comprehensive overview of what has been argued, taking the discussion of *maʿnā* (poetic meaning) to its furthest point. He acknowledges the contributions of early critics, minus their names, in order to expand on a trite and conclusive summary of *sariqāt* theory as given by ʿAbd al-Raḥmān al-Hamadhānī. He offers examples that diversify the thematic proposal and provide other thematic horizons like prose or proverbial sayings exploited by smart poets. Al-ʿAskarī also provides several examples of *akhdh* (partial possession of meaning or expression), and *ḥusn al-itbāʿ* (also: *ittibāᶜ*, neat emulation). Moreover, the *akhdh* category is further divided into substantial sections: there is also *qubḥ al-akhdh* (ugly possession), which occupies the second part of his chapter 6. Relevant to ugly possession is thematic lack, when the latecomer fails to give a verse its due thematic direction, as shown in Figure 2.5. Conversely, good *akhdh* is the one that adds value, as in the examples listed in several critical accounts, but synthesized and brought into patterns by Ibn Aydamir, as shown in Figure 3.2, which presents cases by al-Kumayt, Abū Saʿīd al-Quṭāmī (d. 130/747), Abū Tamām,

[111] See al-Jurjānī, *al-Wasāṭah* (1966), 185.
[112] al-Āmidī, *al-Muwāzanah*, 1:325: إن من أدركته من أهل العلم بالشعر لم يكونوا يرون سرقات المعاني من كبير مساوىء الشعراء وخاصة المتاخرين إذ كان هذا بابا ما تعرى منه متقدم ولا متاخر.
[113] al-ʿAskarī, *Kitāb al-ṣināʿatayn*, 196–238. See also Grunebaum, "Concept of Plagiarism," 235n4.

١٠٦
وكان الفرزدق يقول
وكان ابن هرمة يقول
٦٨

Figure 2.5 Thematic lack

and others. In a word, al-ʿAskarī has the right to claim unprecedented comprehensive focus on categories of *sariqāt* as an intertextual space of multiple directions.[114]

It is very likely that al-ʿAskarī has al-Āmidī and his early contemporaries in mind, among them Qudāmah b. Jaʿfar (d. 337/948), Ibn Ṭabāṭabā al-ʿAlawī, and ʿAbd al-Raḥmān al-Hamadhānī.[115] His approach was different, however, in that he came up with almost the same conclusive remarks, but with a detailed and focused practical criticism that could be seen as foundational to critical poetics. By his time, some phrases and terms that had received the attention of early tenth-century critics were to become common property with respect to previous categories such as *iqtidā*ʾ (following the example of) or *iḥtidhā*ʾ (emulation, close imitation). Before al-ʿAskarī, al-Hamadhānī unequivocally had argued: "Even an eloquent writer, a prominent poet, or an irrefutable orator cannot avoid imitating the ancients, borrowing from recent contemporaries, or following the example of precursors in their invented meanings and stylistic practices." This is his stepping stone, however, allowing him to briefly repeat what is already in the literary marketplace, and to tabulate

[114] al-ʿAskarī, *Kitāb al-ṣināʿatayn*, 196–228, 229–38.
[115] Ibn Ṭabāṭabā al-ʿAlawī died in 322/934, and ʿAbd al-Raḥmān b. ʿĪsā al-Hamadhānī in 320/933.

a terminological basis for the raging discussion of *sariqāt*.[116] Al-ʿAskarī refers to this trite conclusion, introducing it with another: *samiʿtu mā qīl* (literally: I heard what has been said or circulated; an introductory remark that al-Hamadhānī had also used).[117] Thus, one can argue that al-ʿAskarī was aware of a large body of discussions, judgments, terms, and critical and philological positions, and decided to give the whole discussion a focused practical analysis under one single term: *akhdh*. In his chapter 6 with its two sections, al-ʿAskarī tends to bring the whole concern with *sariqāt* to a specific end: the manner and matter of taking over meanings or expressions. Under the good and ugly categories of *akhdh*, al-ʿAskarī provides a map of reading and misreading, which was to occupy Harold Bloom's career centuries later, where the issue of a struggle with strong ancestors remains pivotal, without minimizing the successor's achievements in expanding or changing the direction of poetics in meaning and expression.

The issue of ancestry and precedence is not a trivial matter, not only because philologists and critics argue the case in terms of knowledge accumulation and the ultimate appearance of a large referential corpus, but also because prominent names among ancestors in an age that had witnessed a large portion of orality always comprised a literary history that dwarfed others. Even if we assume that al-Āmidī's suspicions of Abū Tammām's subtle application of minor poets' verses are unfounded and undetected, the milieu where poetry was a dominating cultural commodity allowed fluidity in thriving urban centers. Obscure poets often provide the fodder for major ones. In other words, an active literary ambiance is bound to find ways to explain, justify, or shun processes of use, dependency, or theft.

Slicing Ancestors

Even when there is no evidence of clear-cut plagiarism, raid, or borrowing, there are predilections, dispositions, and inclinations that bring trends and attitudes into the conversation. Modern Arabic poetry, especially since the second half of the twentieth century, readdresses the strong ancestors, not only for poetic meanings and expressions but primarily for their political stand with respect to power. The Dīwān group of the early 1920s, for example, prefers Ibn al-Rūmī for his resonance with its disposition for nature, especially as shown in English

[116] al-Hamadhānī, *Kitāb al-alfāẓ*, viii–ix. See n. 95 in Chapter 1 for the conclusive summation of a theft terminology; presumably reported on the authority of others.
[117] al-ʿAskarī, *Kitāb al-ṣināʿatayn*, 197.

Romantic poetry, a disposition that Yaḥyā Ḥaqqī in *The Saint's Lamp*, for example, assigns to initiation in British culture.[118] These processes of selection, exclusion, or inclusion show an *adab* in motion. If al-Bayātī is blunt in his slicing al-Mutanabbī or T. S. Eliot, Maḥmūd Darwīsh defines his struggle with Imru' al-Qays as poetry-free. Otherwise, how can we explain Darwīsh's "Khilāf ghayr lughawī maʿa Imru' al-Qays" (A Nonlinguistic Dispute with Imru' al-Qays)? He writes:

> So go the way of
> Caesar, behind the smoke that towers over
> time, black. Go the way of
> Caesar, alone, alone, alone,
> And leave us, just here, your language.[119]

Emptied of the person, Darwīsh's "Imru' al-Qays" is a poem that offers an open text to be managed and used. What matters is the poetry, not the person. The late classical Arabic tradition shows a double concern for the person and the poetry, before a radical shift to textual analysis becomes more visible, one that culminates not only in ʿAbd al-Qāhir al-Jurjānī's theory of *naẓm* (compositional structure) but also in the writings of others like Ḥāzim al-Qarṭājannī's (d. 684/1285) discussion of the difference between invention and theft and whatever falls in between. As I have argued elsewhere, the postclassical age widens the prospects of textual space.[120] The increasing emphasis on terms that elude stark or blunt vilification on the basis of an accusation of plagiarism shows not only an open-mindedness but also a resignation to the overwhelming trade in literary merchandise. Hence, the shift to matter at the expense of authors also enables criticism to focus more on stylization and *maʿānī* (meanings and poetic ideas).[121] Nevertheless, this trend cannot be seen as a total departure from the foundational work established by al-Āmidī and al-Qāḍī al-Jurjānī. The concentration on both the person of the poet and the poem derives from al-Qāḍī al-Jurjānī's starting point – that is, *wasāṭah* (mediation) in *al-Wasāṭah*, which entails an objectifying mediational

[118] See al-Musawi, *Islam on the Street*, 41–42, 46–49, 50–52. See also Aḥmad Yūsuf ʿAlī, *Naqd al-shāʿir fī madrasat al-dīwān: Ibn al-Rūmī namūdhajan* (Cairo: Maktabat Madbūlī, 2010).

[119] Maḥmūd Darwīsh, "Khilāf ghayr lughawī maʿa Imru' al-Qays," in *Why Did You Leave the Horse Alone?*, 181–85.

[120] al-Musawi, *Republic of Letters*, 188–89, but also 122–24, 129–30.

[121] Mikhail Bakhtin, in reference to stylization in literature, has written: "The elements of another artist's mode of expression are important to the stylizer, but only as an expression of a particular viewpoint." *Problemy poetiki Dostoevskogo*, 3rd ed. (Azbuka-klassika, 1972), 324, trans. Caryl Emerson as *Problems of Dostoevsky's Poetics* (Minneapolis: University of Minnesota Press, 1984), quoted in The Free Dictionary, s.v. "Stylization," https://encyclopedia2.thefreedictionary.com/Stylization.

process used to weigh claims and counterclaims. As will be discussed further, the name of a poet in classical works appears in titles, even if the name of the poet serves only as a medium to commend or denigrate a specific usage or accusation. Nevertheless, this attention to prominent or controversial names during the heydays of dynasties manifests a competitive literary space presided over by the caliph, the amir, his court, and notables' assemblies. In its multiple processes, recognition entails distinction. Thus, to have al-Mutanabbī or Abū Tammām and al-Buḥturī in a title entails publicity and thence gain in material and symbolic capital. Even having a commanding presence like al-Mutanabbī in a subtitle, as in Abū ʿAlī Muḥammad b. al-Ḥasan al-Ḥatimī's epistle *al-Risālah al-Ḥātimiyyah fīmā wāfaqa al-Mutanabbī fī shiʿrihī kalām Arisṭū*, demands attention even though al-Ḥatimī uses it as a gateway by which he can present, under the rubric of correspondence or plagiarism, his critique of al-Mutanabbī as more of a *ḥakīm*, a thinker or a philosopher, than a poet. More blunt and vindictive is his *al-Risālah al-mūḍiḥah*, which is stark vilification.[122] His *Ḥilyat al-muḥāḍarah* (The Ornament of Discourse) turns out, however, to be the most extensive terminological listing of *sariqāt* that serves Ibn Rashīq's short but sharp chapter in *al-ʿUmdah* (The Foundational Work).

The approach differs to some extent from that of the Ashʿarī theologian al-Bāqillānī (d. 403/1013).[123] The latter's focus on the inimitability of the Qurʾān tends to displace the towering figure of Imruʾ al-Qays and minimize the originality of a poetic harvest, in order to demonstrate that the most recognized poet's odes lack the texture, image, and music that distinguish the Qurʾān as miraculous. With this focus on texts, al-Bāqillānī's reading differs from that of Ibn Sallām (d. 231/845) in *Ṭabaqāt fuḥūl al-shuʿarā* (Classes of Champion Poets),[124] but nevertheless recognizes Imruʾ al-Qays's poetry as texts to be analyzed and occasionally dubbed as reflective of a blemished character.[125] To make a case

[122] For more on the grudge against the poet, see also Amidu Sanni, "The Historic Encounter between al-Mutanabbī and al-Ḥātimī: Its Contribution to the Discourse on *Ghuluww* (Hyperbole) in Arabic Literary Theory," *Journal of Arabic Literature* 35, no. 2 (2004): 159–74. Of relevance is S. A. Bonebakker, *Materials for the History of Arabic Rhetoric from the Ḥilyat al-Muḥādara of Ḥātimī*, MSS 2934 and 590 of the Qarawiyyin Mosque in Fez (Naples: Napoli Istituto orientale, 1975), supplement no. 4, vol. 35, fasc. 3.

[123] Full name: Abū Bakr Muḥammad b. al-Ṭayyib.

[124] Ibn Sallām, *Ṭabaqāt fuḥūl al-shuʿarāʾ*, ed. Maḥmūd Muḥammad Shākir, vol. 1 (Cairo: Maṭbaʿat al-Madanī, 1974).

[125] Gustave von Grunebaum, "Arabic Literary Criticism in the 10th Century A.D.," *Journal of the American Oriental Society* 61, no. 1 (1941): 52, nn. 10–11; 53, nn. 15, 16, 18, 20, 24; 54, n. 26, esp. nn. 27–28.

for this thesis, critics and speculative theologians alike present arguments to deconstruct and reconstitute the canon. Such a fair-minded *adīb* and jurist as al-Qāḍī al-Jurjānī must wade carefully through explosive fields in order to show that nobody, not even Imru' al-Qays, can be free of poetic pitfalls.[126] In all cases, poets and critics take the pre-Islamic poet as their role model for a masterly poetic beginning. The case does not apply to literary and cultural critics like Ibn Qutaybah, who argues against periodization and prioritization of either ancients or modernists.[127] The shift occurs only after the urban rupture that foregrounds Muslim b. al-Walīd, who is, in Ibn Qutaybah's succinct phrasing, "the first who pleasantly polished poetic motifs and refined speech. Abū Tammām relied on him in this and on Abī Nuwās."[128]

أول من ألطف في المعاني ورقق في القول وعليه يعول الطائي في ذلك وعلى أبي نواس

In a slightly different phrasing, Ibn Qutaybah's conclusion can be read as "the first one who produced subtle motifs and refined speech."[129] In other words, while Imru' al-Qays remains as the major poet to be reckoned with, over time there would grow some resistance to his towering poetic presence. Hence, Muslim b. al-Walīd and Abū Nuwās occupied the stage for their poetic naturalness and refinement. The desert rhetoric and wording had to give place to urban delicacy.

The implications of tenth-century writings concerning *sariqāt* are crucial, not only because those writings laid the groundwork for further explorations, but also because the overwhelming predilection for the poetry of the ancients began to be rigorously examined. The renowned Kufic philologist Abū ʿAbdallāh b. Ziyād al-Aʿrābī (d. 231/845), Abū ʿAmrū b. al-ʿAlā' (d. 154/770), and Ibn Sallām's mentor al-Aṣmaʿī (d. 216/831) were all advocates of the ancients at the expense of the emerging talented poets,[130] but, on the authority of Ibn Qutaybah, Abū ʿAmrū b. al-ʿAlā' is reported to have said that the "modernist's verse multiplied and improved so much that he intended to narrate and transmit."[131] Throughout the ninth and tenth centuries, such directions show the difficulty of blanket statements, as the cultural market displays

126 See al-Jurjānī, *al-Wasāṭah* (1966), 4–5.
127 Ibn Qutaybah, *al-Shiʿr wa-l-shuʿarā* (2001), 1:62–63. 128 Ibid., 2:832.
129 Thanks to Geert Jan van Gelder and Wen-Chin for their suggestions respecting the translation of Ibn Qutaybah's saying, and to van Gelder also for locating another variant, in Abū Hilāl al-ʿAskarī, *al-Awāʾil* (Ṭanṭā: Dār al-Bashīr, 1987): أول من خرج اللطيف وعقد المعاني.
130 For examples, see Ṭāhā, *al-Naẓariyyah al-naqdiyyah*, 213–18; Muḥammad ʿAzzām, *al-Naṣṣ al-ghāʾib* (Damascus: Writers' Union Publication, 2001), 86.
131 Ibn Qutayba, *al-Shiʿr wa-l-shuʿarā'* (2001), 1:63.

merchandise of every sort, where fluctuations, deflections, and shifts occur, leaving here and there traces for literary historians to highlight or downplay. At this point, it is worth remembering that Arabic literary history was ahead of the European Renaissance by almost nine centuries, a point that makes comparisons untenable. Nevertheless, Bloom's exception of Shakespeare from the "anxiety of influence" for belonging "to the giant age before the flood" resonates well with classical Arabic philology and literary criticism establishing the exception for Imru' al-Qays as the giant to be imitated, but never surpassed or supplanted. In his *Ṭabaqāt*, Ibn Sallām al-Jumaḥī explains, on the authority of Yūnus b. Ḥabīb, how the giant poet sets the stage not only in his amatory *nasīb*, weeping over the campsite and addressing companions, but also in poetic dexterity, a masterly cadence, and wording.[132]

This does not deny the presence of detractors. The early Abbasid poet Muḥammad b. Yasīr al-Riyāshī (d. after 198/814) alleges that the foremost poet was not immune from borrowing. From among the poet's senior companions, he cites ʿAmrū b. Qamīʾa (d. 540 CE) as a source for poems credited to the strongest poet. Ibn Sallām has the opposite contention, one that rests on tribal efforts to augment the reputation of the lesser-known poet, thereby attaining tribal fame.[133] On the other hand, al-Bāqillānī's approach shows a kind of anxiety in order to present the textual uniqueness and thence inimitability of the sacred text. Although primarily a theologian, who therefore suffers no poetic anxiety in relation to a strong poet, al-Bāqillānī struggles to clear more space for the Qurʾān and its inimitability. Von Grunebaum ranks his text highly for its pioneering "aesthetic investigation and evaluation,"[134] a point that fits well with the ongoing articulation of the limits and prospects of borrowing and thievery in a textually opulent literary market. Apart from movements like *al-muḥdathūn* and the focus on new wording and poetic meanings and ideas, overshadowing figures are bound to generate opposition, which is often centered on issues of originality, imitation, and forthright thievery. Like Ibn Qutaybah before him, al-Qāḍī al-Jurjānī argues against the equation between antecedence and distinction insofar as the ancients are concerned, for "a great portion of their poetry [is] vile and contemptible."[135]

[132] Ibn Sallām, *Ṭabaqāt al-shuʿarāʾ*, ed. Maḥmūd Muḥammad Shākir (Cairo: Dār al-Maʿārif, 1952), 16; for the same passage in a later edition, see *Ṭabaqāt al-shuʿarāʾ* (1998), 37.

[133] Ibn Sallām, *Ṭabaqāt al-shuʿarāʾ* (1998), 32.

[134] Grunebaum, "Arabic Literary Criticism," 52.

[135] al-Jurjānī, *al-Wasāṭah* (1966), 4: وجدت كثيرا من أشعارهم معيبة مُسترذلة، ومردودة منفيّة.

Craft in an Intertextual Space

Some prominent poets were to provoke more accusations than others. Books are devoted to the alleged thievery of Kuthayyir, al-Kumayt, Abū Nuwās, Abū Tammām, al-Buḥturī, and al-Mutanabbī, among others. Accusations of thievery against Ṭarafa and Ḥassān b. Thābit, all the way down to al-Bayātī among twentieth-century poets, and Ibrāhīm al-Māzinī among other writers, run wild, inciting poets and writers to apply some of these terms against immediate contemporaries as well.[136] In all cases, there is a subtle textual dependency that al-Akhṭal (d. 90/708) had already summed up by saying:

نحن معاشر الشعراء أسرق من الصاغة

We poets are even more skillful at thievery than jewelers. [137]

The analogy with jewelers recurs quite often, especially when it comes to versification from prose or epistles; then the poet is, in the words of Ibn Ṭabāṭabā, "like the jeweler who melts silver or gold jewels to create something better."[138] It should not be surprising that this analogy was to survive in other cultures. Thus, England's first poet laureate, John Dryden (d. 1700), believed a "poet was like a gunsmith or watchmaker; the iron or silver was not his own; but they were the least part of that which created the value: the price lay wholly in the workmanship."[139]

In line with competitiveness, Bloom's strong poets "fight to the end to have their initial chance alone."[140] In other words, we need to peel off metaphorical language and speak of a literary marketplace and merchandise. The debate raised by twentieth-century critics like Bloom will surely remain with us as we assess *adab* (i.e., literary production, erudition, etiquette, and knowledge). The questions raised regarding this vast competitiveness take a specifically psychological turn in Bloom's reading, which is extremely significant, to be sure; but the struggle against past masters and antecedent authority that also defines Arab philologists' and critics' enormous corpus in the field of originality, imitation, and *sariqāt* should have been functioning as a generative driving force, and not necessarily a lamentable setback. When focusing on certain highly subjective modes in Romanticism, Bloom cannot hide a sense of discontent: "For all its glories, [Romanticism] may have been

136 See al-Musawi, *Arabic Poetry*; Paniconi, "Reframing Politics."
137 Quoted in Sanni, "Al-Marzubānī in the Context of Arabic Literary Theory: An Analytical Study of al-Muwashshah" (PhD diss., University of London, 1989). 175n67. Other sources claim this was al-Farazdaq's saying (ibid.).
138 al-ʿAlawī, *ʿIyār al-shiʿr*, 78.
139 Quoted from John Dryden's preface to his *Mock Astrologer* in Alexander Lindey, *Plagiarism and Originality* (1952; Westport, CT: Greenwood Press, 1974), 80.
140 Bloom, "A Meditation," 8.

a vast visionary tragedy, the self-baffled enterprise not of Prometheus but of blinded Oedipus, who did not know that the Sphinx was his muse."[141] Conversely, the struggles among poets, critics, and grammarians in the classical and postclassical Arabic literary tradition operate differently, conveying how instances of literary history consolidate a literary theory formation, as Chapter 3 will demonstrate.

[141] Ibid., 10.

3 Grounding Arabic Literary History and Literary Theory

While there is much to agree with in Harold Bloom's conceptualization of poetic anxieties among the English Romantics, I would argue that the struggle with or against masters reads better when placed within the larger semantic field of *adab*.[1] Bloom rightly places his argument within the range of the Romantic movement, which he nevertheless regards as "a vast visionary tragedy." This surmise certainly does not apply to other literary traditions; it definitely does not apply to the Arabic literary tradition, its long history, and preliminary theoretical models, as sparingly presented in Ibn Sallām al-Jumaḥī's (d. 231/846) *Ṭabaqāt fuḥūl al-shuʿarāʾ* (Classes of Champion Poets), where he laid down a poetic ranking proposal, and in al-Farāhīdī's (d. 173/786) prosodic, metric, system in *Kitāb al-ʿayn* (The Source),[2] with its establishment of the standard vowel marks in Arabic writing, along with the study of prosody (*ʿilm al-ʿarūḍ*) and musicology. There are several other books of general cultural and linguistic significance composed around the same time. Ibn Sallām speaks of poetry as craft, without minimizing the milieu as necessarily entangled in the rise of poetic talents. He argues, "poetry requires skillful craft, perceptive subtlety, correctness, and informativeness" (*li-l-shiʿr ṣināʿah wa-thaqāfah*), characteristics which should be known to the learned, *ahl al-ʿilm*.[3] These words bring to the discussion significant issues and modalities for a rising poetic theory; no less important is his attention to the poetry that was laid down by some tribal traditionalists and untrustworthy transmitters. Although Ibn Sallām alerts his readers to the fact that these placed or inserted verses could not delude or deceive the learned among philologists, the notion of the existence of forgery exhilarates the study of *waḍʿ* (fabrication), *intihāl* (self-arrogating others' verses), and *inḥāl* (forging verses under another's name). Indeed, Abū ʿAlī b. al-Ḥasan al-Ḥātimī found in Ibn Sallām's attention to *intihāl* and *inḥāl* not only an important source but also an

[1] See Appendix A. [2] Full name: al-Khalīl b. Aḥmad.
[3] Ibn Sallām, *Ṭabaqāt al-shuʿarāʾ* (1998), 10; further notes will also refer to the 1974 edition. *Thaqāfah* is an inclusive term for manner and matter.

incentive to define these and other terms (see Figure 0.1).[4] Ibn Sallām comes also across examples of *saraq*, *ijtilāb* (procuring support by inserting another's verse), and also *ibtidā*ʿ (inventiveness) in relation to Imruʾ al-Qays (d. 544 CE),[5] as the pioneer in the opinion of Labīd (d. 41/661).[6] The three visible concerns of the book (poetry as craft and informativeness, the informing milieu, and poetic forgery for different reasons including tribal competition), as well as its ranking method, are bound to inform theory for a long time. The sensational issue of forgery drew the attention of many Orientalists, but especially Theodor Nöldeke (d. 1930) and David Samuel Margoliouth (d. 1937); thus, a discussion erupted that reached Arab scholars, especially focusing on Ṭāhā Ḥusayn's (d. 1973) *Fī al-shiʿr al-jāhilī* (Pre-Islamic Poetry), directly or indirectly inviting Arabists, Orientalists, and Arab scholars to develop accordingly their controversial historical and theoretical forays.[7] Margoliouth's article of 1916 and other writings in the *Journal of the Royal Asiatic Society* and entries and books provoked some response,[8] especially from Sir Charles James Lyall in the "Introduction" to volume two of his translation of the *Mufaḍḍaliyyāt* anthology of the most authenticated and celebrated poems (1918), an anthology compiled at the behest of the second Abbasid caliph, Abū Jaʿfar al-Manṣūr (d. 158/775).[9] Lyall refers to Margoliouth as making "an astonishing assertion that the 'early poetry is largely fabrication *modelled on the Koran*.'"[10] The significance of Lyall's response derives from his rigorous analysis, vast knowledge, and appreciation of the subject of his interest, that is, Arabic poetry. The crux of his response rests on both logical analysis and information: "Ḥammād and Khalaf were imitators of a style of composition which was already established long before the

[4] al-Ḥātimī, *Ḥilyat al-muḥāḍarah*, 2:35.

[5] Ibn Sallām, *Ṭabaqāt fuḥūl al-shuʿarāʾ*, 37 (1998), 55 (1974).

[6] Full name: Abū ʿAqīl Labīd b. Rabīʿah.

[7] D. S. Margoliouth, "The Origins of Arabic Poetry," *Journal of the Royal Asiatic Society* 57, no. 3 (1925): 417–49. For an overview, see Basmah b. ʿUthmān Ḥajām, *al-Shiʿr al-jāhilī bayna Ṭāhā Ḥusayn wa-Margoliouth* (Tunis: al-Aṭlasiyyah li-l-Nashr, 2014). See also Munīr Sulṭān, *Ibn Sallām wa-Ṭabaqāt al-shuʿarāʾ* (Alexandria: Manshaʾat al-Maʿārif, 1977), 269–80.

[8] In his notes, Margoliouth wrote: "The subject of this paper was treated by Ahlwardt in a monograph called *Bemerkungen ilber die AechtJieit der alien arabischen Gedichte*, Greifswald, 1872, and by Sir C. Lyall in the Preface to vol. ii of his *Mufaḍḍaliyyāt*. The former is not very confident, and calls attention to some of the matters which have been discussed rather more fully below; Sir C. Lyall deals chiefly with the character of the transmitters, which he rates rather more highly than the present writer." Margoliouth, "Origins of Arabic Poetry," 417.

[9] Charles James Lyall, ed. and trans., The Mufaḍḍaliyyāt: An Anthology of Ancient Arabian Odes. Compiled by al-Mufaḍḍal, son of Muḥammad, according to the Recension and with the Commentary of Abū Muḥammad al-Anbārī, 3 vols. (Oxford: Clarendon Press, 1918–24).

[10] Lyall, introduction to *Mufaḍḍaliyyāt*, xx, n. † (unnumbered).

preaching of Islam."[11] He adds: "the very fact of imitation implies the existence of an original."[12] In a method that accumulates salient features of Arabic poetry, Lyall admits: "We have no materials for constructing a theory for the development of Arabic poetry: its beginnings are lost in the fugitive memory of ages when writing was not in use to record it." However, the "striking and extraordinary feature of the poetic art, of which our poems are specimens, is the strength of conventions by which it is bound."[13] If Ḥammād and Khalaf are held to be suspicious, the unbroken chain of poetry affirms that they were not necessarily the only typical transmitters,[14] and their skill in imitating the ancients or, especially in Ḥammād's case, interpolations were not hard for the learned to detect. Margoliouth refers to this in his 1925 article, "The Origins of Arabic Poetry," without trying to engage with Lyall, whose edition of the anthology in Abū Muḥāmmad al-Qāsim b. Muḥammad b. Bashshār al-Anbārī's (d. 328/940) recension provides commentaries to poems that are thought of as the right and carefully authenticated specimens of an Arab poetic tradition. The history of the *Mufaḍḍaliyyāt* compilation is intriguing, as it was born in a revolutionary hub, when the co-leader of the revolt against the caliphate, Ibrāhīm b. ʿAbdallāh b. al-Ḥusayn, who was hiding in al-Mufaḍḍal's (d. 168/787) house,[15] selected seventy poems of interest from among al-Mufaḍḍal's rich poetry collection, which al-Mufaḍḍal would build on to make his selection later.[16] Al-Mufaḍḍal was the most trusted and knowledgeable authority on ancient poetry, and his book collection should have been among the best, if not the best. As usual, these eighth-century authorities like al-Mufaḍḍal, and also his guest, the co-leader of the rebellion, were no ordinary learned people. Ibn Sallām's mentors and tutors, along with al-Aṣmaʿī, were no less than the most knowledgeable in poetry, the linguist, grammarian, and transmitter of poetry Khalaf al-Aḥmar (d. 180/796), the grammarian, linguist, and sharp critic Yūnus b. Ḥabīb al-Naḥwī (d. 182/798), and the linguist, grammarian, prosodist, and anthologist al-Mufaḍḍal al-Ḍabbī.[17] As a non-Basrah authority from Kufa, the latter is described as the most knowledgeable.[18] During the eighth century, an enormous cultural tree, with branches of tutors and students, occupied a massive space. To list the names of critics,

[11] Ibid., xxi. [12] Ibid. [13] Ibid., xxiv. [14] Ibid., xx.

[15] Full name: Ibn Muḥammad b. Yaʿlah b. ʿĀmir al-Ḍabbī.

[16] The story of the selection and compilation makes an interesting case for poetry and revolution. Al-Mufaḍḍal joined the rebels led by Ibrāhīm and his brother Muḥammad Dhū al-Nafs al-Zakiyyah. See Lyall's marginal note in reference to this narrative as documented by Abū al-Faraj al-Iṣfahānī in his *Maqātil al-ṭālibiyyīn*. Lyall, introduction to *Mufaḍḍaliyyāt*, xiv, n. § (unnumbered).

[17] See further Sulṭān, *Ibn Sallām*, 103–9.

[18] Ibn Sallām, *Ṭabaqāt al-shuʿarāʾ* (1998), 21.

grammarians, linguists, anthologists, literary historians, geographers, and learned people would be daunting.[19] Cultural dynamism in Kufa, Basra, and Baghdad gathered momentum; and part of it involved the transmission of reports, anecdotes, and especially poetry. As will be shown in due course in this chapter, the eighth century witnessed the increasing role of philologists who were bent on establishing poetic genealogies. With suspicions being raised that some transmitters might try their hand at memorized material, a point that will receive further attention, scrutiny was called for, and careful sifting took place. Ibn Sallām makes references to suspicions surrounding some traditionalists accused of unauthenticated reporting and transmission, as was the case of the otherwise knowledgeable Muḥammad b. Isḥāq, whom Ibn Sallām singled out as the first to distort poetry.[20] Although briefly, Ibn Sallām recapitulates an ongoing discussion in which his mentors were involved.

Theoretical Beginnings

As the concern of this chapter is focused on what makes literary history and theory, Ibn Sallām's brief introduction to his selections and ranking of champion poets may serve the purpose, as it focuses on, first, the emphasis on the significance of poetry in the Arabic tradition, as "poetry in pre-Islamic times was the *dīwān* (public register) of their knowledge and the 'utmost compass of their wisdom,' their resource and anchor," or, in Lyall's translation: "with it they began their affairs, and with it they ended them."[21] Second, there is the fact that pre-Islamic Arabs left no *dīwān mudawwan* (written record), and Islamic conquests led to the death of many sources with a fecund memory. Thus, Ibn Sallām's mentor Yūnus b. Ḥabīb records Abū ʿAmrū b. al-ʿAlāʾ's conclusion that "what has reached you of the Arabs' poetry is the least. Had it survived in sufficient quantities, you would have had considerable knowledge and poetry."[22] Nevertheless, and despite the substantial portion that might

[19] See Saniyyah Aḥmad Muḥammad, *al-Naqd al-adabī fī al-qarn al-thānī al-hijrī* (Baghdad: Dār al-Risālah li-l-Ṭibāʿah, 1977); Muḥammad Muṣṭafā Haddārah, *Ittijāhāt al-shiʿr al-ʿArabī fī al-qarn al-thānī al-hijrī* (Damascus: al-Maktab al-Islāmī, 1981); Rashīd ʿAbd al-Raḥmān al-ʿUbaydī, *Mushkilāt al-taʾlīf al-lughawī fī al-qarn al-thānī al-hijrī* (Baghdād: Maṭbaʿat Dār al-Jāḥiẓ li-l-Ṭibāʿah wa-l-Nashr, 1980); Ibrāhīm Shiḥādah Khawājah, *Shiʿr al-ṣirāʿ al-siyāsī fī al-qarn al-thānī al-hijrī* (Kuwait: Sharikat Kāẓimah li-l-Nashr wa-l-Tarjamah wa-l-Tawzīʿ, 1984); Aḥmad Kamāl Zakī, *al-Ḥayāt al-adabiyyah fī al-Baṣrah ilā nihāyat al-qarn al-thānī al-hijrī* (Damascus: Dār al-Fikr, 1961).

[20] He used to say, "I have no knowledge of poetry, I am only a messenger." He was the author of the biography of the Prophet, and very knowledgeable in the history of the Arabs. See Ibn Sallām, *Ṭabaqāt al-shuʿarāʾ* (1998), 11 (editor's note).

[21] Ibid., 24 (1974).

[22] Ibid., 22 (1998), 25 (1974); Lyall, introduction to *Mufaḍḍaliyyāt*, xxvii.

have been lost, Lyall concludes his "Preface" with the following: "No race has ever expressed itself more completely or with greater faithfulness to its national literature, an appreciation of which is therefore indispensable to any adequate view of the part played by the Arabs in the history of Mankind."[23] Third, there were in his own time-knowledgeable authorities, *min ahl al-ʿilm*, such as al-Aṣmaʿī and al-Mufaḍḍal al-Ḍabbī.[24] They are drawn on because they received their training and knowledge from renowned authorities. A genealogy of ancestors is recorded, which Ibn Sallām's book and its editors and detractors helped in constructing.[25] Fourth, tribal competition and the quest for a magnanimous claim to poetry drove some tribes to fabricate poetry and assign it to their poets.[26] Thus, the terms *inḥal* (assigning verses to another), *waḍʿ* (addition of verses to another's poem: fabrication),[27] *ziyādah* (Here: unscrupulous supplementation), *iḥtidhāʾ* (v. *yaḥtadhī*: following closely), and *yaftaʿil* (concocting or contriving) are among the expressions used to account for cases which Ibn Sallām highlights.[28] The book does not spare unscrupulous *ruwāt* (tribal traditionalists; transmitters) the accusation of forgery and dabbling with sources, as this chapter will show. He grants the recurrence of such possibility, especially as these transmitters were among the learned who could find no difficulty in embarking on this *ziyādah*, exempting some Bedouin cases that they might find difficult to augment.[29] Ibn Sallām offers examples for his case study and terms: one on the authority of Abū ʿUbaydah who reports that Ibn Dāwūd b. Mutammim b. Nuwayrah came to Basrah, as Bedouins used to do to get food, and both Abū ʿUbaydah and Ibrāhīm b. Muḥammad b. Nūḥ al-ʿUṭāridī asked him to recite his grandfather's poetry.[30] When he finished, he started adding and forging poetry inferior to that of his (grand)father, but following it closely, mentioning abodes and battles in which Mutammim participated: "We became aware that he contrived" the supplementation to augment his (grand)father's legacy.[31] As for Ḥammād, "he was the first to gather Arabs' poetry and reported its

[23] Lyall, preface to *Mufaḍḍaliyyāt*. [24] Full name: Abū ʿUbaydah al-Naḥwī al-Aṣmaʿī.

[25] See, as examples, ʿAlī Jawād al-Ṭāhir, *Muḥammad b. Sallām wa-kitābuhu Ṭabaqāt al-shuʿarāʾ* (Amman: Dār al-Fikr li-l-Nashr wa-al-Tawzīʿ, 1995); Sulṭān, *Ibn Sallām*; al-Ḥusayn Zarrūq, *Nuṣūṣ al-naqd al-adabī fī Ṭabaqāt fuḥūl al-shuʿarāʾ li-Ibn Sallām al-Jumaḥī* (Fes: Kulliyyat al-Ādāb wa-l-ʿUlūm al-Insāniyyah, 2019); Jihād Majālī, *Ṭabaqāt al-shuʿarāʾ fī al-naqd al-adabī inda al-ʿArab ḥattā nihāyat al-qarn al-thālith al-hijrī* (Beirut: Dār al-Jīl, 1992); Muḥammad ʿAlī Abū Ḥamdah, *Muḥammad b. Sallām al-Jumaḥī wa-kitāb Ṭabaqāt fuḥūl al-shuʿarāʾ: dirāsah naqdiyyah ibdāʿiyyah* (Ammān: Dār al-Bashīr, 1998); Abū Fihr Maḥmūd Muḥammad Shākir, *Barnāmaj Ṭabaqāt fuḥūl al-shuʿarāʾ* (Cairo: Maṭbaʿat al-Madanī, 1980).

[26] Ibn Sallām, *Ṭabaqāt al-shuʿarāʾ* (1998), 32.

[27] In ibid., 46 (1974), *ruwāt* are accused of *waḍʿ* and *ziyādah*. [28] Ibid., 32 (1998).

[29] Ibid., 32, 38. [30] See ibid., 47, n. 4 (1974). [31] Ibid., 32.

occasions. As Abū ʿUbaydah reports on the authority of Yūnus [b. Ḥabīb]."[32] He adds: "he was untrustworthy since he *yanḥal* [assigns verses to another], and augments poems." Thus, tracing *inḥāl* (assigning one's verses to another, often a dead poet) and *intiḥāl* (self-arrogating of another's verses) would be among the landmarks in the scrutinizing process connected with poetry transmission. Although Margoliouth overlooks Ibn Sallām for one reason or another, and relies almost entirely on Abū al-Faraj al-Iṣfahānī in his *Kitāb al-aghānī* (The Book of Songs), his desperate account of discrepancies and unscrupulous "antiquarians" casts doubt on the poetry recorded as of South Arabian provenance, something that is especially so because he gives minimal attention to the counter effort undertaken by specialists to filter the material, according to what Ibn Sallām summarizes as a strategy of *faḥṣ*, *naẓar*, and *riwāyah* (examination, discernment, and transmission on the authority of learned ancestors).[33] Furthermore, Ibn Sallām draws attention to the role of the *ruwāt muṣaḥḥiḥīn* (discriminating or meticulous transmitters) in filtering the poetry, a role which implies a process of authentication, whereby the transmitted material is examined before being assigned a place in the recognized corpus.[34] This must have been on Lyall's mind, when he argued against Margoliouth's hypothesis:

> What we must conclude from the stories about Ḥammād and Khalaf is not that the compositions offered as ancient poems should, on *a priori* grounds, be rejected as spurious, but that they must be carefully scrutinized, with all the evidence of contemporary tradition, and with due regard to their content, style, and individual characteristics, to see if they suggest in any particular case, interpolation, dislocation, or fabrication.[35]

Authentication Processes

Even so, in the end scrutiny entailed an effort to systematize knowledge, including in this case a tabulation of borrowing, allusion, texts, and undertexts or subtexts. Thus, both literary history and literary or cultural theory work hand in hand, especially as a large body of philologists, critics, and cultural historians were transmitters of poetry, while some had their assemblies where poetry was foremost among topics discussed. Thus, Ibn Sallām's attention to cases of *intiḥāl* and *inḥāl* should be seen as a positive driving force toward scrutiny, and not as an open door for

[32] Ibid. [33] Ibid., 33.
[34] Ibid., 22. He uses the case of Ṭarafah (d. 569 CE) and ʿAbid b. al-Abraṣ (d. 554 CE) to point out the little that was authenticated of their poetry.
[35] Lyall, introduction to *Mufaḍḍaliyyāt*, xxi.

Cartesian doubt. Even before Ibn Sallām, pre-Islamic poets reacted against accusations of *intiḥāl.* Literary historians often cite al-Aʿshā Maymūn b. Qays's (d. 625 CE) specific verse denying *intiḥāl.* As these issues and details are the subject of Chapters 4 and 5, it is our concern here to explore the conditions of intertextuality, plain confiscation of another's poetic property, and the shades of repetition or invention and innovation. In all these instances, a human predilection is rarely absent in considering literary history and cultural or poetic theory.

Ibn Sallām's four concerns in his introduction were bound to receive further consideration not only among his contemporaries and ninth–tenth-century philologists, and critics and literary historians, but also in the twentieth century, minus the detailed interest in the transmission chain. While the academy is always in search of topics, the revival of interest in eighth-century cultural life is attuned to a reorientation pursuit, whereby Arabism is an issue. In that domain, authentication, transmission genealogical constructions, and confrontation with detractions, culminating in suspicions of the authenticity of pre-Islamic poetry of South Arabia, assume significance. Thus, a twentieth-century wave of multiple responses emerge as anxieties and navigations among other poetries, especially French, English, and Spanish. These make up a portion of a twentieth-century poetic foray, as will be shown further in this chapter.

As central to a visible mutation in poetics, multiple variations on *saraq* and its associated terms imply an attempt at systematization. While there are anxieties of influence, usually spelled out in defensive refutations, as enumerated by Goldziher,[36] there are often philological or literary recapitulations. The philological contribution constitutes an enormous corpus, especially because enumeration and comparative cataloging of poetic echoes, correspondences, similarities, borrowings, and deliberate duplication are often fused with anecdotes and *majālis* discussions (assemblies or table-talks), such as the ones that relate tricks played on Ibn al-Aʿrabī (d. 231/845) with respect to a deliberately unidentified verse by Abū Nuwās (d. 198/814).[37] Different from these are more systematic readings, usually associated at a later date with ʿAbd al-Qāhir al-Jurjānī

[36] Von Grunebaum's excellent survey and reading in "Concept of Plagiarism" touches on Goldziher's seven types of protesting suspicions or accusations of plagiarism in his article in *Zeitschrift der Deutschen Morgenländischen Gesellschaft* 46 (1892), 235.

[37] Full name: Abū ʿAbdallāh Muḥammad b. Ziyād. See al-Marzubānī, *al-Muwashshaḥ*, ed. ʿAlī Muḥammad al-Bajāwī (Cairo: Nahḍat Miṣr, 1965), 336, for another anecdote that shows Ibn al-Aʿrābī's readiness to comparatively appreciate Abū Nuwās. However, as al-Ṣūlī reports, there were other anecdotes that show the well-known philologist as undisposed to *muḥdathūn*; see al-Ṣūlī, *Akhbār Abī Tammām*, 176; also with reference to Abū Nuwās, see al-Ḥuṣrī al-Qayrawānī, *Zahr al-ādāb*, ed. ʿAlī Muḥammad al-Bajāwī (Cairo: ʿĪsā al-Bābī al-Ḥalabī, 1953), 1:286–87.

(d. 400/1078). He is disconcerted by writings that vault over succinct but popular conclusions, such as al-Hamadhānī's terse summation of the critical corpus on *saraq* in the short preface to his book *Kitāb al-alfāẓ al-kitābiyyah*. ʿAbd al-Qāhir refers to the book as being popular and read by "the youth" in its time.[38] His mention of the book in relation to his own reading of *maʿānī* and *alfāẓ* tends to stress the need to go beyond an outdated discussion already tersely summarized; and instead to turn the attention to structuration, whereby matters of *saraq* are bound to take an intertextual direction rather than a witch hunt for echoes. His few terms (which are to be considered in Chapters 4 and 5) fall within this approach. At this point, even the discussion around *muḥdathūn* (modernists or innovators) and *qudamāʾ* (ancients or conservatives) has its new turns respecting canonicity.

Regardless of what Ibn al-Aʿrābī and even Ibn Qutaybah stand for as canonical standards, ancestry suffers, as al-Qāḍī al-Jurjānī explains: the ancient poets are not beyond blame, a point that he documents with reference to some verses by the "stallion poets." Conversely, al-Qāḍī al-Jurjānī demonstrates a preference for *badīʿ*, as one gateway through which to escape exhausted expressions or even meanings. On the other hand, when it comes to intimate patrons, we may not expect constancy even among the most serene minds, including al-Qāḍī al-Jurjānī himself. The same ranking and prioritization with which he introduces his *Wasāṭah* involves this robust authority in the elevation of his patron as the foremost innovator or inventor of *badīʿ*. Thus, even insightful philologists and critics put their serenity aside and speak of a literary scene as no more than a carbon copy of one single figure, that is, the patron. Al-Qāḍī al-Jurjānī writes in praise of al-Ṣāḥib b. ʿAbbād (d. 385/995) or probably Ibn al-ʿAmīd in order to show the latter's exhaustive stylistic skill and suave thematic fecundity:

فإنْ نحن حاولنا اختراع بديعةٍ حصلنا على مسروقها ومعادِها

If we strive to invent an innovative wording (badīʿatin), we end up only with theft and duplication.

That is, "If we strive to invent an innovative wording (*badīʿatin*), we end up only with theft and duplication."[39] On the other hand, the same verse directs us to the increasing use of specific phrases and terms as part and parcel of specific parlance that permeates the poetry of these critics. In three verses, al-Qāḍī al-Jurjānī brings together the basic tenets of both *naẓm* as sentence structure, and also thievery issues in poetic ideas and wording:

38 al-Jurjānī, *Dalāʾil al-iʿjāz*, 436.
39 Abū Manṣūr al-Thaʿālibī, *Kitāb khāṣṣ al-khāṣṣ* (Beirut: Dār al-Ḥayāt, n.d.), 187–88.

ولا ذنبَ للأفكار أنتَ تركتها   إذا احتشدت لم تحتفلْ باحتشادها
سبقت بأفراد المعاني وألَّ   فتْ خواطرك الألفاظ بعد شرادِها

It is not the fault of the thoughts you left behind
unconcerned as you are with their profusion.
You preceded [others] in unique meanings
while your presence of mind collated fleeing utterances and expressions.[40]

The tendency to aggrandize a name is not unique to al-Qāḍī al-Jurjānī, despite his celebrated sobriety as being *fard al-zamān*, the "unique one in his time."[41] The increasingly distinguished merit of creative inventiveness or *badī*ʿ was to become a marker of distinction, which al-Qādī al-Jurjānī is ready to confer on his contemporary al-Ṣāḥib b. ʿAbbād, but denies to Abū Tammām, for example, because of the latter's alleged artificiality and contrivance.[42] This same celebrated merit is pivotal to the ongoing battle over the body of a poem or a persona. It is often through this gateway that poets receive critics' and philologists' commendation for not duplicating the ancients. As *maʿānī* (poetic ideas and meanings) form a shared textual and conversational space, it is only the medium of utterances, vocal expression, and figures of speech that demonstrate uniqueness. Hence, in the tenth and eleventh centuries the term *badī*ʿ has to assume its ultimate value as a cultural and symbolic distinction. Al-Mutanabbī used it in a panegyric:

ذُكِرَ الأَنامُ لَنا فَكانَ قَصيدَةً   كُنتَ البَديعَ الفَردَ مِن أَبياتِها

If all of creation is compared to a poem
you are its unique *badī*ʿ verse.[43]

These developments are no minor happenings in Arabic literary history, not only because there had been a raging controversy between two positions, *qadīm* and *muḥdath* (antiquity and modernity), but also because this debate had as its juncture and focal point borrowing from or imitation of the ancients and early Islamic poetry. Almost every critic asserts the exhaustion of meanings in pre-Islamic or early Islamic

[40] Ibid. For a different translation, see Aḥmad b. Muḥammad Ibn Khallikān, *Biographical Dictionary* (London: Oriental Translation Fund of Great Britain and Ireland, 1842), 2:221–23.

[41] Abū Manṣūr al-Thaʿālibī, *Yatīmat al-dahr*, ed. Muḥammad Muḥyī al-Dīn ʿAbd al-Ḥamīd (Cairo: al-Maktabah al-Tijāriyyah al-Kubrā, 1947), 4:2; also quoted by Ibn Khallikān, *Biographical Dictionary*, 2:221; or ʿAbbās's edition of Ibn Khallikān's *Wafayāt al-aʿyān* (Beirut: Dār Ṣādir, 2013), 3:279.

[42] For quotes and comments, see Harb, *Arabic Poetics*, 33.

[43] al-Thaʿālibī, *Kitāb khāṣṣ al-khāṣṣ*, 146.

poetry.[44] And since, *saraq* "is an ancient malady" which *muḥdathūn* (modernists) concealed in a number of ways that gave rise to a detailed lexicon,[45] which annoys such a brilliant critic as Iḥsān ʿAbbās,[46] it is incumbent to provide a way out. Hence, al-Qāḍī al-Jurjānī offers a neat and brief list of the modernists' ways of hiding dependency.[47] Moreover, the debate over source material, Genette's hypotext, has remained central to literary and broad cultural disputes as the controversy around Ṭāhā Ḥusayn's *Fī al-shiʿr al-jāhilī* (Pre-Islamic Poetry) shows. Cartesian doubt was not unique to Ḥusayn. As noticed earlier, Ibn Sallām for one voiced concern regarding arbitrary augmentation, but he balanced doubts with the effort of *al-ruwāt al-muṣaḥḥiḥīn* (meticulous transmitters) to filter and authenticate material. The wider implications of distinction and its attending political and social privileges, especially in relation to the Abbasid court or prominent notables, cannot be overestimated, and along with it the search for *al-mubtadaʿ al-mukhtaraʿ* (the invented expression and poetic meaning).[48] No wonder, then, that those raids on even obscure or less prominent poets were, and still are, rampant, and they create a substantial margin in literary history.

Thus, when we look back upon a massive production usually subsumed under the term *sariqāt*, we are bound to agree only partly with Bloom that the struggle *among strong* poets makes up a literary history. As noted previously, there is the other side of this blanket statement: in Arabic literature, and probably in many other ancient and modern ones, minor or less-visible poets often serve as the obscure source material for prominent ones. Al-Āmidī goes so far as to suggest that the less-known poets were a source for Abū Tammām's poetry in matters on heroism and valor: "He picked things from the less productive and obscure poets."[49] The unrecognized creditors are presumed to have made the best part of the poet's selection. The latter's desire to accrue further distinction knows no satiation. In a neat formulation concerning individualism, Michel Foucault makes this statement, which sounds commonplace: "The more one possesses power or privilege, the more one is marked as an individual, by rituals, written accounts, or visual reproductions."[50] Regardless of

[44] See al-Qāḍī al-Jurjānī's apology for "our contemporaries, and the following generations because those who preceded us exhausted meanings, and were ahead of us in using most" (*al-Wasāṭah*, 214–15); al-ʿAlawī, *ʿIyār al-shiʿr*, 13.
[45] al-Jurjānī, *al-Wasāṭah* (1966), 214.
[46] Iḥsān ʿAbbās, *Tārīkh al-naqd al-adabī* (1971; Beirut: Dār al-Thaqāfah, 2nd print, 1978), 39–41.
[47] al-Jurjānī, *al-Wasāṭah* (1966), 214.
[48] Ibid., 186; al-Āmidī, *al-Muwāzanah*, 1:291, 325.
[49] al-Āmidī, *al-Muwāzanah*, 1:55.
[50] Michel Foucault, *Discipline and Punish: The Birth of the Prison*, trans. Alan Sheridan (New York: Random House, 1991), 192.

periods, strong poets would not opt to lose that prestige, even if that entails theft. In al-Marzubānī's (d. 384/993) *al-Muwashshaḥ*, al-Farazdaq is reported to have argued:

خير السرقة ما لم تقطع فيه اليد

> The best thievery is what entails no [judicial] amputation of the hand.[51]

Diverted Theory?

The writings of classical Arab philologists and critics often demonstrate raids and confiscation of the poetries of the amiable or less prominent.[52] The case is even more conspicuous and glaring when explored meticulously in terms of parlance, imagery, enunciations, lexicology, and ideas. In an exhaustive undertaking, classical Arab philologists and scholars also relied on one another to develop over time a coherent system, which I take as central not only to literary history but also to literary theory. Approvals and refutations of each other define a dynamic field, and even value judgments convey a nonconformist climate of ideas, which should be central to the study of literary theory. Al-Marzubānī in his *al-Muwashshaḥ* criticizes his predecessor al-Aṣmaʿī for claiming that nine-tenths of al-Farazdaq's poetry is plagiarized (see Figure 0.2). He counterargues: "There is no doubt that al-Farazdaq did raid some poets in well-known verses, but the above claim is impossible."[53] As a major poet, al-Farazdaq was bound to draw attention to his poetry, which – in several notorious occasions – enlisted *ighārah*, raid, on less intimidating poets whereby a verse or two sounds more in line with his poetry.

On the other hand, even when raiding or seizing by force another poet's verse, as al-Farazdaq did with Ibn Mayyādah's (d. 149/767), poets have made modifications to fit into the new owner's corpus.[54] Differences, as

51 al-Marzubānī, *al-Muwashshaḥ* (1965, Nahḍat Miṣr), 168.

52 al-Marzubānī, *al-Muwashshaḥ* (1965, Dār al-Fikr), 293. For a study of al-Marzubānī, see Amidu Sanni, "Al-Marzubānī in the Context of Arabic Literary Theory: An Analytical Study of *al-Muwashshaḥ*". Sanni concludes that "the characteristic lack of order for which Arabic poetics was known in its nascent stage was remarkably improved by al-Marzubānī. This he was able to do by systematically reorganizing the extant materials as well as by furnishing Arabic literary theory with a logical framework" (ibid., 4).

53 al-Marzubānī in his *al-Muwashshaḥ* (1965, Dār al-Fikr), 293:
ولسنا نشك أن الفرزدق قد أغار على بعض الشعراء في أبيات معروفة، فأما أن نطلق أن تسعة أعشار شعره سرقة فهذا محال.

54 In a well-known narrative, al-Farazdaq heard Ibn Mayyādah – whose grandfather's name was Ẓālim al-Murrī – reciting while surrounded by an audience; punning on the grandfather's name, alternating between the actual name and its equivalent meaning of "tyrant":

well as agreements or mere duplications of one issue of literary thievery or another, form an enormous part of an archive that should caution us whenever we try to check on *sariqāt*. In a rigorous investigation of theoretical inconsistencies, including the large philological corpus on *sariqāt*, Wolfhart Heinrichs asks: "Are there any nuclei of historical reasoning in these treatises on *sariqāt*?"[55] The rhetorical question is already in the minds of many Arab literary historians and critics. Indeed, the late Iḥsān ʿAbbās argues in his 1971 *History of Arabic Literary Criticism* that "the issue of *sariqāt* dominated every other issue in literary criticism, monopolizing every effort, and in this respect it diverted its primary concern from its natural course."[56] Iḥsān ʿAbbās reads the issue from a specific genealogical cultural tree that branches off into multiple philological practices – linguistic, grammatical, theological, philosophical, and literary proper. With a comprehensive overview of the vast scene, Iḥsān ʿAbbās is bound to see the enormous growth of thievery discussions as a serious rupture, a divergence that cuts short the probability of a finished literary theory. As my argument tries to demonstrate, thievery functions as the catalyst that coalesces efforts and incites littérateurs to mobilize their acumen to make a case. The groundwork laid by Ibn Sallām, and later Ibn Ṭayfūr, al-Jāḥiẓ, and Ibn Qutaybah, and the poets themselves, along with the visibility of other literary concerns in the domains of narrative and epistolary, sets the scene for further and more focused tenth-century discussions that cannot be pinned down to specific thematic concerns. Indeed, Iḥsān ʿAbbās is right to be shocked that some critics address *akhdh* (partial seizure or unlawful possession) as if it "were the only principle in the

لو أنّ جميعَ الناس كانوا بربوة وجئت بجَدّي ظِالم وابنِ ظَالم
لظلّت رقاب الناس خاضعةً لنا سُجوداً على أقدامنًا بالجماجم

If all people were on a hillside, and you brought my grandfather,
Ẓālim, the son of Ẓālim,
People's necks would submit to us, lowering/prostrating their
skulls/heads (?) at our feet.

Al-Farazdaq raided the verse, forcing Ibn Mayyādah to give it up, changing only the name Ẓālim with his tribal clan's name: Dārim. The rest of the anecdote details al-Farazdaq's threatening retort and Ibn Mayyādah's reluctant submission. Al-Marzubānī cites this differently, treating it as *majdūl*, when the latter poet, al-Farazdaq, changes a few words to fit it in his poetry, and to gain recognition to the disadvantage of the original, or hypotext. See al-Marzubānī, *al-Muwashshaḥ* (1965, Dār al-Fikr), 144.

A similar case is reported with the poet Shamardal al-Yarbūʿī. See Abū al-Faraj, al-Iṣfahānī, *al-Aghānī*, 13, 357; al-Rāghib al-Iṣfahānī, *Muḥāḍarāt al-udabāʾ*, 1:85. A full citation is in Ṭāhā, *al-Naẓariyyah al-naqdiyyah*, 184–85. It is reported that al-Shamardal also says: "Take it, may God never bless you with it." See Ibn Rashīq, *al-ʿUmdah* (2001), 2:285.

[55] Heinrichs, "Literary Theory," 58.

[56] ʿAbbās, *Tārīkh al-naqd al-adabī* (1978), 39–40.

creative poetic process, to the extent they set rules and gradations for it."[57] The anxiety surrounding the term "thievery" and the focused effort of some littérateurs to manipulate its pejorative connotation illustrate an extremely exciting scene that still calls for research. Heinrichs is not far from this understanding. A scholar of his caliber is certainly aware of the open venues for researchers in this large corpus. As he argues, "In working with specific texts . . . the students of poetry were given another opportunity to develop a kind of historical consciousness, especially since the term *sariqah* is rather loosely applied in these works to denote almost any kind of dependence of a line of poetry on an earlier model."[58] While the issue is admittedly large, especially in terms of reflections on a rapidly growing corpus on thievery and its varieties and terminologies (as there are multiple applications), we must approach it from another perspective, from outside its immediate subject – that is, poetry. As I look upon the thievery controversy beyond the "historical" limit that Heinrichs assigns it,[59] and thence considers antiquity as a starting point for subsequent developments, I take economies of theft as necessarily competitive, and hence dynamic, not static, and lively, not inert. While antecedent authority is often conflated with an established lexicon, and thence with poetic themes and expressions, the latter gradually undergo extension, diversion, slippage, and even rejection. Urbanity, geographical expansion, and consequent lexical interaction and interfusion allow a gradual departure from that antecedence, a self-acquittal of theft, and even some distinction in acclaimed improvement on the original.[60] Thus, thievery gradually loses the stigma of robbery, and appears in a web of terminologies that keep up with a growing tree of practices that find objectification mottos in a few basic maxims.[61] The case is especially so if we look at the matter from Ḥāzim al-Qarṭajannī's (d. 684/1386) perspective with respect to common and shared poetic meanings; as he builds on earlier theorists including al-Āmidī, al-Qāḍī al-Jurjānī, and Ibn Rashīq, to suggest that *saraq* applies only to stealing unique or virgin meanings that are the specific property of a certain poet.

Every instance involving imitation and originality, ancients and moderns, transmission and forgery, selection of relevant literary terms, and the focus on some prominent names accused of invading a relatively unfamiliar poetic production tends toward an institutionalization of

[57] Ibid., 40. [58] Heinrichs, "Literary Theory," 58.
[59] Wolfhart Heinrichs, "An Evaluation of 'Sariqa,'" in "Gli Arabi nella Storia: Tanti Popoli una Sola Civiltà," special issue, *Quaderni di Studi Arabi* 5–6 (1987–88): 358.
[60] See al-Jurjānī, *al-Wasāṭah* (1966), 185, 214, 206.
[61] See Ibn Rashīq, *al-ʿUmdah* (2001), 2:289.

poetic standards. Even as early as the time of Yūnus b. Ḥabīb and Ibn Sallām, this institutionalized space had its reporters, transmitters, narrators, grammarians, and trustworthy authorities. There are rules for assessment that are both ethical and philological. Ibn Sallām mentions how all the learned people of his time were of one opinion, namely, that Khalaf al-Aḥmar was the most discernible and knowledgeable about every verse, and the most sincere and truthful, to the extent that "whenever he transmits or recites poetry, we are unconcerned about not taking it directly from its owner."[62] Ibn Qutaybah also concurs, as "none of those knowledgeable had more poetry than him,"[63] a poetry that is of "high quality." He also adds, "he used to say poetry and assign it to the ancients," that is, *inḥāl.*[64] In other words, the matter here is not about "historical reasoning"; rather, it is about a constitutionalized space that has its arbiters. In a neat surmise that prefaces a comprehensive survey and reading of plagiarism, von Grunebaum cautions against any neglect of an Arab poetic sensitiveness to invention and innovation. He explains: "The Arab audience . . . being highly sensitive to and extremely anxious for those modifications and embellishments of the traditional treatment that, while sometimes hardly noticeable to us, meant for the performing poet the difference between fame and oblivion."[65] The growing awareness of a changing lifestyle, its urban demands, and its new needs is evident not only in what Abū Nuwās says about "*ṣifat al-ṭulūl balāghat al-fadm*" (the description of ruins and campsites is a rhetoric of the sluggish)[66] but also in narrative and chancery belles lettres. In other words, although poetry has remained forever revered, the cultural space offers very competitive genres and styles, as the migration among genres indicates, a point that Ibn Ṭabāṭabā addresses as a navigational space for new generations of poets to use in their search for poetic meanings.[67] Soon after, treatises were written on versification of prose, and prosification of verse. In the mediational space between audiences and poets, philologists, literary critics, polyglots, and *adīb*s used to play a significant role. Even their differences happened to draw attention and entail therefore their recognition or otherwise. This battling and radical competitiveness takes several forms, including the other side of thievery: forgery and counterfeit identity. Arbiters of taste, the inspectors of the

[62] Ibn Sallām, *Ṭabaqāt al-shuʿarāʾ* (1998), 21.
[63] Ibn Qutaybah, *al-Shiʿr wa-l-shuʿarāʾ* (2001), 2:789.
[64] Ibid., 790. Ibn Durayd mentioned that *Lāmiyyat al-ʿArab* is by Khalaf. See ibid., n. 4.
[65] Grunebaum, "Concept of Plagiarism."
[66] Abū Nuwās, *Dīwān*, ed. Ewald Wagne (Beirut: Orient Institut Beirut, 2015), 3:265. Professor van Gelder drew my attention to the fact that *al-qudmī* is mentioned in Ibn Rashīq's *ʿUmdah* and al-Thaʿālibī's *Thimār al-qulūb*.
[67] al-ʿAlawī, *ʿIyār al-shiʿr*, 13.

literary market happened to be on the watch for transgressions, and they were occasionally so carried away by suspicion as to label as thievery even shared orphan verses. This is why robust minds warn against bias, favoritism, interest, and partiality in criticism. Al-Qāḍī al-Jurjānī writes: "be aware that there are critics who are to assess your criticism and are unwilling to give in to partiality as you did."[68] The other case relates to the impact of linguists and grammarians and *transmitters of poetry* on the literary market, and the readiness of some to switch positions from rejection to approval. Al-Qāḍī al-Jurjānī gives, as example, Abū Riyāsh Aḥmad b. Abī Ḥāshim Ibrāhīm al-Shaybānī's (al-Qaysī, d. 339/960) low opinion of the poetry of Abū Tammām and al-Buḥturī. Being an influential *rāwiyah* (transmitter) in the literary market in Basrah, copies of their poetry dwindled "because of the little interest in them."[69] Upon listening to unidentified verses that impressed him, and that he knew later as being by al-Buḥturī, he changed his opinion. Although unrelated to *saraq*, the case is important for the economies of publicity and theft. Hence, the warning against hurried opinion or partiality. Critics, grammarians, and linguists were often uncertain about specific cases that cannot be definite *sariqah*, but more like *ihtidām* – that is, keeping original meaning in a partially new wording.[70] Another point that some tenth-century critics and philologists discussed was the increasing presence of mediocre figures who survive on gossip and accusations of *saraq*. Al-Jurjānī is not alone in his scathing repudiation of anonymous dabblers, as al-Āmidī and a few others before him sound no less annoyed by the unleashed battling and trading in accusatory terms in the literary domain,[71] which, for purposes of cultural dynamics, is an important index of thriving cultural markets, a point that will be discussed in Chapters 4 and 5.[72]

When looked upon panoramically, the large number of writings and discussions of *sariqāt* since pre-Islamic times is as daunting as the large *adab* corpus. Each contribution since pre-Islamic times works as an explosive point in an ever-growing lexical and thematic genealogy, a tree of sorts that shows the inscription of poets, critics, philologists, and learned communities. Terminology down to the twentieth century marks not only shifts of taste but also the informing domain that identifies the recurrence of *ighārah* (literally: raid on poetic meaning; or on both

[68] al-Jurjānī, *al-Wasāṭah* (1966), 411. [69] Ibid., 51.

[70] While referencing al-Ḥātimī and the explanation given by Ibn Rashīq, Bonebakker cites the case of the "megalomaniac" Shumaym al-Ḥilli (d. 601/1204), whom Ibn Saʿīd al-Andalusī (d. 685/1285) mentions in *al-Ghuṣūn al-yāniʿah* and accuses of stealing two lines belonging to al-Nahrajūrī (d. 483/1012–13). See Bonebakker, "Ancient Arabic Poetry and Plagiarism," 74.

[71] For a survey, see ʿAbbās, *Tārīkh al-naqd al-adabī* (1978), 253–336.

[72] al-Jurjānī, *al-Wasāṭah* (1966), 183, 208.

meaning and wording) more often early on when *ghazw* (raid and limited invasion) happened to be among tribal and nomadic lifestyles. On this point of circumstantial evidence, al-Āmidī argues that poets and writers belonging to one period are bound to share poetic meanings.[73] Arbiters have a role to play, but their role is also informed by a cultural ambience. Since the second half of the tenth century, in many branches of knowledge – and Sufism is no exception – there has been a noticeable increase in classification of knowledge as evidenced in professional or teaching guides and manuals. Alongside this increase, there is ease and a tendency to systematize knowledge with insightful clarity that rarely smacks of negativism. A case in point is the terminological zenith in al-Ḥātimī's *Ḥilyat al-muḥāḍarah*, where he endeavors to preserve and systematize what has been in currency since ancient times. His work, as well as what is preserved by al-Marzubānī, receives more trimming and explanation in Ibn Rashīq's significant guide, *al-ʿUmdah*. In the postclassical period, there appear several critics like Ḍiyāʾ al-Dīn b. al-Athīr (d. 637/1239) in *al-Mathal al-sāʾir fī adab al-kātib wa-l-shāʿir* (The Proverbial Saying for the Literary Discipline of the Scribe and Poet), Ḥāzim al-Qartājannī (d. 684/1285), Jalāl al-Dīn Muḥammad al-Qazwīnī (d. 739/1338; better known as al-Khaṭīb al-Dimashqī), and others. They give the *sariqāt* domain a much larger space, better suited to textual navigation. The buildup or accretion and eventual tabulation of the domain offers readers of literary history and theory not only some insight into historical consciousness but also a unique perspective on contextual implications.

Textual Navigations

For some time, writers were unclear about the right approach to embedding (*taḍmīn*) from the text of the Qurʾān. As an example, the first book we are aware of that has *sariqāt* in its title is Ibn Muḥammad b. Kunāsah's (d. 209/824) *Sariqāt al-Kumayt min al-Qurʾān* (al-Kumayt's Thefts from the Qurʾān). It predates a wide range of manuals addressed to scribes on guided borrowing from the Qurʾān, like Ibn Qutaybah's *Adab al-kātib* and in books on prose verse and prose, like Ibn Ṭayfūr's (d. 280/893) *Kitāb al-manthūr wa-l-manẓūm* (Book of Prose and Poetry). There is also *Kitāb intizāʿāt al-Qurʾān*, attributed to Abū al-Qāsim al-Ṣayrafī.[74] The increasing interest in the topic of *sariqāt* takes more nuanced directions, as shown in titles and quotes that have reached us in compendiums, such as

[73] al-Āmidī, *al-Muwāzanah*, 1:61.
[74] Bilāl al-Urfahlī, *Kitāb intizāʿāt al-Qurʾān*, attributed to the Fatimid writer Abū al-Qāsim ʿAlī b. al-Ṣayrafī (Beirut: Dār al-Mashriq, 2020).

Muḥammad b. Aydamir al-Musta'ṣimī's (d. 710/1310) *al-Durr al-farīd wa-bayt al-qaṣīd* (The Unique Pearls and the Outstanding Verse), and before him al-Marzubānī's *al-Muwashshaḥ*, along with several other works. The issue drew the attention of the distinguished linguist and critic Abū Yūsuf Ya'qūb b. al-Sikkīt (d. 244/858).[75] Although unavailable, his *Kitāb sariqāt al-shu'arā' wa-mā attafaqū 'alayh* (Poets' Thefts and What They Commonly Accepted) tends to search for the shared script and transmission in an oral tradition, a position that certainly raises questions about random accusations of plagiarism. On the other hand, while *sariqah* and *ighārah* are among the words used with regard to pre-Islamic poetry, Ibn Sallām al-Jumaḥī adds *ijtilāb* (obtaining support) as used by poets like Jarīr and al-Farazdaq (see Figure 2.2). Both al-Ḥātimī and later Ibn Aydamir, in *al-Durr al-farīd*, were able to collect the sayings or comments by Ibn Ṭayfūr and Yūnus b. Ḥabīb (90–182/708–98). The latter defines *ijtilāb* as an appeal to other people's poetries, and since it is a visible borrowing to make a case, it is not inexcusable. Ibn Sallām quotes Yūnus b. Ḥabīb about a popular verse, reportedly by al-Nābighah al-Dhubyānī (d. 604 CE),[76] but recited by *ahl al-bādiyah* (nomads, non-city dwellers), as being by al-Zibriqān b. Badr.[77] Yūnus explains it as non-*ijtilāb*; instead it is *istizādah* (supplementation) as a proverbial saying, "and Arabs practice that as non-*saraq*"[78] (see Figure 3.2). Ibn Rashīq tends to think of *ijtilāb* as a reprehensible practice – unlike *istilḥāq*, which is acceptable, as, in this case, the later poet is adding to the former's verse[79] (see Figure 5.2). Al-Jāḥiẓ is more disposed to *akhdh* (seizure, taking away) in *al-Bayān*, though the term *sariqah* occurs also in *Kitāb al-ḥayawān*. Historians and critics differ in their approach to the matter of this haunting past, and their terminology indicates an increasing dose of hesitation and sense of responsibility that gradually evolves as the theoretical framework for sustainable poetics. Ibn Sallām employs such idioms as *ijtilāb* (here: obtaining support to fit expressions and images in one's verse), *ighārah* (raid),[80] and also *sariqah*. A relatively latecomer, Ibn Qutaybah has more to say on these matters. He adopts *salkh* (flaying), along with *ittibā'* (following closely) and *akhdh*. He also has important insights insofar as borrowing practices are concerned. When addressing *sariqah* in its visible or subtle forms, he mentions the example of 'Abd al-Ṣamad

[75] *Kitāb sariqāt al-shu'arā' wa-mā ittafaqū 'alayh* (Poets' Thefts and What They Commonly Accepted).
[76] Full name: al-Ziyād b. Mu'āwiyah al-Nābighah al-Dhubyānī.
[77] See al-Ḥātimī, *Ḥilyat al-muḥāḍarah*, 2:58.
[78] Ibn Sallām, *Ṭabaqāt al-shu'arā'*, 38 (1998), 1:58 (1974).
[79] Bonebakker, "Ancient Arabic Poetry," 68.
[80] Al-Ḥātimī cites Jarīr's use of the term against al-Farazdaq, which means he thinks of the practice as reprehensible. *Ḥilyat al-muḥāḍarah*, 2:58–61.

b. al-Muʿadhdhal al-ʿAbdī (d. 240/854), whom he cites in his *al-Shiʿr wa-l-shuʿarāʾ* as the most subtle in his thefts from Imruʾ al-Qays.[81] He notably differentiates between terms like *sariqah* (theft), *salkh* (flaying), and *akhdh*, as the first is a confiscation of a verse; it can be subtle and indiscernible (see Figure 3.2), while the second implies distortion of an original, whereas *akhdh* (seizure), as applied by him, could mean a rewriting of a meaning or even a total confiscation with a change in the rhyming word, as in Ṭarafah's use of Imruʾ al-Qays's known opening verse.[82] Ibn Qutaybah seems to side with Hishām b. al-Kalbī (d. 204/819) and Abū ʿUbaydah (d. 213/828), namely, that Imruʾ al-Qays appropriates the nostalgic yearning and its supplementary weeping at the deserted campsite from another Imruʾ al-Qays b. Ḥārthah b. al-Ḥumām (or Khidhām; or Ḥudhām) b. Muʿāwiyah; hence Imruʾ al-Qays b. Ḥujr's practice partakes of *iḥtidhāʾ* (see Figure 0.1) and *ittibāʿ* (imitation, in the footsteps of, and emulation) of the former. It is a reasonable recognition of antecedent precedence: "Let us weep at the campsite as Ibn Ḥudhām did."[83] There is no claim to originality here, and hence credit goes to Ibn Ḥujr for reviving the memory of a long-departed poet. Moreover, whenever conventional preludes are under discussion, this poetic recognition of antecedent authority should negate claims of thievery. Further, a historicizing process like this documentary reference might have helped Margoliouth out of his labyrinth of suspicions. Imruʾ al-Qays b. Ḥujr also presents the tripartite practice, with its nostalgic prelude as a model or a paradigmatic structure that is associated with states of feeling, "for the superb poet is he who follows these practices."[84] *Ittibāʿ* (emulation) is more in the mimetic tradition of a shared script. One can argue that Ibn Qutaybah is careful not to mix up terms, avoiding blanket judgments, and placing thievery under the rubric of subtle and indiscernible confiscation. The reference to *ighārah* (raid) also occurs quite often, and al-Zubayr b. Bakkār b. ʿAbdallāh al-Qurashī (d. 256/870) has it in a title, as in his *Ighārat Kuthayyir ʿalā al-shuʿarāʾ* (Kuthayyir's Raid on the Poetry of Others), a book that is notorious for its prejudice against the Hashemites and ʿAlī b. Abī Ṭālib, whom Kuthayyir espoused. Does this mean that there was a literary movement that raised issues of poetic subjectivity, ingenuity, originality, and discontinuity or otherwise with the antecedent authority of the Fathers? Certainly. But does this mean there were never such forms of arbitration earlier? Both Ḥassān b. Thābit and Ṭarafah used *sariqah* as a term in defense of their ingenuity and poetic subjectivity. Abū ʿUbaydah substantiates the recurrence of some forms of theft, like the raids

[81] Ibn Qutaybah, *al-Shiʿr wa-l-shuʿarāʾ* (2001), 1:134. [82] Ibid.
[83] Ibid., 1:128. See n. 11 in the Preface for variations in spelling.
[84] Ibn Qutaybah, *al-Shiʿr wa-l-shuʿarāʾ* (2001), 1:74–75.

of the poets of the Ghaṭafān tribe on the poetry of Qurād b. Ḥanash, who was known for high-quality poetry. Even Zuhayr b. Abī Sulmā made use of that poetry, according to Abū ʿUbaydah.[85] In other words, while in the pre-Islamic period there was such a movement to watch and assess poetic production, it was stimulated at a later date as a focal point in literary discussions in the expanding urban centers. Social, economic, and cultural transformations gave birth to new tastes. Thus, Ibn Qutaybah argues the case of Muslim b. al-Walīd on the basis of refinement and gentility in expressions and meanings.[86]

The gradual inclusion and systematization of terminology answers to historical and social changes, not only from Bedouin to urban, quite often noticed by all, especially in al-Qāḍī al-Jurjānī's *Wasāṭah*, but also in line with a tabulation of knowledge, a point that Abū al-Naṣr al-Fārābī's *Iḥṣāʾ al-ʿulūm*, Ikhwān al-Ṣafāʾ's encyclopedia, Muḥammad b. Mūsā Abū Bakr al-Khwārazmī's *Mafātīḥ al-ʿulūm*, al-Iṣfahānī's voluminous *Kitāb al-aghānī* (Book of Songs), and many other specialized books attest to.[87] Indeed al-Qāḍī al-Jurjānī alerts readers not to think of *saraq* only in terms of total confiscation of expression and meaning: there are strategies, including *naql*, thematic or generic transposition, to depart from the original, for instance (see Figure 3.1).[88] Granting that *saraq* is "an old malady," as he argues, and that the modernists were vying to achieve distinction, they were bound "to hide thievery behind *naql*, *qalb* (reversal, transformation), and also by changing the purpose and the structure or arrangement."[89] Gradually, there grows a more systematic effort to tabulate a wide range of variables that come under one term or another. The availability of material and the enormous and fecund domain of interactive and dynamic exchange among poets, ancient and contemporary, were bound to generate a search for the right phrase. The effort to tabulate and classify should be seen as a multidimensional endeavor, not only to list and write down ancient lexical words and forms of speech, appropriate the emerging ones, retain the *faṣīḥ* from the *ʿāmmī* (correct usage in quotidian and common speech), or build up a lexicographical repository and correct corrupt usage whenever possible, but also to provide a thesaurus, as in Ibn al-Sikkīt's *Kitāb al-alfāẓ* and a number of other works.[90]

[85] Ibn Sallam, *Ṭabaqāt al-shuʿarāʾ* (1998), 270n1, where the editor makes a double reference to al-Marzubānī and Abū ʿUbaydah with respect to the case of raids on Qurād b. Ḥanash's poetry.

[86] Ibn Qutaybah, *al-Shiʿr wa-l-shuʿarāʾ* (2001), 2:832. [87] See further Chapter 4.

[88] See al-Jurjānī, *al-Wasāṭah* (1966), 188. [89] Ibid., 214.

[90] Some of these were already referenced before. See Abū Yūsuf Yaʿqūb Ibn al-Sikkīt, *Mukhtaṣar Kitāb al-alfāẓ*, ed. Lūwis Cheikho (Beirut: al-Maṭbaʿah al-Kāthūlīkiyyah, 1897), along with the commentary of al-Tibrīzī in *Kanz al-Ḥuffāẓ*. For more, see

Figure 3.1 *Naql* (thematic transposition)

Prosification and Versification

To review the power of these productions in relation to the *sariqāt* terminological web, which Bonebakker perceives as a labyrinth, it is probably tenable to consider mediums other than the lexical classifications of terms. The issue of *sariqāt* is given a different direction in Ḍiyāʾ al-Dīn b. al-Athīr's *al-Washī al-marqūm fī ḥall al-manẓūm* (The Embroidered Tapestry in Prosification). Good borrowing is justified aesthetically, and Ibn al-Athīr builds on earlier writings to devote pages to issues of *ḥall* and *ʿaqd*, which were by then a common practice among littérateurs. Al-Thaʿālibī's (d. 429/1038) *Nathr al-naẓm wa-ḥall al-ʿaqd* (Prosification of Poetry and the Untying of the Knot) broaches the practice.[91] As I have argued elsewhere, the topic is central to poetics of verse and prose as much as it is to the evolution of literary history and theory. As argued later, many critics are to regard the appropriation of prose

Muḥammad b. Sahl Ibn al-Marzubān (d. ca. 345/956), *Kitāb al-alfāẓ al-kitābah wa-l-taʿbīr*; Qudāmah b. Jaʿfar, *Jawāhir al-alfāẓ*; Ibn Fāris al-Qazwīnī, *Mutakhayyar al-alfāẓ*; ʿAbd al-Raḥmān b. ʿĪsā al-Hamadhānī, *al-Alfāẓ al-kitābiyyah*; Shihāb al-Dīn Ubbadhī (d. 859–60/1455–56), *Bayān kashf al-alfāẓ*; Abū al-Naṣr al-Fārābī, *al-Alfāẓ al-mustaʿmalah fī al-manṭiq*; down to Jirjī Zaydān (d. 1914), *al-Falsafah al-lughawiyyah wa-l-alfāẓ al-ʿArabiyyah.*

91 Full name: ʿAbd al-Malik b. Muḥammad.

images, meanings, and expressions in poetry as *ikhfāʾ* (concealment) of *saraq* (see Figure 4.1).[92] The general proposition for concealment is the fact that *kalām* is welded.

Rather than limiting the discussion to use or misuse of ancient and contemporary repositories of poetry, the field was opened for transference and transposition among genres and mediums. Al-Qāḍī al-Jurjānī thinks of indiscernible theft as *tafannun*, deftness and dexterity that might well fall under the rubric of commendable ones.[93] Although there are already confused accounts of these, as in Ibn Kunāsah's early book on al-Kumayt, the use of the Qurʾān and epistolary writing has evolved as a commendable practice, emphasized and advised in scribal manuals. Ibn ʿAbdakān (d. 270/883), head of the first chancery of Aḥmad b. Ṭūlūn in Egypt, is worth mentioning for the practice of citing Qurʾānic verse and poetry in a prose that has the distinguishable merit of syntactical balance. Ibn Munjib al-Ṣayrafī (d. 542 or 550/1148 or 1155), chief chancery clerk for the Fatimid caliph al-Ḥāfiẓ, was an expert on training ephebes; so were the chief clerk, "exalted shaykh," Abū al-Ḥasan ʿAlī al-Ḥalabī (d. 522/1128), and Muwaffaq b. al-Khallāl (d. 566/1171), chief scribe for the Fatimid caliphs al-Ḥāfiẓ and al-ʿĀḍid. He trained al-Qāḍī al-Fāḍil ʿAbd al-Raḥīm al-Baysānī.[94] Several reasons can explain the significance of this movement in the study of *sariqāt*. It is associated with the rising role of the chancery as a central institution, especially in the Fatimid and Mamluk eras, when the institution witnessed enormous growth.[95] It meant then the need for a highly effective prose that would make use of *ḥall* as a powerful strategy to achieve impact. The divides between use and misuse of ancient and contemporary poetry, alongside Qurʾānic verse, are bound to be blurred even when a better practice is developed. Hence the significance of this space cannot be overestimated: the matter now rests on how good a specific production is in comparison with its basal referent. The matter is as problematic as the Sufi appropriation of poetry,[96] especially its conventional amatory preludes, as shown in the poetry of ʿUmar b. al-Fāriḍ (d. 632/1235), for instance. Is the rewriting of the amatory prelude of the pre-Islamic ode a theft pattern as conservative philologists would like to imply when devising conclusive remarks about *sariqāt*; or is this a *muḥādhāt* (close following) that ʿAbd al-Qāhir al-Jurjānī recommends? The late distinguished Arabist Jaroslav Stetkevych suggests that while

[92] See al-ʿAlawī, *ʿIyār al-shiʿr*, 78. [93] al-Jurjānī, *al-Wasāṭah* (2006), 165, 177–78.

[94] See al-Musawi, *Republic of Letters*, 137–38, where the impact of al-Qāḍī ʿAbd al-Raḥīm is stressed.

[95] al-Musawi, "Pre-modern Belletristic Prose," 105–6.

[96] See Michael A. Sells, ed. and trans., *Early Islamic Mysticism: Sufi, Qur'an, Miʿraj, Poetic and Theological Writings* (New York: Paulist Press, 1996), 56–74.

there is a "self-referential *nasīb* poem," there is also "its disengagement from the structural *qaṣīdah*."[97] Although redirecting the amatory prelude to fit into that Sufi yearning for the heavenly bliss, the "theme of loss and desire" is "closer to the archetype of the *aṭlāl* than it is to the surface metaphor of the beloved."[98] Stetkevych is not far off the motivating force that animates the use of "the Bedouin apostrophe":

> Stop at the abodes and greet the withered
> vernal camping grounds![99]

The combined sense of loss of the beloved and the desire for reunion functions differently for Ibn al-Fāriḍ, whose search is for the divine beatitude. The pre-Islamic prelude and conclusion turn into a frame, or a paradigm to reach that bliss:

> O paradise, which my soul loathed to leave!
> But for the solace of Abode Eternal,
> of sorrow would I die.[100]

Years later, Sharaf al-Dīn Abū ʿAbdallāh Muḥammad b. Saʿīd al-Būṣīrī's (d. 694–96/1294–97) mantle ode reads in the same vein, and indeed follows closely the Sufi model set by Ibn al-Fāriḍ, albeit with a questioning phrasing that is as poignant as Ibn al-Fāriḍ's, yet closer to the epistemic shift that transforms the nostalgic prelude to a yearning for the Divine:

> 1. Was it the memory of those you loved at Dhū Salam
> That made you weep so hard your tears were mixed with blood?
> 2. Or was it the wind that stirred from the direction of Kāẓimah
> And the lightning that flashed in the darkness of Iḍam?[101]

Ibn al-Fāriḍ's original says:

> Was that Layla's fire ablaze in the night at Dhū Salam
> Or was it a lightning-bolt flashing at al-Zawrāʾ, then at al-ʿAlam?[102]

A turning of a prelude and its outcome entails close following of a model, a *muḥādhāt*, or emulation, that nevertheless takes a different thematic direction. While this example is in keeping with generic properties of the prelude, other poets and prose writers made much use of others' expressions or meanings through a subtle transposition among mediums and genres. The transgeneric activity and its variations did not escape the

[97] Jaroslav Stetkevych, *Zephyrs of Najd*, 80. [98] Ibid.
[99] Ibid. Stetkevych's translation from the Dār Ṣādir edition of the *Dīwān*. [100] Ibid.
[101] See: Suzanne P. Stetkevych, "From Text to Talisman"; Stetkevych, *The Mantle Odes: Arabic Praise Poems to the Prophet Muhammad* (Bloomington: Indiana University Press, 2010), 92.
[102] Jaroslav Stetkevych, *Zephyrs of Najd*, 88.

attention of literary critics and philologists. Thus, Ibn Ṭabāṭabā advises poets to "use meanings taken from another genre; and if you come across a meaning in amatory poetry, then transfer it to panegyrics."[103] Probably basing himself on Ibn Qutaybah's attention to indiscernible or discreet *saraq* as exemplified in Abū al-Qāsim ʿAbd al-Ṣamad b. al-Muʿadhdhal's (d. 240/854) poetry,[104] Ibn Ṭabāṭabā seems unconcerned with the moral implications or the issue of recourse to the canon of *ʿamūd al-shiʿr* (the standard model of the ancients). For what comes through in his reading of thievery is how to produce something in a manner that hides dependency. In other words, he is more in line with al-Jāḥiẓ's understanding of the ultimate nature of transference, imitation, duplication, and transformation. It is left to al-Qāḍī al-Jurjānī to situate terminologies in a neat lucid literary argument.[105] Nevertheless, Ibn Ṭabāṭabā's discernment of the inevitable transaction in stylistic and semantic domains explains an ongoing practice while also setting the road for further poetic tactics to escape the accusation of *saraq*. Thus, if there are scarce and few poetic ideas and meanings left for modernists, they should embellish and reproduce these in a new appealing manner. Issues of transference from one territory to another, from panegyrics to lampoon or ghazal (amatory poetry), and so on, can be commendable practices if carried out with both tact and skill.[106]

Reporters, Transmitters-Narrators, and Forgery

No less pivotal to the raging discussion of borrowing and its misuse is the crucial issue of transmission. The discussion takes several directions. There is, for example, corrupt transmission that assigns verses to Abū Tammām or to Abū Nuwās that are either not theirs or are reported with atrocious errors that are at variance with their poetic veracity. Ibn Qutaybah,[107] and before him Ibn Sallām,[108] and later Abū Bakr al-Ṣūlī dealt with this kind of transmission as being misleading and confusing, if not totally unethical at a time of raging accusations of farfetchedness, total abandon of norms, or duplication and thievery.[109]

103 al-ʿAlawī, *ʿIyār al-shiʿr*, 77.
104 Ibn Qutaybah, *al-Shiʿr wa-l-shuʿarāʾ* (2001), 1:134.
105 al-Jurjānī, *al-Wasāṭah* (1966), 183–85, 186–88, 193, 201, 204, 282.
106 Ibid., 76–78.
107 Ibn Qutaybah, *al-Shiʿr wa-l-shuʿarāʾ* (2001), 2:672; see also Ibn Rashīq, *al-ʿUmdah* (2001), 252–57.
108 Ibn Sallām, *Ṭabaqāt al-shuʿarāʾ* (1974), quoted in Ibn Wakīʿ, *Kitāb al-munṣif*, 1:58.
109 See al-Ṣūlī, introduction to *Dīwān Abī Nuwās*, ed. Bahjat ʿAbd al-Ghafūr al-Ḥadīthī (Abu Dhabi: Hayʾat Abū Ẓabī li-l-Thaqāfah, 2010), 31; al-Ṣūlī, *Akhbār Abī Tammām*, 15.

Abū ʿAmrū b. al-ʿAlāʾ agrees, as reported by al-Ṣūlī, stating that "weak narrators-transmitters and unlearned copyists" were behind misrepresentation of Abū Tammām's poetry.[110] Al-Ṣūlī and al-Ḥuṣrī al-Qayrawānī in *Zahr al-ādāb* cite examples of Ibn al-Aʿrābī's prejudice against the modernists, simply because of his normative approach that takes the ancients and their poetry as a role model regardless of the quality of poetry.[111]

In relation to issues of forgery, more serious is *inḥāl*, assigning one's own poetry to the ancients. The difference among philologists in their recognition or denial of *ruwāt* like Khalaf or Ḥammād is not a trivial matter: it is a disagreement in approach.[112] While not denying that Ḥammād, for example, reported his poetry under the names of prominent poets, he is recognized as a superb transmitter.[113] Although a given nowadays, the issue of *inḥāl* happened to be central to the dynamics of poetic property. When looked upon as the act of confiscating the poetry of another in its entirety, it is *intiḥāl*, as in Ibn Rashīq's application in line with pre-Islamic usage. As meant by Ibn Sallām, al-Āmidī, and al-Qāḍī al-Jurjānī, the act of merging the transmitter's poetry with that of the ancients is *inḥāl*, matters that are subsumed under al-Ḥātimī's tabulations of thievery. As referenced earlier, Ibn Sallām says: "The first to collect Arab poetries and narrate their reports was Ḥammād al-Rāwiyah. He was unreliable, and he used to assign the poetry of one to another, and augment poetries."[114] When orality was the rule of the day, poetic augmentation "was not difficult for the learned."[115] The issue turns out to be pivotal to literary mediations. In a rebuttal of those who still speak in terms of a sweeping preference for the ancients, al-Qāḍī al-Jurjānī has this to say in order to raise the complexity and controversial nature of a legacy that could have suffered the meddling of known *ruwāt* and poets:

أُحيلك على ما قالت العلماء في حمّاد وخلف وابن دأب، وأضرابهم، ممن نحلَ القدماء شِعره فاندمج في أثناء شعرهم، وغابَ في أضعافه، وصَعُبَ على أهلِ العناية أفراده وتعَسَّر

I refer you to what the learned said about Ḥammād, Khalaf, and Ibn Daʾb, and their like, who mingled their own poetry with that of the ancients, and let it merge into theirs and get lost in its fold. Hence it was

[110] al-Ṣūlī, *Akhbār Abī Tammām*, 219.

[111] Ibid., 176; see also al-Ḥuṣrī al-Qayrawānī, *Zahr al-ādāb* (1953), 1:241–42. A good brief survey of the camp of grammarians and linguists standing for the ancients as role models is in Ṭāhā, *al-Naẓariyyah al-naqdiyyah*, 90–128.

[112] Bonebakker, "Ancient Arabic Poetry," 86.

[113] Ibid., 88.

[114] Ibn Sallām, *Ṭabaqāt al-shuʿarāʾ* (1998), 32.

[115] Ibid.

difficult for those concerned to identify and differentiate theirs from that of the ancients.[116]

Although known for his *inḥāl*, a *rāwiyah* like Ḥammād is not immune from accusations of stealing from others, according to Ghaylān b. ʿUqbah, Dhū al-Rummah (d. 177/735).[117] In other words, there is much here that raises questions and thence problematizes the deference to ancients. The epithet of *qudamāʾ* (ancients) loses its reported sanctity and integrity, whereas transmitters-narrators as recognized poets appear as the active players in a contested space. *Inḥāl* takes the discussion of *sariqāt* to its extreme, for what is at stake lies at the root of literary history and theory. If the compiler and transmitter of the seven odes of pre-Islamic poetry Ḥammād b. Sābūr, that is, *al-rāwiyah* (d. 156/773), is held to be suspicious, a culprit in this radical movement to destabilize and subvert a revered tradition, his *inḥāl* is more challenging and threatening than any other specific *saraq* application. It is the whole legacy that is under attack, and not a specific verse, poem, and/or poet. Even if we accept the stipulation that at the time there was an ongoing competition between the *ruwāt* (narrators-transmitters) from Basra and those from Kufa that incited much antagonism among grammarians, lexicographers, and linguists, a suspicion was raised by al-Aṣmaʿī and many others all the way down to al-Jurjānī that helped in circulating a narrative of partial *inḥāl*. The matter cannot be laid to rest, as recent publications demonstrate.[118] On the other hand, it is to the credit of Ḥammād and Khalaf al-Aḥmar that they were so capable as to have their claimed poetry merging with that of the ancients. If we accept the accusation of *inḥāl* (insertion of one's poetry in the poetry of another) against one or the other, which many also doubt,[119] this accusation is nevertheless an attestation to a fecund memory, an assimilation of ancient poetry, and hence a rich addition to poetic legacy. Furthermore, *inḥāl*, as argued by Lyall, suggests a prior model, and as such substantiates an existence of a rich ancient poetic tradition.

[116] al-Jurjānī, *al-Wasāṭah* (1966), 17. The full names of poets and transmitters of poetry are Khalaf b. Ḥayyān (d. 180/796), Ḥammād b. Sābūr, who collected the long seven odes (d. 156/773), and ʿĪsā b. Yazīd b. Bakr b. Daʾb (d. 177/793).

[117] See Ṭāhā, *al-Naẓariyyah al-naqdiyyah*, 155.

[118] ʿAbd al-Laṭīf Ḥammūdī al-Ṭāʾī, *Ḥammād al-Rāwiyah: kabīr ruwāt al-shiʿr al-ʿArabī al-muftarā ʿalayh* (Damascus: Dār al-Hilāl li-l-Ṭibāʿah wa-l-Nashr wa-l-Tawzīʿ, 2010); al-Ḥusayn Zarrūq, *Nuṣūṣ al-naqd al-adabī ladā Ḥammād al-Rāwiyah* (Riyadh: al-Majallah al-ʿArabiyyah, 2015).

[119] See al-Ṭāʾī, *Ḥammād al-Rāwiyah*. The title of the book suggests disagreement with Ḥammād's detractors.

The Rise of Disciplines: Poetics and Criticism

More often, arbiters like Ibn al-Aʿrābī, Abū ʿAmrū b. al-ʿAlāʾ, Yūnus b. Ḥabīb, al-Aṣmaʿī, and dozens of others also compete for further recognition, and this explains a chain of duplication, emendation, and difference.[120] There is a long list of rhetors, critics, and poets who also claimed they were unprecedented in one thing or another. Long before Ṣafī al-Dīn al-Ḥillī, who argues in defense of his list of figures and idioms in the appendix appended to his *Sharḥ*,[121] Abū Hilāl al-ʿAskarī argues, "I am unaware of anyone else who classified *sariqāt* in poetry, and gave examples of the sayings of the first initiator and that of the latecomer, and showed the advantage of the first; or the merits of successor. Previous learned authorities used only to indicate points of *saraq*."[122] On the other hand, Aḥmad b. Abī al-Ṭāhir Ṭayfūr (d. 280/893) takes as the base for his study of *sariqāt* the understanding that nobody can escape the presence of the ancients, not only because of strong poets like Imruʾ al-Qays, but also because a substantial amount of material has already become common property, a point that earlier littérateurs like Ibn Sallām took for granted and that other prominent critics of plagiarism, including the systematic critic Ḥāzim al-Qartājannī (d. 684/1285, Tunisia), would rather place under some subheadings like *sharikah* (shared property).

Indeed, our current *adab* discussion, which often focuses on a combined definition of *adab* as ethical comportment, etiquette, refinement, and broad knowledge or *adab* as pure literariness, can find no better opening than *sariqāt*. When brought together in context, gleanings, glosses, or books on *sariqāt* present a foundational literary theory.[123] Especially when carefully placed under specific headings that follow up on a single line of thought, for example, transmissions of a verse or poems, the reader can trace not only deflections, misreading, and misreporting but also the underlying invisible intertextual accommodation, a point that will be shown further in this chapter. Moreover, readers might ask for the reasons behind the shift – which is absolutely epistemological – to *muḥdathūn* (innovators), when Muslim b. al-Walīd, Bashshār b. Burd (d. 168/784), Ibn Harmah (d. 176/792), Salm b. ʿAmr b. Ḥammād al-Khāsir (d. 186/802), Abū Nuwās (d. 198/814),[124] Abū Tammām, al-Buḥturī, and a dozen others all forced on the cultural scene not only new

[120] The anecdote reported by al-Ḥuṣrī al-Qayrawānī in *Zahr al-ādāb* regarding Ibn al-Aʿrābī's admiration of verses by Abū Nuwās, thinking they were by the ancients, tells much about a muddled literary scene. *Zahr al-ādāb*, ed. Zakī Mubārak (Beirut: Dār al-Jīl, 1929), 1:286–87; see also *Zahr al-ādāb* (1953), 1:241–42.

[121] See al-Musawi, *Republic of Letters*, 103–4, 115, 152–53, 227, 239–41.

[122] al-ʿAskarī, *Kitāb al-ṣināʿatayn*, 237–38, quoted in al-Mūsawī, "al-Tarjīʿāt," 63.

[123] See Appendix A. [124] Full name: al-Ḥasan b. Hāniʾ.

poetries but also new terms and applications. Alongside this unique upsurge in urban poetics, new ideas, meanings, and themes in gentle wording and finesse gave impetus to a philological and critical search for reasons behind the move, its tracks of continuity and rupture. This movement, whose burgeoning Ibn Qutaybah associates with Muslim b. al-Walīd, exhilarated the sense of literary property and competitiveness; hence the mounting search for *sariqāt*.[125] Does this development show the treatment of literature as "normative science,"[126] with no sense of historical development, as both Renate Jacobi and Wolfhart Heinrichs suggest? They think that there is a seeming absence of "the dynamic idea of development,"[127] which Heinrichs bemoans. What is missing in the argument is the application of other standards of periodization and transformations. Alongside the discussion of ancients and *muḥdathūn*, there is a different line of thought that sees the literary field as a totality, a common site, with its own past masters and newly emerging powerful names. Subjectivity happened to be central to the scene, and along with it the struggle among subjectivities, ancient and modern. The transaction was never smooth; for even when we consider a modernist like ʿAlī Aḥmad Saʿīd's (Adūnīs) reading of the *muḥdathūn*, we end up reading his own initiation in that phenomenal shift.[128] However, in their double role as poets and critics, people like Abū Hilāl had to revise their reading of *sariqāt*, in view of what they heard among common Baghdadis who were already ahead of them in themes and wordcraft. As much as this admission suggests that the highly learned class was not necessarily in touch with the common people, it also confronts us with the cultural implications of common or personal intellectual property. Abū Hilāl admits, "I was very astonished, and decided not to pass a definite judgment of stealing from a predecessor."[129] On the other hand, literary history in Arabic offers several anecdotes in which poets speak openly about their arduous effort to beat a contemporary to a better phrasing, even if that entails rewording the original with either a refracted meaning

[125] Ibn Qutaybah cites him as unprecedented, or *awwal*; see *al-Shiʿr wa-l-shuʿarāʾ* (2001), 2:832.

[126] Heinrichs, "Literary Theory," 58. [127] Ibid.

[128] I refer here not to Adūnīs's well-known doctoral dissertation, which appeared in book form and emphasized a dialectic of past and present, static and mutable, etc., but to his *Zaman al-shiʿr* (1972; repr., Beirut: Dār al-ʿAwdah, 1983), where he argues his position in response to Yūsuf al-Khāl, Saʿīd ʿAql, and others. The book is an important document. No less so is his *Muqaddimah li-l-shiʿr al-ʿArabī* (1971; Beirut: Dār al-ʿAwdah, 1983), 41–57.

[129] Quoted in *Nuṣūṣ al-naẓariyyah al-naqdiyyah*, ed. Jamīl Saʿīd and Dāwūd Sallūm (Najaf: al-Nuʿmān, 1970), 326, 341, which in turn is quoted in al-Mūsawī, "al-Tarjīʿāt," 63.

or a new expression. In other words, they admit their work as *ṣanʿah* (craft) that works in relation to an available poetic product. Abū Tammām is reported to have said while welting in a *ṣihrīj* (cistern/boiler): "I tried hard to create something like Abū Nuwās's allusion to *al-dahr*'s (lifetime) combined ferocity and leniency, which proved difficult until God enabled me, and I crafted,

شَرَستَ بَل لِنتَ بَل قانَيتَ ذاكَ بِذا　　　فَأَنتَ لا شَكَّ فيكَ السَهلُ وَالجَبَلُ

You hardened, but softened, but blended this and that
for you have undoubtedly the highland and the plain."[130]

The same notion is reported of Jarīr, as he wallowed, welted, rolled in a scorching heat to come across a verse to beat al-Farazdaq's. Transactions take multiple directions, but the most visible is the ongoing negotiation with or importation from other producers.

Hence, the poetic struggle or battleground among contemporaries or in response to the masters' ghosts is no less a matter of skill; and indeed, Abū Hilāl al-ʿAskarī is not far off the mark in calling this endeavor a craft. Abū Hilāl's predecessors such as the poet and philologist ʿAbdallāh b. Aḥmad Abū Hiffān al-Mihzamī (d. 255/871) wrote *Ṣināʿat al-shiʿr*, and early contemporaries like Aḥmad b. Sahl al-Balkhī (d. 322/934), Abū Aḥmad al-ʿAskarī (d. 382/993), and al-Ḥusayn b. Muḥammad al-Khalīʿ (d. 388/865) wrote under the same title, while Abū Saʿīd al-Sīrāfī (d. 368/979) wrote *Ṣināʿat al-shiʿr wa-l-balāghah*, and al-Fārābī (d. 339/950) wrote *Risālah fī qawānīn ṣināʿat al-shiʿr*. Al-Ḥātimī includes this in the title *Ḥilyat al-muḥāḍarah fī ṣināʿat al-shiʿr* (The Ornament of Discourse on the Craft of Poetry). Almost every book on poetry has something on craft and/or thievery. Foremost among earlier ones are Bishr b. al-Muʿtamir's (d. 210/825) *al-Ṣaḥīfah* and Thaʿlab's (d. 291/904) *Qawāʿid al-shiʿr*.[131] Nevertheless, Abū Hilāl al-ʿAskarī's *Kitāb al-ṣināʿatayn* remains the more visible. It is so because he takes craft as a starting point to synthesize the issue of *akhdh*, that is, willful but partial possession of others' poetic meaning or expression, as focal to the discussion of poetic space. His classification of *akhdh* also highlights one of its lauded features when the successor adds value to the original, as in Ibn Aydamir's note on this (see Figure 3.2), a point that later critics like Ḥāzim al-Qarṭājannī give an economic twist in terms of

[130] al-Mūsawī, "al-Tarjīʿāt," 63. The anecdote appears as welting in *bayt muṣahraj* (a room plastered with mortar or quicklime). The reference is to a panegyric addressed to the caliph al-Muʿtaṣim. See *Dīwān Abī Tammām bi-sharḥ al-Khaṭīb al-Tibrīzī*, ed. Muḥammad ʿAbduh ʿAzzām (Cairo: Dār al-Maʿārif, 1964–65), 3:11. I am indebted to van Gelder's note.

[131] Full name: Abū al-ʿAbbās Aḥmad b. Yaḥyā.

Figure 3.2 Improving *akhdh* as adding value

value. Although citing examples from across multiple temporalities, pre-Islamic, Islamic, and Umayyad or Abbasid, the drift of his argument is rather semantic than historical, without bypassing poetic subjectivity. On the other hand, his enhancement of both the conceptualization of poetry as craft that was passingly discussed by others and his textual reading of versification and prosification stand foremost in comparison to early tenth-century suggestions by Ibn Ṭabāṭabā al-ʿAlawī. His analysis bodes well for the emerging practice of both methods by poets and scribes; a practice that later was to draw the attention of al-Thaʿālibī, and several others soon after.

But, to return to von Grunebaum's disappointment at not finding a breakthrough other than encapsulating the available discussion, it is worth looking at Abū Hilāl's claims that his reading differs from others because he is rather concerned with a two-track transaction whereby the successor can be credited with thematic or stylistic improvement. As a synthesizer, he agrees with scholars before him, stating that meanings are commodities available for all, but a poetic meaning turns into meritorious achievement when dressed better and exhibited superbly, a point which recurs in ʿAbd al-Raḥmān al-Hamadhānī's neat summary in the short preface to his *al-Alfāẓ al-kitābiyyah*. The new owner deserves to be credited.[132] He almost echoes al-Qāḍī al-Jurjānī in resolving not to "pass a *saraq* judgment on a successor," after he has heard some Baghdadis reiterating what he thought of as being uniquely his own invention. Ibn Qutaybah's reference to indiscernible *saraq* also occurs in Abū Hilāl's overview. He offers examples of these, such as Abū Nuwās's use of a verse by al-Aʿshā. One can say that Abū Hilāl supplements al-Qāḍī al-Jurjānī's neat terminology with examples.[133] These examples were in circulation, to be sure, in the literary marketplace, but Abū Hilāl places these under the headings *akhdh* and *itbāʿ* (also *ittibāʿ*) (see Figure 3.2). Thus, Salm al-Khāsir "*tabiʿa*" (followed closely) a verse by Bashshār b. Burd, but he excelled in it, and Bashshār could do nothing but admit the improvement. "Son of a ... hijacked my verse."[134] Abū Hilāl is unique in classifying prosification in four models.[135] Even so, how do we justify Abū Hilāl's claim to being unprecedented? Apart from his attention to successors' improvements, like the example in previous paragraphs, he encapsulates the ongoing argument, synthesizes its broad canvas, and drives it more toward intertextuality. It vaults over al-Āmidī's and al-Qāḍī al-Jurjānī's comparisons and mediations, or others' virulent and debasing epistles. His enterprise aims to demonstrate the poetic field as one of exchange, where desire for the other is the driving force.

Poetic or intellectual subjectivity was as real as it is nowadays, and the claim to either originality, inventiveness, or at least mere correspondence and *muwāradah* (coincidental correspondence) remains a powerful marker of authorship. Every other activity assumes significance within a scale and system supervised by the other breed of market inspectors, that is, the philologists, who would gradually give up their role in concession to an increasing number of knowledgeable literary critics. Under pleasant terms like negotiation, imitation, appropriation, addition, and navigation, *sariqāt* began gradually to escape arbitrary judgments in a manner that often meets Ibn Qutaybah's restoration of the practice as art against accusatory connotations.[136]

Competitive Marketplace

Nevertheless, before coming to that, let us consider how prominence is a much-coveted distinction, a merit aspired to by all literary figures. If your contemporaries are reluctant to confer on you the garb of distinction, then you must claim it for yourself. Abū al-Ṭayyib al-Mutanabbī was not alone. The marketplace should be central to our understanding of the

[132] al-ʿAskarī, *Kitāb al-ṣināʿatayn*, 196. [133] Ibid., 197–99. [134] Ibid., 214–15.
[135] Ibid., 216–19. [136] Ṭāhā's phrase, *al-Naẓariyyah al-naqdiyyah*, 188.

evolution of poetry, poetics, and oration, and the formation of such a broad umbrella as *adab*. It is also a reminder that poetry is a commodity in marketplace transactions, a point that English writers, for example, recognize centuries later when considering the libidinal impulse in the economies of desire. The editors of *Economies of Desire at the Victorian Fin de Siècle* quote H. Rider Haggard's protagonist Ayesha in his 1887 *She: A History of Adventure*, where she is made to articulate a statement that applies to all commodity transactions: "the world is a great mart . . . where all things are for sale to whom who bids highest in the currency of desires."[137] Poetry exercises a triple function, not only as a desirable object but also as incentive for magnanimity and achievement. It plays on the desire of both the producer and the recipient, as they are entangled in desiring each other. Thus, the marketplace where poetry used to be recited and competed for was, and still is, a tournament where desires are played out. We often tend to forget that the major poets and arbiters of literary taste happened to attend Sūq ʿUkāẓ and the Mirbad of Basrah, the two major marketplaces for trade, literary competition, and publicity. It is also worth remembering that the root of the name ʿUkāẓ implies conquest and boast. Among its arbiters was no less than al-Nābighah al-Dhubyānī (d. 18/605); pre-Islamic poets took it as their major domain in order to derive what we now call symbolic capital that subsumes meritorial distinction. Al-Mirbad was no less popular; it was attended by Bashshār (d. 168/784) and Abū Nuwās (d. 198/814), and before them Jarīr (d. 110/728) and al-Farazdaq (d. 110/728), alongside critics, grammarians, and philologists, like al-Khalīl (d. 170/786), Sībawayh (d. 180/796), and al-Aṣmaʿī (d. 216/828).[138] In these transactions, and on many other occasions, poets used to reflect on their poetry as the most popular practice, either emphasizing their meticulous skill or disclaiming any raids on the products of others. Ḥassān b. Thābit is reported as saying:

لا أسرق الشّعراء ما نطقوا بل لا يوافق شعرهم شعري

I don't steal from poets their enunciations
their poetry differs from mine

[137] Jane Ford, Kim Edwards Keates, and Patricia Pulham, introduction to *Economies of Desire at the Victorian Fin de Siècle: Libidinal Lives*, ed. Jane Ford, Kim Edwards Keates, and Patricia Pulham (New York: Routledge, 2016), 1.

[138] Indeed in 1983 and on the occasion of the Mirbad Poetry Festival, I initiated the ongoing Mirbad Literary Criticism Circle in Baghdad and supervised its sessions to consolidate poetry and poetics. Almost every prominent writer from all over the world, including Günter Grass, Robert Krotsch, Henry Beisel, Alain Robbe-Grillet, and many others, attended the sessions. My close friend the late Jaroslav Stetkevych never missed a session.

Ṭarafah b. al-ʿAbd claims the same distinctive poetics.

ولا أغير على الأشعار أسرقها　　　غنيت عنها وشر الناس من سرقا

I refrain from raiding poetry to steal
It is dispensable to me, as the worst is the one who steals[139]

It is now also common knowledge that pre-Islamic poets were no less sensitive to accusations of theft or raid on others' verse. The term *saraq* was available then, as it was in Ibn Sallām's times.

The issues of cultural subjectivity, authorship, property, and plagiarism were to undergo transformations in keeping with new and challenging circumstances and the role of the common reading public in the expanding centers of learning, like Damascus, Baghdad in particular, Aleppo, Cairo, Qurtuba, Granada, Qayrawan, Marv, Isfahan, and Samarqand – a point that will receive more attention in Chapters 4 and 6. In all cases, publicity stands out as the venue to connect with others. The poet al-Buḥturī forthrightly condemns obscurity and seclusion as unbecoming of an *adīb*, who for all purposes has to show his learning and poetics. Probably with a verse in mind from the Qurʾān (62:5) that compares those entrusted with the Torah but not making use of it to a donkey loaded with books, he writes:

If the *adīb* accepts a life of obscurity, what benefit will he derive from the *adab* that he has acquired (*al-adab al-mustafād*)?[140]

Publicity is a forceful motivation in the struggle for distinction, a prototype to spectacles and public relations. Obviously, a distinguished *adīb* was then held in very high esteem; and hence the aspiration for distinction in a demanding career entails not only creative productivity but also a thorough knowledge of a large field in order to be qualified for the tightly controlled poetic standards. It is symptomatic of class and cultural distinction to be an *adīb*, and hence Abū Tammām could not digest the idea of a *sarrāj* (saddlemaker) as a poet gifted with the use of "lexical rarities."[141] The reference – and there are many like it – indicates that the literary marketplace was an open space where competitors tried

139 For a general survey of the theory of plagiarism in Arabic, see Maʿtūq, "Al-Sharīf al-Murtaḍā's Contribution," 23–25. On the ownership of the verse, see Bonebakker, "Ancient Arabic Poetry and Plagiarism," 70. See also Sanni, "Al-Marzubānī in the Context of Arabic Literary Theory," 144–45nn14–15.

140 Abū ʿUbādah al-Walīd b. ʿUbayd al-Buḥturī, *Dīwān*, quoted in S. A. Bonebakker, "*Adab* and the Concept of *Belles-Lettres*," in *ʿAbbasid Belles-Lettres*, ed. Julia Ashtiany, T. M. Johnstone, J. D. Latham, R. B. Serjeant, and G. Rex Smith (Cambridge: Cambridge University Press, 1990), 21.

141 Abū Tammām derides the renowned Egyptian poet Yūsuf al-Sarrāj ("the Saddlemaker") for his use of lexical rarities (he has never, he says, heard of

their skill to attract attention, visibility, and thence prominence. Class obstacles were as real then as they are always, as we understand from the books on *adab al-ʿāmmah.*[142] To achieve distinction, some literary figures and poets used to sojourn in cultural centers or make long trips to meet specific names. The Andalusian poet ʿAbbās b. Nāṣiḥ al-Jazīrī (d. 229/844), for example, was in the habit of searching for rising stars in the Arab east. Upon hearing of Abū Nuwās, he headed there to meet the poet and introduce himself as an *adab* seeker.[143] Moreover, the aspiration for excellence operates within a scale whereby masters stand at the summit, to be reached or undermined. Hence, the poet Abū al-ʿAtāhiyah (d. ca. 210/825) felt that his poetry was not as good as that of his contemporaries Bashshār b. Burd and Ibrāhīm b. ʿAlī b. Harmah (d. 176/792), who excelled not only in modernism but also in reaching to the masters' standards.

The Centrality of a Term

In a culture that was so rich with anthologies, classification of material, transmission, and claims to inventiveness and deviations, the existence of systematic or random studies and comments on a recurrent topic like plagiarism should not come as a surprise. The issue was so central throughout the eighth through sixteenth centuries that prominent critics and poets were expected to take part in the discussion; otherwise, they might, rightly or wrongly, incur censure for negligence.[144] Mastery of a cultural scene, acquaintance with literary production, and ability to trace, assess, and filter available material were among the common requirements of littérateurs.[145] These and many other issues surrounding accusations of theft, raids, unacknowledged borrowing, or even prosification or versification thus became pivotal in a competitive cultural scene. Competition was not a temporary issue or merely a matter of concern among a ruler's boon companions. It relates to ranks and merits, gains, and losses. To claim and

a saddlemaker who is also an *adīb*). See Muḥammad Kāmil Ḥusayn, *al-Ḥayāt al-fikriyyah wa-l-adabiyyah bi-Miṣr* (UK: Hindāwī, 2017), 118–19.

142 Fahd, *al-ʿĀmmah bi-Baghdād.*

143 Amidu Sanni, "Arabic Literary History and Theory in Muslim Spain," *Islamic Studies* 34, no. 1 (1995): 93.

144 Abū Bakr Muḥammad b. Yaḥyā al-Ṣūlī (d. 335/946) criticized his teacher Muḥammad b. Yazīd al-Mubarrad (d. 286/899) for overlooking poets' plagiarisms. See Iḥsān ʿAbbās, *Tārīkh al-naqd al-adabī ʿinda al-ʿArab* (Beirut: Dār al-Thaqāfah, 1983), 91. ʿAbbās shows, however, that al-Mubarrad was aware of *sariqāt*. See also Maʿtūq, "Al-Sharīf al-Murtaḍā's Contribution," 19–20n8. For al-Mubarrad's note on Khalaf's *inḥāl* (assigning his poetry to others), see Bonebakker, "Ancient Arabic Poetry and Plagiarism," 88–89, and on Ḥammād, 89n101.

145 al-Jurjānī, *al-Wasāṭah* (1951), 183.

prove uniqueness and difference was, and still is, a mark of distinction. It serves as symbolic capital, a distinguished social status, and material value. As Thomas Mallon puts it, "Plagiarism didn't become a truly sore point with writers until they thought of writing as their trade."[146] The craft as trade entails a necessity to understand it in terms of production for a market. Whether it is the copyist or the patron, there is payment and symbolic capital earned by the author in a transaction whereby a dialectic of value obtains. If the poet gains value for the actual production, the surplus will symbolically go to the caliph, prince, patron, or, financially, to the copyist.[147] These numerous issues and complexities invite us to raise further questions in relation to a massive cultural movement from orality, recitations, dictation, and assemblies to a studious attention to a textually conversational field. The field displays heated or serene debates and vibrant engagements with authorship, imitation and inventiveness, thematic tabulation, terminology classification, and gradual acquiescence to contemporaneity and its claims on writing practices.[148] In this context, both the confusion attending traditionalists' response to unidentified verse recitations and the counter emphasis on "*al-ʿilm bi-l-shiʿr*" (knowledge of poetry) are part of a defensive strategy to confront the rising *muḥdath* tide. Al-Āmidī was not alone in emphasizing the high recognition allotted to the knowledge of poetry, to the extent that "everybody claimed it, and it was practiced by those alien to it."[149] He was building on the views of earlier authorities like Abū ʿAmrū b. al-ʿAlāʾ (d. 154/770) who, in line with the growing needs for a systematic criticism, argues that "those knowledgeable in poetry are even rare than red sulfur."[150] However, this division of labor has its middle ground, as prominent grammarians and linguists like al-Aṣmaʿī prefer the knowledgeable poets in literary tradition, that is, those with fecund memory such as Khalaf al-Aḥmar (d. 180/796).[151] Ironically, this middle ground, one that enlists the support and endorsement of prominent traditionalists, also implies the impossibility of total originality and authenticity. Its most visible *al-shuʿarāʾ al-ruwāt*, after all, are Khalaf and Ḥammād al-Rāwiyah (d. 156/773), who were not immune to accusations of *inḥāl*. It is justifiable therefore to argue the case of plagiarism, not as

[146] Thomas Mallon, *Stolen Words: Forays into the Origins and Ravages of Plagiarism* (New York: Ticknor and Fields, 1989), 4–5.

[147] See Karl Marx, "Theories of Surplus Value," in *Das Capital*, 4 vols., trans. Emile Burns (Moscow: Progress Publishers, 1975), 1:158. He argues a "writer is a productive labourer not in so far as he produces ideas, but in so far as he enriches the publisher."

[148] See n. 35. [149] al-Āmidī, *al-Muwāzanah*, 1:389.

[150] Quoted in Ṭāhā, *al-Naẓariyyah al-naqdiyyah*, 26, from Abū Bakr Muḥammad al-Bāqillānī, *Iʿjāz al-Qurʾān*, ed. Aḥmad Ṣaqr (Cairo: Dār al-Maʿārif, 1954), 310.

[151] See Ibn Qutaybah, *al-Shiʿr wa-l-shuʿarāʾ* (2001), 2:789n2, 790.

an accusatory transaction, but rather a critical activity, a display of knowledge in an increasingly competitive domain.

Excepting forthright theft, I read the seemingly terminological labyrinth that engages with variations on plagiary rubric as an empowering activity, a significant contribution, if not an invigorating dynamic, to a thriving culture. Writings that were on the increase during that period offer a substantial and systematic theorization for the culture industry. The debates surrounding transmission of pre-Islamic poetry and the attacks on some reciters and transmitters could also have been at the base of a rising interest in plagiarism and its varieties. This controversy is of significance in the context of the increasing demand for inscription, dictation, and books as central to urban life and statecraft. Whether we take as examples the Umayyad ʿAbd al-Ḥamīd al-Kātib's (d. 131/749) *Epistle* to fellow scribes or Abū ʿUthmān ʿAmr b. Baḥr al-Jāḥiẓ's (d. 255/868) discourse on the value of books that introduces *Kitāb al-ḥayawān*, the demand for a shared cultural script, at least among the literati, was real and urgent. This shared culture requires the availability of circulated products, be they poems, epistles, narratives, criticism, philological inquiry, and, alongside these scriptoria, rising interests, inhibitions, concerns, exchanges and transactions, thefts, and suspicions.

However, a systematic effort to scrutinize transmission by Khalaf al-Aḥmar or his senior contemporary Ḥammād al-Rāwiyah went hand in hand with an accelerated demand for inscription. With the availability of paper, compilations and anthologies and their like became possible. Theft and its variations were to become an acute issue, an open field for discussion, a forum for literary battles. Such exchanges were needed not only to focus on the probable phenomenal recurrence of this theft or concomitant *adab* applications associated with the rise of tabulation (as shown in Ibn Sallām's ranking of poets), but also because Ibn Sallām's *Ṭabaqāt fuḥūl al-shuʿarāʾ* (Classes [or Ranks] of Champion Poets) applies a process of gradation and builds on his mentor al-Aṣmaʿī's views concerning the prerequisites of the stallion poet.[152] Nonetheless, Ibn Sallām's anthology is of significance because it mentions *sariqāt* or thefts. The concept of "classes" reflects a large urban social stratification of status. What applies to urban populations lends itself to literary culture. Moreover, as a landmark in a movement to anthologize, Ibn Sallām's *Ṭabaqāt* should draw our attention to an enormous cultural production

[152] See Roger Allen, *The Arabic Literary Heritage* (Cambridge: Cambridge University Press, 1998), 366. In al-Aṣmaʿī's words: "No poet will ever become a champion in the realm of poetry till he has performed the ancient poems of the Arabs, listened to accounts, learned topics, and allowed phrases to permeate his hearing" (ibid.).

that required arrangement, systematization, and tabulation. Applied to population, *ṭabaqah* (pl. *ṭabaqāt*) includes such meanings as rank, group, level, building blocks, and so on.[153] As this chapter took as its starting point Ibn Sallām's four concerns, it is worthwhile to synthesize its findings in relation to his book. Although current scholarship shows dissatisfaction with what is perceived as a lack of justification for the anthology, I argue that the title places us onto a hierarchical order that is, in the mode of its time, masculinist. Moreover, and as argued by Roger Allen, "the work of ibn Sallām is often seen as marking a beginning to the development of literary criticism in Arabic since the principles that he adopted marked a process whereby the critical activity and its practitioners began to acquire a separate validity of their own."[154] While posing an important intervention, this conclusion does not exclude the presence of lyricism in poetry as a subjective dynamic, one that prompts a tendency to self-aggrandizement, a point which al-Bāqillānī references in relation to ethical standards.

Bloom proposes a neat intervention regarding increasing lyricism and subjectivity in time, a point that is central to the struggle with precursors. He stipulates that as "poetry has become more subjective, the shadow of the precursor has become more dominant."[155] The shift to subjectivity was already there in pre-Islamic poetry, but the urban environment accelerated it in the poetries of several poets, and especially that of Abū Nuwās, Salm al-Khāsir, Ibn Harmah, Muslim b. al-Walīd, and certainly the galaxy of court poets, like Abū Tammām and al-Buḥturī, down to the sixteenth century. No less subjective were the vagabonds, the *ṣaʿālīk*, the powerful rebels who left behind them an unequal repository of combined personal intimations, wild images, and throbbing rhythm, always tinged with a melancholy that Bloom assigns to "the creative mind's desperate insistence upon priority."[156] Subjectivity demands several inroads, including freedom as the driving motive for the *ṣaʿālīk* in their career as outlaws before and after Islam. Abū Tammām associates travel with renewal: "A man's prolonged stay in the tribe slowly ruins / His stamina and beauty. So go abroad to find renewal." Although less exposed to the accusation of plagiarism, the *ṣaʿālīk* nevertheless also draw on a common register, which is recognized by critics and philologists, starting with Ibn Sallām and not ending with ʿAbd al-Qāhir al-Jurjānī, al-Qazwīnī, Ibn al-Athīr, Ḥāzim al-Qartājannī, and Ibn al-Akfānī (d. 749/1348–49), down to

[153] See Abū al-Naṣr Ismāʿīl b. Ḥammād al-Jawharī (d. 398/1008), *al-Ṣiḥāḥ* (available in multiple editions), which uses *ṭabaqah* in ways that illustrate these meanings.
[154] See Allen, *Arabic Literary Heritage*, 366. [155] Bloom, "A Meditation," 11.
[156] Ibid., 13.

a later period – a recognition that falls within a mediating, but also tenable effort to soften and modify a hardline application of an en bloc accusation of plagiarism.[157] In general, this shared legacy can be seen as a substantial source of poetic capital that is conducive to subjectivity, the struggle for a distinguished space. Self-aggrandizement and its counter opposition proved to be as invigorating as any cultural dynamic. Ibn al-Athīr's *al-Mathal*, for example, provoked several rebuttals.[158] These rebuttals tend to undermine the claim to priority of which Ibn al-Athīr boasts. Reactions occasionally turn into a possessive, but also relentless and ferocious desire demonstrated by both parties, boaster and opponent. Shams al-Dīn Muḥammad b. Ḥasan al-Nawājī's (d. 859/1455) rebuttal of his mentor in *al-Ḥujjah fī sariqāt Ibn Ḥijjah* (The Damning Evidence of Ibn Ḥijjah's Plagiarism) was not the last, not even in the twentieth century.

Twentieth-Century Neo-Classicists

Whether we are referring to the conflict in the first half of the twentieth century between ʿAbd al-Raḥmān Shukrī and Ibrāhīm ʿAbd al-Qādir al-Māzinī of the Dīwān group, or even the later accusations leveled against Adūnīs as *muntaḥlan* (self-arrogating others' verses),[159] terms like *saraq* and *intiḥāl* also occur without due understanding of intertextuality or even awareness of earlier recapitulations by ʿAbd al-Qāhir al-Jurjānī, Ibn al-Athīr, and Ḥāzim al-Qarṭājannī.[160] On the other hand, accusatory discourse survives even in the shadow of an ongoing attention to structuration, and hence intertextuality, and also the attention of some poets and critics to other methods of addressing classical Arabic poetry, a position that is applicable to ʿAlī Aḥmad Saʿīd (Adūnīs).[161] His anthology of Arabic classical poetry as well as his critical studies show him as a neo-classicist whose engagement with classical tradition is mediated through a French literary lens. Moreover, the second half of the twentieth century was to witness a rediscovery of ʿAbd al-Qāhir al-Jurjānī, not only as a rhetor and critic but also as an early structuralist.[162] Furthermore, the

157 On al-Akfānī, see Jan Just Witkam, "Ibn al-Akfānī (d. 749/1348) and His Bibliography of the Sciences," *Manuscripts of the Middle East* 2 (1987): 37–41.

158 See al-Musawi, "Pre-modern Belletristic Prose," 106.

159 Kāẓim Jihād, *Adūnīs muntaḥilan: dirāsah* (al-Dār al-Bayḍāʾ: Afrīqiyā al-Sharq, 1991).

160 See al-Mūsawī's response in "Marjiʿiyyāt." See also al-Musawi, *Arabic Poetry*, 9–10, 13, 32, 99–103.

161 See Adūnīs, *Muqaddimah li-l-Shiʿr al-ʿArabī* (1971; repr., Beirut: Dār al-ʿAwdah, 1983); but especially his *al-Thābit wa-l-mutaḥawwil*, 3 vols. (1974; Beirut: Dār al-ʿAwdah, 1978).

162 See Kamal Abu-Deeb, *Al-Jurjānī's Theory of Poetic Imagery* (Warminster: Aris and Phillips, 1979). Although more concerned with ʿAbd al-Qāhir's emphasis on wonder, Harb's *Arabic Poetics* is worthy of attention.

same period is one of divided ancestry and the selection of specific classical poets at the expense of others. In this instance, the focus is laid on one particular side that fits into one's own poetic era, as the Moroccan Muḥammad Bennīs argues. As ancestors are only names for poems, choosing them is a choice of texts in order to create a textual family, a genealogy of a sort whereby the modern poet selects forebears who meet his or her desires. The tendency to place one's life and career as poet within a genetic tree is not unique to the Moroccan Bennīs. Before him, the Syrian Lebanese Adūnīs had a similar proposal. The emerging textual family plays havoc with the plagiarism lexicon, as words, images, and ideas dance in profusion.

A textual family demands an interaction, one in which only the living poet can slice and claim what he or she desires. Once again, the whole entanglement is driven by desire, a love for the other text/name by which the twentieth-century Arab poet is overwhelmed. Indeed, Adūnīs is not shy in admitting the foreign element as the one informing and energizing his own Arabic poetics. The overwhelming desire for French poetics awakens him to Arabic poetics, leading him therefore to a strategy of prioritization in a dialectic of immobility and mutation. The foreign and the national both appear in this entanglement where Genette's hypotext and hypertext are indistinguishable. Adūnīs writes:

> It was reading Baudelaire which changed my understanding of Abū Nuwās and revealed his particular poetical quality and modernity, and Mallarmé's work, which explained to me the mysteries of Abū Tammām's poetic language and the modern dimension in it. My reading of Rimbaud, Nerval and Breton led me to discover the poetry of the mystic writers in all its uniqueness and splendor, and the new French criticism gave me an indication of the newness of al-Jurjani's critical vision.[163]

As an enlightening moment of intertextual entanglement, this juncture functions as a loaded discovery of an implicating desire for the French poets he enumerates, a desire that provokes a byproduct or subsidiary desire for the Arab poets whom he defines in the same *Introduction to Arabic Poetics*. Adūnīs admits a mediational position between the two textual desirabilities. This same admission incites suspicious critics to designate him as *muntaḥil* (self-arrogating others' poetries).[164] The same critic offers a few examples of mistranslation in a slightly revised

[163] Adaunis, *An Introduction to Arab Poetics*, trans. Catherine Cobham (Austin: University of Texas Press, 1990; Arabic text, 1971; English trans., 1985), 81, quoted in al-Musawi, *Arabic Poetry*, 269.

[164] Jihād, *Adūnīs muntaḥilan*; edited and expanded as *Adūnīs muntaḥilan: dirāsah fī al-istiḥwādh al-adabī wa-irtijāliyyat al-tarjamah*, with an introduction: "Mā huwa al-tanāṣṣ?" (Cairo: Maktabat Madbūlī, 1993).

edition in 1993. One cannot deny that Adūnīs reveals an overwhelming desire to maraud French poetics; a point that also shows in his enthusiastic slicing of the overall corpus of Arab poets. The *Introduction* presents his favorite Arab poets as thematic textualities screened and presented through French magnifying lenses. More relevant and as problematic is his critical rewriting of a history of early Islam soon after the death of the Prophet, and under the Umayyads and Abbasids. Al-Mutanabbī is only a gateway to provide openings for poetic tableaus whereby the poet's own focus on historic ruptures soars high, while the *hawāmish* or margins are only poetic reflections on a long list of select poets' careers. The *rāwī*, as narrator and transmitter, who occupies the right column, provides the outline for these poetic excursions. Al-Mutanabbī's career and poetry is placed at these historical intersections of intrigue and blood. The spatial and temporal recovery turns into a thorny legacy, a burden that lends itself to al-Mutanabbī's poetic career. A poetic rewriting with documentary margins emerges as both a parody of a tradition and an unearthing of its pitfalls. The whole encapsulation of history and poetics escapes the contours of plagiarism while allowing the poet Adūnīs to merge not only into the forerunner as poet and person but also into a controversial corpus. In the concluding section, *tawqī*ʿ *mufrad* ("A Single Voice Signature"), Adūnīs's voice identifies with al-Mutanabbī to ask: Why are you here in this fallow land? The response is one of defiance: to witness a rebirth of the new at the ruins of the past.[165] This short and concluding signature takes as an opening al-Mutanabbī's verse:

إذا ما تأمّلْتَ الزمانَ وصَرْفَهُ   تيَقّنْتَ أنّ الموتَ نوعٌ من القتْلِ

If you ponder time and its vicissitudes
you'll be certain that death is a type of murder

Adūnīs's *The Book Yesterday, the Place Now: A Manuscript Attributed to al-Mutanabbī* is a polyphonic text that escapes accusations of plagiarism while it is an interrogation of repressed historical and poetic engagements. It is his effort to set the record straight under the guise of a recovered manuscript.[166]

This overdose is mitigated in the Moroccan Muḥammad Bennīs's poetry, where he speaks of a personal genetic tree that includes Lorca, Neruda, Ezra Pound, Eliot, Walt Whitman, Mallarmé, and Baudelaire. The group cuts across his lineage to the Arabic poetic script that includes Imruʾ Qays, al-Mutanabbī, Ṭarafah b. al-ʿAbd, Ibn Khafājah, Jamīl Buthaynah, al-Ḥallāj, Abū Ḥayyān, and Arabic poetic *dīwān*s. He sums

[165] Adūnīs, *al-Kitāb ams al-makān al-ān: makhṭūṭah tunsab li-l-Mutanabbī*, 2 vols. (London: Dār al-Sāqī, 1995), 377.
[166] See al-Musawi, *Arabic Poetry*, 81. Also Adūnīs, *al-Kitāb ams al-makān*, 375.

up the intersected trajectory as "a poetic and writing experience of a universal stamp, through which I have become acquainted with poetic time, which is what concerns me in writing."[167] By prioritizing "poetic time" as atemporal and universal, Bennīs eludes what might sound as borrowing or dependency. A universal element is sought in order to release poetry from any temporal stigma in a crowded domain of words, expressions, and meanings with which a poet might grow up.

While it is a given to claim a vast poetic spectrum, a point I addressed in my 2006 book, *Arabic Poetry: Trajectories of Modernity and Tradition*, readings often spill over onto a poem, turning it into a map of reading that eludes the hunt for duplications and presents a poem as a dynamic mosaic of allusions, hints, and names where the poet's persona loses centrality. To demonstrate an intertextual map of allusions, we can focus on two poems: one by the Iraqi ʿAbd al-Wahhāb al-Bayātī (d. 1999), and the other by the Palestinian poetess Fadwā Ṭūqān (d. 2003). In al-Bayātī's "Aisha's Mad Lover," the poet parodies the pre-Islamic seven or ten odes, which were claimed to have been written in gold and suspended from the walls of the Kaaba (Al-Ka ʿbah) in pre-Islamic times. Al-Bayātī's poem is voiced by a displaced lover whose sojourn is not in any land other than textual space:

> The singing of a bird
> woke me up at night, so I went deep with the bird
> into the enchanted unknown
> Aisha could not incarcerate spring oh in her garden
> I saw a flowering branch peeping out into the darkness
> from above the wall of light
> I wept, spring passed and then returned, and I was still at
> the garden gate
> Praying to its flowering branch, to the light that comes
> from within, to the colors
> And carrying my vows to the caliphate's capital
> To the stone of wisdom and myth
> Perhaps the polar star
> Will be my bridge across the infernal river of love
> So as to traverse the deserts
> To walk behind my camel with the dawn ahead of me to Bukhara
> and return, carrying my vows to Damascus
> Pursued, starving for love
> Writing my ten odes (*mu ʿallaqāt*) on its wall

As a parody of the suspended odes of pre-Islamic times that have become central to *ʿamūd al-shi ʿr* (canonized standards in poetry), with the tripartite structure of each ode, al-Bayātī's lyric shares the *raḥīl*

[167] Bennīs, *al-A ʿmāl al-shi ʿriyyah*, 1:15–16.

(journey) motif in order to highlight a romantic agony that finds no settlement other than in a lyrical verse. The poem escapes any search for textual dependency because it is a matrix of dispersion, one where only a yearning for love sounds high.[168]

Trained in the classical tradition by her brother, the poet and professor of Arabic Ibrāhīm Ṭūqān (d. 1941), the Palestinian poetess Fadwā Ṭūqān has the pre-Islamic ode in mind, particularly that of Imruʾ al-Qays, with its famous prelude that calls on companions to stop and weep at the site of the ruins left behind by the departing tribe of those whom he loves. Her poem "Lan Abkī" (I Will Never Cry) is just a reversed voicing of resistance.[169] Its paratextual dedication to the poets of the Palestinian resistance, "a present for the Jaffa meeting, 4/3/1986," is important, as the dedication addresses the resistance poets of that meeting. It entails thereby a thematic reversal of a site confluent with the pre-Islamic nostalgic prelude in order to oppose resignation and nostalgia, and to adopt the ruins of Jaffa under occupation as a reminder of the devastation incurred by European invaders of Palestine driven and funded by prominent European bankers, like the Rothchild family, the fanatic Zionist Sir Alfred Mond (1868–30), and Arthur James Balfour (1848–1930).[170] The dedication as paratext connects and problematizes a site. In Gerárd Genette's words: "The dedication . . . proclaims a relationship, whether intellectual or personal, actual or symbolic, and this proclamation is always at the service of the work, as a reason for elevating the work's standing or as a theme for commentary."[171] Ṭūqān's poem engages with Imruʾ al-Qays's opening lines of the nostalgic prelude, "Stop, and we will weep," but only to a certain extent in order to juxtapose the ruins of Jaffa with what it was before the invasion. Its tripartite structuration follows the pre-Islamic poet's pattern, where there is the campsite provoking sorrow and longing for the departed; followed by journeying in an epical structure, before settling for a promise of return through resistance and struggle.

> Here I am, O beloved ones, extending my hand to yours . . .
> Raising my forehead to the sun, with you,
> Here you are as hard and powerful as our mountains
> As the roses of our homeland

[168] This is my own translation of the first page of al-Bayātī's "Majnūn ʿĀʾishah." A full translation is by Bassam K. Frangieh, as studied in al-Musawi, *Arabic Poetry*, 248–49.
[169] Fadwā Ṭūqān, "Lan Abkī," in *Dīwān Fadwā Ṭūqān* (Beirut: Dār al-ʿAwdah, 2000), 511–17.
[170] Muhsin J. al-Musawi, "The Iraqi Spectres of Marx," *Journal of Contemporary Iraq & the Arab World* 14, no. 3 (2020): 169–88, https://doi.org/10.1386/jciaw_00028_1.
[171] Genette, *Paratexts*, 135.

There is no charge to be leveled against the poet's model; it is independent from its prototype; yet it functions as hypertext for Imruʾ al-Qays's ode, which is now the "literature of the second degree" that leaves only a palimpsest. Furthermore, its prototype, or hypotext, suffers the same slicing of ancestors that defines twentieth-century Arab poetics. Imruʾ al-Qays is only called upon for the nostalgic prelude, and the campsite as the trace of the departing tribe. Thus, despite an ongoing recollection of the poet's oeuvre, there is also a slicing pattern that was there as early as Abū Nuwās's disparagement of the nostalgic prelude, al-Qāḍī al-Jurjānī's critique of the ancients' lapses, and al-Baqillānī's sharp detraction in his *Iʿjāz al-Qurʾān*; a slicing that calls for a nuanced reading of limits, infringements, and intellectual property, as Chapter 4 argues.

4 A Genealogy for Poetic Property

Rights, Infringements, and Arbitration

In an epistemic turn in the ninth century and after, the discussion of ownership in relation to a specific literary production – that is, poetry – had grown into a body of knowledge. This body also involves a diversification of assets insofar as ancient and early contemporary contributions were recognized as part of a large cultural script or cultural tree. There are many insights by Ibn Abī al-Ṭāhir Ṭayfūr and later, Ibn Ṭabāṭabā, al-Qāḍī al-Jurjānī, and even al-Ḥātimī, suggesting that newness and disconnection with antecedent authority is impossible to come by because discourse and speech merge into their like, and yet al-Āmidī and al-Qāḍī al-Jurjānī occasionally mention special and unique applications and themes, a specific (*makhṣūṣ*) usage or verbal and imagist inventory that is one's own private property.[1] Hence, in perusing and analyzing the domain of poetry in particular, we come across both accusatory statements that hunt for echoes or duplications and a philological effort to build up an inventory of terms to account for claims and their refutations. Throughout these periods and ongoing discussions and writings, the underlying desire for another's poetic property is paramount. As Chapter 5 will show, there was among tenth-century critics, down to the thirteen century and after, a tendency to stretch thievery terms to account for a negotiatory space in which repetition and duplication are condoned as long as there is a better value, not only in the new poetic formation (content and form), but also in matters of compilation and culture production.[2] Nevertheless, there is no clear-cut practice, as motivations and applications are often politically or psychologically loaded. The matter became more sensitive, blurred, and elastic among the contemporaries of a specific case, as is demonstrated by the rift among disciples or companions and mentors throughout the fourteenth–fifteenth centuries, a point that will receive further attention in

[1] See al-Jurjānī, *al-Wasāṭah* (2006), 161.
[2] For a detailed study of the ethics of the evolving diversion of assets, see al-Musawi, *Republic of Letters*, 5–6.

Chapter 5 in reference to al-Nawājī, Ibn Nubātah al-Miṣrī, al-Ṣafadī, and Ibn Ḥijjah, for example.

Cultural Diversity

The divide between private and public properties was bound to become central to raging discussions of thievery and its conditions of application. A cultural tree, a genealogy of multiple branches, procreating across lands and identities, has as its root a struggle, or an overwhelming desire, for poetic property rights and their attending cultural, social, and symbolic capital. Hence, a conversation with multiple directions and tones drew the attention of all who were implicated in the literary vocation or *ḥirfat al-adab*, and along with them their audiences. Whether we have in mind scholars like al-Aṣmaʿī with his focus on linguistic correctness and syntactic standardization, or critics like Ibn Qutaybah and al-Jāḥiẓ and their care for depth in ideas and elegance in expression, a literary and grammatical corpus is made available to a specific public that, to borrow Habermas's eighteenth-century European application, "established itself institutionally as a stable group of discussants."[3] The obsession with *adab* – its gifts and ordeals and its triumphs and vagaries – entails not only distinction but also an obsession with its pursuit that often ends in misfortune in a competitive literary market. According to Ibn Abī al-Ṭāhir Ṭayfūr, the poet Abū Yaʿqūb Isḥāq b. Ḥassān al-Khuraymī (d. 278/829) used the term: "I was overtaken – and that was my initiation – . . . in Sijistān, by the obsession with *ādāb*."[4] Ibn Abī al-Ṭāhir referenced it to prove that Abū Tammām seized on this (*akhadha*; literally: took over) in his verse "Whenever a target appeared within reach, I got overtaken by *ḥirfat al-adab*."[5]

Al-Āmidī objects to this, not only because Ibn Abī al-Ṭāhir has confused and misread *ḥirfat al-ʿArab* as used by the poet Abū Tammām with *ḥirfat al-adab*, but also because the phrase is a "common expression shared by people and often repeated by all."[6]

Ḥirfat al-Adab: Obsession with Literary Pursuits

The term *ḥirfat al-adab* is focal to this discussion, as it underwent an epistemic change from an instructional implication relating to tutors and scribes or chancery functionaries to a specifically ninth-century

[3] Jürgen Habermas, *The Structural Transformation of the Public Sphere: An Inquiry into a Category of Bourgeois Society*, trans. Thomas Burger (Cambridge, MA: MIT Press, 1991), 37.
[4] al-Āmidī, *al-Muwāzanah*, 1:121. [5] Ibid. [6] Ibid.

preoccupation with literary pursuits and practices. Its evolving imbrication points to a large semantic field where vying for prominence was, as it is always, the fashion of the day.[7] Indeed to refer to someone as *adrakathu ḥirfat al-adab* (he was obsessed with literary pursuits) also implies misfortune, for as Abū Manṣūr al-Thaʿālibī (d. 429/1038) articulates: *ḥirfat al-adab ḥurfah* (literary pursuits are a misfortune). The turn from instructional service to poetry and literary writing occurred simultaneously when a departure from ancient models gained momentum.[8] It should not be surprising that a late twentieth-century pioneer of poetry like ʿAbd al-Wahhāb al-Bayātī (d. 1999) speaks of this association between poetry and poverty: "From poetry, I inherited: this deadly poverty, / This love, this flame, this murderous sword / With which my throat will be cut one day / For my support of the poor."[9] Moreover, the term also suggests the recognized presence of a group of scholars and littérateurs who take it for granted that they speak for a public.

Authors' practice of addressing anonymous readers or patrons, alongside epistles addressed to named ones, as well as the pairing of advocates in al-Āmidī's *Muwāzanah*, for example, all indicate that this institutionalized group had a substantial role in cultural life. In other words, the author's voice, which is traceable in writings, points to "an institutionalized group [that] claim[s] itself as the mouthpiece of a public."[10] Although largely concerned with almost everything in the field of writing and speech, the group's increasing attention to *saraq* and its variables testifies to an increasing attention to poetry as a cultural commodity. Its owner is a craftsman with a right to a specific production. If the poet is no longer alive or is unable to fight for a right, the arbiters are available to take care of the matter, even when nepotism, bias, or prejudice stand behind one motivation or another. Stripped of its ethical implications and/or pejorative connotations, thievery (*sariqāt*) rises to the standard of a distinctive category in literary criticism. It cuts across popular modes and genres like panegyrics or lampoon, satire, and elegy and demands the attention and participation of every noted critic, philologue,

7 Although the phrase was in use in the second/eighth century by al-Khalīl b. Aḥmad al-Farāhīdī (d. 175/790), as noted by al-Thaʿālibī in *al-Muḍāf wa-l-mansūb*, it became more literary, not educational or instructional, sometime in the third/ninth century: Abū Tammām used it in his poetry in conjunction with poetry as an Arab domain, and the poet Ibn Bassām (d. 542/1147) used it in elegizing Ibn al-Muʿtazz: "There is no this or that blemish in him . . . but he was overwhelmed by the *adab* vocation." See Muḥammad Ṣādiq al-Rāfiʿī, *Tārīkh ādāb al-ʿArab* (Cairo: Maṭbaʿat al-Akhbār, 1911), 1:23.

8 See n. 20 in Chapter 2.

9 ʿAbd al-Wahhāb al-Bayātī, "For Rafael Alberti," in *Love, Death, and Exile*, bilingual ed., trans. Bassam Khalil Frangieh (Washington, DC: Georgetown University Press, 1990), 165.

10 Habermas, *Structural Transformation*, 37.

and grammarian. Its topical domain is inclusive, but it is pivotal as the catalyst and incentive that gathers support around it. It is not enough to claim one's right to a verse or a poem, nor only to market it as a verifiable account to an audience. A reliable authority must stand behind your claim; otherwise, the case remains pending.[11]

A distinct lexical and semantic system joins others in a field that also manifests significant directions, as this chapter plans to show. What emerges as defensive single lines in pre- or early Islamic poetry was to expand into books with a focus on one poet or case, a point that has already been discussed in Chapter 2. These instances – and they are not a few – raised questions about the right terminology, simply because a developing literary theory requires the right critical arsenal. The pejorative term *saraq* (taking over from another's verse some of the wording and the poetic idea), its implications and difference from other terms like *ighārah*,[12] and its conjugations, all underwent interrogation and ultimate replacement with further classifications. So long as there is a shared script, and primarily a shared *kalām* (discourse), there should be common usage that opens the gate for one license or another. Moreover, the epistemological shift cannot be seen as mere quibbles among functionaries, scribes, poets, and philologists. The shift relates to an expanding empire, with its epicenters in Damascus, Basrah, Abbasid Baghdad, Cairo during the Fatimid and Mamluk periods, and in Marv, Samarqand, Isfahan, and many other cities that manifested a visible presence in later periods. These epicenters were the domains of new economies that left nothing untouched. Inventiveness was only in line with drastic societal, political, and ultimately economic transformations that were bound to render ancient lifestyles, as well as speech habits and old writing patterns, obsolete.

A note of caution is in order, however, because the belletristic discursive space does not lose its dominance in the face of revisionist tendencies that touch on a need to refine speech and free it from the burden of an archaic or ancient lexicon. Aḥmad b. Fāris (d. 395/1004), al-Jawharī, al-Hamadhānī, Qudāmah, and other critics and philologists have had their concerns explained in books that deal with a lexical corpus. A revisionist like Abū Bakr Muḥammad b. al-ʿAbbās al-Baghdādī al-Khwārizmī (d. 393/1003?), grand mufti of Baghdad, jurist, and sheikh of the Ḥanafī community, is not far from the mark when he defines the contents of his book *al-Amthāl* as explanatory of a shared disdain for ancient

[11] For a specific controversy that calls upon arbitration, see Naaman, "Plagiarism Controversy."

[12] See Ibn Rashīq, *al-ʿUmdah* (2001), 2:285. *Ighārah* is an enforced self-arrogation and confiscation of another's verse in its entirety (ibid.).

conventions, thinking of the once normative styles as examples of dry, outworn, and outdated practices and habits.[13] Furthermore, *ḥirfat al-adab*, once disdained as no more than tutoring for gain, was to undergo a semantic shift toward literariness while still keeping its stigma as *takassub* (literary mendicancy). As both an obsession and vocation, *ḥirfat al-adab* was poised between the court, with its entourage, surrogates, functionaries, and clientele, on the one hand, and the rising reading public as catered to by copyists and book markets, on the other.[14] As a growing economic force and hence patronage, the latter were to endow the vocation with independence and thus respectability.[15]

Booksellers, Functionaries, and Poets: Defining Plagiarism

As such matters are to receive attention in due course, this introductory note proposes to focus on a semantic genealogy in order to explain the battles among partisans and antagonists as being no mere dilettantish shows or pretentious practices, but as factional literary feuds, entrenched in a culture at the point of defining its poetic geographies, its frontiers, borders, and hinterlands. In other words, the literary culture of the period from the mid-ninth into the tenth century sets the tone and direction for a growing system that we call theory, and which has its epistemic shifts, knowledge constructs, proponents, and publics. Along with its institutionalized groups of philologists, grammarians, rhetors, anthologists, and critics, copyists and booksellers were as important functionaries as bibliophiles and littérateurs. The art of book production and its circulation were increasingly visible, as I have explained elsewhere.[16] While there are no such things as historical demarcations, there are epistemic shifts that feed the forthcoming one. Thus, al-Āmidī needs Ibn Abī al-Ṭāhir (d. 280/893) and his practical criticism insofar as the alleged plagiarisms of Abū Tammām are concerned, not only because al-Āmidī intends the discussion to be a corrective to Ibn Abī al-Ṭāhir in matters that should not fall under the category of plagiarism, since "he confused the unique poetic

[13] See Abū Bakr Muḥammad al-Baghdādī al-Khwārizmī, *al-Amthāl al-muwalladah* (Abu Dhabi: al-Mujamma' al-Thaqāfī, 2003), 68. Another edition of the same work was published by Mūfam li-l-Nashr (Algeria: al-Jazā'ir, 1993).

[14] See Abū Bakr Aḥmad b. 'Alī al-Khaṭīb al-Baghdādī, *Tārīkh Baghdād aw madīnat al-salām*, 14 vols. (Beirut: Dār al-Kitāb al-'Arabī, 1966). A summary of bookshops, their attendees, and names of copyists is available in Wadād Jūdī, "Aswāq al-warrāqīn fī Baghdād fī al-'aṣr al-'Abbāsī" (MA thesis, University of Guelma, 2016–17).

[15] al-Musawi, "Abbasid Popular Narrative."

[16] al-Musawi, *Republic of Letters*, esp. 111–12, 131, 180, 245, but also 2, 4, 7.

meanings with the ones shared among people,"[17] but also because Ibn Abī al-Ṭāhir's book is among the few foundational works that invite interrogation in order to build up a new theoretical base for *muwāzanah* (balanced assessment) as a better criterion for achieving fair considerations of poetry and poetics. Moreover, this engagement with a ninth-century authority buttresses the claim to fairness that al-Āmidī strives to establish against anticipated backlash.[18] Indeed, his method of pairing an already polarized society of two camps for or against a major literary figure also conveys a sense of the literary "public" as a society of discussants, as would be the case in eighteenth-century Europe.[19] As long as al-Āmidī is bent on balancing the two poets Abū Tammām and al-Buḥturī in terms of relevance to the ongoing conflictual paradigm of ancients or moderns, his *Muwāzanah* traps itself in a series of juxtapositions and contradictions.

The critic, and especially a prominent one like al-Āmidī, can claim the role of both judge and jury, an institutionalized role that speaks for both groups, antagonists and protagonists. While seemingly uncovering Ibn Abī al-Ṭāhir's confusion, al-Āmidī offers a corrective that applies what he describes as *al-saraq al-ṣaḥīḥ* (actual plagiarism).[20] Thus, he poses as advisor to a divided audience. As he aligns himself with the experts in *ṣinā'at al-shi'r* (practicing the craft of poetry) and *kalām*,[21] he can conclude that "those who are of a natural disposition and rhetors tend not to prioritize an exhaustive search for meanings and excessive description; they prefer a comprehensive knowledge of meanings, the selection of its best, as the ancients used to do."[22] The problem with the emphasis on "experts" lies in its denial of the vast appeal of poetry. In the words of late twentieth-century critics, to assume that a "fictional truth" "could only be recovered with the help of the analyst's special expertise would be to deny literature's natural power over its readers."[23] Nevertheless, al-Āmidī has experts in mind whenever there is a dispute. Although the ones he rallies on the side of Abū Tammām are fewer in number and of lesser fame than the ones rallied against his poetry,[24] he admits that al-Buḥturī could not resist drawing from Abū Tammām's poetics, a point which later littérateurs like the grammarian and jurist Jamāl al-Dīn Abū 'Amr 'Uthmān b. al-Ḥājib (d. 646/1249) were more inclined to stress in

[17] al-Āmidī, *al-Muwāzanah*, 1:110.
[18] Ibid., 110, 120. His discussion of Ibn Abī al-Ṭāhir's book spans several pages, 110–29.
[19] Habermas, *Structural Transformation*, 37. [20] al-Āmidī, *al-Muwāzanah*, 1:110–20.
[21] Ibid., 394–95. [22] Ibid., 496. The term *'afw* in Ṣaqr's edition means untrodden.
[23] See Michael Riffaterre, *Fictional Truth* (Baltimore: Johns Hopkins University Press, 1993), xvii.
[24] al-Āmidī, *al-Muwāzanah*, 1:19.

a campaign to downplay the poetry of al-Buḥturī.[25] Al-Āmidī's recognition of al-Buḥturī's irresistible desire to invade Abū Tammām's poetry presents a neat and succinct synthesis of the economies of desire that underlines the whole discussion of infringements.

Al-Āmidī: Modalities for Arbitration

Prompted by talent and skill, poets are even more receptive to other poets' unique ideas and rare expressions. Al-Āmidī addresses this issue as one of familiarity and exposure. As befitting a debate, al-Āmidī gives voice to al-Buḥturī's "companion" as the advocate who redraws the matter of *akhdh* (seizure; taking over) as an unwitting transaction: "It is not a matter of blame to seize on poetic meanings, whether intentional or not, when so overwhelmed by the amount of Abū Tammām's poetry to which al-Buḥturī was exposed."[26] As for Abū Tammām, al-Āmidī says with certainty that, as long as he is so knowledgeable and well-read in poetry, his *saraq* is enormous and often indiscernible.[27] In the balance is the critic's objectivity; hence he admits that al-Buḥturī "took possession [*akhadha*] of a substantial portion [a great deal] from the ancients' and moderns' poetic ideas."[28] He is quick to qualify his statement, however, because "I am not supposed to mention *sariqāt* when focusing on their [al-Buḥturī and Abū Tammām's] blemishes."[29] He has a reason for this qualification: "As I mentioned earlier, those whom I have outlived from among the knowledgeable in poetry do not consider thievery in poetic meanings among the worst pitfalls, especially among later poets, as this is a defect from which nobody before or after is free."[30] With this broad canvas thematic justifications can multiply to allow multiple forms of permissible infringements against a tight and rigid hunt for echoes and similarities (see Figure 6.2).

On the same page, al-Āmidī justifies his concern with *sariqāt* in a book that he claims to engage initially with omissions, lapses, oversights, and

[25] Ibn al-Ḥājib's verse runs thus:

والِفتى البحتري سارق ما قا   ل ابن أوس في المدح والتشبيب
كلّ بيت له يجوّد معناه   فمعناه لابن أوس حبيب

And the young Buḥturī stole what
Ḥabīb b. Aws [Abū Tammām] articulated in panegyrics and love.
Every verse where he excels
is by Ḥabīb b. Awas.

See more in the introduction to Ibn Wakī', *Kitāb al-munṣif*.

[26] al-Āmidī, *al-Muwāzanah*, 1:52. [27] Ibid., 55–56. [28] Ibid., 291. [29] Ibid.
[30] Ibid.

defects. If this is the case, why should such a formidable critic and philologist devote more than half of the book to thievery? Why should he apply thievery as a yardstick to evaluate poetry and as a pretext for engaging grammar, diction, meanings, and themes along with philological authorities and literary critics? In a moment of uncertainty following his specifically stated intention to expose al-Buḥturī's enormous *saraq*, al-Āmidī lets his reader into his secret – that is, the motivation behind this painstaking effort to unearth presumed thievery (*sariqāt*). If stealing or modifying and appropriating poetic ideas and meanings is not the worst among poets' flaws, especially in relation to al-Buḥturī, there must be another paramount reason. Indeed, the reason is so urgent as to follow immediately after the declared intention of dealing with al-Buḥturī's enormous thievery. Bent on addressing only what is presumably taken solely from Abū Tammām, al-Āmidī puts aside his admission that al-Buḥturī "*akhadha* … *akhdhan kathīran*" (took possession of a great deal).[31]

The Fight for Distinction: Poetic Naturalness or Newness?

His reasoning is worth our attention in order to consolidate the stipulation that the issue of thievery functioned as the dynamic for literary theory as a consolidated thematic, stylistic, and structural formation that has its epistemic stages where knowledge grids operate with vigor. Let us keep in mind that the formidable critic is making a case for three things: first, to disclose al-Buḥturī's thefts; second, to undermine this proposal by suggesting that thievery should not be central to the discussion because there is always marauding of poetic meanings; and third, he has his reasons to visit this literary space that amounts to no more than refuting "*aṣḥāb Abī Tammām*" (Abū Tammām's advocates).[32] While this last refutation might sound like a fixation, it is pivotal to our understanding of its theoretical implications. He argues, "Abū Tammām's advocates claim that he is unprecedented, and that he is the originator in creativeness and inventiveness."[33] These claims lead the critic to expose what the poet takes from others, and by the same token to demonstrate what al-Buḥturī does as well.[34] To sustain his argument, al-Āmidī admits that he does not cover al-Buḥturī's thefts from others because nobody claims al-Buḥturī as a first, a precedent and pioneer; hence al-Āmidī's attention is confined merely to al-Buḥturī's borrowings from Abū Tammām. What his *Muwāzanah* amounts to in conclusion is a proof that Abū Tammām is not – as presented by advocates – a pioneering innovator and that he is not

[31] Ibid. [32] Ibid. [33] Ibid. [34] Ibid.

an originator of *badīʿ* (unprecedented and innovative style of adornment and creativity) or an inventor of the *badīʿ* mode, a term which ʿAbdallāh b. al-Muʿtazz (d. 296/909) admits is uniquely used by the modernists (*al-muḥdathūn*).[35] Thus, al-Āmidī finds in Ibn al-Muʿtazz's book great support for his goal to undermine for good the claims of originality and inventiveness. He quotes Ibn al-Muʿtazz to argue that "Bashshār, Muslim b. al-Walīd, Abū Nuwās, and those who emulate them and follow in their footsteps are not the first in this art; but it recurs frequently in their poetry, and it becomes known in their time." Moreover, "Ḥabīb b. Aws al-Ṭāʾī [Abū Tammām] was so fascinated by it [*badīʿ*] that it overwhelmed him, driving him to make extensive and diversified use of it, doing well in some verses and badly in others. Such is the outcome of excess, and the payback for extravagance."[36] Ibn al-Muʿtazz asserts that his own undertaking in the book referenced by al-Āmidī was unprecedented in defining *badīʿ* in terms of five constitutive tropes and in applying this definition to the poetry of the modernists (*muḥdathūn*). In a neat clarification, he argues: "*Badīʿ* is a name for the poetic arts usually mentioned by poets and literary critics; as for the learned in language and ancient poetry, they have no knowledge of this name."[37] In other words, al-Āmidī relies on Ibn al-Muʿtazz to augment and consolidate the argument against Abū Tammām as no more than a participant in a movement where he acquires fame for the wrong reasons.

What could make an interesting case here is the certainty that al-Buḥturī was receptive to recitals and presentations, whereas Abū Tammām is "preoccupied throughout his life with selecting and studying poetry."[38] If we accept the hypothesis that "memory-oriented readings displace text-oriented readings,"[39] al-Buḥturī sounds more prone to poetic appropriations and *saraq* (thievery). Even so, al-Āmidī offers a very rich body of poetry that is centered on a discussion of *saraq* as debated and argued at a time when poetry was at its highest point of grandeur as the prominent literary domain among the learned. While pivotal to the critic's argument, *saraq* undergoes a palliation whenever *akhdh* takes over as the appropriate term applicable to both al-Buḥturī and Abū Tammām.[40] In the former's case, al-Āmidī is willing to stretch the term a bit and use *ḥadhā* (*iḥtidhāʾ*), that is, resorting to close

[35] ʿAbdallāh Ibn al-Muʿtazz, *Kitāb al-badīʿ*, ed. Ignatius Kratchkovsky (Beirut: Dār al-Masīrah, 1982), 1.

[36] al-Āmidī, *al-Muwāzanah*, 1:18.

[37] Ibn al-Muʿtazz, *Kitāb al-badīʿ*, 58.

[38] al-Āmidī, *al-Muwāzanah*, 1:55.

[39] Riffaterre, *Fictional Truth*, xviii.

[40] See a random example in al-Āmidī, *al-Muwāzanah*, 1:56–57 (in relation to Abū Tammām), 298–99 (in relation to al-Buḥturī).

emulation: "I think – but God knows best – that he emulates the saying of Shabīb b. al-Barṣā' [d. 100/718?]."[41]

Such an equivocal position is not unique to al-Āmidī. While allowing a subjective strain to intervene in expressions and positionalities, there was among literati at that time an invigorating search for the right terminology to cover a wide swath of poetry and poetics in a lucrative cultural market. All in all, there is a genealogical tree that spreads further in the mid-tenth century to account for a diversified movement in which several participants have multiple concerns. It nevertheless centers on the ethics of writing, intellectual property, ownership, authorship, public space, debts and credits, and the literary profession and its textual space and poetics. The process of surveying the discussions that al-Āmidī references presents a map for reading, an atlas of criticism, debate, disputation, and invigorated poetics. As a consortium of books, this textual space must have been the talk of literati in assemblies and gatherings and in the marketplace where some copyists' shops happened to entertain such gatherings and discussions.[42] It is not surprising that Ibn al-Mu'tazz's *Risālah fī sariqāt Abī Tammām* appears in the discussion when the one-day caliph surprised literati with his book on *badī'* as a practice, not a movement, that gained momentum under new circumstances.[43]

To substantiate the argument at this point and contextualize its *history*, another nod at Abū al-Qāsim al-Āmidī's (d. 371/980) book is needed. He agrees or disputes with early or late contemporaries, like Abū al-'Abbās Muḥammad b. 'Ammār al-Qaṭrabullī, Ibn al-Mu'tazz (d. 296/909), Qudāmah b. Ja'far (d. 337/948), Ibn Ṭabāṭabā (d. 322/934), and certainly Abū al-Ḍiyā' Bishr b. Yaḥyā (d. 371/981), whom he never fails to mention every now and then, before devoting no less than forty pages to dispute Bishr b. Yaḥyā's criticism of al-Buḥturī's alleged *sariqāt* from Abū Tammām.[44] As mentioned before, al-Āmidī's authoritative *Muwāzanah* does not shy away from proclaiming his preference for al-Buḥturī for his "easy wording and accessible meaning, correct casting, right expression, sweet enunciation, malleability, and elegance."[45] This is certainly at variance with Abū Tammām's proneness to "craft obscure meanings that demand the exertion of exploration and thinking."[46] Moreover, al-Buḥturī receives more commendation for being "natural, in line with the

[41] Ibid., 299.
[42] See al-Musawi, *Republic of Letters*, 111–12 (on copying as a lucrative business), 274 (on investing in Ibn al-Ḥajjāj's [d. 391/1001] poetry).
[43] 'Abdallāh Ibn al-Mu'tazz, "Risālah fī sariqāt Abī Tammām," in *Rasā'il Ibn al-Mu'tazz fī al-naqd wa-l-adab wa-al-ijtimā'*, ed. 'Abd al-Mun'im Khafājī (Cairo: Muṣṭafā al-Bābī al-Ḥalabī, 1946), 24.
[44] al-Āmidī, *al-Muwāzanah*, 1:52, 304–42. [45] Ibid., 7. [46] Ibid.

ancients, and as never departing from the established *ʿamūd al-shiʿr*."[47] While seemingly balanced, the assessments can easily lead one to prefer al-Buḥturī to Abū Tammām. While *al-Muwāzanah* asks readers to choose between the two, an outsider cannot overlook the author's interposition.

Al-Qāḍī al-Jurjānī's Mediational Stance: Its Significance for Later Criticism

Before delving into exemplary cases of disputes like that between al-Āmidī and Abū al-Ḍiyāʾ, it is worth mentioning that al-Āmidī was not the only one with a book that has been an important literary and cultural museum, a guide to a movement with its agents and functionaries, poets, writers, and copyists and sellers. Al-Qāḍī al-Jurjānī's *Wasāṭah* is no less so, while al-Marzubānī's *al-Muwashshaḥ* expands the field of conversation by drawing attention to ninth-century contributions that are not extant. Furthermore, specific chapters in books like Abū Manṣūr al-Thaʿālibī's (d. 429/1039) *Yatīmat al-dahr fī maḥāsin ahl al-ʿaṣr* and centuries later Yūsuf al-Badīʿī's (d. 1073/1662) *al-Ṣubḥ al-munbī ʿan ḥaythiyyat al-Mutanabbī* are two cases among many that bridge six centuries and also provide a rounded sketch of the raging battle around a poet whose character and poetry have secured a sustainability of which no poet ever dreams. While the latter is a rounded account of the controversy, the accusations of plagiarism against al-Mutanabbī, and their motivations, al-Thaʿālibī's chapter is more in line with al-Qāḍī al-Jurjānī's *Wasāṭah*,[48] where *sariqah* is sparingly used to allow space for more compromising terms that opt to bring into discussion the power of the verse or its weakness. Pejorative connotations are mostly put aside in favor of a cultural tree that considers fame as necessarily contingent on popularity. Elitism gives way to an audience that sustains literary marketability. When Ḍiyāʾ al-Dīn b. al-Athīr (d. 637/1239) asked the celebrated al-Qāḍī ʿAbd al-Raḥīm al-Bīsānī (d. 596/1199), the minister to Ṣalāḥ al-Dīn al-Ayyūbī (Saladin), about the massive popularity of al-Mutanabbī's poetry in Egypt, he associated popularity with the poetic power to speak for the people, their sentiments and feelings.[49] An aesthetic rather than an ethical shift takes over to reach a nuanced formulation not only in ʿAbd al-Qāhir al-Jurjānī's (d. 471/1078) writings but also in al-Khaṭīb

[47] Ibid., 6. [48] Full name: Abū al-Ḥasan ʿAlī b. ʿAbd al-ʿAzīz.
[49] See Ḍiyāʾ al-Dīn Ibn al-Athīr, *al-Washī al-marqūm fī ḥall al-manẓūm* (Cairo: Quṣūr al-Thaqāfah, 2004), 183; Khalīl b. Aybak al-Ṣafadī, *al-Wāfī bi-l-wafayāt*, ed. Hilmut Ritter (Wiesbaden: Franz Steiner, 1962), 6:208; or see the corresponding passage in the edition published by Dār Iḥyāʾ al-Turāth (Beirut, 2000).

al-Qazwīnī's short intervention that sounds like an afterthought to his popular *al-Īḍāḥ fī ʿulūm al-balāghah*. Furthermore, Ibn al-Athīr's detailed chapter on thievery in *al-Mathal al-sāʾir* (The Popular Model [for the Practice of Secretaries and Poets]) is important for our purpose here, not only because he tries to focus on a few terms but also because of the extensive analysis of them, one that could serve as a monograph on thievery on its own. His key thievery terms are not new, but they are given the attention they deserve before they branch off in other directions and textual examples. Thus, his division of poetic *sariqāt* (*aqsām al-sariqāt al-shiʿriyya*) (see Figure 2.3) is a stepping stone for a departure from that of his predecessors – especially al-Ḥātimī and Ibn Rashīq, who have already offered a lexicon that nobody ever after can overlook. His undertaking aims to situate terminology in the current discursive space of literary criticism. However, he justifies the endeavor because there is a benefit to be gained and a method to be followed.[50] One should keep in mind here Ibn al-Athīr's role in the raging discussion of the requirements of scribes, the training of kuttāb, whose role received significant focus under the Fatimids and Mamluks.[51] Before we look into this development as a structuration that falls within a tendency to justify the belletristic tradition and eventually works within a main discursive space, a genealogical tabulation is in order.

Prioritizing Terminologies: The Slackening of a Pejorative *Saraq*

Visible turns from specific terms in the *sariqāt* corpus could enable us to explore shifts in theoretical thought. ʿAbd al-Qāhir al-Jurjānī's preference for *ḥadhw* or *iḥtidhāʾ* (close emulation), for instance, as comprehensive terms for textual navigation does not overlook such practices like *salkh* (flaying), which he criticizes as the worst in this navigation as it is a servile practice of changing expressions while invading the meaning of the original verse. The grounds for this subsequent articulation are already laid to counter wholesale accusations of plagiarism. One can suggest that the expressed preference for the use of *akhdh* (seizing on only part of either wording or poetic meaning) rather than *saraq*, as shown in Ibn Qutaybah's extensive readings of poetry and poets, demonstrates the adoption of a congenial and acceptable term that is insult-free. Abū Bakr al-Ṣūlī (d. 336/947) tends to highlight *inḥāl* (deliberate assignment

[50] See Ḍiyāʾ al-Dīn Ibn al-Athīr, *al-Mathal al-sāʾir* (Beirut: Dār al-Kutub al-ʿIlmiyyah, 1998), 2:302–54.
[51] See al-Musawi, "Pre-modern Belletristic Prose."

of verses to another) and *intiḥāl* (claiming what is not one's own) in his defense of Abū Nuwās and Abū Tammām (see Figure 4.2).[52] Both terms had been in use since Ibn Sallām, especially in relation to the authenticity of ancient poetry, but powerful poets of the recent past prompt the intervention of scholars in order to resurrect and preserve their actual oeuvre. Thus, after the mid-ninth century, several anthologies of ancient, post-ancient, and modernist poetry began to appear.[53] While indicating an active and invigorating cultural environment, the move to preserve a single poet's verse versus corrupt editions points to the nature of fluidity in the cultural market. An active climate since the late eighth century also meant that poets and littérateurs became interested in emulating or arrogating (*inḥāl*) the poetry of a renowned figure like Abū Nuwās and Abū Tammām. While it might be invigorating, the activity also points to mounting free-market economies in the expanding urban centers. The malleability invokes the participation of other players, the arbiters of taste, who were often beyond the concern of marginal talents, as much as they themselves used to reserve their activity to the study of magisterial figures.

The significance of the move to produce edited and closely authenticated editions of a specific poetic property, copied and sold through the best of "*ahl al-ṣan'ah*" (highly acclaimed professionals),[54] draws attention not only to the rising role of professional scholars like al-Ṣūlī in his edition of Abū Nuwās's poetry, for example, but also to an awareness of the demands of the cultural market. By the same token, this market requires a disciplinary apparatus that might lie outside the *muḥtasib*'s (market inspector) domain. Tenth-century scholars like al-Āmidī and al-Qāḍī al-Jurjānī reiterated the need to intervene and define the role of adept and qualified philologists, littérateurs, or, as al-Ṣūlī calls them, *ahl al-adab*.[55] The same demand for intervention, or policing the cultural market, is bound to drive others to write more books and manuals on terminologies and/or specific renowned poets. This last direction also involves a repetition of applicable terminologies or the multiplication of some, either to defend, mediate, or vilify a renowned figure. Fluidity in literary markets often allows an elastic trading of accusations in order to undermine a name and demonstrate a poet's alleged lack of originality. Even so, if Abū Tammām's poetry invited the challenge, it is bound to drive others to rescue it from stark or even mediated accusations of massive dependency on others. By the same token, for six centuries al-Mutanabbī was to emerge as the focus of several controversies. Terms are also bound to

[52] al-Ṣūlī, introduction, 31.
[53] See Bilal Orfali, "A Sketch Map of Arabic Poetry Anthologies," *Journal of Arabic Literature* 43 (2012): 29–59.
[54] al-Tha'ālibī, *Kitāb khāṣṣ al-khāṣṣ*, 65–82.
[55] al-Ṣūlī, introduction, 37.

multiply beyond those with which we are already familiar. Early on, Ibn Sallām's dictionary is limited to *ijtilāb* (procuring support), *ighārah* (the renowned poet's raid on the poetry of the lesser known), also *sariqah* (theft), and a few others that were listed in Chapter 3. Although al-Jāḥiẓ is more inclined to use the term *akhdh*, like Ibn Qutaybah, the term *sariqah* occurs in his *Kitāb al-ḥayawān*, as noticed by scholars.[56] Quite often *sariqah* and *ighārah* were recurrent in early criticism, alongside the more nuanced application of *akhdh*. Also pertinent to this discussion is Ibn Qutaybah's application of *salkh* (flaying), which is thought of as the worst kind of *sariqāt* among later critics like ʿAbd al-Qāhir al-Jurjānī, as it indicates corruption of an original and inferiority of the new verse. As noted earlier in reference to al-Āmidī and al-Qāḍī al-Jurjānī, there is a counter response to those critics and philologists, who tend to enumerate thematic echoes or common phrases and images as *sariqāt*. A mania for hunting these usages and tracking them down, as if they were not common usage, was the fashion of the day alongside the counter movement to curb and control the literary market. As this issue will be covered in Chapter 5, what invites discussion at this point is the multiplication of terms that derive from primary ones, from variant sources since the late eighth century, and also from pre-Islamic poetry and anecdotes. The effort proceeds to offer a kind of lexicon, such as al-Ḥātimī's *Ḥilyat al-muḥāḍarah*, which Ibn Rashīq uses with reservations to create his own model for literary criticism that adopts ideas more assuredly from al-Qāḍī al-Jurjānī's *Wasāṭah*.[57]

Tabulation: The Effort to Systemize Textual Trading

The mounting search for "plagiarism" and the involvement of many scholars in writing about it could have been reason enough to justify the tendency to tabulate this activity. Tabulation occurs in terms of the conditions of possibility, not only because there is a need for a policing of the literary market but also because the phenomenal recurrence of writings and discussions, in assemblies, markets, and treatises and books that focus on thievery, demonstrates an epistemic transformation, a thriving literary economy where competition is rampant. While significant volumes by al-Āmidī and al-Qāḍī al-Jurjānī, and before them a dozen others, address cases and apply terms, we have *Ḥilyat al-muḥāḍarah fī ṣināʿat al-shiʿr* (The Ornament of Discourse on the Craft of Poetry),

[56] Abū ʿUthmān ʿAmr b. Baḥr al-Jāḥiẓ, *Kitāb al-ḥayawān* (Beirut: Dār al-Kitāb al-ʿArabī, 1969), 311.

[57] al-Jurjānī, *al-Wasāṭah* (1966), 183, 193, 253.

by al-Ḥātimī (d. 388/998), which focuses in the second volume only on terminology.[58] In a later contribution, *al-Risālah al-mūḍiḥah* (The Explanatory [or Explicatory] Epistle), he also provides his version of an encounter with al-Mutanabbī that conveys his anger at what he senses as the poet's vainglory. Tabulation occurs as a scholarly endeavor to organize knowledge and place it within an episteme of knowledge construction that has left nothing untouched.[59] Even Sufism was to undergo organization and regulation, as shown in Abū Naṣr b. ʿAlī al-Sarrāj's (d. 378/988) *Kitāb al-lumaʿ*, ʿAbd al-Karīm b. Hawāzin al-Qushayrī's (d. 465/1072) *Epistle*, Abū Nuʿaym al-Iṣfahānī's (d. 430/1038) *Beauties of the Illustrious*, and others.[60] Al-Qushayrī's epistle offers abundant examples of the stations and states that the Sufi undergoes from the time of initiation as a novice. Rhetoric figures and figurations were to witness multiplication, especially in relation to Abū Yaʿqūb Yūsuf al-Sakkākī's (d. 626/1229) *Miftāḥ* and the *badīʿiyyāt* (odes in praise of the Prophet adorned with an abundance of figures of speech). When we reach ʿAbd al-Ghanī al-Nābulusī (d. 1143/1731), we are in the presence of a large corpus of rhetorical figures and their application.[61] In the end, a lexical activity connected with what was once called *sariqāt* situates itself at the center of the larger constellation of rhetoric. All in all, and in view of such compendiums as Abū al-Faraj al-Iṣfahānī's (d. 356/967) voluminous *Kitāb al-aghānī*, Ikhwān al-Ṣafāʾ's compendium, and al-Muḥassin b. ʿAlī al-Tanūkhī's (d. 384/994) two compilations, we are in the presence of a movement that has its own resonations, motivations, aspirations, and targets that speak of an epistemic shift.

A road map had already been in the making to systematize terminology and engender a theory that could define the variations in recitations, especially in writing. Since book-length analysis provides the established base, critics and scholars have either to add to the lexicon or draw a better sketch that can be workable for all, readers and poets or prose writers alike. Thus, Abū Hilāl al-ʿAskarī (d. 395/1005) has to explain in his *Kitāb al-ṣināʿatayn* (The Book of Two Crafts [Poetry and Prose]) that his

[58] Full name: Abū ʿAlī Muḥammad b. al-Ḥasan al-Ḥātimī.

[59] For more on this, see al-Musawi, *Republic of Letters;* Bilal Orfali, *The Anthologist's Art: Abū Manṣur al-Thaʿālibī and His Yātimat al-dahr* (Leiden: Brill, 2016); Elias Muhanna, *The World in a Book: Al-Nuwayri and the Islamic Encyclopedic Tradition* (Princeton, NJ: Princeton University Press, 2017); Adam Talib, *How Do You Say "Epigram" in Arabic? Literary History at the Limits of Comparison* (Leiden: Brill, 2018).

[60] For selections from these, see Sells, *Early Islamic Mysticism.*

[61] Pierre Cachia, *The Arch Rhetorician or the Schemer's Skimmer: A Handbook of Late Arabic Badīʿ Drawn from ʿAbd al-Ghanī an-Nābulsī's Nafaḥāt al-Azhār* (Wiesbaden: Harrassowitz, 1998).

purpose is not to list objections and accusations,[62] but to present a method and application. Although von Grunebaum thinks there are only "disconnected observations richly illustrated by examples,"[63] Abū Hilāl's notes can make more sense when viewed in the context of his *Dīwān al-maʿānī* (Register [or Repository] of Poetic Meanings and Motifs). Although not the first of its kind, his *Dīwān al-maʿānī* marks a tendency to provide manuals that will help not only epistolary writers and scribes but also poets in search of multiple meanings, either to avoid the stigma of plagiarism or work out a partial or indiscernible theft. On the other hand, the desire to turn away from debates and disputes with or against a poet, which Abū Hilāl claims to attempt, is an effort to objectify the discussion and place notions, motives, and terms within a constellation of its own or in conversation with a large Arabic theory of writing. The aspiration, which might have been lost amid the vast concerns that make up the two crafts under Abū Hilāl's consideration, is no less important for being part of a book on the two dominions, poetry and prose, studied here as crafts.

Thus, as crafts suffer duplication and carbon copying (*naskh*) and need improvements to be marketable, recurrent *maʿānī* (notions, themes, and motives) invite new wording, verbal embellishments, and exchange between one craft and another, or transference from one destination to another. Hence, *ikhfāʾ al-saraq* (applying indiscernible theft) turns into a commendable practice.[64] Abū Hilāl is unequivocally against *qubḥ al-akhdh* (ugly partial takeover), which, apart from total confiscation of theme, motive, and wording (stark *saraq*), could include *salkh* (flaying), which takes the theme or motive with its partial wording.[65] The effort to treat the matter among the requirements of craft frees it from the bondage of personal feuds and their ethical or moral implications; it coincides with similar efforts, especially al-Ḥātimī's *Ḥilyat al-muḥāḍarah* (Ornament of Discourse). The significance of this *Ornament* cannot be overestimated: Indeed, its author has every right to claim its uniqueness. Its earlier composition was probably thirty-five years before its author's death, a point that can place it at the center of the raging debates and discussions of poetry, poetics, ethics, literary criticism, and literary theory. As the most comprehensive study of plagiarism as an art and practice, one that digs deep into sources, including Aristotle's poetics in matters of *istiʿārah* (here: the act of borrowing),[66] al-Ḥātimī's *Ḥilyat al-muḥāḍarah* deserves to be simultaneously a nucleus, a catalyst, and a consortium. In view of

[62] See Grunebaum, "Concept of Plagiarism," 236. [63] Ibid.
[64] al-Jurjānī, *al-Wasāṭah*, 188, 193, 201, 204, 206 (1966), 161–79 (2006).
[65] For Abū Hilāl's six points, see Grunebaum, "Concept of Plagiarism," 237.
[66] See al-Ḥātimī, *Ḥilyat al-muḥāḍarah*, 2:28.

the dearth of its manuscripts, the Andalusian version that traveled to al-Qarawiyyīn (Al Quaraouiyine) Mosque in Fez[67] appears pivotal to our *sariqāt* material, as it has become one of the resources of almost every subsequent work of scholarship on poetics and plagiarism, as carefully documented by its editor, Jaʿfar al-Kattānī. Indeed, the first editor of at least volume twenty-one of *Kitāb al-aghānī* inserted an excerpt from al-Ḥātimī's *Ḥilyat al-muḥāḍarah* that al-Kattānī suspects as a copyist's intervention, because the author of the *Aghānī*, Abū al-Faraj al-Iṣfahānī, was among al-Ḥātimī's sheikhs (mentors). The list of scholars who, acknowledging their source or otherwise, copied, quoted from, or relied on *Ḥilyat al-muḥāḍarah* is too long for our purpose, but it is enough to say that it has remained for ten centuries – and probably not ending with Zakī Mubārak (d. 1952) – as a rich reference.[68]

Al-Ḥātimī's Pioneering Manual

On the other hand, al-Ḥātimī made extensive use of sources, but often with a mention of his authorities who are there to buttress his examples or conclusions. In his chapter 5 of volume two, on "*sariqāt* and *muḥādhāt*" (thievery and close emulation),[69] he explains that a careful tabulation of terminology can be substantiated with examples and supported by references. No wonder, then, that he concludes his introductory note with this claim: "I have defined and divided these categories in an unprecedented manner, and I am unaware of any authorities on poetry who preceded me in their compilation."[70] Those who preceded him left their terminologies spread in their book usually as part of their critical arsenal for specific examples and applications. Thus, al-Ṣūlī, for instance, referenced *ilmām* (indirect inversion of an idea) as it recurred in his uncle's admission that he inverted a saying by the poet Muslim b. al-Walīd in his epistolary writing.[71] Although some later scholars who relied on him, especially Ibn Rashīq, complained of his extravagance in branching off and diversifying terminologies, al-Ḥātimī had his reasons for proving himself as a distinguished authority, an inclination that asserts its legitimacy in a highly competitive age and field. In line with an inclination to be on par with highly acclaimed poets and scholars like al-Āmidī, he manipulates

[67] The University of al-Qarawiyyīn (Al Quaraouiyine), in Fez, Morocco, was founded as a mosque by Fatima al-Fihri in 857–59; it became a leading educational and spiritual center, also known for its manuscript holdings.

[68] See al-Ḥātimī, *Ḥilyat al-muḥāḍarah*, 1:6–13.

[69] His use of *muḥādhāt* anticipates al-Jurjānī, *Dalāʾil al-iʿjāz*, 428.

[70] al-Ḥātimī, *Ḥilyat al-muḥāḍarah*, 2:28.

[71] al-Ṣūlī, *Akhbār Abī Tammām*, 102. His uncle's name: Ibrāhīm b. al-ʿAbbās al-Ṣūlī.

his talents indefatigably in order to draw a map for the widely discussed topic of thievery in relation to the craft of poetry, to which he devotes the first volume. His contention in chapter 5 of the second volume of *Ḥilyat al-muḥāḍarah* rests on a rejection of the popular critical articulations that either claim Arabic as a free zone without borders that permits *saraq* or its variables, or limit thievery to *lafẓ* (expression), not poetic ideas. Whatever has been argued in order to limit the raging thievery discussion, the trading of accusations was bound to undergo systematic interrogation. This questioning is exemplified by rich intertextual documentation and reference. Some philologists, such as the illustrious Abū ʿAlī al-Fārisī (d. 377/987), whom al-Ḥātimī met at the Ḥamdānī court of Prince Sayf al-Dawlah of Aleppo (d. 356/967),[72] were dismayed by excessive investigation of recurrent hints, duplications, expressions, or figures of speech. Abū ʿAlī al-Fārisī opened the gate by suggesting that "there is no *ijtilāb* [procuring support] or *istiʿārah* [here: the act of borrowing], and *kalām* [discourse, written and spoken Arabic] is open to all, and expressions are free."[73] Certainly, Ibn Ṭayfūr's summation that Arabic discursive space is welded and interwoven happened to be a common understanding among literati and scholars like al-Jāḥiẓ (see Figure 4.1).

١١٧

لا يسلم أن يكون كلامه أخذا من كلام غيره وإن اجتهد في الاحتراس
وتخلل طرق الكلام وباعد في المعنى وقارب في اللفظ وأفلت من شباك
التداخل ألا ترى إلى الأعرابي البادي لا يكتب ولا يقرأ ولا يروي ولا يحفظ
ولا يتمثل ولا يحتذي لا يكاد كلامه يخرج عن كلام من كان قبله ولا يسلك
إلا طريقة قد ذللت له فكيف لا يكون ذلك مع المتكلف المتصنع والمتعمد
القاصد ومن ظن أن كلامه لا يلتبس بكلام غيره فقد كذبه ظنه
وفضحه امتحانه ولو نظرنا في معاني الشعر وألفاظ البلاغة حتى نخلص
لكل شاعر أو بليغ ما تبرع فيه من لفظ وتفرد به من معنى لم يشركه فيه
أحد قبله ولا بعده لكان ذلك قليلا معدودا ونزرا محدودا ⑤
ويعم جميع الأسماء المصطلح عليها عند الفضلاء كلها اسم السرقة في الحقيقة

Figure 4.1 Discursive space as interfused textuality

[72] al-Ḥātimī, *Ḥilyat al-muḥāḍarah*, 2:29. [73] Abū ʿAlī al-Fārisī, quoted in ibid., 28.

Armed with a wide-ranging philological arsenal, al-Ḥātimī places *intiḥāl* (arrogating to oneself; confiscating others' verses) (see Figure 0.1) and *istilḥāq* (incurring support; or inserting another's verse in one's poetry as a matter of convenience) at the top of his list.[74] Apart from other possible justifications, his choice and placement of the term *intiḥāl* at the top of his register are not random. He collects available references, ancient and Islamic, to show that not even the prominent poets of pre-Islamic Arabia were immune to *intiḥāl* and *istilḥāq*, a point that supports his contentions and the principle behind his project, while at the same time ironically undermining them. If even eminent poets' poetry could involve thefts or approximations, then the practice entails that *kalām* or discursive space is a free zone, as Abū ʿAlī al-Fārisī concludes.[75] The case of *inḥāl* (assigning verses to another) is no less problematic. Al-Ḥātimī repeats what Ibn Sallām reports with respect to Ḥammād al-Rāwiyah as being the first to collect ancient poetry, but also as untrustworthy for assigning verses to others and augmenting some of them. He also repeats what is reported by al-Mubarrad with respect to Khalaf al-Aḥmar as being amazingly intelligent, knowledgeable in poetics, but also culpable. Al-Aṣmaʿī also incurs similar accusations of *inḥāl*; though the space allocated to *inḥāl* in *Ḥilyat al-muḥāḍarah* remains relatively small.[76] Al-Ḥātimī wishes to stress two things: first, uniqueness and inventiveness are minimal in a widely intermixed lingual space;[77] and second, poets' trading in accusations of *saraq* and *ijtilāb* only supports his underlying premise that *al-tafarrud* (distinctiveness) is far-fetched.[78] One may wonder if this underlying argument had already been on his mind to downplay al-Mutanabbī's towering reputation and the latter's claim to uniqueness, especially as al-Ḥātimī was commissioned to undermine the poet's fame and boastfulness.[79]

Although not necessarily in line with David Samuel Margoliouth (d. 1940) or Ṭāhā Ḥusayn (d. 1973), my argument here takes its cue from al-Qāḍī al-Jurjānī's use of the same case involving deliberate self-arrogation and reassignment as being indicative of the fluidity of a literary zone and its implied struggle, desire, and competition. A free-market economy is in motion, one that cannot be pinned down by categorical dismissals. That Ibn Rashīq is baffled at times by al-Ḥātimī in his *Ḥilyat al-muḥāḍarah* is understandable when we see that al-Ḥātimī or his editor embarks on large quotes from others, with a conclusive remark that runs

[74] al-Ḥātimī, *Ḥilyat al-muḥāḍarah*, 2:30–31. He used the same terms in his list of accusations against al-Mutanabbī.

[75] Abū ʿAlī al-Fārisī, quoted in ibid., 28. [76] al-Ḥātimī, *Ḥilyat al-muḥāḍarah*, 2:35–37.

[77] Ibid., 28. [78] Ibid., 29. [79] See the editor's preface in ibid., 1:12–13.

occasionally against the quote. However, it is reasonable to suggest that he acknowledges that there is indeed an open and fluid space, and that exceptionality is rare. His book is meant to be not only the summary of totalities but also the yardstick for arbitration. As his later work shows, he was prone to target big names, especially al-Mutanabbī, in order to deflate the poet's magnanimous presence. In *Ḥilyat al-muḥāḍarah* his attitude is better articulated in the discussion of *ighārah* (raiding part or all of the poet's expression, or poetic theme and verses), which follows the first two in sequence. Al-Ḥātimī's explanation suggests that *ighārah* means total confiscation, whether with the agreement of the owner or by compulsion (*qasran*).[80] Whenever the tendency is to reword the same theme or *maʿnā*, it is called *naẓar*, while *ikhtilās* implies a different direction that is less amenable to *saraq*. It means repositioning the original motif or meaning; and, in al-Qāḍī al-Jurjānī's reading, it means that the raided *maʿnā* is transposed away from its kind, type, rhythm, and compositional form (*naẓm*).[81]

While it was already a case studied or reported by Ibn Sallām and others, whom al-Ḥātimī mentions, the latter explains the logic, the poetic, and the ethic of this transactional activity. The stronger poet, like al-Farazdaq, hears elegant and impressive verses that are not in line with their own poet's corpus, but they sound more in keeping with the raider's poetry. Thus, he either "raids these with the consent of the lesser poet or forces the latter to cede them."[82] A power politics is in motion whereby the lesser poet buys his peace of mind, avoids the stronger poet's war, and also settles down in resignation. Al-Farazdaq was known for forcing others to give up verses that, in his opinion, were more in line with his poetry, especially as "his magnificent composition" appropriates these so neatly.[83]

To problematize this further, al-Ḥātimī adds that the possibility of a verbal fight between two poets over a verse or a piece of poetry can function as an occasion that invokes each poet's skill in uncovering the weakness of the other. The feud may end up with an agreement that a divine will is to strike the offender dead.[84] No matter how bewildering this may sound, its recurrence raises issues that relate to several things, including discussion of a possibly remarkable inventiveness that produces poetic meanings that are unbeatable for being *maʿānī ʿuqm: al-abkār al-mubtadaʿah* (created virgin meanings),[85] first fashioned by a single poet,

[80] al-Ḥātimī, *Ḥilyat al-muḥāḍarah*, 2:39.
[81] al-Jurjānī, *al-Wasāṭah*, 204 (1966), 178 (2006).
[82] al-Ḥātimī, *Ḥilyat al-muḥāḍarah*, 2:39. [83] Ibid. For examples, see ibid., 40.
[84] Ibid., 41–43. [85] Ibid., 42.

like Imruʾ al-Qays.[86] It is at this point that no one other than their originator can claim them.[87] Al-Ḥātimī's placement of the term at this intersection is part of his strategy to qualify inventiveness as a rarity that may not have been attained by anyone other than the ancients. Even when he applauds *muḥdathūn* as gate openers,[88] his listing of Imruʾ al-Qays's virgin meanings and use and the heavy presence of the ancients suggest that the modernists are at best capping a tradition, improving on it, and accumulating elegant meanings and expressions. He adds *muwāradah* (coincidental correspondence) as a possibility when two poets come up with the same meaning and correspond in wording and expression, quoting in support the often iterated, and also reported earlier, saying of Abū ʿAmrū b. al-ʿAlāʾ "their minds meet by chance on their tongues."[89] A quote from Abū ʿUbaydah Maʿmar b. al-Muthannā (d. 209/824) references Jarīr in his response to al-Farazdaq's assertion that Jarīr's recited verses are actually al-Farazdaq's: "Have you not known that our muse is one and the same?"[90] As these variations fall within a transactional activity, one that in the end substantiates al-Ḥātimī's project to provide an unprecedented catalog, he complements them with the concept of *murāfadah* (verse donation – i.e., ceding verses willingly),[91] as gifts, opening thereby another line in transaction. What we have in these elaborate multiplications are transactional dealings of lending and borrowing, and also of stealth and theft, as befitting a marketplace in a free zone where laws are more social and ethical than legally binding.

As is usual with al-Ḥātimī, while showing his meticulous coverage of a subject that has been growing in importance and value in the literary field, he is not satisfied merely to recover or genealogize material of bygone generations; he must also use every anecdotal narrative to make a point in an area in which he would like to be a reservoir and guide. Especially if it is viewed in terms of his subsequent venture in *al-Risālah al-mūḍiḥah* (The Explanatory [or Explicatory] Epistle), which is meant to place him on par with al-Mutanabbī's magisterial figure, his *Ḥilyat al-muḥāḍarah* (The Ornament of Discourse) deliberately goes over every available term, usually gleaned from the anecdotes that he recovers. Thus, when it comes to *murāfadah* (donation of a few lines to a lesser poet)[92] and its multiple applications and variables, readers cannot avoid

[86] See Ibn Sallām, *Ṭabaqāt al-shuʿarāʾ* (1998), 37, where Abū ʿAqīl Labīd said: "He [Imruʾ al-Qays] preceded Arabs to things that he created, and that the Arabs admired and followed."
[87] See al-Jurjānī, *al-Wasāṭah* (2006), 161.
[88] al-Ḥātimī, *Ḥilyat al-muḥāḍarah*, 2:82. This point is further explained later.
[89] Ibid., 45; Bonebakker, "Ancient Arabic Poetry and Plagiarism," 87.
[90] al-Ḥātimī, *Ḥilyat al-muḥāḍarah*, 2:47. See also n. 102 in Chapter 2.
[91] Ibid., 49.
[92] Ibid., 49–50.

noticing the well-read critic posing as a polymath. Like many of his generation, he fails to explore the reasons as to why some strong poets offer this poetic help. Some of these anecdotes demonstrate that strong poets have cut a style and comportment of their own, to such an extent that another strong poet can easily trace and track down a verse donated to others. In other words, there is a lively climate, a literary and broad cultural marketplace, one where an exchange of gifts takes place gratuitously and as a show of magnanimity. Especially in cases that warrant no accusation of thievery, like *ijtilāb* and *istilḥāq* (borrowing and including a verse as a common exemplary reference),[93] the critic calls on Yūnus b. Ḥabīb and others from among *al-ʿulamāʾ bi-l-shiʿr* (the knowledgeable in poetry) to side with them in stating that these practices are not reprehensible. Although al-Ḥātimī is the first to compile terms and trace their genealogical tree, he avoids as much as possible controversial attitudes. Thus, his list of reprehensible practices (see Figure 4.2) does not side with Abū ʿAmrū b. al-ʿAlāʾ, for example, who dismisses *istilḥāq* and *ijtilāb* as thefts (see Figure 5.2). Nevertheless, his terminological lexicon is rich with ancestral referentiality. It is rare to come across many invented

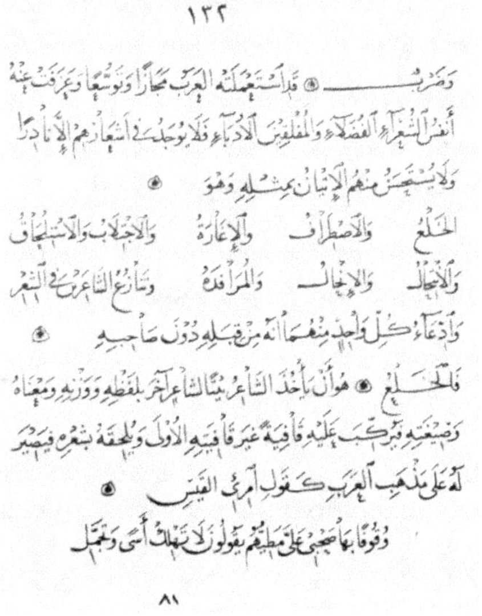
١٣٢

وضرب ــــــــ قد استعملته العرب مجازا وتوسعا وعرفت عنه
أنفس الشعراء الفضلاء والمفلقين الأدباء فلا يوجد في أشعارهم إلا نادرا
ولا يستحسن منهم الإتيان بمثله وهو
الخلع والاصطراف والإغارة والاجتلاب والاستلحاق
والانتحال والإنحال والمرافدة وتنازع الشاعرين في الشعر
وادعاء كل واحد منهما أنه من قبله دون صاحبه
فالخلع هو أن يأخذ الشاعر بيتا لشاعر آخر بلفظه ووزنه ومعناه
وصيغته فيركب عليه قافية غير قافيته الأولى ويلحقه بشعره فيصير
له على مذهب العرب كقول امرئ القيس
وقوفا بها صحبي على مطيهم يقولون لا تهلك أسى وتجمل

٨١

Figure 4.2 Reprehensible practices

93 Ibid., 58.

terms, as the cultural script is so rich with disputes and feuds that critics have no trouble in coming across the appropriate term. The patching or piecing together of bits (*talfīq*) and processes from several verses, including *ilmām* (inversion of a theme) and *naẓar* (a theme redirected in form), can account for cultural dynamics and an invigorating poetic climate in search of a definitive system.[94] While al-Ḥātimī calls upon ancestry in support of his critical effort, a self-augmentation is no less a dynamic. If poets fight for ascendancy and glory, so do critics. Al-Ḥātimī deserves attention because he anticipates Harold Bloom's Romantics, who cannot hide their egoistic, celebratory tone.

Although al-Ḥātimī adds little to the production of idioms, his profuse idiomatic gleanings from anecdotes or even from other critics' contributions help in the organization of a systematic manual and reservoir that will survive in every other discussion of *sariqāt* and its variables or disputations.[95] Dependency on ancestry in this respect undergoes a process of tabulation, as al-Ḥātimī does, for example, when studying *al-iṣṭirāf* (self-attribution of a verse or two from another poet) and *al-ihtidām* (self-attribution with minor change) or *ikhtilās* and *naql* (thematic transference from one domain to another).[96] The anecdotes, which he cites quite often with their funny twist, illustrate a thriving cultural exchange among peers. Although these examples show him as a compiler and literary scholar, he has moved away from a detailed literary study like al-Āmidī's. We are in the presence of a critic and anthologist, while in al-Āmidī's case, we meet a robust literary critic and knowledgeable scholar. This should not minimize al-Ḥātimī's contribution, for the organization of a rich collection of *saraq* material, one that had accumulated over three centuries and was responsible for invigorating literary theorization, anticipates the European tabulation of knowledge centuries later.

Tabulation as an Invigorating Theoretical Dynamic

On the positive side, listing these terms and their variables, as they are shown in a rich poetic tradition that includes reference to poetic and anecdotal feuds, enables later generations of readership and assembly discussions to regenerate further discussions whenever they celebrate a later poetic improvement at the expense of an early originator, or when both the originator and the emulator have the same poetic value. The term *majdūd* (see Figure 4.4) provides a useful way to account for the

94 On patching, see ibid., 90.
95 See the editor's list of contemporary and medieval references and quotes in his preface in ibid., 1:6–13.
96 Ibid., 2:58, 61, 64.

reasons behind the fame attending a belated application when the latter poet endows his new application with vigor or elegance to the disadvantage of the origin, the hypotext. Thus, al-Kumayt and Kuthayyir were known for practices that fall under *majdūd* as a term for fame attending a better application of an original (see also Figure 3.2).[97] Al-Ḥātimī can go out of his way to differ from others, such as his opinion on *al-ishtirāk fī al-lafẓ* (sharing wording and expressions that are common), which cannot be denigrated as *saraq*.[98] He also allows space for equivalence (*takāfuʾ*) between the inventor/innovator and the follower/imitator when the latter is no less a creator, unlike the one who is less equipped (see Figure 4.3),[99] a point that Abū Bakr al-Ṣūlī also discusses.[100] In this discussion he opens a window on anxieties that unveil a poet's struggle to express, beat, or improve on an earlier impressive verse.[101] While invigorative, the anxiety may also derail the possibility of a sustainable poetic. The examples that he has garnered are central to an understanding of the anxiety of influence as both a positive and disruptive force.[102] Tenth-century critics demonstrate an amazing flexibility to allow space for thinking of poetic

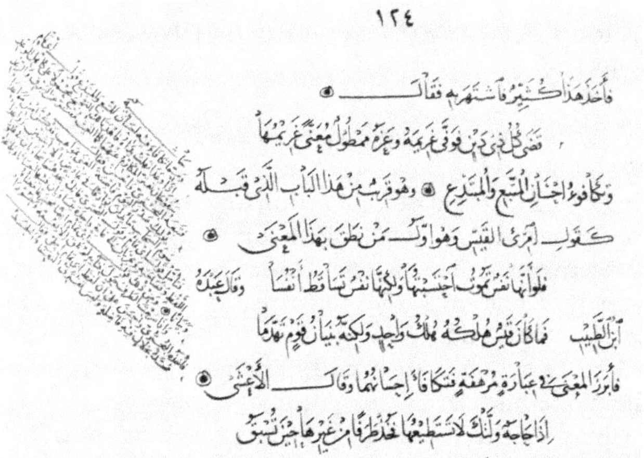
١٢٤

فأخذه كثير فاشتهر به فقال

تقضى كل ذي دين فوفى غريمه وعزة ممطول معنى غريمها

وتكافؤ احسان المتبع والمبتدع وهو قريب من هذا الباب الذي قبله

كقول امرئ القيس وهو اول من نطق بهذا المعنى

فلو انها نفس تموت جميعة ولكنها نفس تساقط انفسا وقال عبدة

ابن الطيب فما كان قيس هلكه هلك واحد ولكنه بنيان قوم تهدما

فابرز المعنى في عبارة مرصفة فتكافا احسانهما وقال الأعشى

إذا حاجة ولتك لا تستطيعها فخذ طرفا من غيرها حين تسبق

وقال عمرو بن معديكرب

إذا لم تستطع شيئا فدعه وجاوزه الى ما تستطيع

٧٧

Figure 4.3 Equivalence in poetic value between the originator and follower (*takāfuʾ*)

[97] Ibid., 67. [98] Ibid., 68. [99] Ibid., 73–74. [100] See further in Chapter 5.
[101] al-Ḥātimī, *Ḥilyat al-muḥāḍarah*, 2:76. [102] Ibid., 74–77.

١٢٣

Figure 4.4 *Al-Majdūd* (fame gained by the follower at the expense of the creator)

equivalence of a former and a later verse as a deft and skillful practice (see Figures 4.3 and 3.2).

In one single succinct and deft reflection on newness and inventiveness, al-Ḥātimī departs from his cataloging or supportive anecdotal reservoir to speak of a thematic and expressive turn in a different direction. He describes it as the "craft of *kalām* constructors [*rāṣṣat al-kalām*], jewelers of meanings, and artful thieves, to conceal thievery, or hide close replication, and to cover subordination and imitation."[103] At this juncture, he applauds the modernists for opening the gate to new meanings and expressions, unearthing the hidden, and awakening the dormant and slothful.[104]

The Consolidation of the Term *Nuqqād* (Critics)

His immediate successor is no less than Ibn Rashīq al-Qayrawānī (d. Sicily, 456/1063–64 or 463/1071),[105] who makes a good case for his recent predecessors al-Qāḍī al-Jurjānī (d. 392/1001)[106] and al-Ḥātimī Ibn

[103] Ibid., 82. This will be replicated by Ibn Rashīq. [104] Ibid.
[105] Full name: Abū ʿAlī al-Ḥasan b. Rashīq al-Qayrawānī.
[106] Grunebaum, "Concept of Plagiarism," 240, confused al-Qāḍī Abū al-Ḥasan ʿAlī b. ʿAbd al-ʿAzīz al-Jurjānī with ʿAbd al-Qāhir al-Jurjānī. In his *al-ʿUmdah*, Ibn Rashīq

Rashīq's relatively succinct review of the issue supports al-Qāḍī al-Jurjānī's reading of *sariqāt*, "as he was better in method and investigation than many who delved into the topic."[107] Ibn Rashīq's opening sentence repeats in meaning and direction al-Qāḍī al-Jurjānī's conclusive remark, namely, that plagiarism is an old malady from which nobody can totally be free. He quotes at length al-Qāḍī al-Jurjānī's statement that it is only when you are familiar with *saraq* – including its divisions and categories – and are aware of its parts and implications that you can be counted among the knowledgeable in *kalām* and critics of poetry.[108] Thus, building on al-Qāḍī al-Jurjānī's discernment and distinction between one term and another, Ibn Rashīq collapses some of al-Ḥātimī's distinctions: he quotes al-Qāḍī al-Jurjānī's definitive statement that a person cannot be claimed to be an authority unless he is capable of distinguishing between the application of terms. Thus, a distinction is called for between *saraq* (thievery) and *ghaṣb* (forceful taking over); between *ighārah* (taking over part but not all of the other's thought)[109] and *ikhtilās* (transferring the borrowed thought to another part of a poem, or to another purpose); and between *ilmām* (antonym of the model's meaning) and *naẓar* (indicative refraction of a theme), or, in ʿAbd al-Karīm al-Nahshalī's (d. 405/1014) understanding of the term in his *al-Mumtiʿ* (The Enjoyable): whatever has its meaning transferred without its *lafẓ*. Ibn Rashīq's long quote from al-Qāḍī al-Jurjānī differentiates shared and common meaning from earlier verbal composition and its contemporary or later duplicators. Neither Ibn Rashīq's nor al-Qāḍī al-Jurjānī's (d. 392/1001) contemporary – that is, al-Ḥātimī (d. 388/998) – can do justice to al-Qāḍī al-Jurjānī because he is foremost in speaking of *al-nāqid al-baṣīr* (the insightful critic) and *nuqqād al-shiʿr* (poetry critics), while his other terms, such as *al-ʿālim al-mubarraz* (distinguished scientist – i.e., expert) and *jahābidhat al-kalām* (the most knowledgeable in philology), are already in use.[110] This is al-Qāḍī al-Jurjānī's stepping stone that allows him to differentiate all the primary terminologies that comprise the theory of plagiarism and become the base for any further reading. This terminological register assumes its major significance because al-Qāḍī al-Jurjānī places it in a literary argument that enhances the discussion as a literary and cultural movement where there are dynamics, but also systems and refractions. His examples for each case of stark theft, indiscernible theft, or

takes verbatim from al-Qāḍī Abū al-Ḥasan ʿAlī's book *al-Waṣāṭah*; the passage can be found in *al-Wasāṭah* (1966), 183–84.

107 Ibn Rashīq, *al-ʿUmdah* (2001), 2:282, 2:280–81; *al-ʿUmdah* (1972), 2:280. Another print is by Maṭbaʿat al-Saʿādah (Cairo, 1955).

108 The passage Ibn Rashīq quotes appears in al-Jurjānī, *al-Wasāṭah* (1966), 280.

109 A word of caution here, as al-Ḥātimī thinks of it as a forceful takeover whenever a strong poet finds the owner's verse more in line with his own poetry.

110 al-Jurjānī, *al-Wasāṭah* (1966), 183–84, 185–86, 188, 193, 201, 204, 206, 208.

improvement on the original flow smoothly to inform and indirectly educate the public. This reading considers al-Qāḍī al-Jurjānī's writing to have either a *tawārud* (coincidental correspondence) with some of al-Ḥātimī's statements or an oblique impact on the latter. Al-Qāḍī al-Jurjānī's critical register and its commanding presence in literary terms and their placement in a flowing literary text suggest this latter explanation, though the exact date of al-Ḥātimī's book could offer another perspective.

With the Qayrawān school, to which Ibn Rashīq belongs, in mind, the latter refers to ʿAbd al-Karīm al-Nahshalī's dismissal of most of these practices as thievery. Al-Nahshalī thinks that *saraq* in poetry means "whatever … has its meaning transferred without its wording."[111] While striving in his critical compendium *al-ʿUmdah* to account for the craft of poetry – that is, poetics and criticism – Ibn Rashīq often refers to "some of the sagacious writers" of later periods to account for popular sayings like ʿAbd al-Raḥmān al-Hamadhānī's summary: "The person who takes over meaning and wording is a thief; but, if he changes some of the wording, he is flaying; and if he is changing some of the meaning to redirect it, this is evidence of skillfulness."[112] Ibn Rashīq qualifies the common reference to poetic meanings, suggesting that "what is meant by invented meanings that invite theft are the directions, organization, and the means to attain them."[113] Underlying the whole argument and terminology is a compelling desire to achieve distinction.

He quotes also from al-Qāḍī al-Jurjānī (and also from al-Āmidī), noting that *saraq* only occurs in invented *badīʿ* by which a poet is distinguished.[114] This is Ibn Rashīq's stepping stone that allows him to use and review al-Ḥātimī's *Ḥilyat al-muḥāḍarah* and "his novel idioms," which Ibn Rashīq deems of "no consequence if placed under scrutiny."[115] His criticism centers not only on al-Ḥātimī's multiplication of terms that are approximate to each other, but also on the misplacement of some.[116] He accepts al-Qāḍī al-Jurjānī's distinction between a shared property, where chances of plagiarism occur, the commonplace and hackneyed, which nobody claims, and the original contribution that in time becomes shared property. In *Qurāḍat al-dhahab fī naqd ashʿār al-ʿArab* (Gold Specks in Appraising the Poetry of the Arabs), Ibn Rashīq claims to have on his side *al-ʿulamāʾ wa-l-nuqqād* (the knowledgeable and the critics), "who say that *saraq* occurs in the rare *badīʿ* and the exceptional."[117] Before focusing on the significant recurrence of the use

[111] Ibn Rashīq, *al-ʿUmdah* (2001), 2:280. [112] Ibid., 281.
[113] Ibn Rashīq, *Qurāḍat al-dhahab*, 55.
[114] Grunebaum, "Concept of Plagiarism," 238, suggests it means "original."
[115] Ibn Rashīq, *al-ʿUmdah* (2001), 2:282. [116] Ibid., 280.
[117] Ibn Rashīq, *Qurāḍat al-dhahab*, 20.

of the term *naqd* and *nuqqād* or *naqadah*, his long opening quote from al-Qāḍī al-Jurjānī's *al-Wasāṭah* allows him to present his own idioms, which nevertheless show no substantial departure from his immediate predecessors. As an informative compendium, his *al-ʿUmdah* is a critical review of the available literature on the topic where he makes use of criticism, especially by al-Qāḍī al-Jurjānī, al-Ḥātimī, and al-Nahshalī. In the chapter titled "*al-Sariqāt wa-mā shākalahā*" (Plagiarisms and Their Like), he expresses the need to tabulate terms in line with al-Qāḍī al-Jurjānī's opening pages on the topic. More important is his endorsement of the latter's view that what was once an invented meaning would become a common use for later generations.[118] No one before al-Qāḍī al-Jurjānī had ever come up with a dialectic formulation that takes into account not only historical processes but also the sociocultural application of linguistic fluidity and transformations. Al-Qāḍī al-Jurjānī argues:

> What deservedly has a claim once to invention and creativity has become publicly available and is not counted as theft in our age, neither is it counted as being "*maʾkhūdhan*" [forcibly seized], even though its origin belongs to the one who is its single inventor, the first one to use and apply it, as in comparing the deserted vanishing ruins with a fading trace.[119]

Ibn Rashīq builds on that and on Ibn Ṭabāṭabā's *ʿIyār*, without specifying his name, to argue that "there is a decrease in invented meanings, and a corresponding one in thievery. If the latter happens, it becomes notorious."[120] This leads him to conclude, in line with predecessors like Ibn Ṭayfūr and later al-Qāḍī al-Jurjānī, that "*kalām* [discourse] derives from discourse, and they are interdependent. The skillfulness displayed in seizing on some new meanings varies."[121] Ibn Rashīq's criticism is explicatory, evaluative, and compendious. He can dismiss Ibn Wakīʿ's *Munṣif* as *ladīgh* (stinging) for being an open and biting attack on al-Mutanabbī, whom Ibn Rashīq counts – alongside Abū al-ʿAlāʾ and, before them, Imruʾ al-Qays and Bashshār – as being foremost in poetic meanings and the accumulation of these meanings in one verse.[122]

These insights fall within the framework of Ibn Rashīq's literary criticism in *Qurāḍat al-dhahab*, which, as its editor notes,[123] accounts for his literary views on "poetic creation," as shown in a genealogy drawn of the first creation of some usage, later use, and application. On the other hand, *al-ʿUmdah* signifies another turn in compendious authoring by the end of the fourth/tenth and early fifth/eleventh century when authors are also editors and compilers. While his idiomatic map echoes others and strives

[118] See al-Jurjānī, *al-Wasāṭah* (1966), 185. [119] Ibid., 184.
[120] Ibn Rashīq, *Qurāḍat al-dhahab*, 22. [121] Ibid., 54. [122] Ibid., 22, 24, 26.
[123] Ibid. See the editor's introduction in ibid., 6.

to collapse some ancillary (or what Grunebaum calls al-Ḥātimī's "newfangled") terminology,[124] its value lies in being a synthesizing point in a theoretical and critical process aimed at providing a dictionary of relevance to Arabic theory. Thus, it has to be made clear to users that what is referred to, by way of an idiom in use such as *iṣṭirāf* (a self-acquisition of a verse by another poet because the later poet finds it more fitting in his poem) (see Figure 4.5), is also called *ijtilāb* and *istilhāq* if it is applied as being proverbial;[125] but if adopted in full, then it falls into the category of *intiḥāl*. He collapses terms like *ighārah* and *ghaṣb*, and almost all others, like piecing together bits from a number of verses, which he places under *talfīq*, *iltiqāṭ* or *ijtidhāb*, and *tarkīb*, as used by others.[126]

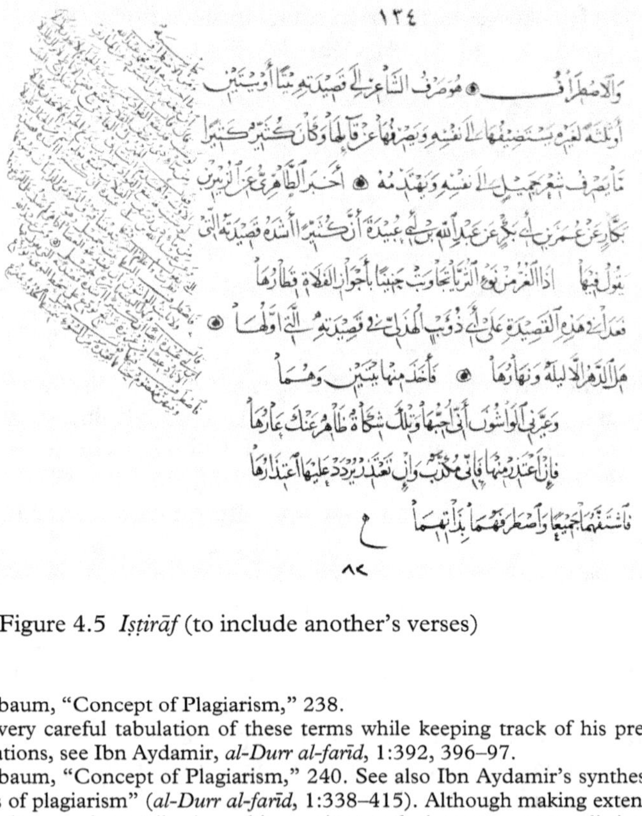
١٣٤
والاصطراف ﴿ هو صرف الشاعر الى قصيدته بيتا او بيتين
او لغيره يستضيفها الى نفسه ويصرفها عن قائلها وكان كثير كثيرا
ما يصرف شعر جميل الى نفسه ويتهدده ﴿ اخبر الطاهري عن الزبير
بكار عن عمر بن ابي بكر عن عبد الله بن ابي عبيدة ان كثيرا انشد قصيدته التي
يقول فيها اذا الغمر من نوء الثريا تحاوبت جنينا باجواز الفلاة قطارها
فعدل هذه القصيدة على ابي ذؤيب الهذلي في قصيدته التي اولها
هل الدهر الا ليلة ونهارها ﴿ فاخذ منها بيتين وهما
وعيرني الواشون اني احبها وتلك شكاة ظاهر عنك عارها
فان اعتذر منها فاني مكذب وان تعتذر يردد عليها اعتذارها
فاشتقهما جميعا واصطرفهما بذاتهما
٨٢

Figure 4.5 *Iṣṭirāf* (to include another's verses)

[124] Grunebaum, "Concept of Plagiarism," 238.

[125] For a very careful tabulation of these terms while keeping track of his predecessors' applications, see Ibn Aydamir, *al-Durr al-farīd*, 1:392, 396–97.

[126] Grunebaum, "Concept of Plagiarism," 240. See also Ibn Aydamir's synthesis of "categories of plagiarism" (*al-Durr al-farīd*, 1:338–415). Although making extensive use of his predecessors' contributions, his succinct and elegant coverage distinguishes his compilation as a significant contribution. See further Geert Jan van Gelder, ed., *Two Arabic Treatises on Stylistics: al-Marghīnānī's al-Maḥāsin fī 'l-naẓm wa-'l-nathr, and Ibn Aflaḥ's Muqaddima, formerly ascribed to al-Marghīnānī* (Leiden: Brill, 1987). Van Gelder adds an introduction, "Ibn Aflaḥ and His *Muqaddima*," 5–14, 26–41; for the Arabic text, see 1–65.

In a short space, the second page of his study of thievery, he sums up the idioms that al-Ḥātimī multiplies.[127] While seemingly too meticulous or superfluous, the effort is pivotal to the economies of theft. If past or current economies require scales, measurements, guidelines, and checks and balances, the literary market must have its own clear criteria. Critics or literary scholars are no longer outsiders; they are the literary market-inspectors who must agree on a set of terms to assess commodities and literary merchandise. On the other hand, the implications of these terms and the practices that called on critics to intervene and tabulate the domain lead us as readers to the motivating and compelling force of a desire for distinction. The availability of an interfused poetic space, the discursive *kalām*, could also, even unwittingly, involve poets in an act of marauding others' poetry.

Discourse on Discourse (*Kalām ʿalā Kalām*) as Justification for Fluidity

In line with al-Qāḍī al-Jurjānī's argument with respect to historical processes and the attending literary and cultural transformations, we as readers assume that another turn has to take over consequent to the organization and arrangement offered by critics and scholars of the eighth to the eleventh centuries. Al-Qāḍī al-Jurjānī does not negate the existence of *saraq*, but he approaches it as an art that he associates with competitiveness for distinction, a point that is already emphasized. As discourse builds on discourse, repetition is inevitable; and hence modernists strive to hide replication (*saraq*) by *naql* (transference) (see Figure 3.1) and *qalb* (reversal of another poet's saying, using some of that first poet's vocabulary, and changing method).[128] By the same token and in the context of idiomacy and specialized parlance, applied replication acquires further improvement and vigor among the elite whenever it enjoys recurrence, and hence distinction as a term. In other words, what was once part of a daily discursive/verbal space gained through recurrence the power of a phrase or term. Thus, even when authors are unconcerned about the thievery controversy per se, these terms find – by force of recurrence – a way into their writing. Al-Sakkākī (d. 626/1229) in his groundbreaking *Miftāḥ al-ʿulūm* (The Key to Sciences),[129] for example, repeats how Dhū

[127] For a guide to these terms and their meanings, see Grunebaum, "Concept of Plagiarism," 238–40. More to the point is Ibn Aydamir's discussion of "categories of plagiarism" in *al-Durr al-farīd*, 1:338–415.

[128] al-Jurjānī, *al-Wasāṭah* (1966), 214; on *qalb*, see ibid., 206.

[129] Full name: Abū Yaʿqūb Yūsuf al-Sakkākī.

al-Rummah – that is, Ghīlān b. ʿUqbah (d. 117/735) – entreated (*istarfada*) the poet Jarīr (d. 110/728), requesting poetic help (*murāfadah*) (i.e., voluntary cession of verses). He therefore inserted (*ḍammanahā*) those verses in his poem.[130]

Instead of further accumulation of new terminology, there arises an effort to direct discussion and attention to rhetoric, whereby a body of figures of speech appears side by side with a long praise poem addressed to the Prophet.[131] The *badīʿiyyah* tradition functions as part of a mounting turn to prose, one that Ibn al-Athīr encourages, as will become clear in due course. Broadly speaking, the dialogue concerning *sariqāt* no longer involves a desperate search for accusations, a leveling of blames, and a hunt for disparagement, as it had once been with al-Ḥātimī and a few others: it becomes more of a domain in rhetoric and structuration. Al-Qāḍī al-Jurjānī and later Ibn Rashīq in *Qurāḍat al-dhahab* had already drawn attention to the *muḥdathūn*'s effort to avert accusations by resorting to transference, reversal, and change in method and structure.[132]

Placing *Saraq* in Innovation and Invention

Thus, it is not surprising that ʿAbd al-Qāhir al-Jurjānī (d. 471/1078) and later al-Khaṭīb al-Qazwīnī (d. 739/1338) place the discussion of *akhdh* and *saraq* in the context of a *badīʿ* tradition. In other words, terminologies take two significant directions that have as their background not only al-Āmidī's, and especially al-Qāḍī al-Jurjānī's, detailed discussions of thievery, but also al-Ḥātimī's *Ḥilyat al-muḥāḍarah* and probably Ibn Rashīq's *al-ʿUmdah*. One direction is a rhetorical turn that highlights *badīʿ* (inventiveness and imaginativeness) in poetry, as espoused structurally by ʿAbd al-Qāhir al-Jurjānī; another is a belletristic one that situates the discussion in the rising tide of belles lettres, a direction that Ibn al-Athīr applies and expands on in a few of his books. Both signify a step forward in developing a literary theory complex that moves further away from controversy, rebuttal, and correction toward a systematized construction of knowledge. ʿAbd al-Qāhir al-Jurjānī's nuanced grammatology channels the reading of *akhdh* (seizure) and *saraq* (theft) as a matter of *ittifāq* (correspondence and similarity).

130 Abū Yaʿqūb Yūsuf al-Sakkākī, *Miftāḥ al-ʿulūm*, ed. Naʿīm Zurzūr (Beirut: Dār al-Kutub al-ʿIlmiyyah, 2nd print, 1987), 580.

131 See al-Musawi, *Republic of Letters*, 39–40, 120–21, 148–50, 161–66; Stetkevych, *Mantle Odes*.

132 See al-Jurjānī, *al-Wasāṭah* (1966), 214; Ibn Rashīq, *Qurāḍat al-dhahab*, 22.

"Know that, if two poets happened to be similar, it is usually in a common theme or in signification."[133] His chapter on "agreement in *akhdh*, *saraq*, *istimdād*, and *isti ʿānah* [i.e., seeking help]" shows his awareness of contemporary popular idioms,[134] but he replaces *istirfād* (procuring assistance) with the last two. He is unequivocal in supporting predecessors' judgment, namely, that a common theme or meaning cannot be part of the discussion of *akhdh* or *sariqah*. Thus, whatever is common knowledge or customary cannot be a reason for accusation, a point emphasized by al-Qāḍī al-Jurjānī.[135] The exception is specific ownership "that has been reached by thought and skill and achieved by diligence and perseverance."[136] This is where "precedence" counts; and hence the ultimate transaction that is either historically efficient as between precursor and successor, or economic between "benefactor and beneficiary."[137]

Opening the Gate: No Creditors and Debtors

In sum, ʿAbd al-Qāhir al-Jurjānī dismisses what is shared and common as not being an issue for prioritization. Instead, he stresses the attentive use of figures of speech and the use of suggestion and allusion that demonstrate skill and personal artistry.[138] While this is only a summary of what earlier authorities had articulated, ʿAbd al-Qāhir al-Jurjānī's phrasing falls within the context of his lexical inventory that synthesizes general and elaborate explanatory statements. Literary criticism assumes specific terminologies that concomitantly release the issue of *akhdh* and *sariqah* from its burdensome paraphernalia. A cautionary remark is worthwhile at this point: ʿAbd al-Qāhir al-Jurjānī does not shy away from using available material, such as Abū Manṣūr al-Thaʿālibī's (d. 429/1039) *Yatīmat al-dahr*, in order to show how the Khālidiyyān Brothers seized on a verse by Ibn al-Muʿtazz (*akhadha ... akhdhan*).[139] Even so, ʿAbd al-Qāhir al-Jurjānī agrees with earlier authorities that *saraq* is applicable only to invented *badīʿ*, or to what he terms *takhyīlī* (make-believe), *khidāʿ li-l-ʿaql* (trickery of the mind), and *ḍarbun min al-tazwīq* (a kind of ornament),[140] which shows a unique unearthing, one "which is to be reached by deep thought and devotional exertion, and only achieved

[133] ʿAbd al-Qāhir al-Jurjānī, *Asrār al-balāghah*, ed. Muḥammad Rashīd Riḍā (Beirut: Dār al-Maʿrifah, 2002), 277; and in the edition published by al-Risālah (Beirut, 2007), 242.
[134] Ibid., 277 (2002), 242 (2007). [135] al-Qāḍī al-Jurjānī, *al-Wasāṭah* (1966), 214.
[136] ʿAbd al-Qā hir al-Jurjānī, *Asrār al-balāghah*, 279 (2002), 243 (2007).
[137] Ibid., 278 (2002). [138] Ibid.
[139] Ibid., 242–43 (2002), 211–12 (2007); al-Thaʿālibī, *Yatīmat al-dahr*, 2:180.
[140] Lara Harb comes up with these translations, which are very close to the author's meaning; see Harb, *Arabic Poetics*, 51, 52.

after deliberation, meditation, and *ḥafr* (excavation)."[141] His practical examples are not confined to comparisons of one poet with another. Examples are only a road map for readers. In his *Dalāʾil al-iʿjāz* he is more specific and more in line with Ibn Qutaybah in indicting *salkh* (flaying).[142] To him, *iḥtidhāʾ* incurs no blame as long as it means following a first poet's style (*uslūb*) or pattern of expression[143] in order to fit into the later poet's poetic meaning.[144] However, another caution is in order at this point. *Uslūb* (style; pl. *asālīb*; also molds)[145] here means "*al-ḍarb min al-naẓm wa-l-ṭarīqah fīhī*" (a form of compositional structure and applied method),[146] but ʿAbd al-Qāhir al-Jurjānī qualifies this further because the phrasing used by ʿAbd al-Raḥmān al-Hamadhānī, in relation to having a *maʿnā* clad in the later poet's wording, should mean not verbal enunciation, but a *ṣūrah* (form) or, in another place, *al-ṭarīqah*, a method of attribution,[147] which, as von Grunebaum rightly deduces, "constitutes literary property, and hence a possible object of plagiarism."[148] On the other hand, if the later poet takes over the idea or poetic meaning and changes some, not all, of its wording, *lafẓ*, it is a blameworthy practice that shows no poetic talent.[149] Although there is no mention of al-Qāḍī al-Jurjānī and his concise phrasing with respect to what he terms *fard mukhtaraʿ* (exceptional invention) and *gharīb mubtadaʿ* (unfamiliar or exceptional innovation),[150] one can tell that ʿAbd al-Qāhir al-Jurjānī's familiarity with al-Qāḍī al-Jurjānī's terminology, and the terminology of other predecessors, does not prevent him from rewording them in order to fit into his systematization of a two-pronged structure that separates the *ʿaqlī*, as inclusive of the customary, commonsensical, proverbial, and revered tradition, from the *takhyīlī* (make-believe). Although von Grunebaum thinks that "his distinction between imitation of style and imitation of *maʿānī* and wording has been discarded without leaving any trace in the final system,"[151] both al-Sakkākī and his explicators or detractors echo some of ʿAbd al-Qāhir al-Jurjānī's phrasing and application.

Al-Qazwīnī's introductory note to "*al-sariqāt al-shiʿriyyah*" regarding common meanings and relevant significations repeats what ʿAbd al-Qāhir

141 ʿAbd al-Qā hir al-Jurjānī, *Asrār al-balāghah*, 279 (2002), 243 (2007).
142 al-Jurjānī, *Dalāʾil al-iʿjāz*, 471.
143 Grunebaum's suggestion in "Concept of Plagiarism," 241.
144 See al-Jurjānī, *Dalāʾil al-iʿjāz*, 428.
145 Heinrichs's application makes no reference to al-Jurjānī, *Dalāʾil al-iʿjāz*, as his focus is on these as molds, as "a result of the intensive and extensive study of earlier poetry on the part of the later poet, and they establish intertextuality even where this is not consciously sought after." Heinrich, "An Evaluation of 'Sariqa,'" 365.
146 al-Jurjānī, *Dalāʾil al-iʿjāz*, 428. 147 Ibid., 437.
148 Grunebaum, "Concept of Plagiarism," 241n71. 149 Ibid.
150 al-Qāḍī al-Jurjānī, *al-Wasāṭah* (1966), 214–15.
151 Grunebaum, "Concept of Plagiarism," 244.

argues in *Asrār*. The significant shift from the precursors' argumentative-explanatory method to a logical reasoning that is relatively free from the names of creditors and debtors is not an ordinary one, especially if we take into account later developments in the readings of al-Qazwīnī's *al-Īḍāḥ* and its explicators. Thus, instead of the common use of *maʿnā* (shared idea or poetic meaning), we have *gharaḍ*, a term that plays in turn on shared or specific use and thematic subgenres that recall *aghrāḍ al-shiʿr*. On the other hand, common meanings or figures of speech (simile, conceit, metaphor, allusion, etc.) are collapsed under *wajh al-dilālah ʿalā al-gharaḍ* (signifiers and signified).[152] As noticed by von Grunebaum, al-Qazwīnī's combined endeavor to work out a synthetic meeting ground between *ʿilm al-maʿānī* and *ʿilm al-naḥw* is "comparatively easy to follow,"[153] especially if, as readers, we keep in mind his indebtedness to ʿAbd al-Qāhir's *Asrār*.[154]

In the footsteps of ʿAbd al-Qāhir, al-Qazwīnī also dismisses shared or common applications and expressions, noting that they are available to all and hence fall outside the domain of *saraq*. Plagiarism is systematically divided into two categories: outward or overt, on the one hand, and discreet or hidden, on the other. Al-Qazwīnī takes the same position as his predecessors in thinking of "seizing on all" of a verse without changing its compositional pattern (*naẓm*) as *madhmūm mardūd* (reprehensible and unacceptable). He adds: "It is so because it is a glaring theft, called replication and arrogation."[155] A partial change in the compositional pattern or expression is given the term *ighārah* (raid) or *maskh* (distortion).[156] He qualifies this as commendable when the successor provides a formation in meaning or expression that is better or is distinguished by brevity or explication. Von Grunebaum sums up al-Qazwīnī's discussion by pointing out that *naskh* as *intiḥāl* is a confiscation of an idea or poetic theme with all or partial wording that retains "the pattern of composition [*naẓm*]"[157] (see Figure 0.1, *naskh* as *intiḥāl*). Included here is the theft of an idea, but one that uses word-by-word synonymous expressions and does not infringe on *naẓm* (compositional pattern).[158]

[152] Compare ʿAbd al-Qāhir al-Jurjānī's chapter on the difference between simile and metaphor, *Asrār al-balāghah*, 202–19 (2002), 242 (2007), with al-Khaṭīb al-Qazwīnī, *al-Īḍāḥ fī ʿulūm al-balāghah*, 2 vols. (each with 6 parts), ed. ʿAbd al-Munʿim Khafājī (Beirut: Dār al-Jīl, n.d.), 2:120–21 (pt. 6); al-Qazwīnī's discussion spans pp. 119–56.

[153] Grunebaum, "Concept of Plagiarism," 244.

[154] See Khafājī's notes in al-Qazwīnī, *al-Īḍāḥ*, 119. Shallāl mentioned this combination in al-Jurjānī, *Asrār al-balāghah* (2002), 202.

[155] al-Qazwīnī, *al-Īḍāḥ*, 122. His phrases are *sariqah maḥḍah* (stark theft), *naskh* (replication), and *intiḥāl* (arrogation to self).

[156] al-Khaṭīb al-Qazwīnī, *Talkhīṣ al-Miftāḥ* (Karachi: Maktabat al-Bushrā, 2010), 142.

[157] Grunebaum, "Concept of Plagiarism," 244. [158] Ibid.

Both *ighārah* (open raid with the consent or otherwise of the owner) and *maskh* are reprehensible because there is a plundering of a poetic idea or *maʿnā* camouflaged as a change in compositional pattern. If the poet only takes over the *maʿnā*, then he is practicing *ilmām* (indirect invasion of a theme) or *salkh* (flaying). Al-Qazwīnī offers an explicit systematization of the hidden theft, which he places under five headings that echo or expand previous tabulations: first, a similarity in meaning, but not a duplication; second, transference, when the poetic meaning of the first poet is moved to another place or redirected to another category; third, the expansion and comprehensibility of the new meaning; fourth, opposition, when the new meaning contradicts that of the first poet; and fifth, an improved, additional meaning.[159] All these practices are acceptable; and, whenever "these or other practices tend to inventiveness and innovation, and [are] more indiscernible as thefts, they are closer to approval."[160] He does not dismiss the possibility that these are coincidental, *tawārud khawāṭir* (coincidental correspondence), with no "intention to take over or steal."[161] On the other hand, *iṣṭirāf* remains reprehensible as long as it means claiming one or more verses from another's poem, with slight changes that might ruin the smoothness of the original, as in Figure 4.5, which cites Kuthayyir's manipulation of Jamīl's verse.

Al-Qazwīnī's reading of thievery as worthy of being associated with the issue of rhetoric, especially figures of speech,[162] assumes further significance when he studies "what connects to this art" – that is, *sariqāt*, like *iqtibās* (unacknowledged insertion of Qurʾān or Ḥadīth) or *taḍmīn* (visible insertion of poetry), *ʿaqd* (versification), *ḥall* (prosification), and *talmīḥ* (allusion).[163] These categories bring al-Qazwīnī's argument closer to the mounting attention that was being given to the systematization of elite prose; they also substantiate the connection between rhetoric and *badīʿ* (newness and inventiveness) and to ʿAbd al-Qāhir's statement that *lafẓ* (expression) follows meaning, not the other way around.[164] Like many other scholars, al-Qazwīnī provides no cultural or intellectual explanation for the relevance of these terms to a broader theoretical stratum. This common attitude is most probably driven by a familiarity with the issue of *saraq* that invites no explanations. Indeed, al-Qāḍī al-Jurjānī had already provided a persuasive argument in presenting a contextual and critical-literary discussion. In terms of economies of theft, however, a note by Ibn Rashīq, namely, that a few of the learned are more inclined to divide a certain term into different applications in order to define its ethics,

159 al-Qazwīnī, *al-Īḍāḥ*, 128; see also ibid., 132, 133, 134. 160 Ibid., 135–36.
161 Ibid., 136. 162 Ibid., 118. 163 Ibid., 137.
164 See al-Qazwīnī, *Talkhīṣ al-Miftāḥ*, 140. This edition also has the Persian examples.

directs us to the other side of the activity, which is rather procedural. Thus, to them, *ighārah* (open raid), for example, is either *iṣṭirāf* (i.e., taking verses from deceased poets) or *ighārah* as a raid on the poetry of the living.[165] It is left to the reader to decide which of these applications is reprehensible or stealthier than the other.

Structurally, and with ʿAbd al-Qāhir's compositional patterns, *naẓm*, in mind, one can argue that al-Qazwīnī brings his systematic analysis of rhetoric and its deft application of a few of the thievery terms in line with the vast development of the belletristic tradition that shifts attention to prose as the inclusive territory that makes use of every other domain. Thus, al-Qazwīnī's discussion of hidden plagiarism shows an indebtedness to Ḍiyāʾ al-Dīn b. al-Athīr, who, in turn, builds on an earlier tradition.[166] The discussion of *sariqah* happens to start with Muḥammad b. Kunāsah's (d. 207/822) confusion of the permissible with the objectionable in *iqtibās* (quotation), with or without indicatives, in his *Sariqāt al-Kumayt min al-Qurʾān*. The developing textual reading of poetic shifts from one application to another, as advised by Ibn Ṭabāṭabā in his support for indiscernible theft or even commendable appropriation of prose, or from one subgenre to another (including from one *gharaḍ* such as panegyric to amatory poetry, or navigationally between poetry and prose), was to receive a good deal of attention when scholars and philologists were at pains to put together a framework for the raging discussion of literary debts and credits in a growing mercantile economy concomitant with the expansion of the empire and its metropolitan centers across the Islamic lands, especially after the fall of Baghdad in 656/1258.

The Shift to Unique Poetic Application

During the Fatimid era (296–566/909–1171), however, serious attention was paid to this navigation among genres and domains, as was required by the state apparatus and its chancery, all in line with the missionary effort that distinguished the dynasty. While reservations were expressed against quotes from the Qurʾān in poetry, there are instances of paraphrase practiced by many, including Abū Tammām.[167] Fluidity between the writing or speaking domains was so much of a given that terminological phrases recur in

165 See Bonebakker, "Ancient Arabic Poetry and Plagiarism," 76.

166 al-Musawi, "Pre-modern Belletristic Prose." See also S. A. Bonebakker, "Poets and Critics in the Third Century A. H.," in *Logic in Classical Islamic Culture*, ed. Gustave E. von Grunebaum (Wiesbaden: O. Harrassowitz, 1970), 108.

167 For more, see Amidu Sanni, "Filiation: The Arabic Theorist's Prescription for Artistic Excellence," *Quaderni di Studi Arabi* 12 (1994): 5.

titles of manuals and books, including al-Thaʿālibī's (d. 429/1038) *Nathr al-naẓm wa-ḥall al-ʿaqd* (Prosification of Poetry and the Untying of the Knot) and Ibn al-Athīr's *Washī al-marqūm fī ḥall al-manẓūm* (The Embroidered Tapestry in Prosification). Thus, when al-Qazwīnī touches on acceptable but indiscernible thievery in the context of discussions of *taḍmīn* (embedding/insertion) as *istiʿānah* (invoking support), or *īdāʿ* (deposit), or even *rafw* (cross-stitching, embroidering),[168] *ḥusn al-sabk* (appealing structure), *ikhtiṣār* (brevity), *īḍāḥ* (explication), and *talmīḥ* (allusion),[169] his attention, as well as that of his explicators like Saʿd al-Dīn al-Taftāzānī (d. 793/1390), functions within a context of a familiar cultural script.[170] He sets the tone for commentators, especially in his emphasis on the means to generate new meanings and expressions, by reproducing meanings and expressions from one territory, such as commonality or banal use (*ʿāmmī mubtadhal*), to something different. There is, however, a figure of speech or usage that is originally *khāṣṣiyan gharīban* (uniquely unfamiliar or strange).[171] This phrasing is not unique to al-Qazwīnī, for al-Qāḍī al-Jurjānī had already written on this shift from one category, like shared and common usage, to al-*mubtadaʿ al-mukhtaraʿ* (the innovated/invented).[172]

Saʿd al-Dīn al-Taftāzānī's *Mukhtaṣar al-Saʿd: sharḥ talkhīṣ kitāb Miftāḥ al-ʿulūm* also places poetic thefts as a *khātimah* (conclusion) to the third craft under discussion – that is, *ʿilm al-badīʿ* (the science of inventiveness).[173] Al-Taftāzānī highlights defamiliarization, something that frees speech and writing from *al-mubtadhal al-ʿāmmī* (the banal, overused, outworn, and common) to become *al-gharīb al-khāṣṣī* (the strange and unique – i.e., *ibtidāʿ*, original invention), a point that is repeated in his abridged and detailed reproductions and commentaries.[174] Von Grunebaum draws attention to an epistemological shift thereafter, for this discussion that takes as a stepping stone al-Sakkākī's (d. 626/1229) *Miftāḥ al-ʿulūm* helped to "cut off independent treatment of the subject and mark the end of the development," which von Grunebaum has outlined.[175] While definitely developed and given

168 See Grunebaum, "Concept of Plagiarism," 245.
169 al-Qazwīnī, *al-Īḍāḥ*, 124.
170 For more on al-Taftāzānī's additional suggestions under allusion, see Grunebaum, "Concept of Plagiarism," 245.
171 al-Qazwīnī, *al-Īḍāḥ*, 121. Al-Qazwīnī elaborates on this in his discussion of figures of speech. See also his *Talkhīṣ al-Miftāḥ*, 141.
172 al-Jurjānī, *al-Wasāṭah* (1966), 185–86.
173 Saʿd al-Dīn al-Taftāzānī, *Mukhtaṣar al-Saʿd: sharḥ talkhīṣ kitāb Miftāḥ al-ʿulūm*, ed. ʿAbd al-Ḥamīd Hindāwī (Ṣaydā: al-Maktabah al-ʿAṣriyyah, 2010), 383, 446.
174 Saʿd al-Dīn al-Taftāzānī, *al-Muṭawwal: sharḥ Talkhīṣ al-miftāḥ* (Beirut: Dār Iḥyāʾ al-Turāth al-ʿArabī, 2004), 710.
175 Grunebaum, "Concept of Plagiarism," 243.

shape, the navigational sites of *sariqāt* display cross-historical and cultural activity whose major players – that is, poets – trade not only in lexical and thematic goods but also in familial and ethical repositories. Al-Qazwīnī, like his precursors, sees no problem in reporting how ʿAbdallāh b. al-Zabayr al-Asadī (d. 75/694) recites to the Umayyad caliph Muʿāwiyah (d. 60/680) a poem that contains verses to be recited soon after by Maʿn b. Aws al-Muzanī (d. 64/683). His explanation runs as follows: "The poetic meaning is mine, but the expression [wording] is his; furthermore, he is my foster brother, and I have the right to his poetry."[176] This statement invokes both *naskh* and *intiḥāl*, but the practice and justification prompt consideration of a certain degree of fluidity, a free-market economy that summons to its side whatever was marketable, including biological or tribal genealogies when the dynastic Umayyad center in Damascus opened the gate to poets and prose writers, encouraging the famed among them to practice whatever could win them to its side. Indeed, Ibn Qutaybah cites the case of the brilliant poet al-Kumayt (d. 126/743),[177] who was known for his alliance with the Alids and was thus a *rāfiḍī*, according to the conservative critic's term.[178] The scholar draws a comparison between his poetry in praise of the Umayyads and that in praise of the Alids in order to conclude that the poetry in praise of the Umayyads is stronger and better. Ibn Qutaybah concludes that earthly gain – that is, gifts from the ruling Umayyads – outweighs the heavenly reward that Islam associates with the Prophet's family (*ahl al-bayt*).[179] From a competitive poetic space involving a first and second poet, a precursor and successor, the argument draws attention to a poet who is involved in a personality split between material and spiritual or immaterial gifts. On the other hand, Ibn Qutaybah's surmise that the poetry addressed to the Umayyads is better than a poetry of mere emotional allegiance is worth considering in terms of transference from one lexical domain to another, from mourning to celebration, and from loss to triumph. A reward exchange is enacted whereby there is splendid poetry with caliphal gifts in mind. Although it is left to the reader to draw a comparison between the two poetic samples of a split personality, we, as readers, assume that the ever-increasing lexicon of *sariqāt* and *badīʿ* is no less applicable to the poetries of a divided self.

[176] al-Qazwīnī, *al-Īḍāḥ*, 122; al-Qazwīnī, *Talkhīṣ al-Miftāḥ*, 140–41.
[177] Full name: al-Kumayt b. Zayd al-Asadī.
[178] Ibn Qutaybah, *al-Shiʿr wa-l-shuʿarāʾ* (2001), 2:581. [179] Ibid., 1:79.

Further Epistemological Shifts: Ibn al-Athīr's Divisions

To understand the economies of what had once been *saraq* and, by the end of the fourteenth century, was a given in ongoing transactions and exchange that have their merits and pitfalls like any market and merchandise, Ḍiyāʾ al-Dīn b. al-Athīr's (d. 637/1239) mid-thirteenth-century interventions are very important. They are so not only because they informed al-Qazwīnī's *al-Īḍāḥ* and *Talkhīṣ al-Miftāḥ* (i.e., al-Sakkākī's *Miftāḥ al-ʿulūm*), and ultimately al-Taftāzānī's commentaries *Mukhtaṣar al-Saʿd* and *al-Muṭawwal*, among others,[180] but also because Ibn al-Athīr happened to be one of the major architects of workable belletristic prose writing. A sharp critic and scholar who claims every now and then that he can improve on whatever is written in prose, Ibn al-Athīr's contributions have a dynamic nature, not only because he lived among early and late formidable contemporaries including al-Qāḍī al-Fāḍil (d. 596/1200), Abū Yaʿqūb Yūsuf al-Sakkākī (d. 626/1229), Shams-i Qays (Shams al-Dīn Muḥammad b. Qays al-Rāzī, d. 629/1232),[181] and Ibn Abī al-Ḥadīd (d. 656/1258), but also because his books and biographical record present him in rigorous conversations with a vibrant culture across the Arabic-speaking world and beyond.

The conversational and anecdotal portion in his literary criticism provides us with what is missing in a seemingly rigid system that al-Āmidī, al-Qāḍī al-Jurjānī, and Ibn Rashīq, among a handful of others, attempted to enliven. His terminology is offered in a series of interpolations and guiding principles for poets and writers as players in a bustling domain. Ibn al-Athīr increases the dose in this respect, by condensing and summarizing terminology under three major headings, adding to them two more that come as complementary and explicatory.[182]

The three divisions are as follows. The first is *naskh* (duplication; in line with al-Mutanabbī's popular response to al-Ḥātimī: "poetry is a trail, and a hoof may tread on the space of another");[183] the second is *salkh* (taking over a portion of the poetic meaning and dressing the old with a new motive); and the third is *maskh* (distortion; turning the original motive

[180] See al-Musawi, *Republic of Letters*, 103, 108–9. Khafājī lists three *mukhtaṣarāt* (abridgments and commentaries) for the *Miftāḥ*, nine *shurūḥ* (commentaries) for al-Qazwīnī's *Talkhīṣ al-Miftāḥ* (see al-Qazwīnī, *al-Īḍāḥ*, 161–62), and six *shurūḥ* for al-Taftāzānī's *al-Muṭawwal*, 162.

[181] For more, see al-Musawi, *Republic of Letters*, 115–16. Shams-i Qays's *al-Muʿjam fī maʿāyīr ashʿār al-ʿAjam* (The Compendium on the Principles of Non-Arabic Poetry [Persian]) is an important contribution.

[182] Ibn al-Athīr, *al-Mathal al-sāʾir*, 2:305, 309.

[183] See Chapter 1. Ibn Rashīq, *al-ʿUmdah* (2001), 2:289.

and poetic idea to a distorted and dreadful one).[184] However, he suggests two more: adding on top of a poetic meaning, and reversing the former *maʿnā* (poetic meaning).[185] He stipulates the need for a very good acquaintance with poetry.[186] He analyzes and supports his divisions not only with examples for each division and its subheadings but also with anecdotal details of what he has perceived, noticed in his travels, or read. Thus, he concludes his preliminary note: "On this topic of poetic plagiarisms, I have provided what has not been made available by others."[187] As von Grunebaum has already mapped out the subheadings,[188] we need to see the significance of the overall discussion of *sariqāt* as it is concluded in Ibn al-Athīr's *al-Mathal al-sāʾir* (The Popular Model [for the Practice of Secretaries and Poets]). The argument leads to a *mufāḍalah* between *arbāb al-nathr wa-l-naẓm* (a scale of preference between the masters of prose and poetry).[189] The argument leads him gradually to conclude that prose is preferable to poetry, primarily because the issue of inimitability in the Qurʾān is reserved for prose.[190] Moreover, the strict rules for excellence in prose are harder to come by, and this is why one can rarely count more than ten great prose writers, while there are numerous poets. As this is a domain that Ibn al-Athīr specializes in, he looks upon prose as an inclusive field and practice that makes use of poetry. In his *al-Washī al-marqūm*, he inserts al-Qāḍī al-Fāḍil's narrative describing his initiation as a luminous prose writer. The Fatimid chief secretary Muwaffaq al-Dīn Yūsuf b. al-Khallāl (d. 566/1170) asks him to prosify (*ḥall*) the poetry he has learned, a practice that was common in the training of initiates.[191] This first step in the art of writing illustrates the direction of Ibn al-Athīr's prioritization. His argument rests on the need to learn poetry by heart in order to strengthen and embellish one's prose writing. The end in mind is prose writing, as it was what was required by the growing state apparatus and chancery. The prose terrain grows in stature as it also provides poets with motifs, ideas, and patterns that feed indiscernible plagiarism. It is not surprising therefore that Ibn al-Athīr devotes a very long chapter in *al-Washī al-marqūm* to the practice of *ḥall al-manẓūm* (prosification).[192] Alongside the fluidity attending the domain of poetry and poetics and the emphasis on a few major poets – and on al-Mutanabbī as the last of the great poets – the shift to prose and the domain of epistolography managed to eclipse the raging controversy for a while.

[184] Ibn al-Athīr, *al-Mathal al-sāʾir*, 2:304–5. [185] Ibid., 305. [186] Ibid.
[187] Ibid., 309. [188] Grunebaum, "Concept of Plagiarism," 243–44.
[189] Ibn al-Athīr, *al-Mathal al-sāʾir*, 2:350. [190] Ibid., 355. [191] Ibid., 180–81.
[192] *al-Washī al-marqūm*, 177–337.

5 Disputed Poetic Territories

Proponents and Interlocutors

There is every reason to start this discussion with a reference to Abū ʿUthmān ʿAmr b. Baḥr al-Jāḥiẓ's (d. 255/868) summary of poetic textual navigation in his *Kitāb al-ḥayawān* (Book of Animals):

> We are not familiar with anyone in this universe who precedes everyone else in a precise comprehensive simile, in a strange and wonderful theme, in a dignified stately meaning, or original invention, and whose contemporaries or successors, if not taking his *lafẓ* [wording and expression] and stealing part of it or claiming it in full, nevertheless invade the meaning and share it. That includes poetic meanings which poets fight to reproduce in different expressions and poetic directions, until no one has more right to that poetic meaning than any other; the successor often denies ever hearing of that meaning, saying it comes to mind effortlessly, as happens with its first initiator.[1]

Although not given to the precise terminologies that would characterize the tenth century, this summary prepares the scene more succinctly for the growth of the discussion of *saraq* (theft) among literati. The recurrence of accusations and their refutations happened to be a feature of a thriving culture when precedence, antecedence, and poetic ownership mattered a good deal. The case is so when perceived in context of the Abbasid empire, when Baghdad, Basrah, and Kufa were metropolitan epicenters that communicated far and wide with other epicenters across the imperial domains. It should not be surprising therefore that the detailed account of *saraq* by Ibn Abī al-Ṭāhir Ṭayfūr is also by the same author who wrote *Kitāb Baghdād* as a history, life, and topography of Baghdad.[2] In that climate where the search for distinction was rampant, he, like a number of others, would like to demonstrate a degree of meticulousness in poetry

[1] Abū ʿUthmān ʿAmr b. Baḥr al-Jāḥiẓ, *Kitāb al-ḥayawān*, ed. ʿAbd al-Salām Muḥammad Hārūn (Cairo: Maṭbaʿat Muṣṭafā al-Bābī al-Ḥalabī, 1938–47), 3:311.

[2] For more on his production and role, see Shawkat M. Toorawa, *Ibn Abī Ṭāhir Ṭayfūr and Arabic Writerly Culture: A Ninth-Century Bookman in Baghdad* (London: Routledge, 2010); *Hilāl Nājī, Aḥmad b. Abī Ṭāhir Ṭayfūr: Ḥayātuhu, dīwānuhu, rasāʾiluhu* (Damascus: Tawzīʿ Dār al-Hilāl, 2008); Aḥmad b. Abī Ṭāhir Ṭayfūr, *Kitâb Baġdâd* (Leipzig: Harrassowitz, 1908), vols. 2 and 6.

and poetics, the domain which happened to be the most attractive to the Abbasid court and upper social strata. His exaggerated search for Abū Tammām's alleged plagiarisms brought him sharp criticism from later littérateurs like al-Āmidī and, soon after, al-Qāḍī Ibn ʿAbd al-ʿAzīz al-Jurjānī, both of whom blamed much of ninth-century criticism for confusing common and shared poetic meanings with *saraq* proper, something that is applicable only to the theft of unique use or original and untouched invention.[3] The epistemic shift, addressed earlier, as conveyed in classification and tabulation of semantic fields, did not bring an end to personal tendencies partaking of partiality, antagonism, and a hunt for alleged plagiarisms. Despite the solid critical effort associated with al-Āmidī, al-Qāḍī al-Jurjānī, Qudāmah b. Jaʿfar, and Ibn Ṭabāṭabā, a rather angry group was antagonized by the wide reputation of Abū Ṭayyib al-Mutanabbī's (d. 354/965) poetry. If the battle and controversy around Abū Tammām centers on a poetics of inventiveness and newness, as discussed by al-Āmidī, the raging controversy around al-Mutanabbī is rather social, political, and personal. Even the seemingly literary gets mixed up with other motivations to undermine the poet's career. Both cases bring to the republic of letters an enormous amount of literary criticism where disputation stands out as dynamic.

Rules for Debates

In either case, disputation spreads as an intriguing feature of a lucrative cultural life. The grammarian and scholar of poetry Yaʿqūb b. al-Sikkīt (d. 244/858) wrote a book whose title may be translated as "Plagiarisms of Poets and What They Agree Upon,"[4] which either was not extant for al-Āmidī and al-Qāḍī al-Jurjānī or is a rather knowledgeable reading of plagiarism in relation to common and shared usage. In contrast, Ibn Abī al-Ṭāhir Ṭayfūr receives great attention, especially as al-Āmidī finds him more in line with his *muwāzanah* (evaluative scale). Ibn Abī al-Ṭāhir accumulates accusations of plagiarism against Abū Tammām. Despite al-Āmidī's reservations, the book provides him with material that can support his effort to demonstrate that Abū Tammām is not the foremost pioneer in innovation and inventiveness and that he only comes after Muslim b. al-Walīd and others. His poetry is more susceptible to criticism for the recurrence of *al-saraq al-ṣaḥīḥ* (actual plagiarisms), which Ibn Abī al-Ṭāhir lists and which al-Āmidī relists to prove his point. Al-Āmidī explains that the critic "is right in some of his findings of *sariqāt*" but wrong in others, because he confused the "*khāṣṣ* [unique and special] in

[3] See al-Āmidī, *al-Muwāzanah*, 1:120–29. [4] al-Nadīm, *Fihrist*, 159–60.

meanings with themes shared among people that cannot count as thievery."[5] This portion covers ten pages in *al-Muwāzanah*.[6] No less than nine pages cover common and shared meanings and, as such, weigh against the tendency to accumulate accusations randomly.[7] On balance, al-Āmidī demonstrates a critical sobriety that should have been convincing to the knowledgeable among literati. It serves, however, as a stepping stone for the assignment of fifteen pages or so to Abū al-ʿAbbās Aḥmad b. ʿUbayd Allāh b. Muḥammad b. ʿAmmār (d. 314/927).[8] The latter's criticism is mainly stylistic and can support al-Āmidī's argument that the poet violates what is normative in Arabic poetry and poetics because of excessive complexity in diction and figures of speech. The reference to Abū al-ʿAbbās's critique is important for preparing a section on al-Buḥturī's thefts from Abū Tammām, as listed by Abū al-Ḍiyāʾ Bishr b. Yaḥyā al-Kātib. As noted earlier, the latter's criticism of al-Buḥturī's thefts from Abū Tammām is counter-argued in terms of what is definitive *saraq* and what is a confused, excessive accumulation of poetic meanings and ideas that make up a shared property. The issue leads al-Āmidī to use tact and careful argumentation to dispute the claims of a well-established contemporary critic and scholar, especially as critical opinion matters much in a highly rewarding field.

Terms for Nonpartial Discussion

Thus, his late contemporary al-Qāḍī al-Jurjānī (d. 392/1001) adds his voice regarding the confusion surrounding allegations of thievery: "When you read what was produced by Aḥmad b. Abī Ṭāhir, Aḥmad b. ʿAmmār on Abū Tammām's plagiarisms, and what was followed by Bishr b. Yaḥyā regarding al-Buḥturī, and Muhalhil b. Yamūt respecting Abū Nuwās, you'll realize the malice of partiality and, conversely, fairness gains more beauty in your sight (*ʿarafta qubḥ āthār al-hawā wa-izdāda al-inṣāf fī ʿaynika ḥusnā*)."[9] Al-Qāḍī al-Jurjānī focuses his response on Ibn Yamūt, justifiably so because the other three have already been discussed by al-Āmidī. He explains, however, that expressions are part of available communication, and if some similarity is traced, it is more often in terms of *iḥtidhāʾ al-mithāl* (following the model).[10] With such tolerance, al-Qāḍī al-Jurjānī sounds more open than al-Āmidī, who has to start the section on al-Buḥturī with the admission that his favorite poet "*akhadha ... akhdhan kathīran*" (seized on ... a big portion), or "has taken from the poetic meanings and ideas

[5] al-Āmidī, *al-Muwāzanah*, 1:110. [6] Ibid., 110–20. [7] Ibid., 120–29.
[8] Ibid., 136–51. [9] al-Jurjānī, *al-Wasāṭah* (1966), 209. [10] Ibid., 211.

of former and later poets a substantial portion."[11] Al-Āmidī is apologetic at this point, because the "scholars of poetry who were still alive in my time (whom I survived) did not see thievery in meanings as the greatest mishap among poets, especially poets of later generations, simply because this is a domain that nobody before or after could have avoided."[12] The suggestion here is important, not only because Ibn Ṭabāṭabā, al-Qāḍī al-Jurjānī, and Abū Bakr Ṣūlī (d. 336/947), along with Abū ʿAlī al-Fārisī, admit the scarcity of new meanings in view of the enormous poetic production that already exists, leading inevitably to duplication of meanings, but also because accusations happen to be the base for disputation. Both al-Āmidī and al-Qāḍī al-Jurjānī argue the issue in detail, but each from a different perspective and position.

As befits a disputed case, al-Āmidī, whose book would influence both contemporaries and later scholars, first submits what has been advocated by Ibn Abī al-Ṭāhir and reported in person by Abū ʿAbdallāh Muḥammad b. Dāwūd b. al-Jarrāḥ (d. 296/909), namely, that he found 600 stolen verses in al-Buḥturī's corpus, and 100 solely from Abū Tammām.[13] Al-Āmidī admits this problem and adds that "it is the worst among a poet's flaws to deliberately take from one single poet and seize on his meanings as al-Buḥturī did with respect to Abū Tammām, even if it is a theft of ten lines; imagine when this theft exceeds a hundred verses!"[14] In the next twenty pages, he lists them,[15] setting one line against another to show definite plagiarisms that cannot be denied. So, if this is the case regarding a poet whom the critic al-Āmidī appreciates for his "extra caution, pleasant deportment, and measured expressions,"[16] why should he embark on a dispute? This is only the preparatory material that the established critic and scholar needs to engage with the contemporary Abū al-Ḍiyāʾ Bishr b. Yaḥyā al-Qīnī al-Naṣībī. Obviously, al-Āmidī expects a backlash, as his rejoinder shows caution in a climate of ideas that is thriving on discussions and disputes, as shown in several compendiums and collections of debates.[17]

Thus, he responds to an implied interlocutor, expecting the person to argue back that al-Āmidī has not exhausted all the plagiarisms cited by

[11] al-Āmidī, *al-Muwāzanah*, 2:291. [12] Ibid. Already noted in Chapter 3.
[13] Ibid., 191. [14] Ibid., 192. [15] Ibid., 304–24. [16] Ibid., 192.
[17] Abū Ḥayyān al-Tawḥīdī includes one debate between Abū Saʿīd al-Sīrāfī and Mattā b. Yūnus in *al-Imtāʿ wa-l-muʾānasah*. The debate was republished in Yāqūt al-Ḥamawī, *Muʿjam al-udabāʾ* (1991), 2:527–45. See also D. S. Margoliouth, "The Discussion between Abu Bishr Matta and Abu Sa'id al-Sirafi on the Merits of Logic and Grammar," *Journal of the Royal Asiatic Society of Great Britain & Ireland* 4 (1905): 79–129.

Abū al-Ḍiyā᾽ Bishr b. Yaḥyā. Al-Āmidī's response to the implied interlocutor runs as follows:

> The case is not so, as I have covered all, and even allowed what might not be counted as thefts, even if the two meanings agree with each other or approximately so, but I put aside the rest of his [Bishr b. Yaḥyā al-Qīnī al-Naṣībī's] findings because he is so unsatisfied with the thefts that careful deliberation confirms so as to multiply what cannot be considered as theft. This runs against his [Bishr b. Yaḥyā al-Qīnī al-Naṣībī's] introduction, which says: The reader of this book should not jump to conclusions, saying that this is taken from that, until contemplating the meaning without the expression and exerting the mind to discern the hidden, for what is stolen in poetry entails the duplication of its meaning without its expression and entails that the new possessor aims far to hide theft.[18]

With this, al-Āmidī assembles his one single but inclusive remark against the contender's excessiveness. At this point, al-Āmidī reiterates his unique phrasing that "plagiarism is only in *al-badīʿ al-mukhtaraʿ* (invented figuration; invented *badīʿ*), which belongs to a specific poet."[19]

In another controversy, none less than the highly regarded and rewarded poet Abū al-Ṭayyib al-Mutanabbī responds to Abū al-Ḥasan al-Ḥātimī, curtly deflating the latter with al-Āmidī's precise maxim while simultaneously reiterating, in another articulation, Ibn Abī al-Ṭāhir Ṭayfūr's succinct phrasing about Arabic as an integrated, mixed discourse: Arab wording and expression hold each other's throat.[20] Along with al-Āmidī's neat maxim, al-Mutanabbī's reiteration is pivotal to disputes and the art of disputation.

However, both are difficult to uphold. Current scholarship, with a foundational base laid by von Grunebaum in his meticulous survey article, has tried in multiple ways to account for Arab authors' engagement with the issue of *saraq*. Even so, it cannot come up with a clear-cut theoretical framework to account for the centrality of *sariqāt* discussions. While there is an acknowledgment that this movement raged for over six centuries, little is done to situate it in socioeconomic terms, or in line with theories of desire. While its advocates and proponents work out the controversy in functional terms, with an increasingly vigorous nod to literary criticism, it is up to later scholars to situate the discussion in context. Intertextuality, phrased differently by Ibn Ṭayfūr and, a century later, al-Mutanabbī as an issue of *kalām* (discourse), requires attention in view of an epistemological shift from anciency to modernism,

[18] al-Āmidī, *al-Muwāzanah*, 2:325. See also a l-Jurjānī, *al-Wasāṭah* (1966), 214, 186; Ibn Rashīq, *al-ʿUmdah* (2001), 2:282. For contemporary scholarship that dwells on *ikhtirāʿ*, see ʿAlī Bin Tamīm, *ʿUyūn al-ʿajāʾib fī mā awradahu Abū al-Ṭayyib min ikhtirāʿāt wa-gharāʾib* (Abu Dhabi: Abu Dhabi Arabic Language Center, 2025), 22.

[19] al-Āmidī, *al-Muwāzanah*, 2:326. [20] al-Ḥātimī, *al-Risālah al-mūḍiḥah*, 143.

from *qadīm* to *muḥdath*, coupled with and manifested in the *badīʿ* movement (innovation and inventiveness, deviation from the former established canon of the poetic precedence of ancients). The *badīʿ* movement unfolds as a prominent shift away from *ʿamūd al-shiʿr* (the standard classical poetic canon) to a contending discourse that was in line with a new way of life, with its caliphal court, entourage, and an intelligentsia that shared and propounded its values.[21] While the conflict between *qudamāʾ* and *muḥdathūn* (ancients and moderns) references and addresses a historical field and its attending semantics, *badīʿ* is a stylistic reformulation of themes, syntax, and structure that has its successes and failures. The *ḥadāthah* movement (modernism) was an inclusive one in a thriving and expanding empire, while *badīʿ* gained visibility within the movement. Its practitioners varied from dissenters to conformists. Its foremost applicant, Bashshār b. Burd (d. 166/783), was a social-political dissenter insofar as power relations are concerned. In other words, the association between *badīʿ* and power cannot be applied consistently to the reading of discursive hierarchies. In a succinct note on the need to retain for language its luster, to rid it of the "rotten fruit dangling from a language [that is] not our language" the poet Mahmoud Darwish (d. 2008) emphasizes what a poetic language requires every now and then to escape stock images and to free itself from an exhausted or outworn convention.[22]

However, this association between modernism, *badīʿ*, and contemporaneity was central to the *sariqāt* controversy, with its philological thrust. As is argued by al-Jāḥiẓ, Ibn Qutaybah, Ibn Ṭabāṭabā, Abū Bakr al-Ṣūlī, al-Āmidī, and al-Qāḍī al-Jurjānī, repetition, duplication, and appropriation of themes are inevitable, a premise that considers further improvements, recreation, transference, and better accrual as signs of accumulative value. Even wording could turn into a commodity when the intertextual space is an arena for use. Wolfhart Heinrichs is probably right in suggesting that critics and scholars stretch the term *saraq* to accommodate a situation where other terms are called for, as summarized by Ḥāzim al-Qarṭājannī when he stresses value as a criterion among users and appliers of themes and images, or even syntax.[23] As *naql* (transferring poetic themes and meanings or their usage from one category to another), for example, escapes that stigma of theft (see Figure 3.1), especially if the poet who performs the action gains a better value, other terms also allow for accommodating applications and endow the material at hand with the

[21] See al-Jurjānī, *al-Wasāṭah* (2006), 24–25; Adūnīs, *al-Thābit wa-l-mutaḥawwil*, 2:109–68; Stetkevych, "Redefinition of *Badīʿ* Poetry."

[22] Mahmoud Darwish, *Memory for Forgetfulness: August, Beirut, 1982*, trans. Ibrahim Muhawi (Berkeley: University of California Press, 1995), 50.

[23] Heinrichs, "An Evaluation of 'Sariqa,'" 361.

characteristics of commodity. The field is a marketplace, and commoditization is a given. Even when critics or scholars resorted to the use of *saraq* as a stigma, they could not overlook current idiom and parlance. Nevertheless, the yardstick established by al-Āmidī and al-Qāḍī al-Jurjānī with respect to inventiveness in the use and application of the new, the *badīʿ*, could not be ignored for long.

Although difficult to abide by, both conclusive remarks on *al-badīʿ al-mukhtaraʿ* (invented figuration; invented *badīʿ*) by al-Āmidī and al-Qāḍī al-Jurjānī can function as a demarcating line, but their perpetuation has remained precarious. Proponents of the attack on al-Mutanabbī like Ibn Wakīʿ and al-Ḥātimī leave the maxims behind. If the attack on Abū Tammām was intended either to negate his precedence in the *badīʿ* tradition or to expose his excessive attempts to invent and reach out for new meanings and expressions, the attack on al-Mutanabbī has multiple facets, as shown in Yāqūt's quote from the transmitter of al-Mutanabbī's poetry, Abū al-Ḥusayn al-Maghribī's book *al-Intiṣār al-munbī ʿan faḍāʾil al-Mutanabbī* (The Informative Backing to al-Mutanabbī's Virtues).[24] Yāqūt introduces the reference and his comment with the following remark: "A most surprising thing that I came across is what I have read" in this book.[25] Yāqūt's note includes al-Maghribī's examples of poetic competitions and tournaments when famous poets were

[24] Full name: Abū al-Ḥusayn b. Muḥammad b. Aḥmad b. Muḥammad al-Maghribī.
[25] Yāqūt al-Ḥamawī, *Muʿjam al-udabāʾ* (1991), 2:527:

ومن عجيب ما مرّ بي: ما قرأته في كتاب الانتصار المُنْبي عن فضائل المتنبي، لأبي الْحُسَيْنِ بْنِ مُحَمَّدِ بْنِ أَحْمَدَ بْنِ مُحَمَّدٍ الْمَغْرِبِيِّ رَاوِيَةِ الْمُتَنَبّي، وكانَ قدْ رَدَّ فيه عَلَى بعْضِ مَنْ زَعمَ أنَّ شِعرَ الْمُتنبّي مسْرُوقٌ من أبي تمَّام والبُحْتُرِيِّ. ولَهُ قصيدةٌ عارضَ بها بَعْضَ قصائِدِ الْمُتَنبّي. وأخَذَ الْمغربيُّ عليهِ فقال: ورأَيْتُهُ وقد استشهَدَ بأبي سعيد السِّيرافِيِّ مُؤدب الأمير أبي إسحاق ابْنِ مُعِزِّ الدَّوْلَةِ أبي الْحَسن بْنِ بُويْهِ، وَذَكر أنَّهُ أعْطاهُ خَطَّهُ بأنّ قصيدتَهُ خيْرٌ من قصيدة أبي الطيّب. قال: ومن جعل الحُكمَ في هذا إلى أبي سَعيدٍ؟ إنما يَحْكُم في الشعر الشعراءُ لا المُؤدِّبَةُ. وبمثل هذا جَرَتْ سُنَّةُ العرب في القديم، كانت تُضْربُ للنابِغَةِ خَيمةٌ من أدَمٍ بسوقِ عكاظ، وتأتي الشعراءُ من سائر الآفاق فتَعْرِضُ أشعارها عليه، فَيحْكُمُ لمن أجادَ، وَخبَرُهُ مع حَسَّانٍ وغيْرِهِ معْروفٌ. ولو كان أعلمُ الناس بالنحو أشعرهم، لكانَ أبو علي الْفَسَوِيُّ أشعر الناس. وما عُرِفَ له من نظْمِ بيتٍ ولا أبياتٍ ولا سُمِعَ ذلك منه

وَأمّا إعْطاءُ أبي سعيد خَطَّهُ، فَيُوشكُ أن يكون من جَنْبِ ما حدَّثني بِهِ المعروفُ بابْنِ الخزَّار الوَرّاق ببغداد، وأبو بكر الْقنطريُّ، وأبو الْحُسَيْنِ بن الخُراسانيّ، وهما ورّاقان أيضاً من جِلّةِ أهلِ هذه الصنعة أنّ أبا سعيد إذا أراد بيع كتاب – اسْتكْتبَهُ بعض تلامذته – حِرصاً على النّفعِ منْهُ، ونظراً في رِقّ المعيشة – كتب في آخره وإن لمْ يَنْظرْ في حرفٍ منْهُ

A most surprising thing I have come across is what I have read in al-Mutanabbī's *rāwiyah* Abū al-Ḥusayn al-Maghribī's book *The Informative Backing to al-Mutanabbī's Virtues*, where he responded to one who claimed that al-Mutanabbī's poetry was stolen from Abū Tammām and al-Buḥturī; and that he [the contender] has a poem that contrafacted some of al-Mutanabbī's poems. Al-Maghribī wrote back: I noticed that he has as an authority on his side, Abū Saʿīd al-Sīrāfī, the tutor for the emir Abū Isḥāq b. Muʿizz al-Dawlah Abū al-Ḥasan b. Buwayh; claiming that the latter told him in writing that his poem is better than al-Mutanabbī's. Al-Maghribī contends that al-Sīrāfī's judgment has no weight, for arbiters on poetry are poets, not tutors.

arbiters, not philologists. Furthermore, Yāqūt consolidates al-Maghribī's response with examples from his own experience with copyists, as will be shown later. Al-Maghribī's book is not extant, and we must conjecture that, since al-Ḥātimī's epistle in its abridged and enlarged versions was the first detailed attack on al-Mutanabbī, he is the person in question. The same epistle presents its writer not only as an ordinary poet but also as a knowledgeable authority on poetry who is unwilling to give credit to others. Begrudging others their reputation, he would not stop at anything other than appearing triumphant.[26]

However, there are reasons for Yāqūt's expressed surprise because the unidentified al-Ḥātimī mentions the improbable support of Abū Saʿīd al-Sīrāfī (d. 368/979) for his poetry against that of al-Mutanabbī. Al-Ḥātimī's frustration – presumably at the age of nineteen – with his inability to cope with prominent scholars and poets at Sayf al-Dawlah's (d. 356/967) court could explain his imaging of the real or imaginary arrogance displayed by the poet laureate al-Mutanabbī, who at the time enjoyed an enormous patronage, much to the chagrin of many, including the prince's relatives, a point I will further explain later. Given to self-aggrandizement, as many accounts demonstrate, al-Ḥātimī directed his autobiographical itinerary to this end: to prove he was on par with the authorities that he had met at Sayf al-Dawlah's court, including grammarians, lexicographers, and men of letters like Abū ʿAlī al-Fārisī (d. 377/987), Abū al-Ṭayyib al-Lughawī (d. 351/962), and Ibn Khālawayh (d. 370/981). In a neat surmise concerning al-Ḥātimī's character, as shown in his epistle, *al-Risālah al-mūḍiḥah*, Bonebakker argues: "The question is whether Ḥātimī's story about his early career can be trusted, since not only the description of his character by his contemporaries, but also the tone of many of his utterances … suggest that he was given to unbridled self-glorification."[27] Bonebakker suggests the likelihood of al-Ḥātimī's being at the court between 337 and 347 AH.[28]

That al-Ḥātimī is the person in al-Maghribī's book is almost certain, as the contender could not be a stellar poet like Abū al-ʿAbbās al-Nāmī, who has a different and less personal approach to the matter, nor a critic and poet like Ibn Wakīʿ, whose book makes no such mention of al-Sīrāfī, or

[26] For a thorough effort to authenticate the different versions of al-Ḥātimī's epistle, see S. A. Bonebakker, *Ḥātimī and His Encounter with Mutanabbī: A Biographical Sketch* (Amsterdam: North-Holland Pub. Co., 1984), 6, 14–15, 16, 18–19, 39. The shorter version is in Yāqūt al-Ḥamawī, *Muʿjam al-udabāʾ*, 5:316–29.

[27] Bonebakker, *Ḥātimī and His Encounter*, 11, nn. 18, 19. For more on this doubt, see ibid., 12, n. 20.

[28] On this autobiographical sketch, see ibid., 11–12, n. 19.

al-Ṣāḥib b. ʿAbbād, whose disillusionment was to occur later. As for Abū Saʿd Muḥammad b. Aḥmad b. Muḥammad al-ʿAmīdī (d. 433/1041) in his *al-Ibānah ʿan sariqāt al-Mutanabbī lafẓan wa-maʿnan* (The Clarification of al-Mutanabbī's Thievery in Form and Content), it is the latest among that group of contenders' writings, to be followed later by Abū Muḥammad Saʿīd b. Mubārak b. al-Dahhān (d. 569/1174) in his *al-Risālah al-Saʿīdiyyah fī al-maʾākhidh al-Kindiyyah min al-maʿānī al-Ṭāʾiyyah* (Saʿīd's Epistle on Seized Meanings by al-Mutanabbī from Abū Tammām) and so on. Being the earliest of the attacks on al-Mutanabbī, which would accumulate over time, al-Ḥātimī's epistle certainly provided others with material, direction, and encouragement.[29] Al-Ḥātimī made references to Abū Saʿīd al-Sīrāfī (d. 368/979) in his extensive account of an encounter that seems to owe a good deal to the imagination.[30] In al-Maghribī's rebuff, al-Ḥātimī made the atrocious claim that the grammarian and linguist Abū Saʿīd al-Sīrāfī, "the tutor for the emir Abū Isḥāq b. Muʿizz al-Dawlah Abū al-Ḥasan b. Buwayh," maintained in his own handwriting that al-Ḥātimī's verse was better than al-Mutanabbī's. Al-Maghribī's rebuttal is understandable, since he himself was the transmitter of al-Mutanabbī's verse. As noted earlier, he also responds that only poets can judge poetry, not tutors, a point to which al-Mutanabbī's apt distinction between the clothier and weaver neatly applies.[31] This distinction, which al-Mutanabbī was reported to have said in response to the emir Sayf al-Dawlah's reference to critics, is worth keeping in mind. The effort to collapse or differentiate between the two crafts never dies (see Figure 5.1). Regardless of al-Maghribī's rebuttal, Yāqūt also relies on well-respected book copyists (*warrāqūn*) who affirm that al-Sīrāfī never wrote in his own handwriting and that the only writing he contributed to his books was his signature, indicating his approval of the books, which

[29] Al-Qāḍī al-Jurjānī seems to suggest something similar, without naming al-Ḥātimī. See *al-Wasāṭah* (2006), 157–58.

[30] Bonebakker, *Ḥātimī and His Encounter*, 16, suggests that the account is "grossly exaggerated."

[31] In an ironic twist, al-Maghribī almost echoes what al-Buḥturī argues in a certain assembly, that those who know poetry are the ones who are driven into its tight straits, meaning poets. Al-Maghribī's statement is quoted by al-Ṣāḥib b. ʿAbbād in his epistle against al-Mutanabbī. See Abū Saʿd Muḥammad b. Aḥmad b. Muḥammad al-ʿAmīdī, *al-Ibānah ʿan sariqāt al-Mutanabbī lafẓan wa-maʿnā*, ed. Ibrāhīm al-Disūqī al-Bisāṭī (Cairo: Dār al-Maʿārif, 1961), an edition that contains al-Ṣāḥib b. ʿAbbād's epistle. See also al-Ḥātimī's *al-Risālah al-mūḍiḥah*, 224, for an earlier contention. For Abū al-Ṭayyib's analogy, see Yūsuf al-Badīʿī, *al-Ṣubḥ al-munbī ʿan ḥaythiyyat al-Mutanabbī*, ed. Muṣṭafā al-Saqqā, Muḥammad Shitā, and ʿAbduh Ziyādah ʿAbduh (Cairo: Dār al-Maʿārif, 1963), 85. The distinction al-Mutanabbī made between the clothier and the weaver was in response to Sayf al-Dawlah's contending suggestion.

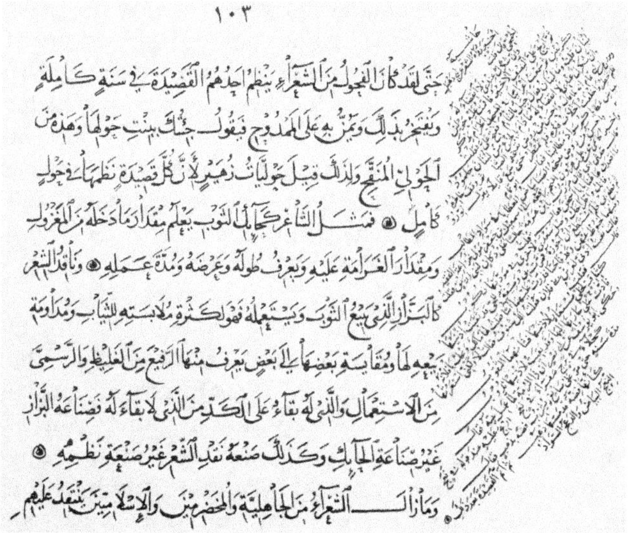

Figure 5.1 Differentiating the craft of poetry from the craft of criticism

had been copied by his students. Yāqūt's interpolation alerts us to the confusion surrounding claims and reports, especially in matters related to thievery as a controversial domain. As a thorny issue that attracted the participation and interest of literati, philologists, and critics, thievery provides a unique cultural forum that goes beyond literariness in its political and economic engagements, involving rulers, their entourage, and assemblies, as al-Ḥātimī's patrons demonstrate. Rulers who were involved in cultural debates that touched on several issues and who were prompted by personal or political motivations must have set the stage for heated debates between contenders and advocates. Poets of al-Mutanabbī's magisterial presence and impact were not ready then to give in to grammarians and linguists, despite Ibn Aydamir's contention that the craft of criticism is harder to accomplish than the craft of poetry.[32]

Exponents, Proponents, and Detractors

In matters of disputation, its politics, and directions, al-ʿAmīdī, not to be confused with al-Āmidī, leveled blame against al-Mutanabbī for alleged plagiarisms, resorting to untheorized accusatory terms with their

[32] See n. 69.

abundance of confusion and deliberate neglect as to what constitutes, as al-Āmidī puts it, *al-saraq al-ṣaḥīḥ* (actual theft). His inventory of what he deems plagiarism or specifically *akhdh* (seizure) of poetic meanings, images, and wording vaults over what predecessors have identified as such when they made a distinction between shared words, meanings, and expressions, on the one hand, and unique inventions especially owned by a certain poet, on the other. That is an issue that al-Āmidī, and more so al-Qāḍī al-Jurjānī, helped to systematize before the matter received the attention of critics who included the issue under the rubric of *badī'*, its register, and its variables.

As noted earlier, fair-minded critics and philologists like Ibn Qutaybah, al-Āmidī, and al-Qāḍī al-Jurjānī argued the issue of creativity, borrowing, and stealing in cultural terms that, for Ibn Qutaybah, operate outside epochs, generations, and tribes or groups. His argument runs as follows: "I haven't applauded the ancients for their antecedence; nor have I held a latecomer in contempt for being so."[33] While al-'Amīdī repeats some of their maxims, he moves beyond them, invoking such hearsay as "a person whom I trust mentioned that, when al-Mutanabbī was killed on the way to Ahwaz, the two *dīwān*s of *al-Ṭā'iyyayn* [Abū Tammām and al-Buḥturī] were found in his saddlebag in his own handwriting, with markers that show every verse he flayed by confiscating its meaning."[34] This is not the only nonsensical piece of hearsay, for the book abounds with them, alongside misquotes and statements reflecting a neglect of historical evidence, as when al-'Amīdī cites the poetry of the fictional Abū al-Fatḥ instead of citing Badī' al-Zamān al-Hamadhānī (d. 398/1007), the author who created Abū al-Fatḥ and who died years after al-Mutanabbī,[35] and hence could not be a source for the latter's poetry.

More confused is al-'Amīdī's muddled tracing of originals when al-Mutanabbī sounds more like the originator of an expression or a meaning, while the other source cited by al-'Amīdī sounds more like a duplicator.[36] Al-'Amīdī's adamant rejection of a poet highly regarded throughout the Muslim world for the simple reason of this popularity and critics' celebration of the power of his verse, expressive poetics, and subtle combination of meaning and expression prevents him from applying a plagiarism register that is already being used by prominent critics.[37] Thus, he rejects *tawārud* because he would like to claim a certain usage as

[33] Ibn Qutaybah, *al-Shi'r wa-l-shu'arā'* (2001), 1:62. [34] al-'Amīdī, *al-Ibānah*, 24–25.
[35] Ibid., 49n1.
[36] See Arthur Wormhoudt, foreword to *The Revelations of the Plagiarisms of al-Mutanabbī* (Oskaloosa, IA: William Penn College, 1974).
[37] On the power and fame of al-Mutanabbī's verse, see Bin Tamīm, *'Uyūn al-'ajā'ib*, 12–13.

deliberate duplication (*al-naskh wa-l-ta ʿammud*).[38] Whenever he comes across *al-ma ʿnā al-badī ʿ* (a new poetic meaning), he grudgingly argues that it might have been possible after "sweating and sleeplessness."[39] Moreover, he adds even more diffidently that such new expressions and meanings are repeated in multiple verses that show al-Mutanabbī's "discursive capacity and creative power." But, rather than crediting the poet with fecundity, al-ʿAmīdī manipulates the idea in order to claim it as a reason for repetitiveness in the discursive tableau, a point that he highlights as a sign of deficiency. He adds depreciatively that there is "a huge disparity between the two."[40] On other occasions, he goes so far as to exclaim, "By God, if a human lit a thousand torches to use their light in order to decipher the ambiguities of this verse, useless as it is, he would end up in failure."[41]

As if this were not enough, he concludes that al-Mutanabbī "was the imitator, not the initiator, the successor, not the predecessor, and he bought his way to people through his easy expressions that touch the soul with sweetness; hence he precedes the rest in elegance, but he distorts patterns and garbles composition."[42] In a neat note on one verse that al-ʿAmīdī harshly criticizes, the editor Ibrāhīm al-Disūqī al-Bisāṭī quotes Abū Manṣūr al-Thaʿālibī's (d. 429/1038) comment on the same verse: "It is the emir [prince] of his poetry, as it has an invented application, good wording, and great invented meaning."[43] This juxtaposition between a highly acknowledged critic like al-Thaʿālibī, on the one hand, and Abū Saʿd Muḥammad b. Aḥmad al-ʿAmīdī, who is less known for literary criticism, on the other, shows an ongoing disparity in dealing with such a controversial domain as *sariqāt*. In his multiple critiques of al-ʿAmīdī, Yūsuf al-Badīʿī finds the former not only deviating and departing from fairness but also vaulting over the system of *sariqāt* already applied by critics;[44] thus al-Badīʿī concludes that al-ʿAmīdī "is so prejudiced as to vilify verses and words already highly acclaimed by all *ahl al-adab* [littérateurs]."[45] In another response, al-Badīʿī adds: "Venom drives al-ʿAmīdī to transform al-Mutanabbī's merits into flaws, and his virtues into vices."[46] Accusatory discourse gets out of hand when a scholar and poet like al-ʿAmīdī accumulates references to marginal poets whose poetry is known only to him in order to suggest that a giant like al-Mutanabbī seized on their meaning or expression, which is possible if we are sure that they were accessible to the target poet. As is noted by the editor

[38] al-ʿAmīdī, *al-Ibānah*, 26. [39] Ibid., 33. [40] Ibid., 42. [41] Ibid., 96. [42] Ibid., 149.
[43] Ibid., 91n1.
[44] Yūsuf al-Badīʿī, *al-Subḥ al-munbī ʿan ḥaythiyyat al-Mutanabbī*, ed. Muṣṭafā al-Saqqā et al. (Cairo: Dār al-Maʿārif, 3rd print, n.d.), 18, 188–221.
[45] Ibid., 251, 265. [46] Ibid., 206.

of *al-Ibānah*, such accumulation presents the author as the advocate and judge in a passage that smacks of willful distortion of al-Mutanabbī's fame.[47]

Thus, when al-Badīʿī responds to al-Mutanabbī's detractors, he explains where the power of al-Mutanabbī resides in matters that detractors charge him with taking from others: "When things reached him, he followed the same poetic method followed by predecessors, but with a difference: he diverted it from what they had applied: he defamiliarized, invented, and hence achieved the sum of the best and appeared as the creator."[48] This runs counter to what al-ʿAmīdī would like to prove – and what he has already concluded in a very reductive manner, saying: "I have examined all his poetry and found that the verses of which his proponents are proud and which become his emblems are duplicates of those of his predecessors, and their poetic meanings are flayed from theirs."[49] What bothers al-ʿAmīdī, as shown in his book, is al-Mutanabbī's popularity, which al-ʿAmīdī has to rationalize in order to justify his thin argument. How is it possible for a poet to achieve such fame if he is not so good? Al-ʿAmīdī comes up with this explanation: "He enhances and complements the meanings that he shares with predecessors, or the ones that he steals from them, as his detractors say, with his magnificent expressive clarity and creative eloquence that make people ignore the poetry of those predecessors and make his poetry memorable as part of people's conversation."[50] What al-ʿAmīdī presents here is a conclusion that runs counter to what has already been defined by scholars like al-Qāḍī al-Jurjānī as *naql* and *majdūd*, which the established literary lexicon defines as commendable practices if the successor or contemporary adds better value to an existing theme or expression. He has no clue as to how *talfiq* (patching), for example, is recognized as commendable whenever a poet gives it a high dose of deftness, dexterity, and meaning.

In a careful reading of some portions of *al-Ibānah*, Heinrichs finds, however, some verses cited by al-ʿAmīdī from al-Mutanabbī's corpus that show a duplication that amounts to *inḥiṭāṭ* (less value) as far as mold and meaning are concerned.[51]

Disparities in a Cultural Market

If al-ʿAmīdī lacks a literary-critical sense and rambles here and there, why should we bother about his intervention? That is because his

[47] al-ʿAmīdī, *al-Ibānah*, 11–12. [48] al-Badīʿī, *al-Subḥ*, 76.
[49] al-ʿAmīdī, *al-Ibānah*, 22. [50] Ibid., 12.
[51] Heinrichs, "Evaluation of 'Sariqa,'" 361–62.

contribution is among the weakest literary interventions that gather to counter the enormous reputation of the poet. It is also a marker of a countermovement leveled against al-Mutanabbī's post-*muḥdath* or *ʿaṣrī* (contemporary) style perpetuated by al-ʿAmīdī and others, all of whom tried hard, but without success, to either deflate the target poet's appealing expressions, or undertake a vain imitation of al-Āmidī's *Muwāzanah*, with its skillful navigation between two positions: either with Abū Tammām or against him. Al-ʿAmīdī fails because his book lacks literary depth, logic, and comprehensive knowledge of the philological scene, qualities that had given al-Āmidī's *Muwāzanah* great leverage. Moreover, the grudge that permeates al-ʿAmīdī's *al-Ibānah* blinds its author to the development of an effective argument. Its advantage lies only in the documentation of verses by poets who are known to him, but less so to the rest of literati.

There is, however, another reason for not neglecting his book in this preparatory discussion of disputations. Although, more often than not, we are listening to his voice speaking for all the poet's adversaries, with little or no space for the poet's advocates, he shares with Ibn Wakīʿ's (d. 393/1003) early vindictive but well-informed account the absence of any ulterior motive other than begrudging al-Mutanabbī his widespread fame. Both al-ʿAmīdī and Ibn Wakīʿ reveal their discomfort with al-Mutanabbī's unprecedented popularity not only with the public but also with poets, critics, and philologists. Among his poetic contemporaries, al-Badīʿī cites Abū al-Ḥasan al-Sarī al-Raffāʾ's (d. 362/973) comment that, in al-Mutanabbī's verse that follows, there is "by God, a poetic meaning which the ancients could not have reached." The verse reads as follows:

وَخَصرٌ تَثبُتُ الأبصار فيهِ كَأَنَّ عَليهِ مِن حَدَقٍ نِطاقا

And a waist that glances are fixed on
as if belted with stares.[52]

The competing poet, Abū al-ʿAbbās Aḥmad b. Muḥammad al-Nāmī, says, "There was left in poetry one untouched corner that al-Mutanabbī was soon to occupy, and I desired to precede him in two unprecedented meanings that he came up with."[53] Al-Nāmī happened to be Sayf al-Dawlah's (r. 333–56/945–67) favorite poet before the advent of al-Mutanabbī.[54] Al-Nāmī's effort to beat al-Mutanabbī in meaning or expression was only part of what was going on in a lively assembly like

[52] al-Badīʿī, *al-Subḥ*, 80. [53] Ibid., 81.
[54] Sayf al-Dawlah's name: ʿAlī b. Abī al-Hayjāʾ ʿAbdallāh b. Ḥamdān.

Sayf al-Dawlah's court.[55] Rewarded for every impressive verse in that assembly, al-Mutanabbī would soon become a focal presence whose detractors were as many as his proponents. Indeed, the assembly was most lucrative, an intellectual and poetic arena that gathered the most prominent scholars and poets of their time. Presided over by the emir, who was himself a knight, a warrior, an impressive poet, and a critic, the assembly served as both a poetic consortium and a tournament. In *Yatīmat al-dahr* (The Orphan [Unparalleled] of the Age), his massive critical study and account of sites and littérateurs, Abū Manṣūr al-Thaʿālibī concludes, with respect to that assembly and court: "There has never been such a gathering of prominent poets and stars of their age at any king's or emir's court, except that of the caliphs, as was the case in his [Sayf al-Dawlah of Aleppo]."[56]

Politics of Allegations

There al-Mutanabbī showed his acumen and unequaled poetic talent. Despite al-Mutanabbī's detractors, Abū Manṣūr al-Thaʿālibī introduces his long chapter on him with the following declaration: "The rarity of the cosmos and the clasp of the time's necklace in the craft of poetry."[57] Almost all the knowledgeable fifty or more explicators of al-Mutanabbī's poetry,[58] of whom al-Thaʿālibī counted more than forty including critical accounts,[59] agree that al-Mutanabbī's best poetry was addressed to the assembly in Sayf al-Dawlah's court. But it was also at that assembly that the elegant and powerful poet, critic, prince, and warrior, the cousin of Sayf al-Dawlah, Abū Firās al-Ḥamdānī (d. 357/968), disputed the often-improvising al-Mutanabbī on his alleged duplication of meaning or expression from many poets. Al-Badīʿī quotes the grammarian and poet Abū Muḥammad Saʿīd b. Mubārak b. al-Dahhān (d. 569/1174), in his *al-Risālah al-Saʿīdiyyah* (Saʿīd's Epistle),[60] where mention is made of the mounting accusations by Abū Firās against al-Mutanabbī. These accusations often took the form of interruptions to the poet's recitation.

[55] In *al-Ṣubḥ*, 80n8, al-Badīʿī quotes from the unavailable *Kitāb al-mufāwaḍah*, by Abū al-Ḥasan Muḥammad b. ʿAlī b. Naṣr al-Mālikī (d. 437/1046), to document the shift of attention from al-Nāmī, who was no less a stallion, to al-Mutanabbī.

[56] Abū Manṣūr al-Thaʿālibī, *Yatīmat al-dahr fī maḥāsin ahl al-ʿaṣr*, ed. Mufīd Muḥammad Qumayḥah (Beirut: Dār al-Kutub al-ʿIlmiyyah, 1983), 1:37. Regarding Sayf al-Dawlah's court and assembly, see ibid., 37–56.

[57] Ibid., 139.

[58] See Shaykh Nāṣīf al-Yāzijī, *al-ʿArf al-ṭayyib fī sharḥ Dīwān Abī al-Ṭayyib* (Beirut: Maṭbaʿat al-Qiddīs Jāwirjiyūs, 1882), 3.

[59] al-Badīʿī, *al-Ṣubḥ*, quoting al-Thaʿālibī, *Yatīmat al-dahr*, 270–72.

[60] Ibid., 87n4.

They accuse al-Mutanabbī of committing *maskh* (distortion) and *saraq* (theft) in his recitation. Abū Firās was so furious as to conclude: "You extol yourself with words stolen from others, and you get the prince's rewards."[61] Thus, in one verse in a famous poem at Sayf al-Dawlah's assembly, al-Mutanabbī says: "If what our envious rival said has delighted you. / A wound does not hurt as long as it pleases you."[62] Although the concluding recited verses won the backing of al-Mutanabbī's patron, Sayf al-Dawlah, the increasing number of attacks from the latter's circle held sway in a lively assembly where the poet's proponents were also among the most illustrious names of that age.[63] Even so, al-Thaʿālibī affirms that reports of al-Mutanabbī's recitations spread everywhere, that his prevalent exemplary sayings made their way throughout the region like the "passage of the moon and sun," and that his verses "traverse lands, urban and Bedouin, nights recite his poetry, and days memorize it."[64] Thus, when he says in his patron's presence: "Time itself is a reciter of my odes; I compose a poem, then time recites," the poet's self-boast has a solid ground in reality.[65] He adds that many of these *qalāʾid* (necklaces) turn into proverbial sayings. Despite this laudatory sentiment, al-Thaʿālibī still devotes pages to the thefts from al-Mutanabbī's poetry and al-Mutanabbī's thefts from others.[66] He qualifies this, adding that al-Mutanabbī improves on importations through pleasantness of expression and dexterity of craft.[67] Even so, in at least one case, al-Thaʿālibī agrees with others that al-Mutanabbī goes beyond *sariqah*, to commit *muṣālaṭah* (seizing on the meaning with all or partial wording), which is usually deemed unacceptable by *al-naqadah* (literary critics).[68] This is an important intervention by al-Thaʿālibī. While *saraq*, according to critics, varies in application and has its acceptable or reprehensible applications, *muṣālaṭah* is inexcusable because it is a confiscation of another's poetic property. It is almost a *khalʿ* (wrenching) when a poet changes only a rhyming word from another's verse, a practice that is reprehensible, especially if it is practiced by a famed poet, as Ibn Aydamir notes (see Figure 5.3). Al-Thaʿālibī's use of the term *naqadah* (critics) sounds to

[61] Quoted in ibid., 87–90.
[62] See the poem, in its original and translation, in A. J. Arberry, ed., *Poems of al-Mutanabbī* (Cambridge: Cambridge University Press, 1967), 70–74.
[63] See al-Thaʿālibī, *Yatīmat al-dahr*, 1:34–37. [64] Ibid., 139.
[65] Stetkevych, *Poetics of Islamic Legitimacy*, 191. The Arabic text is also provided:

وَما الدَّهرُ إِلّاَ مِن رُواةِ قَلائِدي   إِذا قُلتُ شِعراً أَصبَحَ الدَّهرُ مُنشِداً

[66] On thefts from the poet, see al-Thaʿālibī, *Yatīmat al-dahr*, 1:159–64; on his thefts from others, see ibid., 164–71.
[67] Ibid., 171. [68] Ibid., 160.

be in line with an ongoing distinction of the role of critics, a point which Ibn Rashīq's *Qurāḍat al dhahab* accords much attention. The practice of later critics attests to this prominence of the craft of criticism, which Ibn Aydamir describes as the most difficult than the craft of poetry.[69]

A Tournament for Competitors

At this juncture it is worthwhile to check on a few things that relate to the poet and the effort of detractors to downplay his fame with vilifications. Historicizing detractors' epistles and books is one way of understanding an explosive situation where the figure of the poet provokes such an enormous grudge as to challenge others to damage his reputation by any available means, but especially by allegations of thievery, as the most destructive morally, culturally, and – in the poet's lifetime – economically. As noted, al-Qāḍī al-Jurjānī (d. 392/1001) produced his *al-Wasāṭah bayna al-Mutanabbī wa-khuṣūmih* (The Mediation between al-Mutanabbī and His Detractors) at a time when detractors and proponents were transforming the cultural site into contending camps that required some arbitration. Abū al-Ḥasan al-Ḥātimī (d. 388/998) was among the attendees at Sayf al-Dawlah's assembly at an early age, and he, Abū al-Qāsim Ismāʿīl al-Ṣāḥib b. ʿAbbād (d. 385/995), and al-Ḥasan b. ʿAlī al-Tinnīsī b. Wakīʿ (d. 393/1003) were contemporaries. The prince and poet Abū Firās was improvising responses while al-Mutanabbī was reciting a poem of supplication, blame, and self-exaltation. Abū Firās's responses/interruptions relate several verses to ancient and early Abbasid poets, claiming poetic meanings and themes to be taken or stolen from them. In practical terminology, both al-Āmidī and al-Qāḍī al-Jurjānī do not assign weight and value to thematic issues, because they are shared among people, and new generations of poets are impelled to draw on that repository, as Ibn Ṭabāṭabā concludes.[70]

In other words, claims like those of Abū Firās may be dismissed – but not when we understand several points: his claims came as well-informed responses and interruptions, whereby the warrior, poet, and prince was referencing, on the spot, similar verses from this or that poet. In other words, they were not nonsensical interruptions but had the ability to impress attendees by their immediate and spontaneous recall and the apparent similarities that they identify between one image or word, theme or expression, uttered by al-Mutanabbī, and a passage from another poet. Coming from a well-versed poet, whose elegant verse, urbane phrasing, and lyrical power created a terrain that competed intensely with al-Mutanabbī's astounding rhythmic beat, thus producing

[69] Ibn Aydamir, *al-Durr al-farīd*, 1:304. [70] See Chapter 4.

a unison between the urban and Bedouin, Abū Firās's responses were bound to generate a favorable response in a court where Sayf al-Dawlah used to entertain discussions and poetic recitations. Warrior that he was, Abū Firās composed poetry that only occasionally reflected a warlike situation. Moreover, the debate, if we can ever call it such, took place in an assembly that gathered both proponents and opponents. In view of this resistance to the laureate's status, later critics and literary historians began to speak of a divided scene, a two-camp structure, that allowed little space for moderation. Even so, Sayf al-Dawlah's role remained pivotal: Would he align himself with his poet, or with the argument of his cousin? As we know, al-Mutanabbī, as an adept performer in crucial situations, was able to win the ruler to his favor by a series of deflationary verses implicitly targeting his opponent, and by other, more endearing and lyrical ones addressed to the ruler. Despite the positive outcome – namely, rewinning Sayf al-Dawlah's favor – opponents took the lead from there and began to either think of vindictive responses to al-Mutanabbī or systematize a terminology for thievery, in both fact and fiction, as al-Ḥātimī had done before (352/964) in his *Ḥilyat al-muḥāḍarah* (Ornament of Discourse),[71] soon after he met al-Mutanabbī (d. 354/965) and Abū ʿAlī al-Fārisī (d. 377/987) at Sayf al-Dawlah's assembly during 337–41/949–53.[72]

The Embittered Critical Response: al-Ḥātimī

It was probably in that assembly, too, that al-Ḥātimī meditated on a better way to downplay al-Mutanabbī's highly regarded character and poetry. A poet and critic known for his animosity to, and for being disliked by, *ahl al-ʿilm* (the knowledgeable experts), according to Yāqūt,[73] al-Ḥātimī would be a good candidate to battle his target poet.[74] Indeed, in his *al-Risālah al-mūḍiḥah* (Explanatory [or Explicatory] Epistle), al-Ḥātimī shows his dislike not only for the target poet but also for Abū al-Qāsim ʿAlī b. Ḥamzah al-Baṣrī's (d. 375/985) assembly, which he derides as a *sūq* (market). He calls the attendees *ughaylimah* (teens – i.e., of no

71 See al-Kattānī's prefatory note to his edition of *Ḥilyat al-muḥāḍarah*, 7–8.
72 This does not contradict Bonebakker's surmise that al-Ḥātimī joined the court as early as 337–47/948–58.
73 Yāqūt al-Ḥamawī, *Muʿjam al-udabāʾ*, 5:313.
74 Muḥammad Yūsuf Najm develops this point in his introduction to *al-Risālah al-mūḍiḥah*. See Muḥammad Yūsuf Najm, introduction to al-Ḥātimī, *al-Risālah al-mūḍiḥah*, jīm–kāf (this introduction is numbered in Arabic letters).

consequence), unaccepted by experts and untrained in belles lettres.[75] Abū al-Qāsim al-Baṣrī was a friend of the poet, and his assembly was often intended for students of al-Mutanabbī's poetry, who were there to go over, explain, and annotate his available collection. Abū al-Qāsim was also known as a littérateur and philologist of note.

Al-Ḥātimī's introduction to an encounter that had already been planned, orchestrated, and provoked by the ruler and his minister is not only venomous but decidedly negative in intention and design. His *al-Risālah al-mūḍiḥah* shamelessly acknowledges that Abū Muḥammad al-Ḥasan al-Muhallabī (d. 352/963), an Arab statesman, poet, man of letters, and the vizier of the Buyid prince Muʿizz al-Dawlah, is the patron behind this vilifying epistle.[76] The vizier visited al-Mutanabbī in his assembly at al-Baṣrī's house, along with the highly regarded littérateur Abū al-Faraj al-Iṣfahānī (d. 356/967), the author of the voluminous *Kitāb al-aghānī* (The Book of Songs), expecting al-Mutanabbī to reward the courtesy visit with a poem in praise of the vizier, but which the poet did not do.[77] In his *al-Risālah al-mūḍiḥah*, al-Ḥātimī touches on the specific reason for the vizier's anger: al-Mutanabbī "was reluctant to serve him," meaning to write in his praise.[78] He explains how the vizier challenged his companions to denigrate al-Mutanabbī: "Abū Muḥammad al-Muhallabī presumed that nobody could debate and rival him or was capable of uncovering his faults. The prince [Muʿizz al-Dawlah] was upset that a person [al-Mutanabbī] had arrived from the domains [Aleppo] of his arch enemy [Sayf al-Dawlah] without having a person in his own kingdom, equal to him [al-Mutanabbī] in craft, and stature."[79] Al-Ḥātimī adds: "He delegated me to defile him and tear apart his public image, and assigned me the task of tracking down his faults, scrutinizing his poetry, and consequently forcing him to depart Iraq."[80]

In view of the vizier's literary reputation and his companionship with littérateurs, he might have asked for a debate, not a vilification, in line with his interest in literary and cultural disputations that touch on multiple topics. Given to vainglory, al-Ḥātimī probably increased the dose, adding to later editions details and names that could not have been part of the presumed encounter.[81] The challenge finds al-Ḥātimī not only ready but also waiting for such an opportunity after years of a mounting grudge

[75] al-Ḥātimī, *al-Risālah al-mūḍiḥah*, 9; see also ʿUmar Khalīfah b. Idrīs's comment in his introduction to Ibn Wakīʿ, 41.

[76] See further in Sanni, "Historic Encounter"; Bonebakker, *Ḥātimī and His Encounter*, 16.

[77] See Najm, introduction, jīm.

[78] al-Ḥātimī, *al-Risālah al-mūḍiḥah*, 5.

[79] See al-Ḥātimī, *al-Risālah al-Ḥātimiyyah*, in al-ʿAmīdī, *al-Ibānah*, 254. See also Bonebakker's paraphrase in *Ḥātimī and His Encounter*, 16.

[80] al-Ḥātimī, *al-Risālah al-Ḥātimiyyah*, in al-ʿAmīdī, *al-Ibānah*, 254.

[81] See Najm, introduction, nūn.

against the poet laureate, whom al-Ḥātimī thought of as unwilling to support his advancement at the court of Sayf al-Dawlah in 341/951.[82] Al-Ḥātimī's epistle, in both versions,[83] shows how he begrudges the poet's fame and what he considers al-Mutanabbī's arrogance, aloofness, and disregard for others. In passages that follow one another, he discloses his outrage at the poet's grandeur: "He thought that belles lettres is only reserved for him and that poetry is a salubrious sea that reaches no other and a meadow whose flowers are only for him."[84] Apart from their enmity to Sayf al-Dawlah and their failure to secure al-Mutanabbī's encomium, both Muʿizz al-Dawlah and the vizier were enraged to realize that al-Mutanabbī enjoyed a large gathering of prominent littérateurs and students of his poetry at ʿAlī b. Ḥamzah al-Baṣrī's assembly in Baghdad.[85]

Based on the biographical material available about the assembly, Muḥammad Mandūr (d. 1965) concludes that this assembly was much more important than even that of Sayf al-Dawlah and the assemblies in Egypt. "From this assembly particular studies of al-Mutanabbī's poetry got disseminated across the whole Islamic world."[86] In al-Thaʿālibī's account,[87] when in Baghdad (351/962), al-Mutanabbī was undisposed to eulogizing the vizier, and "this was difficult for the vizier to swallow. He tempted Baghdad poets to defame [al-Mutanabbī] and compete in lampooning him; those included Ibn al-Ḥajjāj (d. 391/1001), Ibn Sukkarah, Muḥammad b. ʿAbdallāh al-Zāhid al-Hāshimī (d. 385/995), and al-Ḥātimī." Al-Thaʿālibī adds: "He didn't respond to them, and never thought of doing so, and when he was asked why not, he responded, 'I am already done with such a response by saying to poets who belong to a higher status:

أَرى المُتَشاعِرينَ غَروا بِذَمّي   وَمَن ذا يَحمَدُ الداءَ العُضالا
وَمَن يَكُ ذا فَمٍ مُرٍّ مَريضٍ   يَجِد مُرّاً بِهِ الماءَ الزُّلالا

'Poetasters are tempted to slander me
but who on earth commends an incurable disease?
A person with a bitter, sick mouth
will find sweet water bitter.'"[88]

[82] See Sanni, "Historic Encounter,"163, n. 18.
[83] We have two versions of the epistle. One is al-Ḥātimī, *al-Risālah al-mūḍiḥah*. A different version with fewer details is al-Ḥātimī, *al-Risālah al-Ḥātimiyyah*, in al-ʿAmīdī, *al-Ibānah*.
[84] al-Ḥātimī, *al-Risālah al-mūḍiḥah*, 6 (*al-Risālah al-Ḥātimiyyah*, 253).
[85] See Muḥammad Mandūr, *al-Naqd al-manhajī ʿinda al-ʿArab* (Cairo: Nahḍat Miṣr, 1996), 214–17.
[86] Ibid.
[87] al-Thaʿālibī, *Yatīmat al-dahr*, 1:150–51. For the verse reference in Abū al-ʿAlāʾ al-Maʿarrī's *Muʿjiz Aḥmad*, see Bin Tamīm, *ʿUyūn al-ʿajāʾib*, 215.
[88] *Yatīmat al-dahr*, 1:150.

Like them was Abū al-Ḥasan b. Muḥammad b. Lankak al-Baṣrī (d. 360/970). Al-Mutanabbī's response to his unidentified interlocutors is important as a threshold that can be used to address al-Ḥātimī's epistle, where the latter admits that the vizier, his patron, Abū Muḥammad al-Muhallabī, was waiting for his report after the presumed encounter with al-Mutanabbī,[89] which basically argues against the latter's shared meanings and expressions and labels them under *saraq* (theft), while simultaneously quizzing the poet on varieties of metaphorical application.

Undermining Strategies

In these meetings, al-Ḥātimī's strategy that aimed at tearing down the poet's image rests, first, on listing similarities with other poets; second, on proving that al-Mutanabbī is far below the caliber and acumen of ancient poets; and third, on showing that al-Mutanabbī borrows from and distorts the poetry of recent poets, the *muḥdathūn*, especially Abū Tammām and al-Buḥturī. The claims in the first epistle sound hollow and unreal, if not absurd, claims with which Najm – in his meticulously edited version of the epistle – is uncomfortable.[90] Against the laudatory comments of grammarians, linguists, and poets, al-Ḥātimī presents a poet who is insulted, ridiculed, and rendered helpless and is listening to al-Ḥātimī, who is telling him, "You are a thief, not an originator, and inefficient appropriator," and one who distorts others' poetic meanings – a point that he repeats every now and then, albeit in different phrasing, but to the same end.[91] Although this occurs several times – for the poet is *mustariqun muḥtadhī* (a subtle thief and duplicator), or incapable of invention[92] – nevertheless the occasion does not occur during the encounter at al-Baṣrī's abode, but presumably during the following one in al-Muhallabī's assembly that convened three times, in the presence of many, but especially Abū ʿAlī al-Ḥusayn b. Muḥammad al-Anbārī (d. 384/994), whose admiration for the poet was known;[93] al-Sīrāfī (d. 368/978); Abū al-Fatḥ al-Marāghī; Abū al-Ḥasan al-Anṣārī; ʿAlī b. Hārūn (d. 352/963); and

89 al-Ḥātimī, *al-Risālah al-mūḍiḥah*, 96–97 (*al-Risālah al-Ḥātimiyyah*, 153–270). I am using both. Al-Ḥātimī writes in *al-Risālah al-Ḥātimiyyah*, "I got busy the rest of day with some errand, a case that delayed me a little from attending His Eminence al-Muhallab, but the news reached him, and his messengers called on me at night to come, and I told him the story in full, and he was so pleased and joyful at what happened that he called on Muʿizz al-Dawlah early in the morning to report the entire narrative" (269).

90 Najm, introduction, mīm.

91 al-Ḥātimī, *al-Risālah al-Ḥātimiyyah*, 260–68. See also al-Ḥātimī, *al-Risālah al-mūḍiḥah* (al-Maktabah al-Shāmilah; henceforth: MS), 52, 56. This is a network version that is garbled, with grammatical errors, etc. It is useful in its extra reporting.

92 al-Ḥātimī, *al-Risālah al-mūḍiḥah*, 17, 130.

93 Ibid., 120–56.

ʿAlī b. ʿĪsā al-Rummānī (d. 384/994). The effort to draw comparisons with recent poets and also to claim that the target poet negated knowledge of Abū Tammām was thus part of a vilifying campaign, which – as we understand from the Khālidiyyān Brothers – was not lost on al-Mutanabbī, who dismissed it as absurd.[94] Al-Ḥātimī exposes himself as dedicating time and effort to learning al-Mutanabbī's corpus by heart for the single purpose of demolishing his reputation. Thus, in introducing his first encounter, written down three days after the occasion, al-Ḥātimī presents himself as desperate not only to attack the poet but also to portray himself as a powerful contender: "I bore upon him like a torrent rushing down toward the bottom of the valley."[95] Al-Ḥātimī reiterates: "I know nothing good about your poetry, and I fail to recognize any invention there."[96] As if that were not enough, and contrary to the admiration of the knight, critic, and poet Sayf al-Dawlah, and a number of authorities, including at a later time no less a figure than Abū al-ʿAlāʾ al-Maʿarrī, al-Ḥātimī dismisses claims that the poet has any invented meanings of his own: "These verses, in which you think you excel and surpass all in their meanings, regarding yourself as the lord of their subtleties, were stolen and pasted from those poets who were ahead of you in their compositional order and their invented meanings."[97] He lists what he deems *sariqāt* from al-Buḥturī, Abū Tammām, Jarīr, and al-Ṣanawbarī (d. 334/945),[98] concluding with a verse:

> A youth reciting poetry but,
> so we became aware, steals the stolen.[99]

The traps that al-Ḥātimī sets for himself are several, not only in the sense that he portrays himself as a mercenary commissioned to vilify al-Mutanabbī, using for the task all his knowledge of grammar, eloquence, and rhetorical devices, but also because he vaults over what he has systematically argued in his *Ḥilyat al-muḥāḍarah* (The Ornament of Discourse). Al-Mutanabbī's presumed rejoinder goes as follows: "Be fair, for fairness is your deportment ... and do not let whim muddle your thought; is there ever a person who is free from such a drawback? Who is there who is free from fault: a poet or prose writer, a precursor or successor? I am not an exception."[100] In another version,[101] but also in

[94] This issue is dealt with further later.
[95] al-Ḥātimī, *al-Risālah al-mūḍiḥah*, 10. See Bonebakker's translation, *Ḥātimī and His Encounter*, 17–18.
[96] al-Ḥātimī, *al-Risālah al-mūḍiḥah*, 130.
[97] al-Ḥātimī, *al-Risālah al-mūḍiḥah* (MS), 52.
[98] Full name: Abū Bakr Aḥmad b. Muḥammad b. Marrār al-Ṣanawbarī.
[99] al-Ḥātimī, *al-Risālah al-mūḍiḥah*, 10. [100] Ibid., 78. [101] Ibid., 143; 201 (MS).

Najm's, the target poet's response continues as follows: "And who is unique in invention and innovation? I know of no poet, pre-Islamic or Islamic, who does not follow, imitate, piece together, and appropriate verse."[102] Al-Mutanabbī adds:

> Had you been fair enough to yourself, and abandoned the burdening zeal that weighs you down, you could have found yourself open to disapproval for your record of my poetic faults, drawbacks, and blemishes. That is because he who has so much poetic wealth could be forgiven for little slips. Let me refer to Imruʾ al-Qays, the imam of poets, the creator of poetic meanings, and the precursor in every lucid expression, invented meaning, and innovated simile: he is good in places, average in others, and not so good in some cases as he is perfect in the rest.[103]

The Knights of Poetry

Al-Ḥātimī traps himself in a carefully prepared vindictive presentation, commissioned and paid for, as the recipient of the Buyid ruler Muʿizz al-Dawlah's great reward (*takrumah shadīdah*), a phrasing that Muḥammad b. Aḥmad, the owner of the manuscript, objects to as poorly chosen.[104] According to his account, the target poet, al-Mutanabbī, also falls into several traps. As presented, or at least as al-Ḥātimī would like his patrons and affiliates to believe, the celebrated poet is led into several snares. One of these is al-Mutanabbī's boasting about his precedence in poetic expressions and meanings, a verse that al-Ḥātimī desperately needs in order to counter the claim to originality and precedence. Ironically, al-Ḥātimī in the *Ornament of Discourse* has no objection to the practice of improvement on an original or a collation of multiple verses in one,[105] something that later critics accept as a poetic traction achieved through focused and concentrated patching:[106]

أنَا السّابِقُ الهادي إلى ما أقُولُهُ   إذِ القَوْلُ قَبْلَ القائِلِينَ مَقُول

I am the guiding precursor in my wording
ahead of others in virgin expressions.

Driven as he is in the epistle to downplay the poet's enormous achievement in a successful poetics of dense expressions and poetic themes, al-Ḥātimī jumps on the issue of precedence and originality in the verse as a stepping stone to denigrate the sheer expressiveness as being below the standard of the "knights of poetry." Thus, he brings into the claimed encounter a presumed comparison drawn by al-Mutanabbī between

[102] al-Ḥātimī, *al-Risālah al-mūḍiḥah*, 57. [103] Ibid., 78. [104] Ibid., 96n3.
[105] al-Ḥātimī, *Ḥilyat al-muḥāḍarah*, 2:90. [106] Ibn Rashīq, *Qurāḍat al-dhahab*, 106.

himself and the four pre-Islamic "knights of poetry": Imruʾal-Qays (d. 545), al-Nābighah (d. 604), Zuhayr (d. 609), and al-Aʿshā (d. 629).[107] The poet's reported retort against al-Ḥātimī's list of duplications or borrowings is based on a common understanding among philologists that even though these grand poets are the most celebrated and acclaimed, they are not beyond criticism.

Again, al-Ḥātimī jumps on the occasion to reiterate what irritates him about al-Mutanabbī the person: his self-glorification as someone who treats himself as equal to these four. He seizes the opportunity to argue that the poet has no right to compare himself to these stallions.[108] Al-Mutanabbī only anticipates or sides with a given precept in critical poetic theory, as in al-Āmidī's *al-Muwāzanah*, for example, where improvement and better value negates the issue of anciency and modernity. Reflecting on that explosive cultural climate that al-Ḥātimī sets on fire, al-Qāḍī al-Jurjānī justifies possibilities of equal transactions whereby contemporaries can be on par with the ancients. He also details the pitfalls of sweeping conclusions in his systematic differentiation between *saraq* and common recurrence.[109] His conclusion offers a map for the subject: "If you are fair, then you can apologize for poets of our age or those who follow because precursors exhausted poetic meanings and used most of them; as for the leftovers, they might have been disregarded for a reason, or because of their far-fetched reach, complexity of intention, or inaccessibility." He adds: "If one of us exerts vigor, meditation, and thought in order to come up with a presumably strange [remarkable] poetic meaning and created invention, and composes a verse he thinks of as unique, and goes over the *dīwān*s [collected poetry volumes of others], he may well find it there."[110]

In other words, this is a blanket statement that can adequately refute the stipulations that al-Ḥātimī heaps up to prove his discursive vilification. In response to al-Mutanabbī's few defensive statements, and relentless to the end, al-Ḥātimī turns into a conservative critic who insists on historical precedence as the ultimate value and significance, for his preference lies with the one who has the merit of antecedence.[111] He has already rebuffed a claim that culture and language are open fields. As shown earlier, this response refers to Abū ʿAlī al-Fārisī's conclusive remark that culture and language are open and shared.[112] The same

[107] al-Ḥātimī, *al-Risālah al-mūḍiḥah*, 84–85. [108] Ibid.
[109] al-Jurjānī, *al-Wasāṭah* (1966), 214–15. [110] Ibid.
[111] al-Ḥātimī, *al-Risālah al-mūḍiḥah*, 149–52.
[112] Al-Fārisī opened the gate in suggesting "there is no *ijtilāb* [procuring support] or *istiʿārah* [here: the act of borrowing], and *kalām* [written and spoken Arabic] is open to all, and expressions are free." Quoted in al-Ḥātimī, *Ḥilyat al-muḥāḍarah*, 2:28.

premise that credits antecedent poetic authority with excellence and richness prepares al-Ḥātimī to justify the rise of thievery terminology as necessarily generated to deal with this divide between antecedence and succession.[113] He argues that, had it not been for this prioritization, "there wouldn't be a competitive discussion around *saraq*, procuring support, transference, and stitching or piecing together from several verses."[114] A word that is much to his liking is the one presumably used by the theologian Abū al-Ḥasan al-Anṣārī in al-Muhallabī's assembly in reference to al-Ḥātimī's role and presence in these real or fabricated disputations, *al-tawwāb* (here: one who exhorts penance).[115] Al-Ḥātimī's epistle, as it appears in either version,[116] reveals the extent of the effort that he exerted in order to prove he had the upper hand at the court of al-Muhallabī, the vizier in Baghdad, as a correlative to his obvious failure to secure attention in Sayf al-Dawlah's highly prestigious court. Al-Ḥātimī explains: "I returned home soon after [the presumed encounter at al-Baṣrī's abode] and spent three nights without tasting sleep until the receding stars, fading darkness, and the smile of morning – until the epistle was in shape."[117]

To understand better al-Ḥātimī's self-augmentation and his frustration at Sayf al-Dawlah's assembly and its celebration of others, especially the poet laureate, it is worth bearing in mind his angry but detailed series of accusations in this context. His post–Sayf al-Dawlah career and writing show a tendency to avenge himself on that past and its prominent figures. Thus, he needs al-Muhallabī and his assembly to counter and uproot the image of Sayf al-Dawlah and his court. No wonder, then, that he claims to have been a close companion of the vizier, not only in his assembly but also in his private meetings, and that he was al-Muhallabī's special favorite.[118] This self-glorification, a charade of prestigious career and life, and systematic exhibition of philological knowledge, exposes him as a twisted personality bent on destroying others. To offset a past, it has to replace it with another that would mock al-Mutanabbī in a series of

113 al-Ḥātimī, *al-Risālah al-mūḍiḥah*, 150. 114 Ibid.

115 Ibid., 142; in Islam: the Lord is the Forgiver; in Christian theology: Angel of Penance (forgiver of a sinner), who "extracts thievery."

116 In *al-Risālah al-Ḥātimiyyah*, al-Disūqī al-Bisāṭī, the editor, includes Yāqūt al-Ḥamawī's version, *Muʿjam al-udabāʾ*, 5:316–29. Yāqūt does not reference this version as the *Epistle*; it is a *mukhāṭabah* (here: an encounter) that took place between the two, which, Yāqūt says, "I narrated as I found it" (ibid., 316). *Al-Risālah al-mūḍiḥah* is more extensive, with extra references to scholars who, he claimed, were either present or received it. In his documentation of the author, Yāqūt mentions *Kitāb al-mūḍiḥah fī masāwiʾ al-Mutanabbī* (The Explicatory [or Explanatory] Book of al-Mutanabbī's Vices). Ibid., 314.

117 al-Ḥātimī, *al-Risālah al-mūḍiḥah* (MS), 39; in Najm's edition, *al-Risālah al-mūḍiḥah*, 96.

118 al-Ḥātimī, *al-Risālah al-mūḍiḥah*, 120.

grotesqueries, of which Bonebakker lists a few. "His ridicule of Mutanabbī assumes grotesque proportions when ... he reports that ʿAlī b. Hārūn questions Mutanabbī about three lines which he considers blasphemous."[119] In the next debate out of a total of four, al-Ḥātimī presumably challenges the target poet by saying that, even if Abū Tammām was accused of theft, he "proved himself equal, if not superior, to his models."[120] Furthermore, while describing his own arrival to al-Baṣrī's residence and assembly, "mounted on a beautifully harnessed riding animal and followed by a train of attendants," he describes the target poet's seat as "made out of some worn-out garments or cushions."[121] As if this belittling of the target poet and the host were not enough, al-Ḥātimī reports that ʿAlī b. Hārūn was to "whisper in Ḥātimī's ear that Mutanabbī has bad gums and foul breath."[122] A neurotic character appears that further analysis could disclose better. As we have no information concerning al-Mutanabbī's actual impression of al-Ḥātimī, other than what was reported by al-Thaʿālibī on the authority of others, we can conclude that al-Mutanabbī's disregard for al-Ḥātimī and the Baghdadi group, along with Ibn Lankak, who was in Baghdad at that time, shows that al-Mutanabbī held himself aloof, unwilling to descend to their despicable level. Indeed, al-Ḥātimī's epistle sounds more like an intrusion into an assembly in order to shout a few insults and then leave. It derives significance only from its author's other writings, especially his *Ḥilyat al-muḥāḍarah* (Ornament of Discourse).

The Problematic Position of Ibn ʿAbbād

The extended version of al-Ḥātimī's text that claims three more meetings with al-Mutanabbī at the vizier's assembly may have portions that are a figment of his imagination. Or, if there exist some bits of evidence to suggest otherwise, al-Mutanabbī's responses are repressed so as to give the vizier and his circle an upper hand in debating not only the poet but also the Ḥamdānīs and their highly regarded court in Aleppo. Al-Thaʿālibī's exhaustive account of al-Mutanabbī makes no mention of these presumed encounters other than identifying al-Ḥātimī as being among the group who were incited to insult the poet. He adds:

> Al-Mutanabbī made use of nighttime for his departure from Baghdad, heading to the eminent Abū al-Faḍl b. al-ʿAmīd in a bid to challenge the vizier al-Muhallabī. He arrived comfortably at Arrajān. It was reported that al-Ṣāḥib Abū al-Qāsim wished to have al-Mutanabbī pay him a visit in Iṣfahān and treat him like the chiefs

[119] See Bonebakker, *Ḥātimī and His Encounter*, 48–49. [120] Ibid., 49.
[121] Bonebakker's paraphrase in ibid., 16. [122] Ibid., 49.

of their times whom he addressed. At the time, al-Ṣāḥib was still a youth, and his status was very modest, not a minister as yet. He wrote to al-Mutanabbī, persuading him to pay the visit and share all his [al-Ṣāḥib's] wealth. Al-Mutanabbī ignored his request, not responding to him and heading instead to visit the eminent ʿAḍud al-Dawlah in Shiraz, his trip proving to be both fulfilling and fruitful. Al-Ṣāḥib began to target him with antagonistic darts, noting his drawbacks, blaming him for flaws and faults, even though al-Ṣāḥib was more aware than anyone else of his [al-Mutanabbī's] poetic merits and had memorized more of them than anyone else, using them and adopting them as being exemplary in his lectures and writings.[123]

Nevertheless, al-Ṣāḥib wrote *al-Risālah fī al-kashf ʿan masāwiʾ shiʿr al-Mutanabbī* (The Epistle in Exposing the Faults of al-Mutanabbī's Poetry).[124] There is no comparison between this and other vilifying contributions. As an adept in poetry and culture, a well-raised intellect, and a longtime admirer of al-Mutanabbī, al-Ṣāḥib has to admit that the poet in question is often perfect in compositional patterns, and thus his critique is centered on what he regards as the little that is not as good, for reasons that al-Ṣāḥib supports with examples.[125] When it comes to *sariqāt*, the critic is too smart to get involved in that topic. Thus he offers a blanket stipulation: "As for *saraq*, it is not a matter for reprimand because pre-Islamic and Islamic poetry and poets agree on its nature and limits, but what could be censured and blameworthy would be for him to seize on substantial poetic meanings belonging to al-Buḥturī and others and claiming not to be acquainted with their poetry or aware of their names."[126] There is nothing on the record to substantiate the poet's dismissal of such poets as al-Buḥturī and Abū Tammām, but al-Ḥātimī's previously mentioned rumor,[127] along with Abū Firās's interruptions of al-Mutanabbī's recitations, seems to have left an impression among those souls who were receptive to such an account concerning al-Mutanabbī. In

123 al-Thaʿālibī, *Yatīmat al-dahr*, 1:152.

124 This essay is included in *al-Ibānah*. See al-Ṣāḥib Abū al-Qāsim b. ʿAbbād, *al-Risālā fī al-kashf ʿan masāwiʾ shiʿr al-Mutanabbī*, quoted in al-ʿAmīdī, *al-Ibānah*, 221–50. It is in al-Ḥātimī's *al-Risālah al-Ḥātimiyyah* that the author claimed such a thing, adding that al-Mutanabbī rejoins: "I swear by my own accord I haven't read the poetry of your Abū Tammām" (264). See Yāqūt al-Ḥamawī, *Muʿjam al-udabāʾ*, 5:324, 325, 328.

125 Al-Ṣāḥib's critique of al-Mutanabbī appears in al-Thaʿālibī, *Yatīmat al-dahr*, 1:122, and has been translated by Maurice A. Pomerantz: "It was Ismāʿīl's animosity over this early rebuff that caused him to cast the arrows of slander at al-Mutanabbī, to be attentive to his slips and oversights in poetry and to reproach him for his faults, despite the fact that [Ibn ʿAbbād] was the most knowledgeable of its excellences, had committed the most of it to memory and employed it the most in his speech and writing." See Maurice A. Pomerantz, *Licit Magic: The Life of al-Ṣāḥib b. ʿAbbād (d. 385/995)* (Leiden: Brill, 2018), 51n76.

126 Ibn ʿAbbād, *al-Risālā fī al-kashf*, quoted in al-ʿAmīdī, *al-Ibānah*, 230.

127 See n. 122.

al-Ṣāḥib's note, the conditional *if*, in *in kāna yaʾkhudh* (if he were seizing on), is crucial, because the critic is only responding to others who make such an unfounded claim, contrary to the terms of an ever-growing systematic knowledge as to what constitutes *saraq* and how accountable a poet is for appropriating shared poetic meanings or unique and invented ones. Although Ibn Aybak al-Ṣafadī (d. 764/1363) mentioned in this connection *karārīs* (booklets) by al-Ṣāḥib against al-Mutanabbī, it seems that this is the only one extant.[128]

Worth noting at this point, in justification of the use of the conditional *if*, is what is reported by the Khālidī Brothers.[129] They were writing in reference to what was rumored to be critical of al-Mutanabbī, cited by those who were envious because he belittled the *muḥdathūn* and dismissed well-known rhetors and grammarians.[130] In this connection, the Khālidī Brothers added that they were at Sayf al-Dawlah's assembly reciting a verse and that al-Mutanabbī noticed its similarity to a verse by Abū Tammām. When they looked surprised, al-Mutanabbī rejoined: "Is it possible for an *adīb* [littérateur] not to be familiar with the poetry of Abū Tammām, who is the master for all those who came after?" The Khālidī Brothers told him about the rumor, and he denied it. They added: "Whenever we happened to meet him [al-Mutanabbī], he used to recite for us Abū Tammām's magnificent verse, and he used to transmit all his poetry."[131] This is an important nodal point because a few contemporaries – opponents or spectators – accepted or reported the rumor that al-Mutanabbī had denied any knowledge of Abū Tammām after the war initiated and waged first by Abū Firās, and al-Ḥātimī soon after.[132] Thus, in al-Ḥātimī's version of a claimed meeting at al-Muhallabī's assembly, there is a deliberate falsification of information, especially when he assigns to al-Mutanabbī some highly improbable retort that the poet is unaware of and unfamiliar with the names and poetries of the two prominent poets Abū Tammām and al-Buḥturī. "I am unaware that I have heard of their names except in this place."[133] In another presumed quote, al-Mutanabbī denies both precursors, Abū Tammām and al-Buḥturī, any invented poetic meanings.[134] These obvious falsifications are only a cue for al-Ḥātimī's retort: "Abū Tammām and al-Buḥturī are the poets whose proverbial sayings and favorable expressions you appropriated [*ijtalabta*]

[128] al-Ṣafadī, *al-Wāfī bi-l-wafayāt*, 12:46.

[129] The brothers Abū Bakr Muḥammad and Abū Saʿīd ʿUthmān, the sons of Hāshim, known as the Khālidiyyān, were the litterateurs of Basrah and its poets. They attended Sayf al-Dawlah's assembly and eulogized him. Abū ʿUthmān, the younger of the two, distinguished himself by his prolific memory. He died in 371/981; Abū Bakr in 381/991.

[130] al-Badīʿī, *al-Ṣubḥ*, 142. [131] Ibid., 143.

[132] See Yāqūt al-Ḥamawī's version, *Muʿjam al-udabāʾ*, 5:325.

[133] al-Ḥātimī, *al-Risālah al-mūḍiḥah*, 106. [134] Ibid., 186.

١٣٩

مرّ زنيها والديك يدعو صباحه إذا ما بنو نعش دنوا فتصوبوا

فقال الفرزدق واجتلب البيت الأخير ◉

وإجانة ريّا السروب كأنما إذا غمست فيها الزجاجة كوكب

مرّ زنيها والديك يدعو صباحه إذا ما بنو نعش دنوا فتصوبوا

قال وأحسبه تناول ذلك مغيرا عليه وإن كانت الغارة عارية ولا أراه أورده

إلا اجتلابا واستلحاقا ◉ وقال أبو عمرو بن العلاء ما أرى الاجتلاب

والاستلحاق إلا سرقا ◉ وقد يجتلب الشاعر البيت والبيتين والمعنى

والمعنيين من شعر شاعر آخر إذا كان ذلك الشاعر مخاطبا له وكان موجبا

عن مخاطبته كالذي يلفي في شعر جرير والفرزدق ولا يرى ذلك سرقا

كقول الفرزدق يخاطب جريرا ◉

Figure 5.2 *Istilḥāq* and *ijtilāb*: unacknowledged acquisition as *saraq* in Abū ʿAmrū b. al-ʿAlāʾ's view

and *istalḥaqta* their poetic meanings, but you are much below their standard, like an arrow that falls short of its destination"[135] (see Figure 5.2).

The Disconcerting Fame

Abū al-Qāsim Ismāʿīl b. ʿAbbād, also known as al-Ṣāḥib, could have written or said other things in his assembly of poets, but this could only have lasted for a short time, because soon after his anti-Mutanabbī epistle and or booklets, he compiled al-Mutanabbī's verses on wisdom and exemplary sayings.[136] Throughout his career he also prosified (or dissolved poetry into prose [*ḥall*]) al-Mutanabbī's poetry in his magnificent

[135] Ibid., 106.

[136] Abū al-Ṭayyib Aḥmad b. al-Ḥusayn al-Mutanabbī, *Amthāl Abī al-Ṭayyib al-Mutanabbī: allatī jamaʿahā al-Ṣāḥib b. ʿAbbād li-Fakhr al-Dawlah b. Būyah wa-maʿahā mā dhakarahu al-Thaʿālibī fī Yatīmat al-dahr min maḥāsin amthālihi wa-ḥikamihi wa-mā dhakarahu al-ʿUkbarī min aʿjāz abyātihi allatī dhahabat amthālan*, ed. Muḥammad Ibrāhīm Salīm (Cairo: Dār al-Ṭalīʿah, 1993).

Figure 5.3 Blaming al-Mutanabbī for *khal*ʿ (invading a verse with a new rhyme)

epistolary art. Al-Thaʿālibī presents many of these as examples of what he calls *ghayḍun min fayḍ* (little from a plentiful).[137]

Unlike the annoyance of his contemporaries such as al-Ḥātimī (d. 388/998) and Ibn Wakīʿ (d. 393/1003), al-Ṣāḥib's was alleviated by soothing and deflating responses from some of his circle and also by his position as the companion of his master, Ibn al-ʿAmīd (d. 360/970),[138] who was to be pleased with al-Mutanabbī upon reaching him in Arrajān. Before that, Ibn al-ʿAmīd was ill-disposed toward the poet. According to the grammarian Abū al-Ḥasan ʿAlī b. ʿĪsā al-Rabaʿī (d. 420/1029), one of Ibn al-ʿAmīd's companions once found him displeased and distressed, and the companion thought it was because of the recent death of Ibn al-ʿAmīd's sister. When asked, the latter responded, "The case of this al-Mutanabbī enrages and angers me, and I need to dampen his memory and fame, as more than sixty condolences that I have received start with his verse." The companion

[137] al-Thaʿālibī, Yatīmat *al-dahr,* 1:153–56. See also Amidu Sanni, *The Arabic Theory of Prosification and Versification: On Ḥall and Naẓm in Arabic Theoretical Discourse* (Beirut: Franz Steiner, 1998).

[138] Full name: Abū al-Faḍl Muḥammad b. Abī ʿAbdallāh b. al-ʿAmīd.

rejoined, "You cannot change fate, and the man is lucky in his fame and popularity. It is better not to be occupied with this matter."[139]

Understandably, then, such fame would have enraged competing poets and scholars, some of whom were no less outraged by the poet's close company with grammarians and linguists, who devoted their time to explaining and annotating his verse. Ibn Wakīʿ's *Kitāb al-munṣif li-l-sāriq wa-l-masrūq minhu fī iẓhār sariqāt Abī al-Ṭayyib al-Mutanabbī* (Impartial Assessment of the Plagiarist and Plagiarized in Exposing the Thefts of Abū al-Ṭayyib al-Mutanabbī) proved to be as vindictive as al-Ḥātimī's epistles. Ibn Rashīq's labeling of the book as *ladīgh* (stinging and biting) is most apt.[140] Ibn Sharaf al-Qayrawānī describes Ibn Wakīʿ in his book as "more unjust and cruel than Sadūm" (Qāḍī Sadūm was known for injustice and cruelty).[141] The opening pages do not hide Ibn Wakīʿ's anger at the target poet's fame and his celebration among his supporters and proponents.[142] Ibn Wakīʿ's argument runs against those proponents who claim that al-Mutanabbī was the inventor of and forerunner for new poetic meanings, an opinion that resonates with verse 55 (already cited) where the poet asserts poetic precedence:

أنَا السّابِقُ الهادي إلى ما أقُولُه   إذِ القَوْلُ قَبْلَ القائِلِينَ مَقُول

I am the guiding precursor in my wording
ahead of others in virgin expressions.

Ibn Wakīʿ finds in the verse "vanity and baseless extravagance."[143] With the goal of demonstrating al-Mutanabbī's subservience, not leadership – his being the successor, not the precursor – Ibn Wakīʿ proposes to point out the poet's thefts, especially what he deems despicable and unacceptable *saraq*.[144]

Most of Ibn Wakīʿ's listings fall within verses that have echoes of some antecedents' poetic meanings or images. Thus, ʿAlī b. Manṣūr al-Ḥalabī, known as Ibn al-Qāriḥ (d. 421/1030), concludes that Ibn Wakīʿ was unfair to al-Mutanabbī. When Ibn Wakīʿ read some of his own verses, Ibn al-Qāriḥ alerted him to the fact that they were stolen from other poets. Ibn Wakīʿ rejoined, "I never heard of that." Ibn al-Qāriḥ's intervention at this point is worth citing: "If the case is so, you need to excuse al-Mutanabbī for similar things, without denigrating him or blaming him, as meanings resonate with each other."[145] This interpolation is important because it redirects the conversation to the thrust of Ibn Wakīʿ's indiscriminate

[139] Quoted in al-Badīʿī, *al-Ṣubḥ*, 146–47. [140] Ibn Rashīq, *al-ʿUmdah* (2001), 2:282.
[141] al-Ṣafadī, *al-Wāfī bi-l-wafayāt*, 12:46. See also Ibn Wakīʿ, *Kitāb al-munṣif*, 84.
[142] Ibn Wakīʿ, *Kitāb al-munṣif*, 97–98. [143] Ibid., 99. [144] Ibid., 101.
[145] Ibid., 84, quoted in al-Badīʿī, *al-Ṣubḥ*, 265, 266; and in al-Ṣafadī, *al-Wāfī bi-l-wafayāt*, 12:46.

application of *saraq*. Overlooking what is already argued by al-Āmidī with respect to *ma'ānī* and, before him, by al-Jāḥiẓ, Ibn Wakī' allows his grudge to lead him to accumulate echoes, distant themes, and shared meanings, despite his proclaimed systematization of thievery. This system shares some uniformity with what was current at its time, and hence is part of an ever-growing process of tabulation. The anonymous advocates against whom Ibn Wakī' builds an argument do not fall into two camps, as in al-Āmidī's presentation. Ibn Wakī' lacks the latter's tact and critical expertise. Driven by grudge, he poses as the contender against anonymous proponents. When he turns to expressions, he also accumulates what specialists such as Abū al-Fatḥ 'Uthmān b. Jinnī (d. 392/1002) – in his lost book *al-Naqḍ 'alā Ibn Wakī' fī shi'r al-Mutanabbī wa-takhṭi'atih* (Invalidating Ibn Wakī''s Reading of al-Mutanabbī's Poetry, and Proving Its Faultiness) – reject as misunderstanding and confusion. Ibn Jinnī is, after all, *al-quṭb fī lisān al-'Arab* (the pivot [or pole] in Arabic language) – as al-Tha'ālibī concludes – and is the doyen of belles lettres.[146]

Tabulation for a Purpose

In a neat note by 'Umar Khalīfah b. Idrīs, the editor of the most authoritative text of Ibn Wakī''s *al-Munṣif*,[147] he argues that Ibn Wakī' read Ibn Jinnī's *al-Fatḥ al-wahbī 'alā mushkilāt al-Mutanabbī*,[148] but his responses to Ibn Jinnī's book turn into an insult aimed at grammarians and phonologists. Thus, he says, "And grammar has nothing to do with the craft of poetry; for only thoughtful and introspective minds can reach its meanings," a point that could not have been disconcerting to Ibn Jinnī, whose fame was unparalleled then, as it is now.[149] Moreover, and as al-Thaᶜālibī explains, "He [Ibn Jinnī] accompanied Abū al-Ṭayyib for a long time and explained his poetry and drew attention to its poetic meanings and its grammatical structures and inflection or declension of words."[150]

Thus, Ibn Wakī''s grudge prevents him from providing a nuanced reading,[151] which he could have achieved in view of his accomplishments as poet and scholar. The disparity between the systematization of *sariqāt* terminology and categories, on the one hand, and his own methods of application, on the other, leads to an unfortunate production blinded by

[146] al-Tha'ālibī, *Yatīmat al-dahr*, 1:137. [147] Ibn Wakī', *Kitāb al-munṣif*, 44–45.

[148] Abū al-Fatḥ 'Uthmān Ibn Jinnī, *al-Fatḥ al-wahbī 'alā mushkilāt al-Mutanabbī*, ed. Muḥsin Ghayāḍ (Baghdad: Dār al-Shu'ūn al-Thaqāfiyyah al-'Āmmah Āfāq 'Arabiyyah, 1990).

[149] Ibn Wakī', *Kitāb al-munṣif*, 45. [150] al-Tha'ālibī, *Yatīmat al-dahr*, 1:137.

[151] See Khalīfah b. Idrīs's note in Ibn Wakī', *Kitāb al-munṣif*, 1:17.

the author's determined effort to prove that al-Mutanabbī is below the level of prominent poets.

It is a desperate fight against an overwhelming tide, which al-Thaʿālibī sums up as follows: "In both pre-Islamic and Islamic times there has never been a *dīwān* with so many commentaries and explications as this one."[152] Adamant as Ibn Wakīʿ is, he often runs against the classification that he applies. Thus, if we accept that precursors have left nothing of note to successors, there is no point in claiming that al-Mutanabbī raids the poetry of so-and-so.[153] Moreover, when Ibn Wakīʿ assigns "the most superb of our poets" the art of skillful appropriation and utilization of prose to versify, but depriving al-Mutanabbī of this privilege, he only repeats what Ibn Ṭabāṭabā addresses as a required navigation between poetry and prose, one that is discreet and rewarding.[154] Although Ibn Wakīʿ's work has the merit of a detailed classification in matters that form part of a literary-critical discourse in the writings of Ibn Ṭabāṭabā, al-Āmidī, and al-Qāḍī al-Jurjānī, the effort is conducted in support of his vituperative criticism of al-Mutanabbī, whose enormous popularity everywhere eclipsed all other poets, including Ibn Wakīʿ. Thus, the latter's enumeration of acceptable thieveries is only a tabulation of what was in circulation in the cultural marketplace. These acceptable plagiarisms are as follows: transformation of the first poet's verse to a better one in terms of brevity; improved expressions; neat structure and compositional patterns; switching of genres or themes; and the creation of a new wording from an old one with the same thematic purpose. As for generating better themes in new expressions, a point that was agreed on by all, it is seen as a sign of thoughtfulness, discernment, and perspicacity. As noticed by his Libyan editor, Ibn Wakīʿ's writing has the merit of classifying and systemizing what is available in the market.[155] The possibility of an equal standing in production between the originator and follower, where priority is given to the creator, which Ibn Wakīʿ lists as his eighth point, can be a subject of dispute, as the cultural corpus during that time was more inclined to innovation and newness.[156] In the introduction to *Kitāb al-munṣif*, ʿUmar Khalīfah b. Idrīs argues that the author is more serene and meticulous in the first volume, but not so in the second volume, which deals with al-Mutanabbī's verse addressed to Sayf al-Dawlah.[157]

Ibn Wakīʿ's list of unacceptable plagiarisms sounds more like a list of justifications for what he intends to level against al-Mutanabbī's poetry.

[152] Quoted in al-Badīʿī, *al-Ṣubḥ*, 269. [153] Ibn Wakīʿ, *Kitāb al-munṣif*, 102.
[154] al-ʿAlawī, *ʿIyār al-shiʿr*, 78. See also Ibn Wakīʿ, *Kitāb al-munṣif*, 70.
[155] Ibn Wakīʿ, *Kitāb al-munṣif*, 66. [156] Ibid., 73. [157] Ibid., 54–55.

The effort was in line with the criticisms al-Ḥātimī and his camp. The latter were desperate to accumulate accusations in a heated climate that was triggered not only by the target poet's magisterial presence and performance at Sayf al-Dawlah's court but also by his boastful verses that speak of his person and his poetry as both unique and a gate-opener in expression and enlightenment.

In line with a tendency to classify and tabulate a massive poetic production that has its own resonances, echoes, and repetitions, Ibn Wakīʿ's account for literati of unacceptable or despicable plagiarisms includes long-windedness as opposed to the original's brevity; low and vulgar meaning in contrast with the rigorous and decent meaning of the first; the ugly and inordinate in meaning and composition in contrast with the tidy and pleasant; invective instead of encomium; heavy and ugly rhythms and rhymes as opposed to the pleasant and smooth cadence of an original; inappropriate elision; failure to keep up to the standard of an original wording; a despicable and dry rhyme instead of the pleasant one of an original; distortion and inadequacy; and theft of wording and meaning, which is the worst kind of theft.[158] While there is a correspondence between Ibn Wakīʿ and al-Ḥātimī in the classification and systematization of the subject of *saraq* – driven probably by a grudge that motived them at some time in order to downplay Abū al-Ṭayyib al-Mutanabbī's fame, if not to demolish it – the mechanism at hand is the presentation of their discursive invective in a scholarly garb persuasive to the educated public.

It seems that there were other writings critical of al-Mutanabbī that are thematically and stylistically in conversation with each other. The book by the "stallion" poet Abū al-ʿAbbās al-Nāmī is one of them. The epistle is no longer extant, but we have references to it and quotes from it in Ibn Wakīʿ's *Kitāb al-munṣif*. In these references the epistle sounds like another criticism of al-Mutanabbī's poetry. Given the historical details about al-Nāmī being replaced by al-Mutanabbī as Sayf al-Dawlah's laureate, rivalry is only reasonable. On the positive side, it seems that al-Nāmī's epistle is in keeping with his character as a great and well-respected poet who, unlike al-Ḥātimī, would not go low and slander his rival's personality. He deals with what he deems thefts. While this act testifies to the fact that competitiveness generates jealousy, it cannot raise any surprise among readers. What raises astonishment, however, is the fact that Ibn Wakīʿ refutes many of al-Nāmī's citations, faulting him every now and then. Thus, ʿUmar Khalīfah b. Idrīs, the editor of *Kitāb al-munṣif*, cannot hide his surprise, especially after comparing these refutations with Ibn Wakīʿ's "defense of insipid things in al-Mutanabbī's corpus that are

[158] Ibid., 68, 124–32.

criticized by several critics simply because al-Nāmī cites them as objectionable."[159] Since we know that Ibn Wakī' went to Aleppo and praised Sayf al-Dawlah, it is probable that Ibn Wakī' met al-Nāmī there and also that he returned with some grudge against him. While this is a conjecture that some critics, including the editor, share, it is as valid as any in a competitive climate where support from a highly recognized poet could change fortunes.

The Discursive Tenth Century

The larger context was certainly the raging discussion of thievery, especially in relation to the eminent Abū Tammām and al-Buḥturī. Every term and application, but especially in al-Qāḍī al-Jurjānī's *al-Wasāṭah*, has a place and meaning that following scholars might apply, qualify, or explicate. Al-Ṣūlī (d. 335/946),[160] who tutored the future caliph al-Rāḍī (d. 329/940), must have been as important in his notes on plagiarism and defense of Abū Tammām and Abū Nuwās as al-Āmidī was in his subtle defense of al-Buḥturī.[161] In other words, his remarks as well as those of Ibn Ṭabāṭabā add a significant portion to the growing plagiarism corpus, and their writings were accessible to Ibn Wakī' and al-Ḥātimī. Indeed, Ibn Wakī' could have made use of al-Ṣūlī's view, which sides with *al-muḥdathūn* (modernists). Al-Ṣūlī upholds the premise that "the wording of the *muḥdathūn* since the age of Bashshār is directed at more innovative meanings, accessible expressions, and gentle language, even though we credit the ancients with precedence."[162] Moreover, al-Ṣūlī agrees with al-Āmidī and, especially, Ibn Ṭabāṭabā – who are free from the grudge factor – that, as themes are often exhausted, it is feasible to give credit to the modern poet who completes an existing poetic theme, adds to it, and clothes it in expressive and figurative language.[163] Al-Ṣūlī asserts that if there is a *poet who should not be accused of saraq, it is Abū Tammām*, "for the abundance of his *badī'*, inventiveness, and independency."[164] Since the underlying premise is antecedence/precedence, the possibility of a similarity between two poets in meaning and expression presumes prioritization of the older, as the latecomer is often the one who borrows or seizes on themes and wording. If both poets who share the similarity belong to one age and period, then the owner is the one whose poem is in line with his register.[165]

[159] Ibid., 29. [160] Full name: Abū Bakr Muḥammad b. Yaḥyā al-Ṣūlī.
[161] Muḥammad b. Yaḥyā al-Ṣūlī, *Sharḥ al-Ṣūlī li-Dīwān Abī Tammām*, ed. Khalaf Rashīd Nu'mān (Baghdad: Wizārat al-Thaqāfah wa-l-I'lām, 1978).
[162] al-Ṣūlī, *Akhbār Abī Tammām*, 16. [163] Ibid., 53; al-'Alawī, *'Iyār al-shi'r*, 76.
[164] al-Ṣūlī, *Akhbār Abī Tammām*, 100. [165] Ibid., 100–101.

Al-Mutanabbī's proponents include illustrious names like Ibn Jinnī, al-Sarī al-Raffāʾ, the Khālidī Brothers (the Khālidiyyān), and a bit later, Abū al-ʿAlāʾ al-Maʿarrī (d. 449/1058) – and many others whom al-Thaʿālibī also lists. They form a camp that counteracts the adversarial side in the battle of words. Poets and prose writers who use his verse are numerous. The acknowledged high quality of al-Mutanabbī's verse, which even detractors recognize, was bound to permeate the poetic scene. Hence, poets who memorized his verse could not avoid taking from his expressions and poetic meanings.

Even so, being on the side of al-Mutanabbī in the continuing battle against opponents does not entail a uniform stand or peaceful front. *Saraq* occurs whenever there is competition and rivalry for rewards. The celebrated al-Sarī al-Raffāʾ was such a case,[166] as he also offers a unique example of how poets will battle each other in the competitive domain of poetry and search for recognition and rewards. Al-Raffāʾ's case can serve as a nexus for a thriving culture where talent can ensure rewards without detracting from one's literary prestige. Thus, his use of al-Mutanabbī's verse was rarely lamented. He was, after all, the compiler of Kushājim's (d. 360/970) poetry.[167] The latter was an illustrious poet, a compiler of a multivolume book on earthly pleasures and pleasantries, and the royal chef in Sayf al-Dawlah's kitchen. What is worth attention, however, is that al-Raffāʾ inserted verses from the poetry of the Khālidī Brothers in that volume in order to direct criticism against them as plagiarists in the ongoing exchange of vilifications against each other.[168] As nobody would accuse Kushājim of theft, the Khālidī Brothers would carry the stigma. While devoting a chapter to the Khālidī Brothers' thefts from al-Raffāʾ and their raids (i.e., seizing most of the first poets' poetic meaning) on his verse,[169] al-Thaʿālibī also noticed similar verses in their handwriting claimed by both sides. He rhetorically asks: Is it *tawārud* (coincidental similarity), or *muṣālaṭah* (appropriation of another poet's verse)?[170]

Al-Thaʿālibī provides an important source on al-Raffāʾ and his rivals; and he finds a disparity between, on the one hand, two collections dictated by and copied from Abū Bakr al-Khwārizmī and the volume brought to the former by Muḥammad b. Ḥāmid al-Khwārizmī and, on the other hand, the book in the poet's handwriting. The latter contains

[166] al-Thaʿālibī, *Yatīmat al-dahr*, 2:141–58.

[167] Full name: Abū al-Fatḥ Muḥammad b. Maḥmūd b. Shāhāk al-Ramlī.

[168] al-Thaʿālibī, *Yatīmat al-dahr*, 2:138. See Naaman, "Plagiarism Controversy"; Jocelyn Sharlet, "Inside and Outside the Pleasure Scene in Poetry about Locations by al-Sarī al-Raffāʾ al-Mawṣilī," *Journal of Arabic Literature* 40, no. 2 (2009): 133–69; Sharlet, "The Thought That Counts: Gift Exchange Poetry by Kushājim, al-Ṣanawbarī, and al-Sarī al-Raffāʾ," *Middle Eastern Literatures* 14, no. 3 (2011): 235–70.

[169] al-Thaʿālibī, *Yatīmat al-dahr*, 2:139. [170] Ibid.

several additions.[171] Although al-Thaʿālibī thinks highly of al-Raffāʾ and his magnificent poetic meanings,[172] he describes al-Raffāʾ's *sariqāt* as subtly interwoven in neat verses. He uses three terms to account for these thefts: *saraq*, *akhdh*, and *ʿaks* (indirect inversion of meaning).[173] Ironically, however, to be visibly present in the ongoing battle of thievery means achieving some distinction. Had al-Raffāʾ been a mediocre poet, nobody would have paid much attention to his raids or the raids of others on his poetry. The same is applicable to the Khālidī Brothers. When the bibliophile Ibn Isḥāq al-Nadīm (d. 385/995) addresses the topic of *sariqāt*, in his compendious *Kitāb al-fihrist*, he lists fourteen books by eminent scholars. The books and their authors demonstrate how controversial the topic had been until the end of the tenth century. In other words, it was in the heyday of the Arab Islamic empire that books devoted to the issue and its disputed territories multiplied. The association between this multiplication and cultural invigoration points to a thriving life of prestation and rewards. Assemblies happened to be also a source not only for blooming criticism and cultural industry but also for debates where poets, philologists, and patrons demonstrated both a keen interest in this battle for distinction and a genuine search for resourcefulness and inventiveness. This heated discussion, which would continue for some time, was bound to wane and slacken off, but never die out.

With the breakup of governorates from the deteriorating center of the caliphate in Baghdad and the rise of other epicenters, new reading publics multiplied, and booksellers and copyists found it worthwhile to encourage compendiums, treasuries, and other forms of compilation that care less for property rights as long as the material is made available under its authors' names.[174] Along with this transformation, to borrow or steal material is no longer a serious matter that requires arbitration, especially as the issue of *saraq* belongs to a past when competitiveness was an issue among strong poets and when patronage happened to be central to this competitiveness. More important is the radical shift in the structure of the Islamic empire, the breakaway of governorates, emirates, kingdoms, and states, which, while accelerating the search for prestation and rewards, allowed an increasing space for chancery professionals. Even poets were enrolled in chancery jobs that required prose writing. As has been argued

[171] Ibid., 140. [172] Ibid., 158. [173] Ibid., 141.

[174] For more, see al-Musawi, *Republic of Letters*, 111–12, 131–32, 166–67, 180–81, 245, 257; Beatrice Gruendler, *The Rise of the Arabic Book* (Cambridge, MA: Harvard University Press, 2020); Konrad Hirschler, *The Written Word in the Medieval Arabic Lands* (Edinburgh: Edinburgh University Press, 2012).

elsewhere,[175] writings celebrating the priority of prose began to appear whenever the texture of poetry began to fuse into the ongoing untying and dissolution of verse.

Moreover, other forms of poetry writing began to flourish, while the legacy of invented figuration became less of a dynamic and more or less a given in the search for virtuosity and elegance, as exemplified in the writings of al-Qāḍī al-Fāḍil ʿAbd al-Raḥīm al-Bīsānī. In other words, alternative forms of disputation and debate were to take over, and *saraq* as an issue would become a merely a stigma-free starting point in the reading of stylistic techniques that take *badīʿ* (innovated figuration) for granted. Thus, the issue of *saraq* lost the taint of theft and became more often an appendix to the study of *badīʿ*, as noted in Chapter 4. Al-Mutanabbī's poems remained a common legacy, cherished, celebrated, and discussed, as al-Thaʿālibī argued and foresaw, stating that "there is no other than the poetry of al-Mutanabbī that came to be so talked about and circulated among the literati in poetry and prose."[176] As for the poet himself, he foresaw that in his verse:

أَنَامُ مِلْءَ جُفُوني عَنْ شَوَارِدِهَا　　　وَيَسْهَرُ الخَلْقُ جَرّاهَا وَيَخْتَصِمُ

I sleep in sublime unconcern for the words which wander abroad,
whilst others are sleepless on their account, contending mightily.[177]

The battle around his poetry and character never ends, and, although twentieth-century poets like al-Bayātī (d. 1999) might object to his panegyrics, this very slicing of poetry and character indicates a certain ambivalence that can never negate the object of desire. As an index of Arabic poetry, thought, and self-imaging, writings about him cover all periods, reaching into the twenty-first century with the birth of new forums devoted to him. The accusatory discourse of the mid-tenth century resides in the background, while books by ʿAbd al-Wahhāb ʿAzzām and others dismiss that discourse as mere quibbles.[178]

This unprecedented battle around al-Mutanabbī, which goes beyond the controversy over innovation and inventiveness and the issue of originality, authenticity, and replication as applied to the poetries of Abū Tammām and al-Buḥturī, was to subside in the thirteenth to fifteenth centuries. As I have argued elsewhere, alternative transactions were in

[175] See al-Musawi, "Pre-modern Belletristic Prose"; al-Musawi, "Vindicating a Profession."
[176] al-Thaʿālibī, *Yatīmat al-dahr*, 1:269.
[177] Arberry, *Poems of al-Mutanabbī*, 72–73. Needless to say, the power of the poet's wording and imaging gets lost in translation.
[178] ʿAbd al-Wahhāb ʿAzzām, *Dhikrā Abī al-Ṭayyib baʿd alf ʿām* (Cairo: Dār al-Maʿārif, 1968).

effect. There is first a different understanding of terms that was bound to produce some repercussions, although often with loose application of *saraq*:

> The licensing process (*ijāzah*, a license to transmit) in [al-Mutanabbī's] day underwent some drastic shifts in application. It became not the result of a choice between, on the one hand, authoritative *riwāyah* or transmission based on *samā*ʿ (certified audition) from the immediate author and, on the other hand, *dirāyah* (cognizance) as basically grounded in understanding and reasoning, but rather a confrontational posture, as was the case between ibn Nubātah and al-Ṣafadī and also between Ḥasan Shams al-Dīn al-Nawājī (799–859/1386–1455) and his mentor and fellow-scholar, Abū Bakr ibn Ḥijjah al-Ḥamawī (767–837/1366–1434).[179]

The shift to the confrontational only indicates another grid of correspondence and intertextuality among contemporaneous texts that happened to emerge from close and intimate connections among authors. The prolific Abū Bakr b. Ḥijjah al-Ḥamawī (d. 837/1434) documented Ibn Nubātah al-Miṣrī's (d. 768/1366) *ijāzah* (license to transmit) to the polymath Ibn Aybak al-Ṣafadī (d. 764/1363), as the authority to report and document the former's poetry and criticism. The intimacy could have involved the polymath in internalizing and absorbing Ibn Nubātah's writing in such a way as to provoke the latter to write his *Khubz al-shaʿīr* (Barley Bread, i.e., eaten and despised), accusing al-Ṣafadī as an ungrateful property invader. More controversial is the case of Ḥasan Shams al-Dīn al-Nawājī (d. 859/1455), who copied in his own handwriting his mentor Ibn Ḥijjah's *Qahwat al-inshā*ʾ (The Intoxication of Chancery). Nevertheless, he wrote a harsh criticism of Ibn Ḥijjah as plagiarist.[180] As a very learned scholar, al-Nawājī should have been aware of the classifications of plagiarisms, but he lists a number of these thematic echoes and seeming replications under *akhdh* (seizure). On occasion, he draws attention to the stark replication of definitions and statements from Ṣafī al-Dīn al-Ḥillī's (d. 749/1349) *al-ʿĀṭil al-ḥālī* in Ibn Ḥijjah's *Bulūgh al-amal fī fann al-zajal*.[181] Although seemingly receding into the background in comparison with the increase in contemporaneous confrontational sites, the major figures around whom discussions happened to be rampant were not eclipsed. Abū Muḥammad Saʿīd b. Mubārak b. al-Dahhān's book that is exclusively

[179] al-Musawi, *Republic of Letters*, 122.

[180] *Kitāb al-ḥujjah fī sariqāt Ibn Ḥijjah*, manuscript, undated, MS Arab 285, Houghton Library, Harvard University, http://nrs.harvard.edu/urn-3:FHCL.HOUGH:2600641.

[181] For a reading of al-Nawājī's vilification, see Hakan Özkan, "Donkey or Thief: Defamation or Well-Deserved Criticism? An-Nawāǧī and His Treatise *al-Ḥujjah fī sariqāt Ibn Ḥijjah*," in *The Racecourse of Literature: An-Nawāǧī and His Contemporaries*, ed. Alev Masarwa and Hakan Özkan (Baden-Baden: Ergon Verlag, 2020), 83–94.

devoted to al-Mutanabbī's *saraq* was only a late twelfth-century contribution in the ongoing discussion that, as noted earlier, Ḥāzim al-Qarṭājannī (d. 684/1286) summarized under four workable and transactional categories: *ikhtirā*ʿ (invention); *ishtirāk* (sharing the same value in meaning or mold); *istiḥqāq* (deservedly owned for its extra value); and, in a case in which the *maʿnā* is below the standard of the source, *inḥiṭāṭ* (a degeneration in value).[182] Ibn Aydamir comes with a better explanation when he studies *khal*ʿ (confiscation of a verse with the imposition of a different rhyme, as usually practiced among the literati).[183] He thinks al-Mutanabbī's *khal*ʿ of Marwān b. Abī Ḥafṣah's verse that starts with *wa-innī la-tughnīnī* (It suffices me . . .) should not have been practiced by a renowned poet whose fame is unequalled.[184] Around the major poets, and al-Mutanabbī in particular, there grows a large philological corpus that thirteenth–fifteenth-century concurrent confrontations enrich with a shift toward dissonance among mentors and disciples (see Figure 5.3).

As I address this stage in his popularity, and the ups and downs in the narrative of poetic and literary thievery in relation to intertextual absorption, appropriation, and the role of artificial intelligence in new types of infringements on intellectual property rights, both in the Preface and the Conclusion, it is worthwhile to consider whether al-Mutanabbī's verse is an exercise in vainglory, as Ibn Wakīʿ would like us to believe, or it is deservedly popular, as is testified to by multiple books in Andalusia, Muslim Spain, and elsewhere. The Andalusians take his uniqueness for granted, with one of them also addressing accusations against him.[185] Even so, the Andalusian intervention has something exceptional about it, because it is presented from a perspective that also strives to carve an independent path of its own, free to some extent of the heavy presence of the Eastern flank in the production of the first centuries of Andalusian culture.

182 See Heinrichs, "Evaluation of 'Sariqa,'" 361. For these and other issues and references, see Chapter 4. For a quote from Ḥāzim al-Qarṭājannī's *Minhāj al-bulaghāʾ*, see Bin Tamīm, *ʿUyūn al-ʿajāʾib*, 14.

183 Ibn Aydamir, *al-Durr al-farīd*, 1:388–89.

184 Ibid., 389.

185 Ibn Bassām al-Naḥwī, *Sariqāt al-Mutanabbī wa-mushkil maʿānīhi*, ed. Muḥammad al-Ṭāhir b. ʿĀshūr (Tunis: al-Dār al-Tūnisiyyah li-l-Nashr, 1970).

6 The Waning Economies of Textual Theft

The Andalusian Shift

While discussion of plagiarism in the Arab East has raged continually, as is shown in a continuing and ongoing publication of books, articles, and current social media communications,[1] the matter was not as visible in Andalusia, even at the heyday of cultural life in Córdoba, Seville, Toledo, and Granada. There must be some reasons behind such a noticeable lacuna, especially in view of thriving cultural production and dynamic assemblies. Even if we assume that the cultural issue of generational shifts from anciency to modernity, from *qudamāʾ* to *muḥdathūn*, and the latter's practice of *badīʿ*, was not as acute and visible in Andalusia, this could not be a well-rounded justification for a relative, though not total, absence of a theoretical dynamic such as thievery and its terminological classifications.

To address the matter as a complex and not as a trivial issue, one of no actual consequence for a booming culture, we need to keep in mind that al-Jazīrah – that is, the Iberian entity in its Andalusian formation – was never disconnected from the flourishing caliphal and emirs' centers of the Arab Eastern flank. Specific cases of traveling books and the migration of scholars, singers, critics, poets, and musicians are well known.[2] More

[1] The following titles show various engagements with thievery that span modes, periods, and techniques: Muḥammad Muṣṭafā Haddārah, *Mushkilat al-sariqāt fī al-naqd al-ʿArabī: dirāsah taḥlīliyyah muqāranah* (Beirut: al-Maktab al-Islāmī, 1975); Muṣṭafā Saʿdanī, *al-Tanāṣṣ al-shiʿrī: qirāʾah ukhrā li-qaḍiyyat al-sariqāt* (Alexandria: Tawzīʿ Munshaʾat al-Maʿārif, 1991); Badawī Aḥmad Ṭabānah, *al-Sariqat al-adabiyyah: dirāsah fī ibtikār al-aʿmāl al-adabiyyah wa-taqlīdihā*, 2nd ed. (Cairo: Maktabat al-Anjilū al-Miṣriyyah, 1969); Maḥmūd Miṣfār, *al-Tanāṣṣ bayna al-ruʾyah wa-l-ijrāʾ fī al-naqd al-adabī: muqārabah muḥāyithah li-l-sariqāt al-adabiyyah ʿinda al-ʿArab* (Sfax, 2000); ʿĪd Balbaʿ, *Ukdhūbat al-tanāṣṣ: murājaʿāt uslūbiyyah fī al-sariqāt al-shiʿriyyah* (Tanta: Dār al-Nābighah, 2019); Dāʾūd Sallūm, *al-Sariqāt al-fanniyyah li-l-āthār al-adabiyyah: sariqāt al-Duktūr Muḥammad Nabīl Ṭarifī anmūdhajan* (Baghdad, 2005); ʿAbd al-Razzāq Bilāl, *Jadaliyyat al-taʿāluq al-naṣṣī bayna al-sariqāt al-adabiyyah wa-l-tanāṣṣ: muqārabah iṣṭilāḥiyyah* (Fes: Dār Mā baʿda al-Ḥadāthah, 2009).

[2] See Salma Khadra Jayyusi, ed., *The Legacy of Muslim Spain*, 2 vols. (Leiden: Brill, 1992), vol. 1, esp. Robert Hillenbrand, "'The Ornament of the World': Medieval Cordoba as a Cultural Centre," 112–35, and Abbas Hamdani, "An Islamic Background to the Voyages of Discovery," 273–306. An extensive reading is offered by Muḥammad Bin

pertinent are the traveling books that are central to theoretical disputations and implications of *saraq*. Jaʿfar al-Kattānī, the editor of al-Ḥātimī's *Ḥilyat al-muḥāḍarah* (The Ornament of Discourse), showed that al-Ḥātimī's manuscript from Fèz is of an Andalusian origin.[3] The Western flank's indebtedness to al-Ḥātimī's study of poetics and elaborate classification of terms for *sariqāt* is extensively shown not only in Ibn Rashīq's *al-ʿUmdah*, but also in Ibn Ḥazm's (d. 456/1064) encyclopedic *Jamharat ansāb al-ʿArab* (The Sum of Arab Genealogies), and in Abū ʿUbayd al-Bakrī's (d. 487/1094) *Samṭ al-laʾāliʾ fī sharḥ amālī al-Qālī* (The Pearls Strung in Explicating al-Qālī's Dictations).[4] We know that the caliphal guest of honor, Ismāʿīl b. al-Qāsim Abū ʿAlī al-Qālī (d. 356/967), brought along with him books from Baghdad, including poetic *dīwān*s. Many other scholars from al-Andalus were frequent visitors to Baghdad.[5]

Thievery Terminology between Ibn Rashīq and Ibn Sharaf

On the other hand, the renowned poet and critic Jaʿfar b. Muḥammad b. Sharaf (d. 460/1067), who settled in Andalusia, alludes to what the celebrated poet Abū al-Ḥasan Muḥammad b. Lankak al-Baṣrī (d. 360/970) claims in his grudging notes that al-Mutanabbī stole poetic meanings and ideas from Abū al-Qāsim Naṣr b. Aḥmad al-Khubzaruzī (also written al-Khubz Arzī, d. 330/939), the illiterate but famed poet of Basrah.[6] While not mentioning al-Mutanabbī by name, Ibn Sharaf implies as much: "Some of our great poets who were his [al-Khubzaruzī's or al-Khubz Arzī] contemporaries confiscated one part of the verse [*ihtadama*] [and] something of his poetic form and structure and assimilated [*ihtaḍama*] bits of his meanings. Thus [these thefts were] rarely noticed."[7] In another place in his brief critical survey, Ibn Sharaf relies heavily on what has already been argued in the Arab East regarding thievery. He presents what is probably a summary of the brief review offered by his fellow countryman, contemporary, and once rival, Ibn Rashīq. Ibn Sharaf considers thievery to be a defect in poetry, a point that leads him to draw a pithy typology that can be paraphrased as follows: There

Sharīfah, *Abū Tammām wa-Abū al-Ṭayyib fī adab al-Maghāribah* (Beirut: Dār al-Gharb al-Islāmī, 1986).

[3] Jaʿfar Kattānī, *Ḥilyat al-muḥāḍarah fī ṣināʿat al-shiʿr* (Baghdad: Wizārat al-Thaqāfah wa-l-Iʿlām-Dār al-Rashīd li-l-Nashr, 1979), 1:9.

[4] See ibid., 7–8. [5] For more, see Bin Sharīfah, *Abū Tammām*, 10–112.

[6] Jaʿfar b. Muḥammad Ibn Sharaf, *Dīwān al-Khubz Arzī Naṣr b. Aḥmad al-Baṣrī* (Damascus: al-Āmāl al-Jadīdah, 2019).

[7] Jaʿfar b. Muḥammad b. Saʿīd Ibn Sharaf, *Rasāʾil al-intiqād*, ed. Ḥasan Ḥusnī ʿAbd al-Wahhāb (Beirut: Dār al-Kitāb al-Jadīd, 1983), 34–35; see also Charles Pellat's edition of the same work (Alger: Éditions Carbonel, 1953), 36, quoted in ʿAbbās, *Tārīkh al-naqd al-adabī* (2006), 469. Another edition is by Maṭbaʿat al-Muqtabis (Damascus, 1911).

are thieveries of expression; and there are thieveries of poetic meanings, which occur more often because they are easily concealable. There are total or partial thieveries of meaning; some abridge expression but complement meaning, a practice that is the best in the domain of thieveries. Conversely, an increase in expression and a failure in meaning is the worst type of theft. On top of this is plain thievery, one that involved the theft of total meanings and expressions. Ibn Sharaf culminates this summary with a commendation of the victim as the better poet who excites desire, not the thief. As an example, he cites Abū Nuwās's thievery from the poet Abū al-Shīṣ al-Khuzāʿī (d. 196/811).[8] Summaries like this demonstrate how, by the mid-eleventh century, thievery as a subject is no longer a rife conversation. If Ibn Rashīq's summary of basic *saraq* terminology follows al-Qāḍī al-Jurjānī's succinct account, Ibn Sharaf's is probably the briefest after that of al-Hamadhānī, the author of *al-Alfāẓ al-kitābiyyah*. Here Iḥsān ʿAbbās's explanation of Ibn Rashīq's summary, which can apply to the waning interest in plagiarism, is worth citing: "There is a strong belief that Ibn Rashīq has not paid much attention to thievery because he was certain that *sariqāt* has been a common trend in contemporary poetic practice."[9]

Apart from casual allusions to probable duplication of ideas and forms from the Eastern centers of Islamic civilization, no pressing case of plagiarism was brought against a specific poet or prose writer. The eighth-to-fourteenth-century disputations of the cultural market in the Arab East are simply not there. Even if we take the Andalusian Ḥāzim al-Qarṭājannī's short treatment of *sariqāt* into account, it is more or less an afterthought, as pointed out in Chapter 5, in line with an ongoing theoretical discussion that makes it incumbent upon scholars and critics to have their say on a matter so central to literary and cultural theory.[10]

As a poet, Ḥāzim al-Qarṭājannī was not oblivious to the sweeping infusion of Eastern Arabic poetics, to such an extent that his poetry betrays an assimilation of the poetries of such figures as Abū Tammām.[11] This conspicuous absence of a body of disputation that claimed the participation and attention of poets, critics, and philologists should involve its own Andalusian causes, especially if we take for

[8] Ibn Sharaf, *Rasāʾil al-intiqād*, 59–60.
[9] ʿAbbās, *Tārīkh al-naqd al-adabī* (2006), 463.
[10] For more on Ḥāzim al-Qarṭājannī as theorist, see G. J. H. van Gelder, "Critic and Craftsman: al-Qarṭājannī and the Structure of the Poem," *Journal of Arabic Literature* 10 (1979): 26–48.
[11] Bin Sharīfah, *Abū Tammām*, 70, quoted from Abū al-Ḥasan ʿAlī Ibn Bassām al-Shantarīnī, *al-Dhakhīrah fī maḥāsin ahl al-jazīra*, ed. Salīm Muṣṭafā al-Badrī (Beirut: Dār al-Kutub al-ʿIlmiyyah, 1998), 1:5–6; and from Abū al-Qāsim Muḥammad al-Sharīf al-Sabtī, *Rafʿ al-ḥujub al-mastūrah*, ed. Muḥammad al-Ḥajuwī (Rabat: Wizārat al-Awqāf wa-l-Shuʾūn al-Islāmiyyah, 1997), 1:84–89, 2:8, 33–34.

granted the availability of material from the Eastern flank of Arab culture, attested to by the large number of temporary Andalusian residents in urban centers such as Basrah, Kufa, Baghdad, Aleppo, Damascus, and Cairo. No less so are such compilations as those made by the caliphal guest of honor Abū ʿAlī al-Qālī (d. 356/967) and by the Córdoba poet and scholar Ibn ʿAbd Rabbihi (d. 328/940) in his *Unique Necklace*. Indeed, such a comprehensive treasury as Abū ʿAlī al-Ḥasan b. Bassām al-Shantarīnī's (d. 542/1147) *al-Dhakhīrah fī maḥāsin ahl al-Jazīrah* (i.e., al-Andalus), which was compiled and written when he was in Córdoba, could not avoid extensive references to the Eastern flank. Although its ultimate purpose is to highlight the cultural, especially literary, achievements of Andalusians, the endeavor makes substantial reference to poets and writers from the Arab East. Furthermore, he resorts to the terminological corpus on *sariqāt* to show every now and then a thorough navigational exchange between the two geographical locations.

Exploding the Geographies of the Center and Periphery

This exchange or movement suggests the need for a reference to what Ibn Bassām recalls in his mention of Abū ʿAlī al-Qālī's surmise while he is heading from Baghdad toward Andalusia and then to Qayrawan, Tunisia, which was at that time a hub of cultural activity. Before reaching Qayrawan, however, al-Qālī thought that the farther people are from the Abbasid center, and from Qayrawan, the duller and more incomprehensible they become, "depending on proximity or distance."[12] He adds, "I concluded that the people of al-Andalus could be just as dull and incomprehensible, if not more so; I thought I must need a *turjuman* [interpreter] there."[13] Ibn Bassām reports that, while there in Andalusia, al-Qālī was so impressed by Andalusians, their intelligence, and their reasoning, that he apologized, concluding: "At the time my knowledge was based on transmission and reporting, not grounded in familiarity and experience."[14]

The spatial dimension in al-Qālī's report is a loaded parameter, one that may resonate, though differently, with Arnold van Gennep's surmise found in the second chapter of his *Rites of Passage*, where the *marge*,[15] liminality, or transition from one location to another has a sacrality of a sort, a threshold preparation. In al-Qālī's case, the initial surmise and his

[12] Ibn Bassām, *al-Dhakhīrah*, 1:5–6. [13] Ibid., 6. [14] Ibid.
[15] Arnold van Gennep, *The Rites of Passage*, 2nd ed. (1960; Chicago: University of Chicago Press, 2019), xix.

retraction of it because it was based on hearsay rather than informed knowledge of Andalusia demonstrate a transformation in understanding the ultimate space as one of integration. In these spatial rites lands beyond Qayrawan function as thresholds that usher him into something that needs no *turjumān*. Ibn Bassām's reference to al-Qālī's early misunderstanding and subsequent recognition functions as an entry into Ibn Bassām's voluminous treasury of Andalusian culture. It serves as a doorway to his approach to intercultural grids that define Andalusian culture, while also highlighting its distinctive contributions. As shown in his abundant critical and historical survey of people and trends in al-Andalus over five centuries, interculturality does not shy away from allusion to texts and names from the Arab Eastern flank, especially Basrah and Baghdad. In fact, his approach reads literary thievery in terms of value as laid down later by his fellow countryman Ḥāzim al-Qarṭājannī (d. 684/1286).

Ibn Bassām, the compiler and author of *al-Dhakhīrah*, not to be confused with his namesake "Ibn Bassām al-Naḥwī" who wrote a small book on al-Mutanabbī's literary thefts,[16] proves to be tactful in his approach to a few terms from *sariqāt* terminology, such as *akhdh*, *ḥall*, *naql* (thematic and stylistic redirection of a poetic meaning and expression),[17] and *ihtidām*,[18] where value is contingent on application. Resemblance in diction and poetic themes derives value and significance only in the case of improvement. Speaking of the vizier Abū al-Walīd Muḥammad b. ʿAbd al-ʿAzīz al-Muʿallim, for instance, he praises him for *faḍl al-tawlīd* (the advantage of recreation/regeneration of meaning) and *ḥusnun min al-naql* (flair in thematic and stylistic redirection).[19] Thus, he is pleased with Ibn Rashīq's verse preferring blackness to whiteness, which Ibn Bassām defines through comparison to earlier poetry on the same topic by Easterners and Andalusians as being *al-mutaʾakhkhir al-sābiq* (the improving latecomer).[20] However, Ibn Bassām sides with Ibn al-Rūmī's (d. 283/896) use of simile to describe a smile in commending blackness in the verse "Yaftarru dhāka al-sawād ʿan yaqaqin" (blackness opens on bright whiteness in her mouth as symmetrical even pearls), because the whole verse depends on a beginning that "draws the attention of listeners and induces appreciation."[21] Beginnings matter whenever they resonate not only with each verse ending but also with the poem's concluding verse, as is the case in Ibn al-Rūmī's (see Figure 6.1).

[16] al-Naḥwī, *Sariqāt al-Mutanabbī*. [17] al-Ḥātimī, *Ḥilyat al-muḥāḍarah*, 2:82.

[18] Either "taking over less than one verse" or, in Ibn Rashīq's usage, the use of a similar structure and meaning; see Ibn Bassām, *al-Dhakhīrah*, 1:218; Grunebaum, "Concept of Plagiarism," 239.

[19] Ibn Bassām, *al-Dhakhīrah*, 2:80. [20] Ibid., 1:91. [21] Ibid., 92.

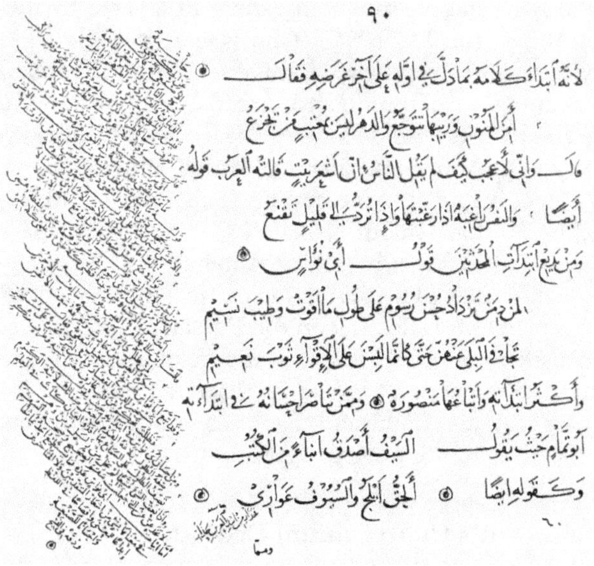

Figure 6.1 Poetic openings resonating with endings

Thus, while creating a genealogy of *badīʿ* application and the use of simile and metaphors that celebrate blackness, Ibn Bassām vaults over accusations of *akhdh* (poetic seizure), emphasizing instead poetic value as a criterion that should take into account readers' and listeners' reception. This is a significant approach. Although it carried a tinge of al-Qāḍī al-Jurjānī's appeal to readers to think of thievery accusations in a broad context of intercultural space,[22] Ibn Bassām's specific attention to readership redirects thievery's semantic applications to present what we reference nowadays as intertextuality, and which the classicists speak of in terms of an interfused discursivity.

Ibn Bassām is no less keen to trace *ḥall* (prosifying verse) in the prose writings of the minister and writer Abū al-Mughīrah ʿAbd al-Wahhāb b. Ḥazm (d. 438/1046–47) – specifically, in his description of death. Ibn Bassām considers the elaborate virtuosity in this discourse to be "*maḥlūl* [prosified] from the saying of Abū al-Ṭayyib":

وما الموت إلا سارق دق شخصه   يصول بلا كف ويسعى بلا رجل

Death is but a frail person
marauding with no hand and striving with no leg.[23]

[22] al-Jurjānī, *al-Wasāṭah*, 214–15 (1966), 185–86 (2006).
[23] Ibn Bassām, *al-Dhakhīrah*, 1:96.

He also finds al-Mutanabbī's poetic meaning in a verse by the poet al-Muʿtamid b. ʿAbbād (d. 488/1095), who was also the last king of the dynasty in Seville.[24] However, he recapitulates in order to explain that the above poetic meaning is a common and shared one.[25] Abū al-Mughīrah's poetry cannot escape Ibn Bassām's detective work that traces inspiration back to the poetries of Abū Tammām, al-Buḥturī, and al-Ṣanawbarī.[26] In these acts of detection no less interesting is the one by Abū al-Qāsim Muḥammmad b. ʿAbd al-Ghafūr al-Kalāʿī (d. 542/1165), the author of *al-Intiṣār li-Abī al-Ṭayyib* (Victory for al-Mutanabbī; i.e., siding with . . .) and *Iḥkām ṣanʿat al-kalām* (The Perfection of the Discursive Craft). In the latter book, he is probably reflecting on Ibn Bassām's detection of Abū al-Mughīrah's prosification, punning on the teknonym of the latter's "*mughīrah*" and the thievery term *ighārah* (literally: raid), for it is rare to find an epistle by Abū al-Mughīrah "that does not invade (*mughīrah*), or take over the meaning of the poetry of Abū al-Ṭayyib."[27]

Ibn Shuhayd's Contrapuntal Critique

Ibn Bassām is more attentive and celebratory when mentioning Abū ʿĀmir Aḥmad b. ʿAbd al-Malik b. Shuhayd (d. 426/1035), because "in merit he was on par with the highest class of Baghdadi poets."[28] The comparison is important because the Baghdadi literary elite is often cited as being the highest in standards and output. Ibn Shuhayd's high literary and cultural status as minister, poet, and essayist endows his writings and poetry with a power that is usually acknowledged in evaluating the cultural scene in Andalusia. Ibn Bassām is not oblivious to this fact. There is an association between status and vigor, and Ibn Shuhayd's verdict concerning his Andalusian contemporaries therefore carries weight, even when the tide in public opinion is positively inclined toward its celebrated littérateurs. Thus, when it comes to Abū al-Qāsim Ibrāhīm b. al-Iflīlī (d. 441/1049), a highly acclaimed commentator on al-Mutanabbī's poetry, Ibn Shuhayd includes him in "a group of tutors in our Córdoba . . . who found books in *badīʿ* and criticism and understood from them only what a Yemeni ape understands from dancing to a tune."[29] Ibn Shuhayd castigates Ibn al-Iflīlī for an egoistic attitude that downgrades others so as to present himself as uniquely eminent in grammar, argumentation, theological discourse, and poetics: "He is

[24] Ibid., 96. [25] Ibid., 97.
[26] Ibid., 108. Full name: Aḥmad b. Muḥammad b. al-Ḥusayn b. Marrār al-Ṣanawbarī.
[27] Abū al-Qāsim Muḥammad b. ʿAbd al-Ghafūr al-Kalāʿī, *Iḥkām ṣanʿat al-kalām*, ed. Muḥammmad Raḍwān al-Dāyah (Beirut: Dār al-Thaqāfah, 1966), 141.
[28] Ibn Bassām, *al-Dhakhīrah*, 1:136. [29] Ibid., 148.

singly disposed to stand alone as the best in al-Andalus with no rival. Thus I feel he should reside in Galicia, or in a land far from Islamic territory, to be there by himself, where no orator can be heard nor a poet can evoke such a positive citation."[30] Even so, Ibn Shuhayd does not denigrate Ibn al-Iflīlī and the "gang of tutors,"[31] but accuses them of an acquired and learned knowledge that failed to come to their rescue in assemblies and discussion circles, where only naturalness, spontaneity, and genuineness matter.[32] However, Ibn al-Iflīlī was highly regarded as a main link in the chain of transmitters of the poetries of both al-Mutanabbī and Abū Tammām based on the widely discussed and celebrated handwritten copies introduced by Abū ʿAlī al-Qālī.[33] If al-Baṣrī's assembly was pivotal to the dissemination of al-Mutanabbī's poetry, al-Qālī's was even more so.[34]

While a bit too critical of Ibn al-Iflīlī, Ibn Shuhayd is not immune from implications of indebtedness to other poets from the Abbasid region, or from among Andalusian contemporaries. Thus, Ibn Bassām quotes his verse while describing a war situation where horses strive to reach the war zone even when forced to crawl. His comment runs as follows: "This verse shows how Abū ʿĀmir [Ibn Shuhayd] fails to come up with a good *saraq* or to be on par with al-Mutanabbī's highly admirable verse. 'If their hooves slip, you make them creep on their bellies, / as dappled snakes slither uphill.'"

إذا زَلِقَتْ مَشّيْتَها ببُطونِهَا كمَا تَتَمَشّى في الصّعيدِ الأراقِمُ[35]

Abū al-Ḥasan Ibn Bassām's celebration of Ibn Shuhayd introduces his subtle reading of *saraq*, which is often camouflaged under the rubric of value, there being indiscernible or discreet *saraq* (covert), which varies between high and low. He argues the case as follows:

> As mentioned regarding the stratagem used by crafty poets in the forcible seizure [*akhdh*] of poetic meaning minus form, there is a resort to amplification if the precursor is pithy. Can't you see Abū ʿĀmir's [Ibn Shuhayd]

[30] Ibid., 149. [31] Ibid., 151. [32] Ibid. [33] Bin Sharīfah, *Abū Tammām*, 20–22.
[34] Ibid.
[35] Ibn Bassām, *al-Dhakhīrah*, 1:196. Thanks to Andras Hamori for multiple suggestions. Another possible interpretation: "If horses slip, you walk them on their bellies / as if they were snakes sliding a plateau." Wormhoudt translates this as follows: "When they slip you make them go on their bellies / like the snakes slither on the surface." Arhtur Wormhoudt, *The Diwan of Abu Tayyib ibn al-Husayn al-Mutanabbi: Translated from the Text of Abu al-Hasan Ali ibn Ahmad al-Wahidi al-Naishaburi (d. 468/1075)* (Oskaloosa IA: William Penn College, 1971), 160. In a 1995 version, this reads: "When they slip you make them go / On bellies like snakes slither on slopes" (205). Another is James Warren's 2022 translation: "They slipped – you made them on their bellies go, / As serpents slink along the ground below." James F. Warren, trans., *Al-Mutanabbi: The Complete Poems*, vol. 3 (Washington, DC: Cultural Books, 2022), 27.

saying when hearing Yūsuf b. Hārūn al-Ramādī (d. 403/1012): "I have never seen lovelier than eyes smiling / on the eve of departure, opening on once hidden pearls."[36]

He adds that Ibn Shuhayd adopts the same meaning in five verses, adding that "such a construction allows forgetting the ploy of prolongation."[37] This doesn't mean that al-Ramādī, great poet that he is, is beyond blame. Ibn Bassām argues that his "verse is taken from Ibn ʿAbd Rabbihi's saying 'As though sorrow plunges into her eyelids / bringing you scattered pearls.'"[38]

وكأنّما غاص الأسى بجفونها   حتى أتاك بلؤلؤٍ منثورا

Ibn Bassām explains his reasons for elevating al-Ramādī's verse: "Al-Ramādī craftily claims pearls and replaces plunging with smiles, and hence the fine placement of the eye-smile metaphor, instead of a usual mouth smile; this is done through the medium of pearls, which functions doubly for eyes and mouth. He duplicated [*nasakha*] the meaning in full, and totally and conversely transformed it [*qalabahu qalban*]."[39] Although this intervention comes as part of a laudatory reflection on Ibn Shuhayd, it presents Ibn Bassām as an expert in the application of *saraq* terminology to Andalusian poets. Aware of the *sariqāt* corpus by al-Āmidī, al-Qāḍī al-Jurjānī, al-Ḥātimī, and Ibn Rashīq, Ibn Bassām nevertheless demonstrates an exceptional mastery of practical criticism and textual application. His scattered references to *sariqāt* downplay or water down its heavy presence in the disputations of the Arab East.

While this instance of practical criticism is worth special mention in the Andalusian archive of *saraq*, there are many references to variations in application, consisting of *qalb* (contrary meaning to the original) and *naql* (transference of the original meaning to a different poetic subgenre or location). Activity in this web of correspondence and exchange provides an intertextual space, a shared script that reflects a dynamic culture. Vaulting over random accusations of thievery, Ibn Bassām links a certain verse, its poetic meaning, or even its expression to a textual spectrum that navigates East and West. When, for example, Ibn Bassām provided a biographic poetic critique of Abū al-Walīd Aḥmad b. Zaydūn (d. 463/1071), he introduces Ibn Zaydūn as a statesman, a brilliant poet and prose writer, one of the few who are unrivaled in their poetics of elegance, depth, distinctiveness, and power.[40] In this shared script, however, Ibn Zaydūn is not immune from instances of borrowing. Ibn Bassām

[36] Ibn Bassām, *al-Dhakhīrah*, 1:197. [37] Ibid., 198. [38] Ibid. [39] Ibid.
[40] Ibid., 207.

divides occurrences of *saraq* between *lafẓ* (wording or expression) and poetic meaning. Thus, Ibn Zaydūn's metaphorical reference to "borrowing blackness of heart and eyesight" (*qad istaʿāra sawād al-qalb wa-l-baṣari*) leans on and reflects that of Abū al-ʿAlāʾ al-Maʿarrī (d. 449/1057) in his line "He wishes for night's darkness to last / with intense blackness of heart and vision."[41]

When it comes to poetic meanings, Ibn Bassām lists several from Abbasid poets, especially Abū Tammām, al-Mutanabbī, al-Buḥturī, the Andalusian Ibn Darrāj al-Qasṭallī (d. 421/1030), the Kufi-Baghdadi poet Rāshid Abū Ḥukaymah (d. 420/1029–30), and others. Instead of using common terminologies for borrowing, Ibn Bassām uses *nāẓirun ilā* ("discreetly traceable to," or "echoing," as in al-Ḥātimī's *naẓar*; it can also mean "striving toward equivalence").[42] He also uses common terms like *ilmām* in his reference to a verse that has a similar meaning in Ibn al-Muʿtazz's verse,[43] and *iḥtidhāʾ* to indicate the use of a certain mode of expression already used by a precursor or contemporary in order to render a meaning.[44] Every now and then he departs from such terms so as to show that a hemistich is *muqtaṭaʿ* (copied from a source).[45] Even so, Ibn Bassām keeps up with the *saraq* lexicon, placing it within a balanced review of merits and drawbacks. Thus, when providing an overview of Ibn Zaydūn, he concludes, in the middle of a lengthy study of the poet and essayist,[46] that the latter, "despite substantial worthiness, commits much *ihtidām* in prose and poetry."[47] *Ihtidām* is a serious accusation, though committing *ihtidām* is less objectionable than committing other categories of *saraq* already explained in Chapter 4. It is so because – as its connotative application indicates – *ihtidām* destroys another poet's verse by taking over part of it.[48] In other instances – and they are many – Ibn Bassām is satisfied with a casual reference suggesting that the following verse is from the sayings of Abū al-Ṭayyib al-Mutanabbī[49] or is a *nāẓirun* (from *naẓar*, a subtle pointing to an expression) to a specific verse by the latter poet.[50] Other tracings relate to the poetry of Ibn Hāniʾ al-Andalusī (d. 360/970–71), Muḥammad al-Tuhāmī al-Qayrawānī al-Qābsī (d. 403/1012–13), or the like.[51]

[41] Ibid., 214. [42] Ibid., 214, 220. See also al-Ḥātimī, *Ḥilyat al-muḥāḍarah*, 2:86.
[43] Ibn Bassām, *al-Dhakhīrah*, 1:225. *Ilmām* occurs when the poet reverses a poetic meaning of another poet's verse, or, in al-Nahshalī's terms, the transference "of a poetic meaning without its original wording." See Ibn Rashīq, *al-ʿUmdah* (2001), 2:283.
[44] Ibn Bassām, *al-Dhakhīrah*, 1:229. See also Grunebaum, "Concept of Plagiarism," 241.
[45] Ibn Bassām, *al-Dhakhīrah*, 1:230. [46] Ibid., 218.
[47] It is "taking over less than one verse," as in Ibn Rashīq's understanding; *al-ʿUmdah* (2001), 2:283.
[48] See also Grunebaum, "Concept of Plagiarism," 239.
[49] Ibn Bassām, *al-Dhakhīrah*, 1:234. [50] Ibid., 235. [51] Ibid.

Ibn Bassām's Treasury and *Sariqāt* Lexicon

In other poetic citations, Ibn Bassām is unwilling to spare the target poet from an accusation such as the following: "And this is Ibn Darrāj al-Qasṭallī's verse in its totality"; yet Ibn Bassām does not name it *sariqah*.[52] This departure from the bluntness of al-Ḥātimī's discourse is important for our understanding of the waning economies of theft. As the ultimate purpose for compiling such a treasury of the merits of Andalusia in Arab cultural production is to underline merits and points of strength without overlooking echoes, similarities, and variations of *saraq*, the *Dhakhīrah* treasury picks its style neatly to conform with a distinguished and pleasant Andalusian style. To balance its material, the treasury has to make two significant contributions, which its author and compiler, Ibn Bassām, highlights as guiding principles. There is first the basic understanding that the poetries of Abū Tammām and al-Mutanabbī make up part of the *maḥfūẓ* (memorized) and celebrated legacy among Andalusians and Moroccans, as the poetry of the two renowned poets was taught in the mosques of Córdoba, Seville, Valencia, and other cultural centers.[53] Thus, Ibn Bassām explains, collapsing both al-Qāḍī al-Jurjānī's and al-Mutanabbī's conclusions: "I cannot be absolute in saying this one has taken over part of either wording or meaning [*akhdh*] from that one, as correspondence in thoughts and notions occurs, and a hoof may tread on the space of another. Poetry is a tournament, and poets are knights."[54]

On the other hand, and as was noticed by Muḥammad Bin Sharīfah, ʿAlī b. Aḥmad b. Saʿīd b. Ḥazm (d. 456/1064) is as absolute (as was ʿAbd al-Karīm al-Nahshalī [d. 403/1013] before him) in rejecting *muwāradah* (correspondence in thought), for

> what is being mentioned by *al-mutakallimūn fī al-ashʿār* [critics of poetry] under *muwāradah*, where they argue that poets' thoughts agree with others in several verses, are unfounded and unreasonably fabricated statements, as they are only thefts and *ghārāt* [forced resignation of verses to a powerful poet who finds them more fitting into his poetry[55] or acts of taking over most poetic meanings].[56]

Along with ʿUmar b. al-Ḥasan b. Diḥyah al-Kalbī (d. 633/1235) and others, Ibn Bassām shows *sariqāt* as a domain of conversational grids that are indicative of an intertextual space. Poets simply endow the practice with common references that were acceptable in their time. Thus, when reviewing the poetry of Abū Bakr ʿUbādah b. Māʾ al-Samāʾ (d. 422/1030), omitting his *azjāl* and *muwashshaḥāt* (strophic [girdled] poems), Ibn

[52] Ibid., 231. [53] See Bin Sharīfah, *Abū Tammām*, 20–22.
[54] Quoted in ibid., 68, from Ibn Bassām, *al-Dhakhīrah*.
[55] See al-Ḥātimī, *Ḥilyat al-muḥāḍarah*, 2:39. [56] Bin Sharīfah, *Abū Tammām*, 68.

Bassām encounters poetic meanings that recur in the poetries of al-Mutanabbī, Ibn Sharaf, al-Maʿarrī, and others. He recapitulates that "these are recurrent meanings and ideas; and their *alfāẓ* [wording and expression] are common, even if ʿUbādah b. Māʾ al-Samāʾ associates these with different meanings."[57] Desire finds nourishment in this memorized legacy, and it is up to the poet to redirect its course.

This undertaking has the advantage of showing the cultural field as one of refinement where competition was not as aggressively pursued as it was in the Eastern flank. Multiple princely courts, mosque assemblies, and other coteries allowed a space for all, while leading scholars endowed some of their disciples with more recognition as the licensing process allowed. As succinctly shown by Muḥammad Bin Sharīfah, there are genealogical trees for the transmission of the poetry of Abū Tammām and Abū al-Ṭayyib al-Mutanabbī and, by implication, for the interaction with or departure from their poetics. If both poets were central to the thievery controversy, and hence to Arabic literary and cultural criticism, their relocation inside the Andalusian culture initiated further engagement with their poetry, as well as liberation from them.

Thus, the second principle that we can glean from Ibn Bassām's *maḥāsin* (treasury of virtues and beauties) is proposed with regard to Abū Bakr ʿUbādah b. Māʾ al-Samāʾ. Ibn Bassām claims him to be the master who sets the form and rules for the art of *tawshīḥ*, "as if it were not heard from any other, and only transmitted by him, and he was so well known for it that it incapacitated him, and overshadowed many of his merits."[58] While Ibn Bassām dismisses any further focus on the art because the meters and internal rhyming of *muwashshaḥāt* (strophic [girdled] poems) "fall outside the purpose of this *dīwān* [*al-Dhakhīrah*], as most of them are unlike the Arab prosody of poetry,"[59] he joins many in believing that this art is an Andalusian property. Indeed, as the refined Ayyubid poet Ibn Sanāʾ al-Mulk (d. 608/1211)[60] notes in the preface to his unique and pioneering *Dār al-ṭirāz fī ʿamal al-muwashshaḥāt* (The House of Brocade on the Composition of *Muwashshaḥāt*),[61] these poetic excursions stand for "what precursors left untouched for successors; through them the latecomer surpasses [in invention] the predecessor."[62] As the first book-length study of its kind, Ibn Sanāʾ al-Mulk's contribution came at a critical

57 Ibn Bassām, *al-Dhakhīrah*, 1:296. 58 Ibid., 292. 59 Ibid.

60 Full name: al-Qāḍī al-Saʿīd Abū al-Qāsim Hibat Allāh.

61 See Dwight F. Reynolds's significant contribution, *Medieval Arab Music and Musicians: Three Translated Texts* (Leiden: Brill, 2022). Reynolds suggests this phrasing: "The latter have outstripped the former" (174).

62 Ibn Sanāʾ al-Mulk, *Dār al-ṭirāz fī ʿamal al-muwashshaḥāt*, ed. Jawdat al-Rikābī (Damascus: Dār al-Fikr, 3rd print, 1980), 29.

juncture when the raging discussion of borrowing and *saraq* from antecedent poetic authority witnessed multiple directions within the same temporal frame of reference, as shown in Chapters 4 and 5.

This is why Ibn Bassām's intervention sixty-four years earlier than Ibn Sanā᾿ al-Mulk is important for this discussion. He provides a historical frame of reference for these metric units or stanzaic forms: "The first who came up with metric measures for these *muwashshaḥāt* in our land and invented its style, as I was told, was Muḥammad b. Maḥmūd al-Qabrī, the Blind."[63] He adds that "Ibn ʿAbd Rabbihi, the author of *The Unique Necklace*, was the first to practice this kind of *muwashshaḥāt*"; but Yūsuf b. Hārūn al-Ramādī (d. 403/1012) made extensive use of *taḍmīn* (insertion),[64] in the so-called *markaz* (center) or *kharjah*. As it is important to relate this controversial issue to the waning economies of theft, let me cite the whole passage:

> The *muwashshaḥāt* are rhythms that the people of al-Andalus used copiously in the [erotic genres of] *ghazal* and *nasīb*, with the result that carefully guarded bosoms and even hearts are broken upon hearing them. The first to compose the rhythms of these *muwashshaḥāt* in our country, and to invent their method of composition, as far as I have determined, was Muḥammad b. Maḥmūd al-Qabrī, the Blind. He used to compose them after the manner of the hemistichs of classical Arabic poetry (except that most of them were [composed] after the manner of the nonexistent hypothetical meters that are not used [in classical Arabic poetry]), by quoting colloquial Arabic and Romance diction, which he called the *markaz* [= *kharjah*], and basing the *muwashshaḥa* upon it without any internal rhyming in [the *markaz*] or in the *ghuṣn*s [branches]. It has been claimed [as an alternative tradition] that Ibn ʿAbd Rabbihi, the author of the *Kitāb al-ʿiqd*, was the first to compose *muwashshaḥāt* of this type among us. Then Yūsuf b. Hārūn al-Ramādī appeared. He was the first to extend the use of internal rhyming into the *markaz*es, employing it at every caesura he encountered, but in the *markaz* exclusively. The poets of our age followed this pattern, such as Mukarram b. Saʿīd and Abū al-Ḥasan's two sons. Then there appeared our ʿUbādah [b. Māʾ al-Samāʾ (d. 422/1030)], who invented the technique of *taḍfīr*; that is to say, he reinforced the caesurae in the *ghuṣn*s by adding internal rhyming to them, just as al-Ramādī had reinforced the caesurae in the *markaz*.[65]

The overview is worth examining, not only because of the reference to *taḍmīn*, which could mean an interruption or a threshold for the insertion

[63] The right name could be: Muqddam b. Muʿāfā al-Qabrī (d. 300/912).

[64] Translated in the text as "caesurae," and in *sariqāt* terminology as the insertion, from another source, of some expressions as a way of confirmation, according to Ibn al-Athīr. See Grunebaum, "Concept of Plagiarism," 244.

[65] Ibn Bassām, *al-Dakhīrah*, 1:292. This translation is taken from Samuel G. Armistead and James T. Monroe, "Beached Whales and Roaring Mice: Additional Remarks on Hispano-Arabic Strophic Poetry," *La Corónica* 13 (1985): 212–34; re-quoted in James T. Monroe, "*Zajal* and *Muwashshaḥa*," in *The Legacy of Muslim Spain*, 1:398–419, 410.

of colloquial Arabic, of words from a Romance dialect, and of surviving indigenous expressions in the *markaz* or *kharjah*. While more in line with the erotic prelude tradition in Arabic poetics, its structure is uniquely Andalusian. The *muwashshaḥ* also assumes this intertextual space because it sounds like street songs, to be sung and played among locals, who by that time used to insert words culled from everyday speech that could also partly acknowledge the principles of Arabic prosody. The act of expressing *tawshīḥ* in a *muwashshaḥah* demolishes al-Ḥātimī's restrictive "new-fangled terminology,"[66] for the form and content belie any accusation of theft. One sample of the *kharjah*, or exit, by al-Aʿmā al-Tuṭīlī,[67] will suffice, where he writes:

> Meu l-ḥabīb enfermo de meu amar.
> Que no ha d'estar?
> Non ves a mibe que s'ha de no llegar?
>
> My beloved is sick for love of me.
> How can he not be so?
> Do you not see that he is not allowed near me?[68]

The art speaks to a wider audience, and in a larger cultural context where transactions take place between the creator, performer, and audience. In terms of matter and manner, we are in the presence of a locally oriented practice, one that responds to the expanding needs and concerns of city dwellers. Al-Ḥātimī's terminological limits lose their power in a totally different construction that might borrow in its *kharjah* (exit) indigenous (Romance) and Arabic colloquial or street language. If we think of this poetic growth in terms of a legacy that relies heavily on an available corpus of Arabic literature, we find this departure in line with what appeared also in the Eastern flank and was analyzed systematically by the poet and rhetor Ṣafī al-Dīn al-Ḥillī (d. 750/1349) in his *al-ʿĀṭil al-ḥālī wa-l-murakhkhaṣ al-ghālī* (The Unadorned Now Bedecked and the Cheapened Made Costly), where he studies the "seven arts."[69] In a brief but invaluable summary, Roger Allen explains:[70]

> Al-Ḥillī divides the categories of the poem in two different ways according to variations in metre and rhyme, and according to language. Three are said

[66] See Grunebaum, "Concept of Plagiarism," 238.
[67] al-Aʿmā al-Tuṭīlī, *Dīwān*, ed. Iḥsān ʿAbbās (Beirut: Dār al-Thaqāfah, 1963), 261–62, quoted in James T. Monroe, *Hispano-Arabic Poetry: A Student Anthology* (Berkeley: University of California Press, 1974), 248–51. See Appendix B for a perfect *muwashshaḥ*.
[68] Armistead and Monroe, "Beached Whales and Roaring Mice," 250n16.
[69] Safī al-Dīn ʿAbd al-ʿAzīz b. Sarāyā al-Ḥillī, *al-ʿĀṭil al-ḥālī wa-l-murakhkhaṣ al-ghālī*, ed. Ḥusayn Naṣṣār (Cairo: al-Hayʾah al-Miṣriyyah al-ʿĀmmah li-l-Kitāb, 1981).
[70] Roger Allen, *The Arabic Literary Heritage: The Development of Its Genres and Criticism* (Cambridge: Cambridge University Press, 1998), 134.

"*muʿrabah*," meaning that they require the use of fully inflected literary Arabic within which, as he colorfully notes, any lapse is unforgivable: *qarīḍ*, *muwashshaḥ*, and dubayt (also known as rubāʿī [quatrain]).

Allen adds:

Three other types are termed "*mulḥūnah*," implying that a kind of language unacceptable to the grammarians is the norm: the *qūmā*, the *zajal*, and the *kān wa-kān* ("once upon a time"). ... For one type of poem, the *muwāliyā*, al-Ḥillī suggests that either kind of language is permitted, although the colloquial level is said to be more prevalent.

In both cases, there is a departure from a dominating prosody, and, along with it, from the stupendous production of books and treatises or accounts that take trading among verses as a field of exploration.

Ibn Sanāʾ al-Mulk's interventions are worth considering in this respect. The art of *tawshīḥ* (writing *muwashshaḥ*) may rely heavily on classical prosody, but it also resorts to a seemingly unsystematic mixture of metrics that are nevertheless sustained by other variables that could only be applied by the most knowledgeable masters of the art, such as al-Tuṭīlī and Abū Bakr Yaḥyā b. Muḥammad b. Baqī (d. 545/1150). Quite often the poet makes use of a verse by Kushājim or Ibn al-Muʿtazz in order to bolster the *muwashshaḥ*. In such cases, the lyrical verse of antecedent authority helps set the tone and generate the erotic pleasantries that distinguish the art. The nature of the art as a different metrical and thematic practice, its acquisition of a mode, and its resurrection of erotic lyricism all belie any accusation of *saraq*.

I will quote from Ibn Sanāʾ al-Mulk on these issues. As mentioned earlier, the author of *Dār al-ṭirāz fī ʿamal al-muwashshaḥāt* (The House of Brocade on the Composition of *Muwashshaḥāt*) summarizes the appearance of these strophic poems by saying that they elude categorization, for there is solemnity and jest, prose and poetry, a phenomenon "with which the Maghreb [here Andalusia] shines as it arose on its horizon; and its people became the richest for gleaning the treasure that the days had stored for them, the metal of which people remained unaware."[71] In another passage from the same text, in Dwight Reynolds's translation, Ibn Sanāʾ al-Mulk states:[72]

The people of the West brought them [*muwashshaḥāt*] to the East and *the poets have left them to be mended.* They are the jewel of our age, the Babel of magic, the

[71] Ibn Sanāʾ al-Mulk, *Dār al-ṭirāz*, 30.
[72] Reynolds, "The House of Brocade on the Composition of *Muwashshaḥāt*," in *Medieval Arab Music and Musicians*, 174.

amber of Shihr, the aloe wood of India, the wine of Qufs, the gold nuggets of Algarve, the measure of minds, the gauge of intellects, and the essence of essences.

The author reflects on the ever-worrying concern that lies behind poetic anxiety, a concern eloquently pronounced by the pre-Islamic poet ʿAntarah b. Shaddād's (d. 608) verse "Have the poets left anything to be mended?" Ibn Sanāʾ al-Mulk further explains:[73]

They entertain and enchant, they cause despair and bring hope, they fascinate and captivate, they bring release [from cares] and yet preoccupy, they are sociable, but shy away. They are frivolity, all of which is serious, and seriousness, all of which is frivolous. They are poetry that the eye perceives as prose and prose that discerning taste perceives as poetry.

His attention is drawn to the *kharjah* in its foreign expression, especially if its wording is also excessively nonsensical and obscene. The *kharjah* is also the *muwashshaḥa*'s "sweetness, and salinity, its musk and amber,"[74] and "it [the *kharjah*] is the conclusion, but also the precedent, even if it comes last, because it is the part that first captures the composer's mind in preparation for the rest."[75] Indeed, Ibn Sanāʾ al-Mulk looks upon the *kharjah* as the defining section of a *muwashshaḥ*, on condition that it has the obscenity of Ibn al-Ḥajjāj's verse and the colloquialism of Ibn Quzman's *zajal*: "The *kharja* is the final common-rhyme section of the *muwashshaḥ*. It should be *Ḥajjājī* in its vulgarity and *Quzmānī* in its colloquialism, burning hot, finely sharpened, [filled with] expressions of the masses and the slang of the lower classes."[76] Its significance drove "most valiant composers," *washshāḥīn*,[77] to make use of (*akhdh*) a well-known verse to be the *kharjah*, as Ibn Baqī does with this verse by Ibn al-Muʿtazz:

علموني كيفَ أسلو، وإلاّ،   فخذوا عنْ مقلتيّ الملاحا

Teach me how to forget or
keep these enticing beauties away from my sight.

Another recourse, also resorted to by Ibn Baqī, is to take over (*akhdh*) a verse from Kushājim, spreading the theme and words in a *muwashshaḥa*

[73] Ibid. [74] The combination of salt and sweet recurs in usual conversation.

[75] Ibn Sanāʾ al-Mulk, *Dār al-ṭirāz*, 43:
وقد تكون الخرجة عجمية اللفظ بشرط أن يكون لفظها أيضاً في العجمي سفسافاً نفطياً، ورمادياً زطياً. والخرجة هي أبزار الموشح وملحه وسكره ومسكه وعنبره، وهي العاقبة وينبغي أن تكون حميدة والخاتمة بل السابقة وإن كانت الأخيرة، وقولي السابقة لأنها التي ينبغي إن يسبق الخاطر إليها، ويعملها من ينظم الموشح في الأول، وقبل أن يتقيد بوزن أو قافية، وحين يكون مسيباً مسرحاً ومتبحبحاً منفسحاً.

[76] Reynolds, "House of the Brocade," 182. References to Ibn Ḥajjāj (d. 391/1001) and Ibn Quzmān (d. 555/1160), respectively: "Ḥajjājī" and "Quzmānī."

[77] Ibid.

section and duplicating the sense and sound so as to fit into his art.[78] Kushājim's verse reads in Arabic:

يقولون تب والكأس في كف اغيد   وصوت المثاني والمثالث عال
فقلت لهم لو كنت أضمرت توبةً   وأبصرت هذا كله لبدا لي[79]

In Dwight Reynolds's translation, it reads:

They say, "Repent!" while the wine cup was in the hand of a young beauty // and the sound of the second and third strings of the lute rang out

I said to them: "If ever I were even to consider repenting // having seen all of this – well, this would be the moment!"[80]

Ibn Baqī's *akhdh* reads as follows:

قالوا ولَم يقولوا صواباً
أفنيت في المجون الشبابا
فقلت لو نويت متابا
والكأس في يمين غزالي   والصوت في المثالث عال   لبدا لي[81]

They said, but they did not speak the truth:
"In frivolity you have wasted your youth!"
I said, "If ever I intended to repent
While the wine cup was in my gazelle's right hand // and a song on the lute's third string rings out // well, this would be the moment!"[82]

Ibn Sanāʾ al-Mulk was so enthralled with the *kharjah*, with its foreign or lewd drift, that he authored two *muwashshaḥāt*, probably learning Persian for their sake so as to Persianize the *kharjah*.[83] As the Romance dialect was almost impossible to master, Persian was an available alternative.[84] In line with what is argued in the prefatory *Khuṭbat al-kitāb*, its design and purpose, several incitements and motivations lie behind this applied defamiliarizing exit. Ibn Sanāʾ al-Mulk asserts the power of the *kharjah*, exit, as the locus and nexus of the *muwashshaḥ*. It is so not only because it has a startling effect, but also because it is an invitation to go back to the opening of the poem. This is why Ibn Sanāʾ al-Mulk speaks of it as the succulent piece that settles in the poet's mind and sense even before

[78] Ibn Sanāʾ al-Mulk, *Dār al-ṭirāz*, 45. [79] Ibid.
[80] Reynolds, "House of the Brocade," 186. [81] Ibn Sanāʾ al-Mulk, *Dār al-ṭirāz*, 45–46.
[82] Reynolds, "House of the Brocade," 187. [83] Ibid., 181–85.
[84] Ibn Sanāʾ al-Mulk, *Dār al-ṭirāz*, 183. Also, *Fuṣūṣ al-Fuṣūl*, 2005, 375. Here is Ibn Sanāʾ al-Mulk's own *kharjah* in Persian (which seems garbled), followed by its Arabic equivalent:

وانتي كي بوسة بمن داذ   دها انكسترين
او إزكواي دست من باش   ببوسته شبين

أتعرف من أعطاني القبلة؟   ما زلت أتذكره
وهذا الذي أنعم علي   بالقبلة احترمه

the beginning and sections of the *muwashshaḥ*. Hence, it is a culmination and summation of the whole. A total effect is to be attained, driven, as it were, by a subtle mix of poeticity that craves what is appealing and relatively new. There is, therefore, the desire to re-create the lyrical property of another famed name, a desire that is a display of both affection and spite; but there is also the cautious confiscation of another's property. In conclusion, the *muwashshaḥ* settles comfortably into an in-between space, with the *qaṣīd* on one side and street songs and *azjāl* on the other. Ibn Bassām's reading of its presence in Andalusia is therefore significant.

No less relevant is the presence of Ibn ʿAbd Rabbihi in Ibn Bassām's reading. Since he is recognized as being the first to practice writing a *muwashshaḥah* with a *kharjah* that recurs like a refrain, his invention is worth taking very seriously, not only because this feat is coupled with a vast knowledge and an acute sense of what is worth collecting for his Andalusian audience from the literature of the Arab Eastern flank, but also because his *Unique Necklace* functions as a reservoir for the growing Andalusian readership. Thus, in this joint endeavor, intended to sustain commensurability and adequate exchange between Arab Eastern and Western flanks and to bring about a new practice of poetic invention that could have in its introductory part a reminiscence of the *kān wa-kān* (once upon a time), Ibn ʿAbd Rabbihi is not only a poet, anthologist, gatekeeper of a tradition, and perpetuator of knowledge; he also carves out an exit from the Eastern Arab indulgence in a competitive cultural market. With ingenuity and a vast acquaintance with the culture of the Eastern flank, his presence at the very inception and threshold of the phenomenal rise of the *muwashshaḥ* should encourage readers to search for other terms in order to account for the transactional economies of "theft" in Andalusia. It is not competitiveness but desire that propels a flowing poetic movement. Moreover, his probable grandson Muḥammad b. ʿAlī b. ʿAbd Rabbihi al-Ḥafīd (d. 602/1225) would take over the belles lettres role, write a book explaining al-Mutanabbī's poetry, and name it *Sharḥ al-mukhtār min shiʿr Abī al-Ṭayyib al-Mutanabbī* (Commentary on Selected Poetry from Abū al-Ṭayyib al-Mutanabbī). The book is part of a whole chain of Andalusian and Moroccan commentaries that constitute a substantial cultural engagement with al-Mutanabbī's poetry, a point that will be addressed under "The Slender Andalusian *Saraq* Lexicon".

Ibn Bassām's treasury has several advantages, but the most visible are his quotes from Andalusian writers and poets. Some of these touch on originality and inventiveness in order to ward off accusations of thievery in its multiple implications as highly developed in the Arab East. Examples are many, but I will cite Abū Ḥafṣ b. Burd al-Aṣghar's (d. 418/1039) *Sirr al-adab wa-sabk al-dhahab* (The Golden Mold of the Core of Belles

Lettres): "Everything I have narrated is my creation; and all that is laid down is what I have crafted, as I haven't exploited others' input or ignored it, nor betrayed their trust; but I have adorned it [my narrative] with poetic sections that are rich in superb wisdom and can pass as proverbial sayings by celebrated poets and the worthy learned."[85] Both the disclaimer and attestation underscore the distinctive Andalusian delicacy in managing a field that is intertextually woven. To ward off any accusation of theft, such disclaimers imply that there is an awareness of plagiarism as a controversial subject. Even so, there was a discussion of the *sariqāt* as applied to the popular poetries of Abū Tammām and al-Mutanabbī.

The fourth part of *Jawāhir al-ādāb wa-dhakhā'ir al-shu'arā' wa-l-kuttāb* (The Jewels of Belles Lettres and Poets' and Writers' Treasuries) by Muḥammad b. ʿAbd al-Malik al-Sarrāj (i.e., Ibn Bassām Shantarīnī al-Naḥwī) deals with alleged thieveries in the poetry of al-Mutanabbī. In Muḥammad Bin Sharīfah's *Abū Tammām wa-Abū al-Ṭayyib fī adab al-Maghāribah*,[86] the author points out that this Shantarīnī was not Ibn Bassām al-Shantarīnī the compiler and author of *al-Dhakhīrah*. Al-Naḥwī's four-part manuscript is an abridgment of Ibn Rashīq's *ʿUmdah* and has the advantage of correcting the latter in some places while coming up in this fourth part with "useful additions." Al-Naḥwī was a renowned grammarian and philologist and the mentor of the famous Egyptian grammarian Abū Muḥammad ʿAbdallāh b. Barrī al-Maqdisī (d. 582/1187). Leaving al-Andalus and settling in Egypt, he wrote texts that show more involvement in philological research on the Arab East. As noted by Iḥsān ʿAbbās, there is a difference between the two Shantarīnīs in their selections of thefts and their sources.[87] On the other hand, Ibn al-Sarrāj al Shantarīnī al-Naḥwī is credited with collecting, classifying, and tabulating accusations of theft that are scattered in several Eastern sources.[88] He therefore provides handy material for commentators. The editor of al-Naḥwī's *Sariqāt al-Mutanabbī wa-mushkil maʿānīh*, Ibn ʿĀshūr, suggests that al-ʿUkbarī could have made use of this in his popular commentary on al-Mutanabbī's poetry.[89] Ibn ʿĀshūr also explains the theoretical thread that underlines the collection and organization of verses:

> Know that what littérateurs consider thievery rests on the understanding that a poet seizes on a poetic meaning in a precursor's verse and deliberately includes it in his own.

[85] Ibn Bassām, *al-Dhakhīrah*, 1:305.
[86] Bin Sharīfah, *Abū Tammām*, 132–33. Iḥsān ʿAbbās has already raised doubts about authorship, as there is nothing to indicate it is by Ibn Bassām. See ibid., 134; ʿAbbās, *Tārīkh al-naqd al-adabī* (1978), 506–7, 507n4.
[87] ʿAbbās, *Tārīkh al-naqd al-adabī* (1978), 134.
[88] Bin Sharīfah, *Abū Tammām*, 135.
[89] al-Naḥwī, *Sariqāt al-Mutanabbī*, lām.

He adds:

> *Akhdh* [possessing forcibly; seizing on] and *saraq* are of two kinds: visible and discreet. The visible is when the meaning is taken in full, with its expression or part of it; it is despicable if the meaning is taken without change. If the latecomer produces a better verse than a precursor's, it is laudable; otherwise, it is reprehensible.[90]

The wording in Ibn ʿĀshūr's foregoing quote is worth considering, as he draws attention to only two terms from the *sariqāt* terminology, *akhdh* and *saraq*, which occur in al-Naḥwī's fourth part on *sariqāt*. On the other hand, Ibn Bassām al-Shantarīnī, the compiler and author of *al-Dhakhīrah*, lays more emphasis on several terms, especially *naẓar* (subtle and discreet allusions to a meaning), and *ihtidām* (confiscating a slice of a verse).[91] Although unobtrusive, al-Naḥwī often includes a citation that may disagree with commentaries by Abū al-Ḥasan ʿAlī b. Aḥmad al-Wāḥidī (d. 468/1076) and Abū al-Baqāʾ al-ʿUkbarī (d. 616/1219)[92] – for example, so as to agree with Ibn Jinnī's highly reputable but controversial readings of al-Mutanabbī's poetry.[93] Thus, al-Naḥwī selects verses that receive controversial commentaries, often discreetly objecting to some.[94] In most citations, there is a vague resemblance in meaning that is free of duplication of all or part of a wording, a matter that is often thought of in terms other than blunt thievery. As meanings are common and available to all, the focus is laid on wording and expression, its duplication or contrary application. Thus, when al-Naḥwī cites al-Mutanabbī's comparison and contrast between the deserted abodes of the nostalgic prelude and the continued psychic inhabitation of the heart, he fails to see beyond a partial thematic resemblance with Abū Tammām's use of abodes, thereby overlooking the other significant objectification of the correlative abode of heartfelt loss:

[90] Ibid., kāf. [91] See al-Ḥātimī, *Ḥilyat al-muḥāḍarah*, 2:86, 64.

[92] Both have their highly reputed commentaries on al-Mutanabbī's poetry: Abū al-Baqāʾ al-ʿUkbarī, *Dīwān Abī al-Ṭayyib al-Mutanabbī*, ed. D. Kamāl Ṭālib (Qum, 2015); *Sharḥ Dīwān al-Mutanabbī*, ed. ʿAbd al-Raḥmān al-Barqūqī (Qum, 3rd print, 2015). Another edition is *Dīwān Abī al-Ṭayyib al-Mutanabbī*, ed. Muṣṭafā al-Saqqā, Ibrāhīm al-Ibyārī and ʿAbd al-Ḥafīẓ Shalabī (Cairo: Muṣṭafā al-Bābī al-Ḥalabī, 1936). Al-Wāḥidī's commentary is *Dīwān Abī al-Ṭayyib al-Mutanabbī*, ed. Frīdarikh Dītrīṣī (Berolini: Mittler, 1861). Another is *Dīwān al-Mutanabbī*, ed. Muṣṭafā Rajab (Dasūq: Dār al-ʿIlm wa-l-Īmān, 2019). Of significance is *al-Lāmiʿ al-ʿazīzī*, by Abū al-ʿAlāʾ Aḥmad b. ʿAbdallāh al-Maʿarrī, ed. Muḥammad Saʿīd al-Mawlawī (Riyadh: Markaz al-Malik Fayṣal, 2008).

[93] Abū al-Fatḥ ʿUthmān Ibn Jinnī, *al-Fasr: sharḥ Ibn Jinnī al-kabīr ʿalā Dīwān al-Mutanabbī*, ed. Riḍā Rajab (Damascus: Dār al-Yanābīʿ, 2004). See also Ibn Jinnī, *al-Fatḥ al-wahbī*.

[94] See, for example, al-Naḥwī, *Sariqāt al-Mutanabbī*, 7, n. 1.

لَكِ يا مَنازِلُ في القُلوبِ مَنازِلُ أَقفَرتِ أَنتِ وَهُنَّ مِنكِ أَواهِلُ

Abodes, you have in the hearts abodes
You have become deserted, but they are inhabited by you.[95]

Al-Naḥwī cites the following verse from Abū Tammām, which has a similar meaning, but with a totally different but plain expression:

وقفت وأحشائي منازل للأسى به وهو قفر قد تعفت منازله

Sadness overwhelmed my being as I stopped at the deserted abodes.[96]

In a different context, Abū Tammām's verse that draws Huda J. Fakhreddine's attention could have been the base for a better comparison, and a redirected association:

لا أَنتَ أَنتَ وَلا الدِيارُ دِيارُ خَفَّ الهَوى وَتَوَلَّتِ الأَوطارُ

You are not you, the abodes are not the abodes,
Passion has faded, desires have turned away.[97]

The compiler's lexicon of traces avoids the available plagiarism terminology and is often satisfied with "this is from the saying" of so-and-so.

However, there are many examples that show a striking similarity to a source. Thus, al-Mutanabbī's verse:

ومن صحب الدنيا طويلا تقلبت على عينه حتى يرى صدقها كذبا

To be in the company of this world for so long should reveal it as fickle
even its sincerity looks devious.

Al-Naḥwī adds:
This is from Abū Nuwās's poetry:

إذا امتحن الدنيا لبيب تكشفت له عن عدو في ثياب صديق

When a sensible person tries the world, it exposes itself
to him as a foe in the garb of a friend.[98]

While these two verses invite a critical opinion in order to demonstrate that Abū Nuwās's verse sounds better in wording and meaning, al-Naḥwī

95 Huda J. Fakhreddine, *Metapoesis in the Arabic Tradition: From Modernists to Muḥdathūn* (Leiden: Brill, 2015), 58. A different phrasing is as follows: "You deserted abodes / are still abiding in the heart." Fakhreddine draws a good comparison between the two most obvious instances of loss. Wormhoudt translates as follows: "For you O campsites there are camps in the hearts / You become waste, but they are peopled by you." *The Diwan*, 73.
96 al-Naḥwī, *Sariqāt al-Mutanabbī*, 106.
97 Fakhreddine, *Metapoesis in the Arabic Tradition*, 58.
98 al-Naḥwī, *Sariqāt al-Mutanabbī*, 14.

lets the issue rest. He cites other examples, like this verse, for example, which al-Mutanabbī addresses to Sayf al-Dawlah:

إذا شد زندي حسن رأيك في يدي ضربت بنصل يقطع الهام مغمدا

When you brace my forearm with your high esteem
I will strike them with a sword that, even sheathed, splits skulls.[99]

He states that al-Mutanabbī is quoting Abū Tammām, without adding that there is *ihtidām* (use of part of the meaning and wording of the original) whereby he has put the source to a better use in a specific personalized plea for support:

يسر الذي يسطو به وهو مغمد ويفضح من يسطو به غير مغمد[100]

It gladdens the one who assails with it sheathed
and exposes the one who assails with it unsheathed.

Al-Naḥwī repeats common or shared applications without going into the implications of an improvement in meaning and wording, which is more visible in al-Mutanabbī's verse. In other words, these citations focus on semantic parallels with less care for value, something that is vigorously maintained as a criterion in assessments of improvements on the original or otherwise. One can argue that al-Naḥwī, who is merely collecting what is being traded in the competitive cultural market of thefts, is unwilling to use stark, accusatory terms like the ones in al-Ḥātimī's *al-Risālah al-mūḍiḥah*. The refined Andalusian background endows such compilations with subtlety and tact, as though approving of Ibn al-ʿAlāʾ's popular formula of *muwāradah*, al-Jāḥiẓ's on the availability of meanings and ideas to all, or al-Mutanabbī's premise of discursive entanglement.[101]

The Slender Andalusian *Saraq* Lexicon

While we rarely come across al-Ḥātimī's trading in accusations among Andalusians, the attention to patterns of this process of trading in the Arab Eastern flank, especially focused on the familiar and towering names of poets, is watered down to fit Andalusian taste. Thus, even when Ibn Sharaf would like to endorse Ibn Lankak's claim that al-Mutanabbī has practiced *saraq* from Abū al-Qāsim Naṣr b. Aḥmad al-Khubzarruzī al-Khubz Arzī, he refrains from naming al-Mutanabbī.[102] On the other hand, Ibn ʿAbd Rabbihi prefers *istiʿārah* (here: borrowing), stressing that the most subtle of these borrowings are the ones that are transferred

[99] Stetkevych, *Poetics of Islamic Legitimacy*, 191.
[100] al-Naḥwī, *Sariqāt al-Mutanabbī*, 37. [101] See Chapters 1 and 4. [102] See n. 7.

from one genre and sematic field to another: from prose to poetry and vice versa.[103] Throughout, he applies the term *istiʿārah* in cases that usually receive harsher treatment in the cultural market of the Arab East.[104]

Abū ʿĀmir b. Shuhayd offers a more complicated case, not only because of his sustained support of naturalness and spontaneity in poetry and discourse, but also because his preference for contemporaneity involves harsh criticism of the "gang of instructors," including the highly reputed grammarian and philologist Abū al-Qāsim b. al-Iflīlī,[105] the author of a celebrated commentary on Abū al-Ṭayyib al-Mutanabbī. While Ibn Shuhayd was an admirer of the latter and also of the historian and essayist Ibn Ḥayyān, who thinks very highly of Ibn al-Iflīlī as the master of Arabic language philology,[106] his attention is focused on spontaneity. In many places in Ibn Shuhayd's *Risālat al-tawābiʿ wa-l-zawābiʿ* (The Treatise of Familiar Spirits and Demons), the narrator of this witty and erudite treatise invokes the spirits of his forebears to offer a few suggestions regarding spontaneity and genuineness. There, the narrator cites examples of poetic pieces that generate impressive meanings, including *al-maʿānī al-ʿuqm* (unique or virgin meanings, inaccessible to duplication).[107] The narrator touches on *al-dunū minhu wa-l-ilmām bih* (approximating a meaning and inverting it),[108] a point that a shaykh who instructs his son in poetics takes to heart as being pivotal to poetic dynamism. The shaykh, probably the author's surrogate, as a practitioner of poetry advises his son to avoid a unique meaning, "already reached by a precursor." If the precursor "has already done well with its structure and refined its wording," it is better to avoid it, or "if there is an urgency to do so, change its prosody," so as "to activate your naturalness and strengthen your stamina."[109]

Ibn Shuhayd provides a case for naturalness and spontaneity that recalls al-Āmidī's in his defense of al-Buḥturī. This stance – which also shows his preference for forebears, who alone can license poets – necessarily runs counter to the tenets of grammarians regarding organization and rules, which provoke his bitter and sarcastic tone. On the other hand, it matches an ongoing transactional literary activity in the engagement with the Eastern flank's overwhelming cultural production. However, Iḥsān ʿAbbās calls for a systematic application of rules respecting *al-akhdh* and *saraq*. He argues that: "If Eastern poetry was in need of rules to organize *akhdh*, then Andalusian poetry should have been even more in

[103] See ʿAbbās, *Tārīkh al-naqd al-adabī* (2006), 478–79.
[104] See Ibn ʿAbd Rabbihi, *The Unique Necklace*, vol. 2, trans. Issa Boullata (Reading, UK: Garnet Publishing, 2009), 81, 185, 189, 300–302, 312.
[105] See Ibn Bassām, *al-Dhakhīrah*, 1:239, 240–41. [106] Ibid., 281–82. [107] Ibid., 286.
[108] See al-Jurjānī, *al-Wasāṭah* (1966), 253, 428; Ibn Rashīq, *al-ʿUmdah* (2001), 2:287.
[109] I Cited in ʿAbbās, *Tārīkh al-naqd al-adabī* (Dār al-Shurūq edition), 485.

need of them because its ongoing growth depends on new anxious pulses that keep flowing from the East."[110] As shown earlier, the effort to maintain the highest standards was upheld, but it is situated within the larger conversation among texts, thereby accommodating the Andalusian need for further distinction. As is the case in a lucrative marketplace, you take from another in order to produce better merchandise or at least to be competitively on par. Commentaries, treasuries, and assemblies were at the heart of this marketability. Thus, even commentaries on al-Mutanabbī are not exempted. Both Ibn al-Iflīlī and al-Kalāʿī, who was a philologist and literary critic, have their commentaries that highlight the power of meaning and wording in al-Mutanabbī's poetry, a point that was well-taken by several commentators, tipping the scale for the poet, who was not immune to the vilification of a few detractors.

Before checking on these texts as they relate to the issue of *sariqāt*, I should argue the case raised by Iḥsān ʿAbbās as being an issue of gravitation toward, and a desire to depart from, that overwhelming but cherished legacy. The tension is nowhere more apparent than in Ibn Bassām's *al-Dhakhīrah*. Whenever a poet or writer from al-Andalus is mentioned, that citation is always placed in a context of negotiation with poets from the Eastern flank, along with others from al-Andalus. The trend is meant to suggest a comparatist scale by which a specific Andalusian poet or writer is shown to be deservedly on par with highly recognized Eastern figures. The whole negotiatory effort tends to minimize the harsh application of *saraq*, an inclination that is shown succinctly in Ibn Rashīq's (d. 456/1064, Sicily) short account in his *ʿUmdah* and in *Qurāḍat al-dhahab* (Gold Specks [or Nuggets] on Appraising the Poetry of the Arabs).[111] He admits that he is more in line with al-Qāḍī al-Jurjānī's approach and terms. He argues that "theft is only in cases of *badīʿ nādir* [a rare *badīʿ*, the exceptional, that shows in expressions – i.e., *alfāẓ*]."[112] He thinks that, as "inventiveness in meaning dwindles, *sariqāt* [plural] also decrease, and receive notoriety when they occur."[113] He admits two significant shifts that have been in active motion for a long time: the availability of an overwhelming poetic legacy and memorization (*ḥifẓ*). Both are bound to entail deliberate or unwitting recollection and application in an integrated discursive space. An alternative to stark thievery is a re-creative strategy that resorts to patching from several verses, *talfīq*, in

[110] ʿAbbās, *Tārīkh al-naqd al-adabī* (2006), 482.
[111] Konrad Hirschler translates the title as *The Clipped Gold Piece [on Criticizing the Arabs' Poems]*. See Konrad Hirschler, *Medieval Damascus: Plurality and Diversity in an Arabic Library: The Ashrafiya Library Catalogue* (Edinburgh: Edinburgh University Press, 2016). Thanks to Geert Jan van Gelder for pointing this out.
[112] Ibn Rashīq, *Qurāḍat al-dhahab*, 20. [113] Ibid., 20.

a collation of expressions, to create a new verse,[114] a technique at which such great poets as al-Mutanabbī and Abū al-ʿAlāʾ al-Maʿarrī excel.[115] This is a significant process practiced by the Andalusian literary market, not only because *al-kalām min al-kalām maʾkhūdh* (integrated discursive space), but also because a new generation of meanings culled from multiple sources indicates a genuine poetic effort that is almost *ikhtirāʿ* (invention).[116] Furthermore, in the same place, Ibn Rashīq argues the significance of this effort in a marketable transaction. First, because a skillful applicant of *talfīq* stands alone as a representative of a collective group of poets; and second, because a skillful user like al-Mutanabbī shows a mastery of a consortium of poetic meanings in minimal wording. Hence, Ibn Rashīq concludes that experts prefer al-Mutanabbī to others because he exemplifies poetic brevity.[117] Especially in *Qurāḍat al-dhahab*, Ibn Rashīq is more concerned with poetic creativity. The terminological labyrinth, which Bonebakker takes as a title for an article,[118] is redrawn in Ibn Rashīq's *Qurāḍat al-dhahab*, where he emphasizes patching and piecing together in a vast discursive sphere.

In the same tradition, Ḥāzim al-Qarṭājannī (b. 608/1211, Cartagena, Andalus; d. 684/1286, Tunisia) also reiterates that the highest standard in poetry is attained when a new meaning is obtained. He agrees that what emerges from this discursive integration amounts to a rare meaning that poets avoid because it is too obvious to pass unnoticed.[119] Despite the historical span between Ibn Rashīq and al-Qarṭājannī, there is flexibility toward *saraq* in their approach that can help us understand the Andalusian style that functions between Ibn ʿAbd Rabbihī's application of "borrowing" and Ibn Rashīq's and Ibn al-Iflīlī's *ilmām* (thematic inversion). Ibn Rashīq deconstructs some terms like *ijtilāb* (procuring support). He situates the phrase outside the definition of *saraq* because it is a matter of deliberate preference for another poet's verse that he finds more fitting in his poem, similar to what Jarīr did with verses by al-Maʿlūṭ b. Badal al-Saʿdī (d. 9/630).[120] In *Qurāḍat al-dhahab* Ibn Rashīq also avoids the use of *akhdh* in order to claim as more appropriate the new term *fatḥ* (opening up), suggesting that he is unprecedented in this usage. The precursor or contemporary may introduce a specific usage or

[114] Ibid., 106; al-Ḥātimī, *Ḥilyat al-muḥāḍarah*, 90.
[115] Ibn Rashīq, *Qurāḍat al-dhahab*, 106. [116] Ibid. [117] Ibid.
[118] Bonebakker, "Ancient Arabic Poetry and Plagiarism."
[119] See ʿAbbās, *Tārīkh al-naqd al-adabī* (2006), 563; Ḥāzim al-Qarṭājannī, *Minhāj al-bulaghāʾ wa-sirāj al-udabāʾ*, ed. al-Ḥabīb b. Khujah (Tunis: al-Dār al-Tūnisiyyah, 1966), 192–93.
[120] Ibn Rashīq, *Qurāḍat al-dhahab*, 85.

thematic concern without exhausting it. The latecomer comes upon some poetic ideas or wording and expressions that invite expansion, intensification, or inversion, deflection, and inflection. He cites as examples a verse by Abū Nuwās that led to Ibn al-Muʿtazz's adoption and another by Imruʾ al-Qays that enables al-Farazdaq's expression.[121]

Ḥāzim al-Qarṭājannī's intervention fits in with this line of filtering the fierce cultural battle of the Eastern flank on plagiarism. Although marginal to his discussion of poetic aesthetics, his perception of theft in terms of a canvas of applications also resonates with a dismissal of any aggressive treatment of *sariqāt*. Hence his formula for a guided conversation functions within the discussion of invention, insertion of proverbial sayings, shared meanings, and *saraq*. Ibn al-Iflīlī (d. 441/1050), an early contemporary to Ibn Rashīq, could have been the source for late eleventh- and twelfth-century scholars' concerns with this issue and its ramifications in literary and cultural marketability, especially since many of his students were notable philologists. One of Ibn al-Iflīlī's disciples, Abū al-Ḥajjāj Yūsuf, known as al-Aʿlam al-Shantamarī (d. 476/1084), who wrote his own *sharḥ* of Abū Tammām's poetry, also completed his mentor's unfinished *Sharḥ shiʿr al-Mutanabbī*.[122]

The controversy around Abū Tammām and al-Buḥturī was bound to spill over in al-Andalus, where, in Seville and the Andalusian West in general, al-Buḥturī was celebrated for his naturalness.[123] Along with transmissions of Abū Tammām's poetry by the Baghdadi traveler Abū al-Yusr Ibrāhīm b. Aḥmad al-Riyāḍī (d. 298/911), as documented by Ibn al-Abbār,[124] there were also ʿUthmān b. al-Muthannā (d. 273/886), the Córdoba scholar, tutor, and poet, and the celebrated poet Muʾmin b. Saʿīd, who used his circle to teach Abū Tammām's poetry, as he mentioned that he had met the poet and was licensed to transmit his poetry.[125] There were other Andalusians who met Abū Tammām and transmitted his poetry. A more solid copy of the poet's corpus was the one in two drafts by Abū ʿAlī al-Qālī, one in the poet's own handwriting and another inscribed by al-Qālī on the authority of Abū Muḥammad ʿAbdallāh b. Jaʿfar b. Darastawayh (d. 347/958). Ibn al-Iflīlī would soon make a copy from al-Qālī's copy of the handwritten one by Abū

121 Ibid., 43, 48.

122 Abū al-Qāsim Ibrāhīm Muḥammad b. Zakariyyā Ibn al-Iflīlī, *Sharḥ shiʿr al-Mutanabbī*, ed. Muṣṭafā ʿUlayyān (Beirut: Muʾassasat al-Risālah, 1992), 1:65.

123 See Bin Sharīfah, *Abū Tammām*, 52–56.

124 See Ibid., 10n3, where there is a reference to this case in Shaykh Aḥmad b. Muḥammad al-Maqqarī, *Nafḥ al-ṭīb min ghuṣn al-Andalus al-raṭīb*, ed. Iḥsān ʿAbbās (Beirut: Dār Ṣādir, 1968), 3:134–35. Abū al-Yusr was originally from Baghdad, settled in Qayrawan, and held high offices.

125 See ibid., 13–14.

Tammām, a copy that was to be the most popular among his students and disciples.[126] What becomes a pattern in poetic structures was a form of *iḥtidhā'* (stylistic emulation) that relies on Abū Tammām's celebrated openings to build their own (see Figure 6.1).[127] Apart from *mu'āraḍah* (contrafaction), which was followed by Ibn 'Abd Rabbihi and others who came under his influence, especially in panegyrics,[128] we find prose writers who prosify Abū Tammām's poetry, such as Abū Ḥayyān, who also alludes to the way that the former's verses contain "allusions that often escape the attention of his authenticating editors."[129]

Ibn al-Iflīlī, whom Ibn Shuhayd blames for a self-centered demeanor, happened to be one of the most influential in spreading the poetries of Abū Tammām and Abū al-Ṭayyib al-Mutanabbī. In his carefully written introductory study to Ibn al-Iflīlī's *Sharḥ* of al-Mutanabbī's poetry, the editor, Muṣṭafā 'Ulayyān, notices that, although al-Mutanabbī "was impacted by the poetic ideas of precursors, Abū al-Qāsim al-Iflīlī touched on the matter of borrowing in a balanced way." He explains: "While not denying such an influx, or use of their poetic ideas, Ibn al-Iflīlī economizes on such connotations, distinguishing what is common and shared that is much in use and has become a trodden track from the rare and special, or newly invented."[130] In line with the compiler's attention to al-Mutanabbī's poetics of enhancement, Muṣṭafā 'Ulayyān asserts the tendency to accept the popular premise that it is a sign of poetic innovation to turn shared meanings into rare inventions. He quotes from *al-Wasāṭah* to explain the emerging "invented new."[131] Ibn al-Iflīlī's terms denoting al-Mutanabbī's use of precursors' poetic meanings are limited to *ilmām*, *naḥw* (following), and *ijmāl* (collation). These terms touch on meanings and hence have no weight in the study of *sariqāt*.[132] While Ibn al-Iflīlī avoids the mention of the term *saraq*, his editor still thinks that the three terms "mean partial use of meaning, minus expression."[133] Muṣṭafā 'Ulayyān is right, however, in thinking that *ilmām* is accepted as theft-free, and it is "the easiest to be used against al-Mutanabbī's verse" in relation to a verse by al-Nābighah because "he took the meaning and ran with it in a totally divergent expression."[134] In sum, Muṣṭafā 'Ulayyān believes that Ibn al-Iflīlī is reluctant to accuse al-Mutanabbī of thefts, "either by maintaining silence regarding verses where *saraq* occurs, or redirecting the term *saraq* differently."[135] Muṣṭafā 'Ulayyān goes out of his way, however, to criticize Ibn al-Iflīlī for not sustaining *manhaj al-qiwāmah* (trusteeship

[126] Ibid., 15–17. [127] Ibid., 32–34. [128] Ibid., 56, 68, 70. [129] Ibid., 74.
[130] Muṣṭafā 'Ulayyān, introduction to al-Iflīlī, *Sharḥ shi'r al-Mutanabbī*, 1:113.
[131] Ibid. [132] Ibid., 114. [133] Ibid. [134] Ibid., 115, 118. [135] Ibid., 115.

obligation), for not pointing out *saraq* cases.[136] Again, while Abū al-Ṭayyib al-Mutanabbī, like other prominent poets, relies on his fecund memory, and his early companionship to the best *warrāqīn* (copyists) in Baghdad, his lexicon can never be free from poets' expressions and meanings. His inversions of the original meanings are already placed outside objectionable territory, as is made clear in *al-Wasāṭah*. All in all, al-Mutanabbī is lauded for better expressions than the acclaimed sources. As we have noticed, even a bitter critic like al-ʿAmīdī can admit that these powerful and highly impressive expressions distinguish the poet's style. His verse seems "to soar in the clouds, like eagles," which his detractors think of as thievery, whereas Ibn Sharaf applauds it for a reason. While poets who take the verse meaning from al-Nābighah, for example, attain less value than the latter's verse in meaning and expression, al-Mutanabbī "augmented the meaning and signified that the birds [eagles] had fed on the enemies of the subject of praise," as Ibn Sharaf argues. Thus, the latter thinks of the poet as the "felicitous benefactor."[137] In all cases, and despite the common toning down of plagiarism accusations, Abū Tammām, al-Buḥturī, and al-Mutanabbī were part and parcel of an Andalusian memory and repertoire, an overwhelming presence that often drove poets like Aḥmad b. Ṭalḥah al-Shaqrī to shout down such a presence: "You make a hell of talk about Ḥabīb [Abū Tammām], Buḥturī, and al-Mutanabbī, and among you are poets who have come up with what they had never reached."[138] The same toning down was more or less a phenomenon even in Kamāl al-Dīn Abū al-ʿAbbās Aḥmad al-Sharīshī's (d. 619/1223) highly regarded *sharḥ* (commentary) on al-Ḥarīrī's *Maqāmāt* (Assemblies). In *maqāmah* 23, "al-Shiʿriyyah" (On Poetry [or On Poetics]), we have Abū Zayd al-Sarūjī, and his presumed companion as son, complaining to the judge of his son's plagiarism of his poetry.[139] This becomes the occasion for explaining to the governor twenty cases, divided into ten commendable *sariqāt* and ten reprehensible ones. These focus more or less on either strengthening meaning and expression or falling short in both. Ibn Wakīʿ has already addressed that, but al-Sharīshī al-Andalusī presents the discussion in relation to his own milieu to show that poets compete in value, a competition that is stimulating but not detrimental. Ibn

136 Ibid. 118.

137 Ibn Sharaf, as quoted from his *Risālat al-tawābiʿ wa-l-zawābiʿ*, by Muṣṭafā ʿUlayyān, 117.

138 Quoted in Bin Sharīfah, *Abū Tammām*, 77 n131.

139 Abū al-ʿAbbās Aḥmad b. ʿAbd al-Muʾmin al-Qaysī al-Sharīshī, *Sharḥ Maqāmāt al-Ḥarīrī*, 4 parts in 2 vols., ed. Muḥammad ʿAbd al-Munʿim Khafājī (Cairo: ʿAbd al-Ḥamīd Aḥmad Ḥanafī, 1952), 1:203–49, esp. 204–5, where *saraq* terms are listed.

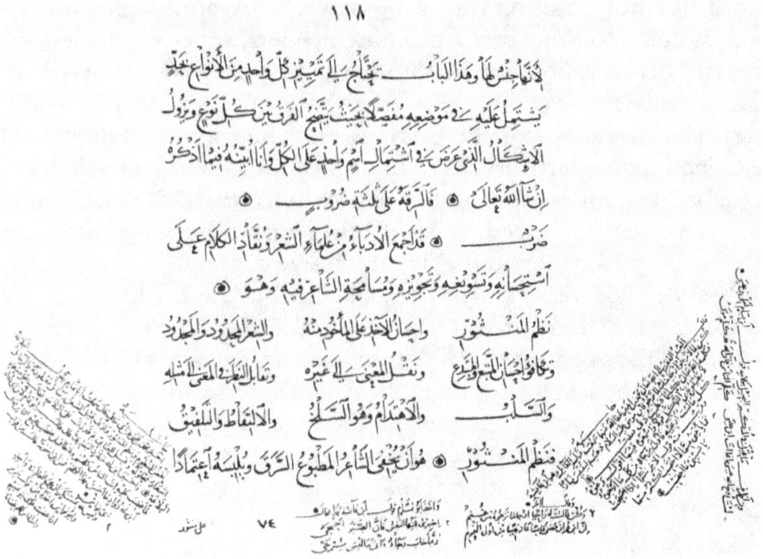

Figure 6.2 Permissible infringements

Wakī‘'s book is the main source for al-Sharīshī's reading of poetry and theft. Whenever a question is raised by the judge, al-Sharīshī jumps on that to provide explanations. When the judge in the *Maqāmah* (no. 23) asks if the *saraq* shows as *maskh* (distortion), *salkh* (flaying; partial theft), or *naskh* (duplication), al-Sharīshī relies on Ibn Wakī‘ to give detailed explanations of these terms with examples that are recurrent in studies of *saraq*.[140] Throughout, permissible infringements are carefully presented in terms of improvement and better value (see Figure 6.2). There is a difference between those produced in the Arab East and the ones that show an Andalusian bent. In his examples he compares Andalusian poetry with antecedent Eastern poets. The comparison rests on analogical citations where resemblance is visible.[141] Al-Sharīshī's undertaking should not be underestimated. While the *maqāmah* on poetics fits well onto the Andalusian economies of desire, its involvement of the judiciary in the discussion of theft accusations presents a contrapuntal criticism. It parodies the Eastern flank's raging disputations, exhausts its limits, and replaces it in the

[140] Ibid., 205.

[141] See Bin Sharīfah, *Abū Tammām*, 71, where he makes a reference to al-Sharīshī. There, Bin Sharīfah alludes to the Andalusian poets' poetic meanings that rely on Abū Tammām, though in a different form, *naẓar*.

cultural market as a matter of conflictual desire. As usual, the names of Abū Tammām and al-Mutanabbī signify a literary tradition in motion.

The record of Abū al-Ṭayyib al-Mutanabbī in al-Andalus is more varied. Ibn al-Iflīlī's *Sharḥ* (commentary on his *dīwān*) derives significance from his independent stature, which was taken by Ibn Shuhayd and others to be bigotry. His thorough grounding in Arabic-Islamic philology and his training by some of the well-reputed Andalusian scholars endow his style with vigor, logic, and variety. His *Sharḥ* received the commendation of many, including ʿAlī b. Aḥmad b. Ḥazm, who lists it as part of his documentation of the virtues of Andalusian culture – though he reconsidered that commendation in his nonextant book: *A Rejoinder to Ibn al-Iflīlī's Sharḥ Dīwān al-Mutanabbī.*[142] The rejoinder provoked a response from one of Ibn al-Iflīlī's many students, ʿAbdallāh b. Aḥmad al-Nabbāhī.[143] Andalusian scholars who wrote, taught, or used Ibn al-Iflīlī's commentary are important, not only because they signify the role played by this commentary and its impact on other commentaries, but also because the commentary plays a central role in redirecting the conversation from the Arab East on plagiarism and its terminological variables away from Andalusian poets.[144] Ibn al-Iflīlī's widely circulated commentary left its stamp on other significant commentaries, like al-ʿUkbarī's (d. 616/1219) *Sharḥ al-Tibyān.*[145] Taken together, these commentaries and their visible disregard for the raging battle over al-Mutanabbī's proclaimed plagiarisms fit into the whole Andalusian ambiance, which tends to boost achievement rather than track down echoes. While Ibn Bassām records several cases on "borrowing" from, or "*ḥall*" of, al-Mutanabbī's verses in prose writings, they are marginal to the more immediate task of showing the virtues of Andalusian culture.

In other words, despite the raging discussion of al-Mutanabbī and the tendency of some detractors to prove he is *mustariqun muḥtadhī* (a plagiarist/duplicator), as al-Ḥātimī contends in *al-Risālah al-Ḥātimiyyah,*[146] the Andalusian attitude bypasses this debate, to focus more on what his poetry has to offer, as shown by Muḥammad Bin Sharīfah.[147] The latter tried to find a strong reason to explain an astounding tradition of commentary focusing on al-Mutanabbī in particular. He offers this explanation: "The interest in al-Mutanabbī used to get sturdier and more visible whenever strong rulers appeared, as they were in need of poets who could be on par with al-Mutanabbī in his panegyrics, so as to have their own deeds celebrated and their achievements written down."

[142] Ibn al-Iflīlī, *Sharḥ shiʿr al-Mutanabbī*, editor's note, 1:121n1. [143] Ibid., 121.
[144] See ʿUlayyān, introduction, 1:124–34.
[145] Abū al-Baqāʾ ʿAbdallāh b. al-Ḥusayn ʿUkbarī, *Sharḥ al-Tibyān li-l-ʿUkbarī ʿalā Dīwān Abī al-Ṭayyib Aḥmad b. al-Ḥusayn al-Mutanabbī* (Cairo: Dār al-Ṭibāʿah, 1870).
[146] See Chapter 5. [147] Bin Sharīfah, *Abū Tammām*, 93–167.

Thus, Muḥammad Bin Sharīfah contends, Ibn Hāni' (d. 362/973) was "the Moroccan Mutanabbī" during the reign of the Fatimid al-Mu'izz, while Ibn Darrāj thrived during al-Manṣūr b. 'Āmir's reign and "'in the Andalusian land was like al-Mutanabbī in al-Shām.'"[148] This high praise is firmly in line with the rising cultural tide that tended to place Andalusian culture and literature on par with that of the Arab East.

An anxiety of influence, authorship, or sovereignty was so widely felt that treatises and compilations were written to place Andalusian production in a position comparable to that of the Arab East. As discussed in its own time, the matter was not merely intended to display the production of Andalusian luminaries, for anxiety also involves a kind of wrestling with an imposing Arab Eastern culture that fed generations of scholars and readers through thriving cultural assemblies. This entanglement follows several trajectories. Accreditation from renowned Eastern poets or prose writers, for example, was often reported in order to legitimize a name or mode. This also required solutions to local issues. Before celebrating Andalusian writers, Abū Muḥammad 'Alī b. Aḥmad b. Sa'īd b. Ḥazm (d. 456/1064) has first to settle a problem in his milieu, which he criticizes for a latent inability to celebrate local and national talents. In *Risālah fī faḍl al-Andalus* (An Epistle on the Virtue of al-Andalus), Ibn Ḥazm presents a discursive account that conveys an anxiety of influence that strives to make a case for an Andalusian cultural wealth, while drawing a comparison every now and then not only with Arab Eastern poets and writers but also with geographical locations and centers. The *Epistle* was presumably written in response to the Qayrawānī scribe Ibn al-Rabīb (d. 430/1039).[149] The latter addressed a letter to Abū al-Mughīrah 'Abd al-Wahhāb b. Ḥazm, the cousin of 'Alī b. Aḥmad b. Sa'īd b. Ḥazm, bemoaning Andalusians' failure to recognize their own talented writers, poets, and scientists. The letter also blames the Córdoba poet and writer Ibn 'Abd Rabbihi because "he overlooks the merits of his land and the magnanimity of rulers." Ibn al-Rabīb adds that the book later suffered neglect because of this lack. Ibn Ḥazm uses Ibn al-Rabīb's letter as the incentive for the composition of his *Epistle* in order to express his displeasure that Andalusians cannot recognize talent in their land. "They disparage a [scholar's] productivity, vilify its merits, and hunt for errors and mishaps, especially during one's lifetime. If he excels in production, they'll label him as being *sāriqun mughīr wa-muntaḥilun mudda'in* [a plagiarist, plunderer, and preposterous confiscator]."[150] Ibn Ḥazm's

[148] Ibid., 164–67. The inside quote is from al-Tha'ālibī, *Yatīmat al-dahr*.
[149] Full name: Abū 'Alī al-Ḥasan b. Muḥammad, known as Ibn al-Rabīb.
[150] al-Maqqarī, *Nafḥ al-ṭīb*, 3:166–67 (ch. 7). For a detailed account of this issue, see Mateusz Wilk, "In Praise of al-Andalus: Andalusi Identity in Ibn Ḥazm and al-Shaqundī's

Epistle derives its value from taking this presumed vilification of talent as a stepping stone to demonstrate the existence of writers and poets who are on par with their Eastern counterparts. This comparison initiates other responses and rejoinders with more elaboration on talented Andalusians who deserve a recognition like the one accorded to their peers in the Arab Eastern flank.[151] This anxiety sounds magnified and even ironic in view of a list of comparisons with names from the Eastern flank, as it implies a thorough knowledge of these names in a shared script with readers and listeners. By the same token, this awareness entails an assimilation of material from that script. Although Ibn Ḥazm cites Andalusian commentaries and theological works – especially Abū ʿAbd al-Raḥmān Baqī b. Mukhalid's commentary on the Qurʾān, which he deems preferable to the ones by al-Ṭabarī and others,[152] for example – he still thinks of Iraq as "the destination for migrating minds and the anchor of knowledge and its upholders."[153] Even so, he collects a long list of grammarians and philologists whom he thinks are no less than the disciples of Muḥammad b. Yazīd al-Mubarrad. He is more fervent, however, when it comes to the literary field, as he demonstrates pride in referring to poets of his time:

> Even if we have no other stallion than Aḥmad b. Muḥammad b. Darrāj al-Qasṭlī, he is no less important than Bashshār, Ḥabīb [Abū Tammām], and al-Mutanabbī. But what if we have, along with him, Jaʿfar b. ʿUthmān al-Ḥājib, Aḥmad b. ʿAbd al-Malik b. Marwān, Aghlab b. Shuʿayb, Muḥammad b. Shukhayṣ, Aḥmad b. Faraj, ʿAbd al-Malik b. Saʿīd al-Murādī, as each one of them is awe-inspiring and an untamed stallion.[154]

This epistle, with its early criticism of a certain vindictive discourse against talented Andalusians and its subsequent enumeration of talented littérateurs, philologists, compilers of poetic anthologies, speculative theologians, historians, scientists, and philosophers, sets a conversational domain that shows an enormous anxiety of extensive proportions. We have not many sources to lead us to the degrading comments to which he alludes; but his mention of *saraq*, *ighārah*, *intiḥāl*, and *iddiʿāʾ* (preposterous claim) is informative enough to show his awareness of the mounting *sariqāt* lexicon. The anxiety rests on the restlessness felt by many but explained by Ibn Bassām in his prefatory justification of his project: "The people [littérateurs] of this land could not but follow those of the East."[155] Such anxieties helped to generate a struggle aimed at proving independency and excellence. Iḥsān ʿAbbās, the

Treatises," *Imago Temporis, Medium Aevum* 4 (2010): 141–73. The letters are published in full in al-Maqqarī, *Nafḥ al-ṭīb*, 3:156–224.

151 See Ibn Saʿīd's marginalia in al-Maqqarī, *Nafḥ al-ṭīb*, 3:179–86; Abū al-Walīd Ismāʿīl b. Muḥammad al-Shaqundī's (d. 629/1232) epistle in ibid., 186–222.

152 al-Maqqarī, *Nafḥ al-ṭīb*, 3:168. 153 Ibid., 177. 154 Ibid., 178.

155 Ibn Bassām, *al-Dhakhīrah*, 1:1.

late insightful critic and literary historian, thinks differently, because, as noticed earlier, "its [Andalusian poetry] growth depends in every age on the new gushes in its nerves that keep flowing from the East."[156] The issue is no longer a case of indictment, for, as long as *nuqqād* (critics) and literary theorists, or *ahl al-adab* (litterateurs), have already spoken of a reprehensible or commendable *saraq*, the matter is taken out of the ethical and moral domain and placed in an aesthetic territory that invites critical opinion. Critics' involvement rests on evaluative criteria whereby the struggle for excellence functions not only in an economic transaction of debt and credit but also as an urgent desire to surpass, or be equal to, the forerunner.

The Other Side of Spatial Poetics

In all cases, the anxiety that generates such wide discussion can be readdressed in terms of desire as a complex of attraction and resistance and of dependency and freedom. Very much in need of merited cultural admiration, the Andalusian littérateur accepts the grounding in Eastern culture as a given, one that invites further internal growth and enhancement as brought about by the land, its people, and events. In this struggle the reward consists of the emergence of a lively and rich culture that combines the power of legacy with the offerings of al-Andalus. As much as Andalusian memory infuses the poetry of Lorca with rejuvenation and its lyricism and concretization of color, it also nourishes Maḥmūd Darwīsh with a comparable frame of land, nature, and identification. Thus, he says, "Land, like language, is inherited."[157] The land and its people and culture sustain a memory and draw thereby an underlying history that is, paradoxically, feeding the Eastern flank. The massive poetic and novelistic engagements with Andalusia signify a major marker of modern Arabic tradition.

Darwīsh's recollection of Andalusia is worth considering as a formative intertext, a point that rarely fades in his poetry. "Nothing can take away from you the Andalusia of old times," he writes in "Tamārīn ūlā ʿalā qīthārah Isbāniyyah" (Preliminary Practices on a Spanish Guitar).[158] The overwhelming desire for Andalusia concretizes itself in a spatial poetics that connects the two regions of Palestine and Andalusia not as a matter of loss and dejection at the site of a deserted encampment but instead as

[156] ʿAbbās, *Tārīkh al-naqd al-adabī* (2006), 482.

[157] Mahmoud Darwish, "The Tragedy of Narcissus, the Comedy of Silver," in *The Adam of Two Edens*, ed. Munir Akash and Daniel Moore (Syracuse, NY: Syracuse University Press, 2000), 174, quoted in al-Musawi, *Arabic Poetry*, 1. Also translated by Fady Joudah as "The Tragedy of Narcissus: The Comedy of Silver," *Words Without Borders*, October 1, 2009, https://tinyurl.com/3bxvn6v8.

[158] There is a slightly different translation in Jeff Sacks's edition of *Why Did You Leave the Horse Alone?*

poetry that redraws both to persist as a presence despite heavy odds. Andalusia functions as a motif, a catalyst, and a poetics of poignancy. Thus, this recollection is always associated with music, with the *muwashshaḥ*, and the Nahāwand *maqām*, with its low-key musical note.[159] In his *dīwān* titled *Limādhā tarakta al-ḥiṣān waḥīdan* (1995; in English: *Why Did You Leave the Horse Alone?*), Darwīsh writes: "Only the Nahāwand musical notes / will ever take from you the Andalus of time / and the Samarqand of yesterday."[160] Darwīsh's Andalusian world is one of poetry where the *muwashshaḥ*, the guitar, and Lorca come together to redraw Granada as a land of bliss. This intertext eludes the search for raids or echoes; there is instead a dense poetics that generates another showing Palestine to be a deeply rooted presence of music, color, poetry, life, and a land of plenty, a field of oranges, olives, figs, and ritual.

No wonder that the late Palestinian poet Nazīh Khayr (d. 2008), who is no less poetically enmeshed in a wide intertext of quotes, engages with some of Darwīsh's poems in order to offer another variation on *muwashshaḥ* and Nahāwand.[161] In their poetry, the *muwashshaḥ* that Ibn Sanāʾ al-Mulk celebrates as uniquely Andalusian recurs for a reason. They might have the author of "The House of Brocade" in mind, as he argues: "With them the West [Andalusia] has become the East, for they arose on the West's horizon and shone forth from there."[162] More important, he takes these *muwashshaḥāt* as the yardstick to measure people's intellect and exuberance: "Nothing indicates more clearly that someone's intellect is praiseworthy, their understanding noble, their character superior, and their mind superb than knowledge of *muwashshaḥāt*."[163] Hence, their musicality and lyricism permeate Palestinian poetry, but especially that of Darwīsh and Nazīh Khayr. It is not only the recurrence of the term that signifies a permeation; rather, what natters here is the lyrical mode and its attending sense of trampling over an encroaching occupation. Hence, an intertext exists that eludes a simple search for echoes in a poetry that soars high in pain or rupture. This is how the two Andalusian guitars exchange a *muwashshaḥah*, and this is how the *muwashshaḥ* has a Monday and the Nahāwand mode a Sunday in his poem "Ayyām al-ḥubb al-sabʿah" (The Seven Days of Love).[164] Instead of the ramifications of a historical or theological

[159] See "Maqam Nahawand," Maqam World, www.maqamworld.com/en/maqam/naha wand.php.

[160] See Darwish, *Why Did You Leave the Horse Alone?*, 160–61.

[161] Hatem Jawiya, "A Study of the Collection *I Inherited from You Maqām al-Nahāwand* by the Late Great Poet Nazih Khair" [in Arabic], Bukja, February 16, 2022, www.bukja.net/ar chives/1046494.

[162] See Reynolds, "House of Brocade," 174–75. [163] Ibid., 175.

[164] Darwish, "Ayyām al-ḥubb al-sabʿah," in *Why Did You Leave the Horse Alone?*, 164–71.

genesis, there is a scale of musicality that aligns love, rapture, and subtle romantic agony.

Throughout Darwīsh's *Aḥada ʿashara kawkaban* (1992; in English: *Eleven Planets*) and *Why Did You Leave the Horse Alone?* the conflation with Andalusian space and culture functions in an exuberant, but subtle interrogative, poetic enunciation as both intertextual inroads and a series of reflections on loss of land under a fiercely enforced settlers' occupation.[165] Probably like Lorca, but with a dense poetic acquaintance with the lands and cultures of Andalusia and Palestine, Darwīsh gives the whole discussion of textual infringements a massive turn whereby the rustle of language matters. More than any of his former collections, both *Eleven Planets* and *Why Did You Leave the Horse Alone?* vibrate and surge with Andalusian Palestinian semiotics, landscape features, and music. One cannot distinguish between Granada and occupied Palestinian cities or villages like his Birwa:

> How can I write my people's testament above the clouds when they
> abandon time as they do their coats at home, my people
> who raze each fortress they build and pitch on its ruins
> a tent, nostalgic for the beginning of palm trees? My people betray my
>   people
> in wars over salt. But Granada is made of gold,
> of silken words woven with almonds, of silver tears
> in the string of a lute. Granada is a law unto herself:
> it befits her to be whatever she wants to be: nostalgia for
> anything long past or which will pass. A swallow's wing brushes
> a woman's breast, and she screams: "Granada is my body."
> In the meadow someone loses a gazelle, and he screams, "Granada,
>   my country."
> And I come from there . . .[166]

The migration of words between his language and Lorca's is even more pronounced, as his poetic mission as chanter is akin to Lorca's:

> I will shed my skin and my language.
> Some of my words of love will fall into
> Lorca's poems: he'll live in my bedroom
> and see what I have seen of the Bedouin moon.[167]

One may argue against including Darwīsh in a chapter on the waning mention of *saraq*. Many other modern Arab poets are no less engaged with

[165] Maḥmūd Darwīsh, *Aḥada ʿashara kawkaban* (Beirut: Dār al-Jadīd, 1992).
[166] Mahmoud Darwish, *Eleven Stars over Andalusia*, trans. Mona Anis, Nigel Ryan, Aga Shahid Ali, and Ahmad Dallal, in "Oblivion," special issue, *Grand Street*, no. 48 (1994): 102.
[167] Ibid., 103.

Lorca,[168] but the voices of Lorca and Darwīsh merge in unison, and hence the reader can find in Darwīsh's poetry a newly emerging poetics, a subtle conflation that defies for good the traditional terminology of *saraq*. It is the rustle of language that assumes density and music in this exchange of locations, features, icons, tones, reverberations.[169] We are no longer discussing the trading in accusations, for what is pronounced is a fusion in poetics, expressions, feelings, and ambiance. It is not surprising, then, that the interface between the Nahāwand *maqām* and the *muwashshaḥ* is a navigation between Arab East and Eest, a conflation whereby Palestine stands out as the nexus and catalyst.

To understand Darwīsh's unique application of Andalusia, which eludes specific comparativist reading, and thus confuses those fishing for echoes, borrowings, and thefts or infringements,[170] let us look at what I defined once as his poetics of collision and restlessness, resignation and trepidation, juxtaposition and symmetry, anger, and harmony. There is (1) a "rhetorical poetics of shock and resistance, (2) a dialogical poetics of multiple layering and voicing to account for the complexity of the ongoing loss, (3) a poetics of transcendence that valorizes the word in a cultural context, and (4) a poetics of absence to speak of exile and the human condition."[171] His thorough acquaintance with Andalusia, and specifically with Granada and the deception and loss that elicited Abū ʿAbdallāh's "last sigh of the moor," occurs only in his post-Oslo poetic rejoinders.[172] Otherwise it is through Lorca and Granada's landscape that his Andalusian lyrics problematize identity, names, flags, language, *muwashshaḥ*, songs, residential keys, and gestures of resistance or surrender. To see his poetics in the context of accusations of textual infringements, we need to remember that he anchors his poetics not only in Mesopotamian lore, which often covers the whole region east of the Mediterranean, as in the *Epic of Gilgamesh*, but also in current settler colonization, as shown in his volume *Why Did You Leave the Horse Alone?* Hence

[168] See, for example, Rasheed El-Enany, "Poets and Rebels: Reflections of Lorca in Modern Arabic Poetry," in "Ethnicity in World Politics," special issue, *Third World Quarterly* 11, no. 4 (1989): 252–64; al-Musawi, *Arabic Poetry*, 144–46.

[169] "The rustle of language" is a translation of a phrase used by Roland Barthes in one of his essays. The phrase became the title of a collection of his articles. See *The Rustle of Language*, trans. Richard Howard (Berkeley: University of California Press, 1989), 76–81.

[170] See, for example, Sāmī Mahdī's article that responds to those who accuse the poet of theft, confusing thereby intertextuality and fusion with *saraq*: "Darwish's Accusers Ignore His Use of Quotations: Mahmoud Darwish's Poetry between Plagiarism and Intertextuality" [in Arabic], alrakoba.net, December 3, 2012, https://tinyurl.com/4s45ydax. See also "Mahmoud Darwish's Poetry between Plagiarism and Intertextuality" [in Arabic], *al-Quds al-Arabi*, December 3, 2012, https://tinyurl.com/mw582m93.

[171] al-Musawi, *Arabic Poetry*, 24–25.

[172] See Samuel England, "After Nostalgia: Revisiting Palestine's Poetics of al-Andalus," *Journal of Arabic Literature* 55, no. 1 (2024): 2–25.

the recurrence of such motifs or dominants as Anat, the Sumerian symbol of motherliness, along with the carefree guitar player, the custodian of gypsy lore. Lorca shows often in association with this lore, but also as "a public intellectual."[173] Apart from the collapse of senses for which Lorca is known in poetic depictions, there is the chanter, especially in his gypsy lyrics.

This chanter appears in Darwīsh's poetry as a poetic vocation, one in which poetry identifies with music, as in Lorca's. Darwīsh explains: "Lorca used to test both the appeal to the taste and the poem itself in recitation. He was searching for the direct connection between sound and heart, for poetry is not a visual art. There must be an ear, a rhythm."[174] Recitation and performative poetics entail a living experience whereby Arab culture, and along with it the poetry of modern Spain, becomes his negotiatory textual space, which needs to be free from the occupation and its multiple facets of siege. In the performative act of recitation, the poet needs the audience as much as the latter needs the poet, because the stakes are high and the systematic obliteration of topographical sites, signs, names, and people requires a counter action, including asserting the role of culture. The legacy of the past, which draws the poet and permeates an invigorated poetics, impels interrogating analogies, including the issue of loss. Should poetics sustain a textual presence of what is physically lost? "Was Andalusia here or there? On earth, / or only in poems?"[175] In these moments of resignation, Darwīsh leans on an Andalusian legacy:

> I've got nothing left but my ancient armor
> And my saddle worked in gold.
> I've got nothing left but a manuscript by Averroes,
> The Necklace of the Dove, various works in translation.[176]

It is not difficult to see that the poet has in mind al-Mutanabbī's poem that addresses Abū Shujā' Fātik, whereby he places himself on equal footing with the emir in terms of gift exchange:

> لا خَيلَ عِندَكَ تُهديها وَلا مالُ فَليُسعِدِ النُطقُ إِن لَم تُسعِدِ الحالُ

> You have no steeds to offer, neither do you have money
> Let utterance help if status doesn't.[177]

173 al-Musawi, *Arabic Poetry*, 27.
174 Ibid., 146. See Maḥmūd Darwīsh, *'Ābirūn fī kalām 'ābir* (Beirut: Dār al-'Awdah), 173–74, 175.
175 Darwīsh, *'Ābirūn fī kalām 'ābir*, 162; Darwish, "Eleven Planets in the Last Andalusian Sky: One Day I'll Sit on the Sidewalk," in *Adam of Two Edens*, 150. These received wide circulation; see "Eleven Stars over Andalusia," *Grand Street*, www.grandstreet.com/gsissues/gs48/gs48c.html.
176 Darwish, "Eleven Planets in the Last Andalusian Sky," 158.
177 Quoted in al-Musawi, *Arabic Poetry*, 134. The reference is to Abū al-Baqā' al-'Ukbarī's edition of al-Mutanabbī's *Dīwān* (Beirut: Dār al-Ma'rifah, n.d.), 3:276.

As I have argued in *Arabic Poetry: Trajectories of Modernity and Tradition*, Darwīsh's connection with Andalusia sums up an acculturated poetic career where classical tradition, Andalusia, and the poetry of Badr Shākir al-Sayyāb become a textual space, larger than Genette's hypotext, one that Darwīsh can draw on whenever elated or distressed. In his poem "Eleven Planets in the Last Andalusian Sky," included in his 1992 collection *Aḥada ʿashara kawkaban* (Eleven Planets), Andalusia is not a mere memory; it is a culture that is alive and invigorating. What applies to Andalusian poets and littérateurs who could not easily disentangle their poetry from a memorized legacy is applicable here to the poet who cannot escape the Andalusian presence. His grounding in classical and Andalusian poetic traditions enables him to navigate easily among tropes, poetic themes, images, and the cadence and exuberance of the *muwashshaḥāt*. Hence, Andalusia survives in his poetry as an inbuilt formation that cannot be dislodged, especially in times of discord.[178] All in all, Andalusia is poetry and poetics: "Only the notes of the Nahāwand will take away from you the Andalusia of old times,"[179] he says in his "Preliminary Practice on a Spanish Guitar."

One can argue the case of intertextual space along the lines set by Arab classists, namely, that Arabic discursivity is an entangled web, and hence only specific and visible transgressions or violations are worth mentioning. The Andalusians were aware of that, as their learning and production demonstrate. Hence, their legacy is an invitation to intertextualize in order to invigorate poetics and escape limits. Although a substantial part of that Andalusian light and glory was lost after the disintegration and defeat of the "petty" states and the onslaught of the northern powers, Andalusia appears in several modern accentuations and contexts. While Jurjī Zaydān (d. 1914) locates characters in historical narratives that rely on Andalusian and Moroccan historians, Raḍwā ʿĀshūr (d. 2014), for example, takes a different direction decades later (1994–95) that is more in line with a postcolonial inquiry that departs from Homi Bhabha's ambivalence, but is more informed by current perspectives on power politics.[180] Despite military prowess, the conquerors appear as bigots with no understanding of the sciences achieved and developed in Andalusia. Thus, books of chemistry, philosophy, and medicine were held suspect, and tons of library holdings were set on fire, along with their authors and custodians, who were charged with

[178] Darwish, *Adam of Two Edens*, 249.
[179] Mahmoud Darwish, "Preliminary Practice on a Spanish Guitar," in *Why Did You Leave the Horse Alone?*, 158–63.
[180] Raḍwā ʿĀshūr, *Thulāthiyyat Gharnāṭah*, 5th ed. (Cairo: Dār al-Shurūq, 2005); vol. 1 trans. William Granara, *Granada* (Syracuse, NY: Syracuse University Press, 2003).

sorcery by the Inquisition. The witch hunt was enormous and devastating. By then, and throughout the years following the fall of Granada (January 2, 1492), a brutal Inquisition was initiated. The cultural loss is certainly much more daunting than the political and geographical. Poets have this in mind, and what is recalled blends with past and present legacies that occupy modern and postmodern poetries where *talfīq* (patching) is no longer a violation or a textual transgression. As argued earlier, patching in the hands of the expert can generate exuberant poetry, as Ibn Rashīq argues with respect to al-Mutanabbī and al-Maʿarrī. In her powerful trilogy *Granada*, Raḍwā ʿĀshūr recalls a past not as a matter of loss, but rather as a matter of stimulation and incitement with which the cultural scene has to engage and converse, and which it must also recapitulate.[181] Does this trilogy recall or even hint at Palestine? Even if there is a shade of reminiscence in the Egyptian intellectual and scholar's narrative, it is not its purpose to go in that direction – even though her husband, the Palestinian poet Murīd al-Barghūthī (d. 2021), suffered estrangement and deportation, which he poetically revived in his unique autobiography after being allowed to visit his homeland and take a glance at the changing landscape under occupation. His *I Saw Ramallah* (1997; English translation: 2000, introduced by Edward Said) complements ʿĀshūr's trilogy, and both present two directions and realities, one of loss, and another of enforced Western settlement, which strives through mechanisms of misinformation and a war machine to abolish Palestinianism. Ironically, a new public awareness explodes a bluffing discursivity. Like the *Granada* trilogy, a wave of poetry and song leans on an Andalusian legacy to build up an intertextual space of broad Arab identitarian politics, but specifically a Palestinian one that consolidates its essence through more than one rapport. Every now and then there is an elegiac mode, a lamentation of betrayal or negligence. On balance, however, there is in this intertextual space a formative dynamic that borrows from Andalusia, more than the Sufism of Ibn ʿArabī, as in Muḥammad Ḥasan ʿAlwān's narrative of the Sufi master's autobiographical itinerary in *Mawt ṣaghīr* (2016; in English: *Small Death*)[182] or in al-Shūshtarī's (d. 668/1269) *zajal* on the dismissal of worldliness.[183] Do

[181] For a detailed study of al-Andalus across narratives, see Christina Civantos, *The Afterlife of al-Andalus: Muslim Iberia in Contemporary Arab and Hispanic Narratives* (New York: State University of New York Press, 2017).

[182] Muḥammad Ḥasan ʿAlwān, *Mawt ṣaghīr* (London: Dār al-Sāqī, 2016); in English: Mohammed Hasan Alwan, *Ibn Arabi's Small Death*, trans. William M. Hutchins (Austin: Center for Middle Eastern Studies, University of Texas at Austin, 2021).

[183] See England, "After Nostalgia."

these recapitulations complement the waning interest in *saraq* in Andalusia? They do assert a navigation between East and West that explodes the heated discussions of poetic limits and boundaries. An intertextual space appears larger than geographies and presents textual and cultural fusion and exchange as a matter of fact, proved and sublimated in poetry.

Conclusion

A Sense of Unending

A topic of such enormous presence in the literary and cultural lives of societies could not be concluded. As long as humanity and speech survive, possibilities of dialogic, multilingual, conversational, and borrowing sites remain a fact of the human condition. Survival entails repetition. This is not opening the gate to textual and documented thefts that take over not only meanings and expressions, which have been the focus of some Arab classicists between the sixth and eighteenth centuries, but also segments and portions of another's intellectual property. While the early focus of those classicists on meanings and expressions was dismissed by many philologists and critics during those august periods of dialogue, visible self-arrogation of works or pieces and portions of them still provokes condemnation. Even artificial intelligence tries to evade en bloc thefts. On the other hand, intertextual space, the weaving of speech and writing from the available material that feeds memory and research, is another issue that Arab classicists and current scholarship recognize as a fact of survival. But this is not the direction of this unending. Nor is it the emphasis on the significance of the topic for the humanities.

While we address lingual and textual continuities, we are as yet unconversant with the terminological arsenal that has grown over centuries. In his specific concern with the Romantics' struggle with their strong predecessors in the realm of poetry, Harold Bloom finds a few (Latinized) Greek terms to accommodate the range of these poets' responses to strong ancestors and their consequential anxieties: *tessera*, or supplementation; *clinamen*, or departure from the strong father; *kenosis*, simple denial of an influence; *daemonization* of the ancestor – attributing their power to something outside of them; and *askesis*, the dismissal of a trace to prove originality, which is just the opposite of paying homage, *apophrades*. These terms are rarely used thereafter. Similarly, the large Arabic terminological corpus is often left behind; and only *saraq*, or *ighārah* or *saṭw* (robbery), recur, as shown in early twentieth-century controversies. The availability of the small amount of information in a rarely researched issue keeps scholars away from the more demanding effort of accommodating the classical to the modern urge to develop a workable parlance in an increasingly demanding space, one where jargon, lies, marauding artificial intelligence, and pervasive permeation in all aspects of life pose a challenge. In 1995, into a study presented to the Thirteenth Jarash Festival symposium on the late Iraqi poet ʿAbd al-Wahhāb al-Bayātī's (d. 1999) use of myth, allusion, and image, a substantial number of classical *saraq* idiomacy finds its way.[1] The combined application of classical and modern terms seems to have worked out smoothly, especially when the application draws on popular and somehow appealing quotes from the studied case or poet. On the other hand, artificial intelligence feeds on what is available in cyberspace, including specific virtual feeds, and hence an increasing application of the terminological arsenal will soon find its way to this space.

This is only one case, among many others, that invites further exploration. There is first the intertextual space that is a common ground between ancients and moderns. Shared in theory, it is a battleground where contemporaries, French and others, speak of the text as a woven mosaic that is in conversation with other texts in which memory, readings, and robbery occur. If some post-classicists used to dismiss lenient phrasing of infringements as one way of escaping the use of harsh terms, modern theorists like Roland Barthes and Julia Kristeva think of intertextuality as the right term to accommodate an ongoing discursivity. We know that the tenth-century al-Qāḍī al-Jurjānī warns against a too specific targeting of meanings and wording in poetic production. As he points out, such a trend amounts to a suggestion that all discourse is theft. Nevertheless, intertextuality and transtextuality are terms that anticipate media permeation of speech and writing. The matter might get out of control – a point that worries academic institutions, propelling them to flag *integrity* as a counter premise with respect to "teaching in the age of artificial intelligence (ChatGPT, et al.)," a point that is stressed in universities' guidelines. In this context, discursive space requires a level of vigilance that the term "intertextuality" might not necessarily accommodate. What are the limits of intertextuality? How is it possible to track down the permissible and reprehensible? Does the metafictional, or metapoetics, entail self-plagiarism? Have Barthes and Kristeva, among others, had in mind the inevitability of dependence on a tradition – Latin in their case – in terms of terminology, ideas, wording, and almost the whole discursive space? While there is this current awareness of probable

[1] Muḥsin Jāssim al-Mūsawī, " Taqallubāt al-usṭūrah wa-l-talmīḥ," in *al-Muʾaththirāt al-ajnabiyyah fī al-shiʿr al-ʿArabī al-muʿāṣir*, ed. Fakhrī Ṣāliḥ (Amman: al-Muʾassasah al-ʿArabiyyah li-l-Dirāsāt, 1995), 105–42.

infringements on intellectual property, scholarship can no longer relegate this impending violation and its cultural history to the margin.

Like Barthes, Kristeva, Riffaterre, and Genette, we are handed what has been circulating in scholarship, a place where readers become complicit in a cultural rupture, an uncertain position, and where all involved are caught in between a tradition of rich contributions – albeit with limitations – and an emerging one that turns its back on it, and instead relies almost totally on the seemingly significant breakthroughs. As usual with emergent trends, limits are tenuous, and theories are easy to articulate as long as they are free from what Goethe once termed the outworn garb of the European Middle Ages. A carefree presentation is on the market. The same critique applies to scholars of Arabic or Islamic studies. They circulate what is available in the current marketplace of idiomacy. In other words, theory, including the cultural and literary, must reckon with the complications of *saraq*, or theft, and unfair textual practice that only acknowledgment can rectify.[2] If we agree that the discussion of this *saraq* – that is, intertextuality nowadays – is central to theoretical thinking, or should be so, the next step is to introduce it at the center of our discussions and speculation since the European institutionalization of literature.[3] The Arabic tradition has a different timeline, as manuals on *adab* began to appear early on in the ninth century.

The other side is even more serious: complicity! I take two texts that alert us to the ramifications of this complicity. Texts have to converse with other texts, plainly or discreetly, but they can also refer to a blindness that is worse than any glaring theft or confiscation. It is the blindness to the grafted text of erasure, the celebration of European settlements built on Palestinian sites, that allows corporate media journalists and reporters to take for granted the apparent tourist site, callously vaulting over the erosion of lands and people that should have become at least the palimpsest for this irresponsible journalism. This is not an intrusive remark on the issue of borrowing and intertextuality, and theft. This concluding note chooses only two examples to show the interchangeability between texts and contexts, poetry and physical erosion of landmarks, people, and urban and rural spaces as devised by the tycoons of settler colonialism. There is first "The Birwah Prelude" by the late Palestinian poet Maḥmūd

[2] This piece, however, is not a reflection on Frank Kermode's famous book in narrative theory, *The Sense of an Ending: Studies in the Theory of Fiction* (Oxford: Oxford University Press, 1967).

[3] On this point, see Jeffrey J. Williams, *The Institution of Literature* (New York: State University of New York Press, 2002); Jon Mee, ed., *Institutions of Literature, 1700–1900* (Cambridge: Cambridge University Press, 2022). On the turn to literariness, see Appendix A.

Darwīsh. It is not another "halt" at a deserted campsite;[4] it is a re-creation of the town of Birwah, his birthplace, that was invaded and occupied, like many other villages, some of which were erased to the ground. The "Prelude" functions as a double bind. The graphic and geographic recall of his own village finds its pre-occupation status textualized against the Western journalist whose account is a tourist's description of what is established by the corporate capital as a tourist site, memory free, callous, and inhuman. Not even a hypotext, for the journalist Birwah is what is made by corporate capital and European settlers. "Ṭalaliyyat al-Birwah," or "The Birwah Prelude,"[5] recalls the nostalgic prelude of the pre-Islamic odes, which laments a departure of the beloved's tribe. It certainly engages with Imru' al-Qays's iconic prelude to expose the brutality of settler colonialism, its travestied mythos to deceive desperate seekers, its mechanisms of deception and brutality, and its vast investment in corporate capital war machines. As I have argued in *Arabic Disclosures: The Postcolonial Autobiographical Atlas*, "the poet shows how the media is camouflaged by the colonizer."[6] Furthermore, a "history is kept apart by two incommensurable poles: a compromised, uncritical journalist who is wholly interested in highways and construction plans run by global capital, and a native who is totally negated, along with land and property."[7]

Its irony plays on Genette's hypo- and hypertext, for Birwah is not a palimpsest, not in the poem, as it regains its native presence to be juxtaposed with the journalist's lifeless account, as being no more than yet another commercial advertisement. The poem only leans on the pre-Islamic ode in an ironic twist so as to re-create the birthplace against actual erasure and occupation.

Dependence on the pre-Islamic ode might present a hypotext, but the graphic resurrection of life and space annuls the circulated "fact on the ground." Conversely, irresponsible journalism is a site of shame, because it is complicit in settler colonialism, which Darwīsh's later collections, especially *Why Have You Left the Horse Alone?*, address.[8] Instead of uncovering the brutal and devastating invasion, facilitated by bankers and colonialists, reprehensible journalism tends to erase even the palimpsest, the fading site under the heavy-handedness of the war machine. Darwīsh's "Birwah Prelude" is an ideal locus for the exploration of the theft of texts, lands, and memory. In this single ode, which Darwīsh wrote a few years before his lamentable death, he brings the basal

[4] For a translation and reading, see al-Musawi, *Arabic Literature for the Classroom*.

[5] The ode is in Maḥmūd Darwīsh's last *dīwān, Lā 'urīd li-hādhī al-qaṣīdah an tantahī* (Beirut: Mu'assasat Darwīsh al-Ahliyyah, 2013).

[6] al-Musawi, *Arabic Disclosures*, 19. [7] Ibid. [8] See nn. 157–60 in Chapter 6.

nostalgic prelude from the pre-Islamic ode to the present occupation and colonization of Palestine. While he borrows nostalgic reminiscences from ancient poetics, the prelude in his poem problematizes the deportation and murder of thousands of Palestinians as carried out by an aggressive inhuman war machine, fed and led by vicious corporate cartels. It also interrogates the hypo/hyper binary and involves readers in a combined intertext, pretext, and space. It outgrows indebtedness to the tradition of *ṭalal*, the ruins of the fading campsite, to reerect it differently as the reality that defies sham journalism and its functionaries. Liberated from the terminology of tangled theft, the prelude directs attention to the larger and bloody theft of lands, their topoi and iconic markers, and the instigated murder of thousands so as to leave script and land receptive to invaders. Birwah is alive in Darwīsh's poem, because it builds on an ode tradition in order to debunk the attending nostalgia and eroticism, and reinstate the village that he knows, alive in a poetics grafted on to the tourist site that in the poem is now a palimpsest.

The second example is from an Algerian narrative. Kateb Yacin's *Nedjma* (1956) predates the formal independence of Algeria (1962). It takes the French occupation, its enclaves at the expense of Algerian population, destruction of mosques and learning sites, as an undertext, a subtext, or a palimpsest. Occupation constitutes the trace that every page struggles to erase in order to figure out a future text, one that cannot be totally free of the contamination of contact with the invader that implicates urban populations in hybridity. Nedjma herself is a hybrid product of an Algerian father and French mother. No matter how forceful it is, and how liberating, the text itself is indebted to the French new novel, "Nouveau Roman," a movement in which Yacin also participated, during its development and circulation as a mode of writing. As a novel, *Nedjma* survives and builds on several palimpsests: songs, canticles, gossip, autobiographic sketches, recollections of life amid the growing population of French settlers (*pieds noirs*), and the ultimate treatment of Algerians as foreigners in their own land and culture. These are no mere retrievals of local rituals and practices; they are empowering dynamics invoked against the competing colonialist effort to erase their presence. Settler colonialism, the French settlements, treated Algerians as outsiders unless they accepted a role of total subordination, a willing erasure of identity. Thus, while the novel *Nedjma* lives on subgenres and local tradition, these palimpsests gain power when aligned with the mounting struggle for liberation. Drawn as a fierce battle over language and land, both hypotext and hypertext wrestle for ascendance. The novel admits hybridity as a given, and the hypotext and hypertext are often blurred as in the character of Nedjma, but the momentum of songs, conversations, and action signals a triumphal march.

Whether addressed in poetry and poetics – classical, postclassical, or modern – the issue of contamination is applicable to texts, contexts, scripts, lands, and people. What was once a discursive discussion, an issue of gifts and rewards, a rife struggle for distinction, gets more traction in a postcapitalist era when texts are no longer an exercise in verbosity, but a nexus for exposure. Dependence on native lore and canticles, local landscape, and biographical or autobiographic signatures helps in the retention of a homeland against systematic erosion. No longer a passing discussion of a marginal issue, the study of intertexts and the traces of interchangeabilities in discursive scripts emerges as being more demanding. In a deft narrative reclamation of native rituals, topoi, and cultural signatures, *Nedjma* allows the mounting alignment between poetry, songs, and canticles to confront the imposed French annexation of Algeria. In this narrative, they force occupation to give way to what its authority – for over 130 years – has turned into a mere fading trace, a palimpsest. Like any settler colonialism, the French occupation tried for many years to generate a myth of an Algerian geographic belonging to France, a myth that started with Napoleon's invasion of Egypt (1798), as articulated in the introduction to the *Description of Egypt*. The emerging text, now the novel *Nedjma*, is grafted on to a history of bloody occupation.

These two texts, from two sites in the struggle for freedom, present a complexity where basal and grafted texts fight for control, complicating thereby the whole discussion of borrowing and contamination. They alert us to the fact that intertextuality or borrowing, grafting, and thievery are no mere textual exercises. They invite everyone to place the economies of intertextuality and borrowing at the nexus of politics.

Appendix A: *Adab*

Etymology

Adab (root: *a-d-b*) is aptly defined by Abū al-Naṣr Ismāʿīl b. Ḥammād al-Jawharī (d. 393/1002) in his *Ṣiḥāḥ* as "*adab al-nafs wa-l-dars*" (self-refinement and erudition). He cites for "dars," *darastu al-kitāb darsan* (i.e., I studied the book meticulously). The emphasis is laid on a two-dimensional process: social-moral-ethical; and learning. He differentiates this from **adb**, wonder; but *adaba* means to host; and *ādib*: host; hence *maʾdabah* or *maʾdubah*: banquet, or meaty repast. He also differentiates this from ***daʾb***, taken earlier to mean ancestral custom, as noticed by Nallino. This can be a summation of what has already been in circulation when the use of the term *adab* entails erudition, good manners, and etiquette. The association with banquet or feast goes back to an ongoing Arab custom, and hence Ibn Qutaybah (d. 276/889) compares his book *ʿUyūn al-akhbār* (Quintessential Reports) in its variety, purpose, and social life and learning to a feast.

Use and Evolution of the Term

It should not be surprising that the term ***adab*** has been drawing so much attention. While some scholars are driven by a desire to settle for some ultimate conclusions, others are drawn to it as a crucial signifier of a shift from one epistemology of the universal and particular to one of compartmentalization and social science. In its early use in pre- and early Islamic times, ***adab*** was an inclusive term, with a vast semantic range. In multiple practices, emphasis is laid on language as quintessential to ***adab***, for, as Ibn Yazīd al-Mubarrad (d. 285/898) argues in his *al-Fāḍil*, "it serves to embellish man's writing, and sweetens speech." The late thirteenth and early fourteenth century also witnessed more emphasis on the literariness of the term. Muḥammad b. Aydamur (or Aydamir, as he had it; d. 710/1342), who made good use of earlier authorities in his *al-Durr al-farīd wa-bayt al-qaṣīd* (The Unique Pearls and the Outstanding Verse), devotes a long section to *adab* where he lays emphasis on language and grammar, before elaborating on the role of litterateurs, especially the *nuqqād* (critics) as the most qualified in deciding the value of poetic and literary production. The application is broad enough to accommodate a late, but no less inclusive, use by Ibn Ḥajar al-ʿAsqalānī (d. 852/1449), who defines ***adab*** as "resorting to laudability in word and action." Elaborating on Nallino's significant historical exploration of the term since pre-Islamic times, Bonebakker adds, explains, and also grapples with the term. The attempt to come to grips with the rich itinerary and its multiple recurrences in verse and prose over long periods should not be expected to dwindle. The best that all ancient and modern poets, writers, and scholars can suggest is to speak of it as equivalent to knowledge, or to what scholars like Bonebakker and George Makdisi rephrase as the humanistic tradition. This could easily find a place in a book like Abū ʿAbdallāh Muḥammad b. Aḥmad b. Yūsuf al-Khwārizmī's (d. 387/997) *Mafātīḥ al-ʿulūm* (The Keys of Sciences) or, before him, Muḥammad b. Yazīd al-Mubarrad's *al-Kāmil*, Ibn Qutaybah's *ʿUyūn al-akhbār*, al-Jāḥiẓ's (d. 255/869) *Bayān*, and much later al-Māwardī's (d. 450/1058) *Adab al-dunyā wa-l-dīn* (*Adab* of Worldliness and Religion). In this connection the use of the term in manuals for or epistles to professional secretaries is quite fitting, such as ʿAbd al-Ḥamīd al-Kātib's (d. 132/750?) epistle, Ibn Qutaybah's *Adab al-kātib*, and or even in anthologies like Abū Isḥāq Ibrāhīm b. Muḥammad al-Bayhaqī's (third/ninth century to early fourth/tenth century) *al-Ādāb*. Variations in concept or focus on one group or concern are also available, as in Kushajim's (d. 350/961) *Adab al-nadīm* (The *Adab* of the Boon-Companion), or *Adab al-ḥisbah*, or as chapters in Ibn ʿAbd Rabbihi's (d. 328/940) *al-ʿIqd al-farīd* (The Unique Necklace), which has as titles *adab al-akl* (table manners) or *adab al-nikāḥ* (proprieties of matrimony). In the effort to differentiate between ***ʿilm*** and ***adab***, Ibn Qutaybah refers to a quotable saying that assigns to the *ʿālim* specialization in a branch of knowledge, while to the *adīb* a variety or miscellany of knowledge. Indeed, his analogy of *ʿUyūn al-akhbār* as banquet is meant as such. Al-Jāḥiẓ provides the example for the *adīb*. Abū Bakr b. Shaybah (d. 235/849) includes a miscellany of learning in his *Muṣannaf* under the heading of ***ʿilm al-adab***. The tendency toward harboring a miscellany is already to be found in al-Mubarrad's *al-Kāmil* as a composite book "of various *ādāb*: prose, good verse, famous proverbs, eloquent homilies, and a selection of celebrated speeches and stylish letters." In his *ʿUyūn al-akhbār* (Quintessential Reports) Ibn Qutaybah states that he undertook "to compose a book on knowledge and the straightening of tongue and hand for secretaries deficient in *taʾaddub*." In a word, a tendency to compose works on miscellaneous branches of knowledge is the most defining aspect of ***adab***. It is inclusive of what prominent nineteenth-century figures see as a three-dimensional understanding. Under the term ***adab*** are anecdotal and anthological compendiums that were obviously in demand to meet the rising needs of a growing urban society. Yāqūt has the experts in *adab*, that is, *adībs*, in his compendium *Irshād al-arīb ilā maʿrifat al-adīb* (Guidance of the Intelligent to Learned Men). There is also a moral dimension that rarely departs from an Islamic ethic; and there is emphasis on learning and erudition, including poetry, literary or mainly good prose, alongside philological explorations taken to be basic to understand the Qurʾān and Ḥadīth.

There were instances when ***adab*** was used to refer to literary knowledge. Bashshār b. Burd (d. 168/784) used it in reference to his poetic achievements; while Abū Tammām (d. 231/ 845) was reported to have derided the Egyptian poet Yūsuf al-Sarrāj, known for his new lexical explorations, suggesting that a saddlemaker cannot be an ***adīb***. Al-Buḥturī (d. 284/897) argues that an *adīb* should make his erudition known to people. In another instance, we have the Andalusian ʿAbbās b. Nāṣiḥ (d. 238/852) who made a trip to benefit from Abū Nuwās's ***adab***. This is an important nexus, for ***adab*** inclusive of learning and eloquence had already provoked the fears of jurists and religious circles who found the *adībs* popular with the court and prominent dignitaries. According to Muḥammad b. Yūsuf al-ʿĀmirī (d. 381/992), they accused "littérateurs of either seeking praise for eloquence and clarity, or people who are after knowledge as veneer, a means to attain success and rank through the appeal to the mighty and noble." Ibn Sanāʾ al-Mulk (d. 608/ 1212) stresses the association between finesse and literary/poetic sense in his *Dār al-ṭirāz*: "As for he who is ignorant of them [*muwashshaḥāt*] after hearing them, his ignorance is witness to the fact that he has a rigid character, an inflexible personality, coarse manners, an immature disposition, is unrefined of thought, of brutish designs, is someone who has not yet awakened to the presence of literature/politesse [*adab*], and can lay no claim whatsoever to graciousness"(Dwight Reynolds's trans., 175). Many books also have *adab* in their titles, and we have, as an example from Andalusia, Abū Ḥafṣ b. Burd al-Aṣghar's (d. 418/1039) *Sirr al-adab wa-sabk al-dhahab* (The Golden Mold of the Core of Belles Lettres).

As for the ill-fated, that is, the "men of letters," those overtaken by a compelling literary disposition (*adrakathum ḥirfat al-adab*), who suffered (the misfortune of letters or wordcraft), the term ***adab*** was recurrent in the classical period. From Andalusia, Ibn Baqī (d. 545/1150) decries this misfortune, and writes, "Lines of poetry shall weep out ... for an Arab lost among foreigners." He was not alone, as the phrase is often found in biographies and anthologies.

In an interesting gloss, Janusz Danecki noticed a lack in the integrated study of both lexicology and ***adab***; which is true in comparison with the interest in ***adab*** and Islamic ethics, and ***adab*** in the humanities. It is often suggested that there is a disparity, if not a disconnect, between Ḥadīth and ***adab***. This underlines an ongoing subscription to a European enlightenment discourse: in Islamic cultures, the Prophet resumes a visible presence throughout the medieval (i.e., postclassical) period, as the *badīʿiyyāt* testify. Although urban concerns were as conspicuous in the classical period, there was always an emphasis on language and poetry as necessary for the study of the Qurʾān and Ḥadīth. ***Adab*** as learning and poetics implies a greater focus on its immediate concerns, and this is to be resumed under Arab modernity, as can be noticed in al-Ṭahṭāwī's writings or in Buṭrus al-Bustānī's "Khuṭbah fī adab al-ʿArab." Openness to new things and epistemologies entails no binary polarities. Its use in Ṭāhā Ḥusayn's writings tends to be specifically literary, but not so in the writings of his contemporary Muḥammad Ṣādiq al-Rāfiʿī. The shift to literariness occurs epistemologically. Whether global, or local, philological endeavor and the classification of sciences, coupled with the impending industrial, economic, and concomitant colonial educational policy and the imposition of its curricula, would confine ***adab*** to literariness. In all cases, ***adab*** continues to play out in language as masculine. Long ago, Muḥammad b. Mūsā al-Damīrī (d. 808/1405) summarizes it in *Ḥayāt al-ḥayawān al-kubrā* (Animal Life), stating in the introduction, "*al-Adab dhakar*" (*Adab* is male).

Relevant Articles and Contributions

Allan, Michael. "How *Adab* Became Literary: Formalism, Orientalism and the Institutions of World Literature." *Journal of Arabic Literature* 43, nos. 2–3 (2012): 172–96.

Bonebakker, S. A. "*Adab* and the Concept of *Belles-Lettres*." In *ʿAbbasid Belles-Lettres*, edited by Julia Ashtiany, T. M. Johnstone, J. D. Latham, R. B. Serjeant, and G. Rex Smith, 16–30. Cambridge: Cambridge University Press, 1990.

Bonebakker, S. A. "Early Arabic Literature and the Term *Adab*." *Jerusalem Studies in Arabic and Islam* 5 (1984): 389–421.

Bonebakker, S. A. "Variations on the Theme of *Ḥirfat al-Adab*." *Quaderni di Studi Arabi* 20, no. 21 (2002–3): 17–38.

Danecki, Janusz. "Early Adab and Grammar." In "Gli Arabi nella Storia: Tanti Popoli una Sola Civiltà." Special issue, *Quaderni di Studi Arabi* 5, no. 6 (1987–88): 189–95.

Gelder, Geert Jan van. "Ibn Qutayba." In *Encyclopedia of Arabic Literature*, 2 vols., edited by Julie Scott Meisami and Paul Starkey, 1:361. London: Routledge, 1998.

Gelder, Geert Jan van. *Of Dishes and Discourse: Classical Arabic Literary Representation of Food*. Richmond, Surrey: Curzon, 2000.

Heinrichs, Wolfhart. "The Classification of the Sciences and the Consolidation of Philology in Classical Islam." In *Centres of Learning and Location in Pre-modern Europe and the Near East*, edited by Jan Willem Drijvers and Alasdair A. MacDonald, 119–40. Leiden: Brill, 1995.

Holmberg, Bo. "*Adab* and Arabic Literature." In *Literary History: Towards a Global Perspective*. Vol. 1, *Notions of Literature across Times and Cultures*, edited by Anders Pettersson and Gunilla Lindberg-Wada, 180–205. Berlin: De Gruyter, 2006.

Ibn Aydamir, Muḥammad b. Sayf al-Dīn. *al-Durr al-farīd wa-bayt al-qaṣīd*. Edited by Fuʾād Sazkīn. Frankfurt: Maʿhad Tārīkh al-ʿUlūm al-ʿArabiyyah wa-l-Islāmiyyah fī Iṭār Jāmiʿat Frānkfūrt, 1988.

Kilpatrick, Hilary. "Adab." In *Encyclopedia of Arabic Literature*, 2 vols., edited by Julie Scott Meisami and Paul Starkey, 1:54–56. London: Routledge, 1998.

Mayeur-Jaouen, Catherine, ed. *Adab and Modernity: A Civilizing Process? (Sixteenth–Twenty-First Century)*. Leiden: Brill, 2020.

McLarney, Ellen. "Freedom, Justice, and the Power of *Adab*." *International Journal of Middle East Studies* 48, no. 1 (2016): 25–46.

al-Musawi, Muhsin J. "Abbasid Popular Narrative: The Formation of Readership and Cultural Production." *Journal of Arabic Literature* 38, no. 3 (2007): 261–92.

al-Musawi, Muhsin J. *The Islamic Context of the Thousand and One Nights*. New York: Columbia University Press, 2009.

al-Musawi, Muhsin J. *The Medieval Islamic Republic of Letters: Arabic Knowledge Construction*. Notre Dame, IN: University of Notre Dame Press, 2015.

Sacks, Jeffrey. "Futures of Literature: *Inhitat, Adab, Naqd*." *Diacritics* 37, no. 4 (2007): 32–55.

Salvatore, Armando. "Secularity through a 'Soft Distinction' in the Islamic Ecumene? *Adab* as a Counterpoint to *Shariʿa*." In "Islamicate Secularities in Past and Present." Special issue, *Historical Social Research* 44, no. 3 (2019): 35–51.

Sperl, Stefan. "Man's 'Hollow Core': Ethics and Aesthetics in *Ḥadīth* Literature and Classical Arabic *Adab*." *Bulletin of the School of Oriental and African Studies* 70, no. 3 (2007): 459–86.

Appendix B: The Perfect *Muwashshaḥ*

ضاحكٌ عن جُمانْ   سافرٌ عن بدر   ضَاقَ عنهُ الزمان   وَحواهُ صَدْري

آهْ ممَّا أجِدْ   شفَّني ما أجدُ
قامَ بي وقعَدْ   باطشٌ متئِدُ
كلما قلتُ قدْ   قال لى أين قَدُ

وَانثنى خُوطَ بانْ   ذا مَهزٍّ نَضْرِ   عابَثَتْهُ يَدَان   للصّبَّا والقَطْرِ

ليس لي منك بُدْ   خذ فؤادي عنْ يَدْ
لم تدع لي جَلدْ   غير أني أجهَدْ
مَكرعٌ مِنْ شهَدْ   واشتياقي يَشْهَدْ

ما لِبِنْتِ الدِّنان   وَلِذاكَ الثّغْرِ   أين محيا الزَّمان   من مُحيَّا الجمر

بي هوى مُضْمَرُ   ليتَ جَهدي وَفقُهْ
كلمَّا يَظهَرُ   ففؤادي أفقُهْ
ذلك المنظرُ   لا يُداوى عشْقُه

بأبي كيفَ كانْ   فلكيٌّ دُرِّي   راق حتى أسْتبَان   عُذرُهُ وعُذْري

هل اليكَ سبيلْ   أوْ إلى أنْ أيْأسا
ذبتُ إلا قليلْ   عَبْرةً او نَفَسَا
ما عسى أن   أقول ساءَ ظني بعسى

وانقضى كلُّ شانْ   وأنا استَشْرِي   خالعاً منْ عِنَانْ   جَزَعي أو صَبري

ما عَلى مَنْ يَلو   مْ لو تَنَاَهى عَنّي
هلْ سوَى حبِّ ريمْ   دينُهُ التَجني
أنا فيهِ أهِيمْ   وَهْوَ بي يُغنيّ

قَدْ رأيتكْ عيان   ليس عليك ستدريْ   سَيطول الزمانْ   وستنسى ذكري

Al-Aʿmā al-Tuṭīlī

Laughing out of pearls, A full moon appears, Surpassing Time Though held in my heart.

Alas for my woe! I pine in distress!
I danced to her tune; A gentle assailant.
If I say: "At last," "How d'you know?" says she.

A Swaying willow Green, supple, and fresh Teased by the hands of the breeze and the rain.

I cannot resist you: Take my heart in abasement
Put an end to the patience Which I try to maintain.
You, fresh spring of honey My yearning bears witness

To the daughter of jugs And to that sweet mouth. What's the face of all Time To the flush of that wine?

All my love I conceal, could my efforts end it!
When it starts to arise, Its horizon's my heart.
That beautiful vision Leaves my passion unhealed

O, why, by my father, Did a pearly bright star Shine forth and reveal Her excuse and my plea?

Is there no way to you? Must I always despair?
I wept not a little; Tears flowed and I sighed;
I thought what to say; "Perhaps" makes me sad,

Since all comes to nought. Yet, am I headstrong; I gallop loose reined, Unbridling restraint.

It harms not my blamer That she keeps avoiding,
Yet for the love of a doe Whose habit's accusing
I'm possessed by despair, while she sings this ditty:

"I see that you're pining; I say, what's with you, man; You know Time will pass And you will forget me."[1]

[1] Monroe, *Hispano-Arabic Poetry*, 252 (translation modified); al-Tuṭīlī, *Dīwān*, 253–54.

Bibliography

ʿAbbās, Iḥsān. *Tārīkh al-naqd al-adabī*. Amman: Dār al-Shurūq, 2006.

ʿAbbās, Iḥsān. *Tārīkh al-naqd al-adabī ʿinda al-ʿArab*. Beirut: Dār al-Thaqāfah, 1983.

Abu-Deeb, Kamal. *Al-Jurjānī's Theory of Poetic Imagery*. Warminster: Aris and Phillips, 1979.

Abū Ḥamdah, Muḥammad ʿAlī. *Muḥammad b. Sallām al-Jumaḥī wa-kitāb Ṭabaqāt fuḥūl al-shuʿarāʾ: dirāsah naqdiyyah ibdāʿiyyah*. Amman: Dār al-Bashīr, 1998.

Abū Nuwās. *Dīwān*. Edited by Ewald Wagner. Beirut: Orient Institute Beirut, 2015.

Achaari, Mohammed. *The Arch and the Butterfly*. Doha: Bloomsbury Qatar Foundation Publishing, 2015.

al-Achʿarī, Muḥammad. *al-Qaws wa-l-farāshah: riwāyah*. Beirut: al-Markaz al-Thaqāfī al-ʿArabī, 2013.

Adūnīs, *An Introduction to Arab Poetics*. Translated by Catherine Cobham. Austin: University of Texas Press, 1990.

Adūnīs, ʿAlī Aḥmad Saʿīd. *Muqaddimah li-l-shiʿr al-ʿArabī*. 1971. Reprint. Beirut: Dār al-ʿAwdah, 1983.

Adūnīs, ʿAlī Aḥmad Saʿīd. *al-Thābit wa-l-mutaḥawwil: baḥth fī al-ibdāʿ wa-l-ittibāʿ ʿinda al-ʿArab*. Beirut: Dār al-Sāqī, 2002. First published 1974.

al-ʿAlawī, Ibn Ṭabāṭabā. *ʿIyār al-shiʿr*. Edited by Ṭāhā al-Ḥājirī and Muḥammad Zaghlūl Salām. Cairo: al-Maktabah al-Tijāriyyah, 1956.

al-ʿAlawī, al-Muẓaffar b. al-Faḍl. *Naḍrat al-ighrīḍ fī nuṣrat al-qarīḍ*. Edited by Nuhā ʿĀrif Ḥasan. Damascus: Majmaʿ al-Lughah al-ʿArabiyyah bi-Dimashq, 1976.

Alem, Raja. *The Dove's Necklace: A Novel*. Translated by Katharine Halls and Adam Talib. London: Overlook Press, 2016.

ʿĀlim, Rajāʾ. *Ṭawq al-ḥamām*. Casablanca: al-Markaz al-Thaqāfī al-ʿArabī, 2010.

Allan, Michael. "How Adab Became Literary: Formalism Orientalism and the Institutions of World Literature." *Journal of Arabic Literature* 43, nos. 2–3 (2012): 172–96.

Allen, Roger. *The Arabic Literary Heritage: The Development of Its Genres and Criticism*. Cambridge: Cambridge University Press, 1998.

Allen, Roger. *The Arabic Novel: An Historical and Critical Introduction*. Syracuse, NY: Syracuse University Press, 1995.

Allen, Roger. "The End of the Nahḍah?" In *Arabic Literature in a Posthuman World*, edited by Stephan Guth and Teresa Pepe, 3–12. Wiesbaden: Harrassowitz Verlag, 2019.

Allen, Roger. "Fiction and Publics: The Emergence of the 'Arabic Best-Seller.'" In "The State of the Art in the Middle East." Special issue, *Middle East Journal* (2009): 8–12.

Alwan, Mohammed Hasan. *Ibn Arabi's Small Death.* Translated by William M. Hutchins. Austin: Center for Middle Eastern Studies, University of Texas at Austin, 2021.

ʿAlwān, Muḥammad Ḥasan. *Mawt ṣaghīr.* London: Dār al-Sāqī, 2016.

al-Āmidī, Abū al-Qāsim al-Ḥasan b. Bishr. *al-Muwāzanah.* Edited by Aḥmad Ṣaqr. Cairo: Dār al-Maʿārif, 1961.

al-Āmidī, Abū al-Qāsim al-Ḥasan b. Bishr. *al-Muwāzanah bayna shiʿr Abī Tammām wa-l-Buḥturī.* 2 vols. Edited by Ahmad Ṣaqr. Cairo: Dār al-Maʿārif, 1972.

al-Āmidī, Abū al-Qāsim al-Ḥasan b. Bishr. *Tabyīn ghalaṭ Qudāmah b. Jaʿfar fī naqd al-shiʿr.* N.p., n.d.

al-ʿAmīdī, Abū Saʿd Muḥammad. *al-Ibānah ʿan sariqāt al-Mutanabbī lafẓan w-maʿnā.* Edited by Ibrāhīm al-Disūqī al-Bisāṭī. Cairo: Dār al-Maʿārif, 1961.

Arazi, A. "Waḍḍāḥ al-Yaman." In *Encyclopedia of Islam.* Edited by P. Bearman, Th. Bianquis, C. E. Bosworth, E. van Donzel, and W. P. Heinrichs. 2nd ed. Leiden: Brill, 2012. http://dx.doi.org/10.1163/1573-3912_islam_SIM_7798.

Arberry, A. J., ed. *Poems of al-Mutanabbī.* Cambridge: Cambridge University Press, 1967.

El-Ariss, Tarek. *Leaks Hacks and Scandals: Arab Culture in the Digital Age.* Princeton, NJ: Princeton University Press, 2019.

El-Ariss, Tarek. *Trials of Arab Modernity: Literary Affects and the New Political.* New York: Fordham University Press, 2013.

Armistead, Samuel G., and James T. Monroe. "Beached Whales and Roaring Mice: Additional Remarks on Hispano-Arabic Strophic Poetry." *La Corónica* 13 (1985): 206–42.

al-ʿAskarī, Abū Hilāl. *al-Awāʾil.* Tanta: Dār al-Bashīr, 1987.

al-ʿAskarī, Abū Hilāl. *Dīwān al-maʿānī.* Edited by Aḥmad Salīm Ghānim. Beirut: Dār al-Gharb al-Islāmī, 2003.

al-ʿAskarī, Abū Hilāl. *Kitāb al-ṣināʿatayn: al-kitābah wa-l-shiʿr.* Edited by ʿAlī Muḥammad al-Bajāwī and Muḥammad Abū al-Faḍl Ibrāhīm. Beirut: al-Maktabah al-ʿAṣriyyah, 1998.

al-Aṣmaʿī, ʿAbd al-Malik b. Qurayb. *Fuḥūlat al-shuʿarāʾ.* Beirut: Dār al-Kitāb al-Jadīd, 1980.

ʿAzzām, ʿAbd al-Wahhāb. *Dhikrā Abī al-Ṭayyib baʿd alf ʿām.* Cairo: Dār al-Maʿārif, 1968.

ʿAzzām, Muḥammad. *al-Naṣṣ al-ghāʾib.* Damascus: Writers' Union Publication, 2001.

al-Badīʿī, Yūsuf. *al-Subḥ al-munbī ʿan ḥaythiyyat al-Mutanabbī.* Edited by Muṣṭafā al-Saqqā et al. Cairo: Dār al-Maʿārif, 3rd print, n.d.

al-Baghdādī, Abū Bakr Aḥmad b. ʿAlī al-Khaṭīb. *Tārīkh Baghdād aw madīnat al-salām.* 14 vols. Beirut: Dār al-Kitāb al-ʿArabī, 1966.

Bakhtin, M. M. "Forms of Time and of the Chronotope in the Novel: Notes towards a Historical Poetics." In *The Dialogic Imagination: Four Essays*, trans. Caryl Emerson and Michael Holquist, 84–258. Austin: University of Texas Press, 1994.

Balbaʿ, ʿĪd. *Ukdhūbat al-tanāṣṣ: murājaʿāt uslūbiyyah fī al-sariqāt al-shiʿriyyah.* Tanta: Dār al-Nābighah, 2019.

al-Bāqillānī, Abū Bakr. *Iʿjāz al-Qurʾān.* Edited by Aḥmad Ṣaqr. Cairo: Dār al-Maʿārif, 1954.

al-Barqūqī, ʿAbd al-Raḥmān. *Sharḥ Dīwān al-Mutanabbī.* Qum, 3rd print, 2015.

Barth, John. "Literature of Exhaustion." The Atlantic Monthly, August 1967, 29–35.

Barth, John. "The Literature of Replenishment." *The Atlantic Monthly*, January 1980, 65–71.

Barthes, Roland. *Image – Music – Text.* Translated by Stephen Heath. New York: Hill and Wang, 1977.

Barthes, Roland. *Mythologies.* London: Paladin Grafton Books, 1973.

Barthes, Roland. *The Pleasure of the Text.* New York: Hill and Wang, 1975.

Barthes, Roland. *The Rustle of Language.* Translated by Richard Howard. Berkeley: University of California Press, 1989.

Bauer, Thomas. *Altarabische: Dichtkunst eine Untersuchung ihrer Struktur und Entwicklung am Beispiel der Onagerepisode.* Wiesbaden: Harrassowitz Verlag, 1992.

Bauer, Thomas. "Literarische Anthologien der Mamliikenzeit." In *Die Mamliiken: Studien zu ihrer Geschichte und Kultur*, edited by S. Conermann and A. Pistor-Hatam, 71–122. Hamburg: EB-Verlag, 2003.

al-Bayātī, ʿAbd al-Wahhāb. *Love, Death and Exile.* Translated by Bassam Khalil Frangieh. Washington, DC: Georgetown University Press, 1990.

Bennīs, Muḥammad. *al-Aʿmāl al-shiʿriyyah.* 2 vols. Casablanca: Dār Tūbqāl, 2002.

Berman, Jacob R. *American Arabesque: Arabs Islam and the 19th-Century Imaginary.* New York: New York University Press, 2012.

Bilāl, ʿAbd al-Razzāq. *Jadaliyyat al-taʿāluq al-naṣṣī bayna al-sariqāt al-adabiyyah wa-l-tanāṣṣ: muqārabah iṣṭilāḥiyyah.* Fes: Dār Mā baʿda al-Ḥadāthah, 2009.

Bin Shallāl, ʿIṣām. *Naqd al-naqd wa-tajalliyātihi fī al-turāth al-naqdī wa-l-balāghī.* Algiers: Editions Difaf, 2021.

Bin Sharīfah, Muḥammad. *Abū Tammām wa-Abū al-Ṭayyib fī adab al-Maghāribah.* Beirut: Dār al-Gharb al-Islāmī, 1986.

Bin Tamīm, ʿAlī. *ʿUyūn al-ʿajāʾib fī mā awradahu Abū al-Ṭayyib min ikhtirāʿāt wa-gharāʾib.* Abu Dhabi: Abu Dhabi Arabic Language Center, 2025.

Bitton, Simone, dir. *Mahmoud Darwich. Et la terre comme la langue.* Paris: Point du Jour International, 1997.

Bloom, Harold. *The Anxiety of Influence: A Theory of Poetry.* 2nd ed. Oxford: Oxford University Press, 1997.

Bloom, Harold. "The Internalization of Quest-Romance." In *Romanticism and Consciousness: Essays in Criticism*, edited by Harold Bloom, 3–24. New York: W. W. Norton, 1970.

Bloom, Harold. "A Meditation upon Priority and a Synopsis." In *The Anxiety of Influence: A Theory of Poetry*, 5–92. New York: Oxford University Press, 1973.

Bloom, Harold. *The Western Canon: The Books and School of the Ages*. New York: Riverhead Books, 1995.

Bonebakker, S. A. "*Adab* and the Concept of *Belles-Lettres*." In *ʿAbbasid Belles-Lettres*, edited by Julia Ashtiany, T. M. Johnstone, J. D. Latham, R. B. Serjeant, and G. Rex Smith, 16–30. Cambridge: Cambridge University Press, 1990.

Bonebakker, S. A. "Ancient Arabic Poetry and Plagiarism: A Terminological Labyrinth." *Quaderni di Studi Arabi* 15 (1997): 65–92.

Bonebakker, S. A. "Early Arabic Literature and the Term *Adab*." *Jerusalem Studies in Arabic and Islam* 5 (1984): 405–10.

Bonebakker, S. A. *Hātimī and His Encounter with Mutanabbī: A Biographical Sketch*. Amsterdam: North-Holland Pub. Co., 1984.

Bonebakker, S. A. Materials for the History of Arabic Rhetoric from the *Ḥilyat al-Muḥādara* of Ḥātimī. MSS, 2934 and, 590 of the Qarawiyyin Mosque in Fez. Naples: Napoli Istituto orientale, 1975. Supplement no. 4, vol. 35, fasc. 3.

Bonebakker, S. A. "Poets and Critics in the Third Century A. H." In *Logic in Classical Islamic Culture*, edited by Gustave E. von Grunebaum, 85–112. Wiesbaden: O. Harrassowitz, 1970.

Bonebakker, S. A. "Variations on the Theme of 'Ḥirfat al-Adab.'" *Quaderni di Studi Arabi* 20–21 (2002–3): 17–38.

Bourdieu, Pierre. *Language and Symbolic Power*. Translated by Gino Raymond and Matthew Adamson. 7th ed. Cambridge, MA: Harvard University Press, 2003.

Bourdieu, Pierre. *The Rules of Art: Genesis and Structure of the Literary Field*. Translated by Susan Emanuel. Stanford, CA: Stanford University Press, 1996.

Brugman, J. *An Introduction to the History of Modern Arabic Literature in Egypt*. Leiden: Brill, 1984.

Cachia, Pierre. *The Arch Rhetorician or the Schemer's Skimmer: A Handbook of Late Arabic Badīʿ Drawn from ʿAbd al-Ghanī an-Nābulsī's Nafaḥāt al-Azhār*. Wiesbaden: Harrassowitz, 1998.

Chakraoui, Rym. "Arabic Narrative in American Voices." *Journal of Arabic Literature* 55 (2024): 253–85.

Civantos, Christina. *The Afterlife of al-Andalus: Muslim Iberia in Contemporary Arab and Hispanic Narratives*. New York: State University of New York Press, 2017.

Conte, Gian Biagio. *The Rhetoric of Imitation: Genre and Poetic Memory in Virgil and Other Latin Poets*. Translated by Charles Segal. Ithaca, NY: Cornell University Press, 1986.

Culler, Jonathan. *The Pursuit of Signs: Semiotics, Literature, Deconstruction*. Ithaca, NY: Cornell University Press, 2002.

al-Daghmūmī, Muḥammad. *Naqd al-naqd*. Rabat: College of Arts Publications, 1999.

al-Dahhān, Sāmī, ed. *Kitāb al-tuḥaf wa-l-hadāyā*. Cairo: Dār al-Maʿārif, 1956.

Danecki, Janusz. "Early Adab and Grammar." *Quaderni di Studi Arabi* 5 (1987): 189–95.

Darwish, Mahmoud. *Eleven Stars over Andalusia*. Translated by Mona Anis, Nigel Ryan, Aga Shahid Ali, and Ahmad Dallal, in "Oblivion." Special issue, *Grand Street*, no. 48 (1994): 100–111.

Darwish, Mahmoud. "Khilāf ghayr lughawī maʿa Imruʾ al-Qays." In *Why Did You Leave the Horse Alone?*, translated by Jeffrey Sacks, 181–85. Brooklyn: Archipelago Books, 2006. First published 1995 in Arabic.

Darwish, Mahmoud. *Memory for Forgetfulness: August, Beirut, 1982*. Translated by Ibrahim Muhawi. Berkeley: University of California Press, 1995.

Darwish, Mahmoud. "The Tragedy of Narcissus, the Comedy of Silver." In *The Adam of Two Edens*, edited by Munir Akash and Daniel Moore, 174–88. Syracuse, NY: Syracuse University Press, 2000.

Darwish, Mahmoud. "The Tragedy of Narcissus: The Comedy of Silver." Translated by Fady Joudah. Words Without Borders, October 1, 2009. https://tinyurl.com/3bxvn6v8.

Darwish, Mahmoud. *Why Did You Leave the Horse Alone?* Translated by Jeff Sacks. Brooklyn: Archipelago Books, 2006.

Darwīsh, Maḥmūd. *ʿĀbirūn fī kalām ʿābir*. Beirut: Dār al-ʿAwdah, 1987.

Darwīsh, Maḥmūd. *Aḥada ʿashara kawkaban*. Beirut: Dār al-Jadīd, 1992.

Darwīsh, Maḥmūd. *Lā urīd li-hādhī al-qaṣīdah an tantahī*. Beirut: Muʾassasat Darwīsh al-Ahliyyah, 2013.

Darwīsh, Maḥmūd. *Li-mādhā tarakta al-ḥiṣān wāḥidan*. Beirut: Riad al-Rayyes, 1995.

Darwīsh, Maḥmūd. *al-Rasāʾil*. Haifa: Arabesque Publishing House, 1989.

Darwīsh, Maḥmūd. *Ward aqall*. Beirut: Dār al-ʿAwdah, 1986.

De Quincey, Thomas. "The Palimpsest of the Human Brain." In *Suspiria de Profundis*, pt. 1, in *The Collected Writings of Thomas De Quincey*, edited by David Masson, 14 vols., 13:340. Edinburgh: Adam Charles Black, 1889–90.

Derrida, Jacques. *Given Time: I. Counterfeit Money*. Chicago: University of Chicago Press, 1994.

Derrida, Jacques. *Of Hospitability: Anne Dufourmantelle Invites Jacques Derrida to Respond*. Translated by Rachel Bowlby. Stanford, CA: Stanford University Press, 2000.

DeYoung, Terri. "A New Reading of Badr Shakir al-Sayyab's 'Hymn of the Rain.'" *Journal of Arabic Literature* 24 (1993): 39–61.

Dieterman, Lucian. "The Destroyed Villages of the Nakba: Mahmoud Darwish on Visiting al-Birweh after 1948." Jerusalem Fund, May 18, 2015. https://tinyurl.com/33zt28wa.

Eliot, T. S. "The Burial of the Dead." In *The Waste Land*, 9–16. New York: Boni and Liveright, 1922.

Emerson, Ralph Waldo. "Gift." In *The Logic of the Gift*, edited by Alan D. Schrift, 25–27. London: Routledge, 1997.

England, Samuel. "After Nostalgia: Revisiting Palestine's Poetics of al-Andalus." *Journal of Arabic Literature* 55, no. 1 (2024): 2–25.

Fahd, Badrī Muḥammad. *al-ʿĀmmah bi-Baghdād fī al-qarn al-khāmis al-hijrī*. Baghdad: Maṭbaʿat al-Irshād, 1967.

Fakhreddine, Huda J. *Metapoetics in the Arabic Tradition*. Leiden: Brill, 2015.

al-Fārābī, Abū al-Naṣr. *al-Alfāẓ al-mustaʿmalah fī al-manṭiq*. Beirut: Dār al-Mashriq, 2008.

Ford, Jane, Kim Edwards Keates, and Patricia Pulham, eds. *Economies of Desire at the Victorian Fin de Siècle: Libidinal Lives*. New York: Routledge, 2016.

Foucault, Michel. *Discipline and Punish: The Birth of the Prison*. Translated by Alan Sheridan. New York: Random House, 1991.

Gelder, G. Jan van. "Arabic Poetics and Stylistics according to the Introduction of *al-Durr al-Farīd* by Ibn Aydamur." *Zeitschrift der Deutschen Morgenländischen Gesellschaft* 146 (1996): 381–414.

Gelder, G. Jan van. "Critic and Craftsman: al-Qarṭājannī and the Structure of the Poem." *Journal of Arabic Literature* 10 (1979): 26–48.

Gelder, Geert Jan van. "Ibn Qutayba." In *Encyclopedia of Arabic Literature*, 2 vols., edited by Julie Scott Meisami and Paul Starkey, 1:361. London: Routledge, 1998.

Gelder, Geert Jan van. *Of Dishes and Discourse: Classical Arabic Literary Representations of Food*. Richmond, Surrey: Curzon, 2000.

Gelder, Geert Jan van. "The Poet as a Body-Builder: On a Passage from al-Ḥātimī's *Ḥilyat al-Muḥāḍara*." *Journal of Arabic Literature* 13 (1982): 58–65.

Genette, Gérard. *Palimpsests: Literature in the Second Degree*. Translated by Channa Newman and Claude Doubinsky. Lincoln: University of Nebraska Press, 1997.

Genette, Gerard. *Paratexts: Thresholds of Interpretation*. Translated by Jane E. Lewin. Cambridge: Cambridge University Press, 1997.

Gibb, H. A. R. "Studies in Contemporary Arabic Literature." *Bulletin of the School of Oriental Studies* 7, no. 1 (1933): 1–22.

Gruendler, Beatrice. *The Rise of the Arabic Book*. Cambridge, MA: Harvard University Press, 2020.

Grunebaum, Gustave E. von. "The Concept of Plagiarism in Arabic Literary Theory." *Journal of Near Eastern Studies* 3, no. 4 (1944): 234–53.

Habermas, Jürgen. *The Structural Transformation of the Public Sphere: An Inquiry into a Category of Bourgeois Society*. Translated by Thomas Burger. Cambridge, MA: MIT Press, 1991.

Haddārah, Muḥammad Muṣṭafā. *Ittijāhāt al-shiʿr al-ʿArabī fī al-qarn al-thānī al-hijrī*. Damascus: al-Maktab al-Islāmī, 1981.

Haddārah, Muḥammad Muṣṭafā. *Mushkilāt al-sariqāt fī al-naqd al-ʿArabī: dirāsah taḥlīliyyah muqāranah*. Beirut: al-Maktab al-Islāmī, 1975.

Ḥajām, Basmah b. ʿUthmān. *al-Shiʿr al-jāhilī bayna Ṭāhā Ḥusayn wa-Margoliouth*. Tunis: al-Aṭlasiyyah li-l-Nashr, 2014.

al-Hamadhānī, ʿAbd al-Raḥmān b. ʿĪsā. *Kitāb al-alfāẓ al-kitābiyyah*. Edited by Father Luwīs Shaykhū. Beirut: Maṭbaʿat al-Ābāʾ al-Yasūʿiyyīn, 1911.

Hamori, Andras. *The Compositions of Mutanabbī's Panegyrics to Sayf al-Dawla*. Leiden: Brill, 1992.

al-Ḥamūd, ʿAlī b. Muḥammad. *Athar al-Qurʾān al-karīm fī shiʿr Abī Tammām*. Damascus: Dār al-Fikr, 2018.

Harb, Lara. *Arabic Poetics: Aesthetic Experience in Classical Arabic Literature*. Cambridge: Cambridge University Press, 2020.

al-Ḥātimī, Abū al-Ḥasan ʿAlī. *Ḥilyat al-muḥāḍarah*. Edited by Jaʿfar al-Katānī [or al-Kattānī]. Baghdad: Dār al-Rashīd, 1979.

al-Ḥātimī, Abū al-Ḥasan ʿAlī. *al-Risālah al-Ḥātimiyyah*. Amman: Dār Yāfā, 2024.

al-Ḥātimī, Abū al-Ḥasan ʿAlī. *al-Risālah al-mūḍiḥah*. al-Maktabah al-Shāmilah.

al-Ḥātimī, Abū al-Ḥasan ʿAlī. *al-Risālah al-mūḍiḥah fī dhikr sariqāt Abī al-Ṭayyib al-Mutanabbī wa-ṣāqiṭ shiʿrihi*. Edited by Muḥammad Yūsuf Najm. Beirut: Dār Ṣādir li-l-Ṭibāʿah wa-l-Nashr, 1965.

Heidel, W. A. Review of *Das Plagiat in der griechischen Literatur*, by Edward Stemplinger. *Classical Philology* 8, no. 3 (1913): 251–52.

Heinrichs, Wolfhart. "The Classification of the Sciences and the Consolidation of Philology in Classical Islam." In *Centres of Learning: Learning and Location in Pre-modern Europe and the Near East*, edited by J. W. Drijvers and A. A. MacDonald, 119–39. New York: Brill, 1995.

Heinrichs, Wolfhart. "An Evaluation of 'Sariqa.'" In "Gli Arabi nella Storia: Tanti Popoli una Sola Civiltà." Special issue, *Quaderni di Studi Arabi* 5–6 (1987–88): 357–68.

Heinrichs, Wolfhart. "Literary Theory: The Problem of Its Efficiency." In *Arabic Poetry: Theory & Development*, edited by G. E. von Grunebaum, 16–69. Wiesbaden: Harrassowitz, 1973.

al-Ḥillī, Ṣafī al-Dīn ʿAbd al-ʿAzīz b. Sarāyā. *al-ʿĀṭil al-ḥālī wa-l-murakhkhaṣ al-ghālī*. Edited by Ḥusayn Naṣṣār. Cairo: al-Hayʾah al-Miṣriyyah al-ʿĀmmah li-l-Kitāb, 1981.

Hirschler, Konrad. *Medieval Damascus: Plurality and Diversity in an Arabic Library: The Ashrafiya Library Catalogue*. Edinburgh: Edinburgh University Press, 2016.

Hirschler, Konrad. *The Written Word in the Medieval Arabic Lands*. Edinburgh: Edinburgh University Press, 2012.

Holmberg, Bo. "Adab and Arabic Literature." In *Literary History: Towards a Global Perspective*, edited by Anders Pettersson, Gunilla Lindberg-Wada, Margareta Petersson, and Stefan Helgesson, 180–205. Berlin: de Gruyter, 2006.

Ḥusayn, Muḥammad Kāmil. *al-Ḥayāt al-fikriyyah wa-l-adabiyyah bi-Miṣr*. UK: Hindāwī, 2017.

al-Ḥuṣrī al-Qayrawānī. *Zahr al-ādāb*. Edited by Zakī Mubārak. Beirut: Dār al-Jīl, 1929.

al-Ḥuṣrī al-Qayrawānī. *Zahr al-ādāb*. Edited by ʿAlī Muḥammad al-Bajāwī. Cairo: ʿĪsā al-Bābī al-Ḥalabī, 1953.

Hutcheon, Linda H. "Literary Borrowing ... and Stealing: Plagiarism Sources Influences and Intertexts." *ESC: English Studies in Canada* 12, no. 2 (1986): 229–39.

Ibn ʿAbd Rabbihi. *The Unique Necklace*. Vol. 2. Translated by Issa Boullata. Reading, UK: Garnet Publishing, 2009.

Ibn Abī al-Iṣbaʿ, al-Miṣrī al-ʿAdwānī, Zakī al-Dīn Abū Muḥammad ʿAbd al-ʿAẓīm b. ʿAbd al-Wāḥid b. Ẓāfir b. ʿAbdallāh. *Taḥrīr al-taḥbīr fī ṣināʿat al-shiʿr wa-l-nathr*. Edited by Ḥafnī Muḥammad Sharaf. Cairo: Lajnat Iḥyāʾ al-Turāth, n.d.

Ibn al-Athīr, Ḍiyā' al-Dīn. *al-Jāmi' al-kabīr fī ṣinā'at al-manẓūm min al-kalām wa-l-manthūr*. Edited by Muṣṭafā Jawād and Jamīl Sa'īd. Baghdad: Maṭba'at al-Majma' al-'Irāqī, 1956.

Ibn al-Athīr, Ḍiyā' al-Dīn. *al-Mathal al-sā'ir*. Beirut: Dār al-Kutub al-'Ilmiyyah, 1998.

Ibn al-Athīr, Ḍiyā' al-Dīn. *al-Washī al-marqūm fī ḥall al-manẓūm*. Cairo: Quṣūr al-Thaqāfah, 2004.

Ibn Aydamir [Aydamur], Muḥammad al-Musta'ṣimī. *al-Durr al-farīd wa-bayt al-qaṣīd*. Edited by Kāmil Salmān al-Jabūrī. Beirut: Dār al-Kutub al-'Ilmiyyah, 2015.

Ibn Bassām, Abū al-Ḥasan 'Alī al-Shantarīnī. *al-Dhakhīrah fī maḥāsin ahl al-jazīrah*. Edited by Iḥsān 'Abbās. Beirut: Dār al-Thaqāfah, 1979.

Ibn Bassām, Abū al-Ḥasan 'Alī al-Shantarīnī. *al-Dhakhīrah fī maḥāsin ahl al-jazīra*. Edited by Salim Muṣṭafā al-Badrī. Beirut: Dār al-Kutub al-'Ilmiyyah, 1998.

Ibn al-Iflīlī, Abū al-Qāsim b. Muḥammad Zakariyyā. *Sharḥ shi'r al-Mutanabbī*. Edited by Muṣṭafā 'Ulayyān. Beirut: Mu'assasat al-Risālah, 1992.

Ibn Ja'far, Qudāmah. *Jawāhir al-alfāẓ*. Cairo: Maktabat al-Khānjī, 1932.

Ibn Jinnī, Abū al-Fatḥ 'Uthmān. *al-Fasr: sharḥ Ibn Jinnī al-kabīr 'alā Dīwān al-Mutanabbī*. Edited by Riḍā Rajab. Damascus: Dār al-Yanābī', 2004.

Ibn Jinnī, Abū al-Fatḥ 'Uthmān. *al-Fatḥ al-wahbī 'alā mushkilāt al-Mutanabbī*. Edited by Muḥsin Ghayāḍ. Baghdad: Dār al-Shu'ūn al-Thaqāfiyyah al-'Āmmah Āfāq 'Arabiyyah, 1990.

Ibn Khallikān, Aḥmad b. Muḥammad. *Biographical Dictionary*. London: Oriental Translation Fund of Great Britain and Ireland, 1842.

Ibn Kunāsah, Muḥammad 'Abdallāh. *Sariqāt al-Kumayt min al-Qur'ān wa-ghayrihi*. N.p., n.d.

Ibn al-Marzubān, Muḥammad. *Kitāb al-alfāẓ: al-kitābah wa-l-ta'bīr*. N.p., n.d.

Ibn al-Mu'tazz, 'Abdallāh. *Kitāb al-badī'*. Edited by Ignatius Kratchkovsky. Beirut: Dār al-Masīrah, 1982.

Ibn al-Mu'tazz, 'Abdallāh. "Risālah fī sariqāt Abī Tammām." In *Rasā'il Ibn al-Mu'tazz fī al-naqd wa-l-adab wa-l-ijtimā'*, edited by 'Abd al-Mun'im Khafājī, 19–31. Cairo: Muṣṭafā al-Bābī al-Ḥalabī, 1946.

Ibn al-Muzarra', Muhalhil b. Yamūt. *Sariqāt Abī Nuwās*. Edited by Muḥammad Muṣṭafā Haddārah. Cairo: Dār al-Fikr al-'Arabī, 1957.

Ibn Qutaybah, Abū Muḥammad 'Abdallāh b. Muslim. *al-Shi'r wa-l-shu'arā'*. Edited by Aḥmad Muḥammad Shākir. Cairo: Dār al-Ma'ārif, 1982.

Ibn Qutaybah, Abū Muḥammad 'Abdallāh b. Muslim. *al-Shi'r wa-l-shu'arā'*. Edited by Aḥmad Muḥammad Shākir. Cairo: Dār al-Ḥadīth, 2001.

Ibn Rashīq, Abū 'Alī al-Ḥasan al-Qayrawānī. *Qurāḍat al-dhahab fī naqd ash'ār al-'Arab*. Edited by al-Shādhlī bū Yayā. Tunis: al-Sharikah al-Tūnisiyyah li-l-Tawzī', 1972.

Ibn Rashīq, Abū 'Alī al-Ḥasan al-Qayrawānī. *al-'Umdah*. Edited by Muḥammad Muḥyī al-Dīn 'Abd al-Ḥamīd. Cairo: Maṭba'at al-Sa'ādah, 1955.

Ibn Rashīq, Abū 'Alī al-Ḥasan al-Qayrawānī. *al-'Umdah*. Edited by Muḥammad Muḥyī al-Dīn 'Abd al-Ḥamīd. Beirut: Dār al- Jīl, 4th print, 1972.

Ibn Rashīq, Abū ʿAlī al-Ḥasan al-Qayrawānī. *al-ʿUmdah*. Edited by Muḥammad Muḥyī al-Dīn ʿAbd al-Ḥamīd. Beirut: Dār al-Jīl, 1981.

Ibn Rashīq, Abū ʿAlī al-Ḥasan al-Qayrawānī. *al-ʿUmdah fī maḥāsin al-shiʿr wa-ādābihi wa-naqdihi*. Edited by ʿAbd al-Ḥamīd Hindāwī. Beirut: al-Maktabah al-ʿAṣriyyah, 2001.

Ibn Sallām, Abū ʿAbdallāh Muḥammad al-Jumaḥī. *Ṭabaqāt fuḥūl al-shuʿarāʾ*. 2 vols. Edited by Maḥmūd Muḥammad Shākir. Cairo: Dār al-Maʿārif, 1952.

Ibn Sallām, Abū ʿAbdallāh Muḥammad al-Jumaḥī. *Ṭabaqāt fuḥūl al-shuʿarāʾ*. Vol. 1. Edited by Maḥmūd Muḥammad Shākir. Cairo: Maṭbaʿat al-Madanī, 1974.

Ibn Sallām, Abū ʿAbdallāh Muḥammad al-Jumaḥī. *Ṭabaqāt fuḥūl al-shuʿarāʾ*. Edited by Shaykh Muḥammad Suwayd. Beirut: Dār Iḥyāʾ al-ʿUlūm, 1998.

Ibn Sanāʾ al-Mulk. *Dār al-ṭirāz fī ʿamal al-muwashshaḥāt*. Edited by Jawdat al-Rikābī. Damascus: Dār al-Fikr, 3rd print, 1980.

Ibn Sharaf, Jaʿfar b. Muḥammad b. Saʿīd. *Dīwān al-Khubzaruzzī Naṣr b. Aḥmad al-Baṣrī. Dīwān al-Khubz Arzī* Damascus: al-Āmāl al-Jadīdah, 2019.

Ibn Sharaf, Jaʿfar b. Muḥammad b. Saʿīd. *Rasāʾil al-intiqād*. Edited by Ḥasan Ḥusnī ʿAbd al-Wahhāb. Beirut: Dār al-Kitāb al-Jadīd, 1983.

Ibn al-Sikkīt, Abū Yūsuf Yaʿqūb. *Mukhtaṣar Kitāb al-alfāẓ* ed. Luwīs Cheikho. Beirut: Al-Maṭbaʿah al-Kāthūlīkiyyah, 1897.

Ibn Wakīʿ, al-Ḥasan b. ʿAlī. *Kitāb al-munṣif li-l-sāriq wa-l-masrūq minhu*. Edited by ʿUmar Khalīfah b. Idrīs. Benghazi: Qār Yūnis University Press, 1994.

Infante, Guillermo Cabrera. *Three Trapped Tigers*. Translated by Suzanne Jill Levine and Donald Gardner. New York: Harper and Row, 1971. First published 1967.

ʿĪsā, ʿAbd al-Khāliq. "Intertexuality in Abū Tammām's Poems." *Al-Azhar* 14, no. 2 (2012): 431–46.

al-Iṣfahānī, Abū al-Faraj. *al-Aghānī*. Edited by ʿAbd al-Sattār Farrāj. Beirut: Dār al-Thaqāfah, 1955–61.

al-Iṣfahānī, al-Rāghib. *Muḥāḍarāt al-udabāʾ*. 4 vols. in 2. Beirut: Maktabat al-Ḥayāt, n.d.

al-Jāḥiẓ, Abū ʿUthmān ʿAmr b. Baḥr. *al-Bayān wa-l-tabyīn*. Edited by Ḥasan al-Sandūbī. UK: Hindāwī, 2017.

al-Jāḥiẓ, Abū ʿUthmān ʿAmr b. Baḥr. *Kitāb al-ḥayawān*. Edited by ʿAbd al-Salām Muḥammad Hārūn. Cairo: Maṭbaʿāt Muṣṭafā al-Bābī al-Ḥalabī, 1938–47.

al-Jāḥiẓ, Abū ʿUthmān ʿAmr b. Baḥr. *Kitāb al-ḥayawān*. Beirut: Dār al-Kitāb al-ʿArabī, 1969.

Jawiya, Hatem. "A Study of the Collection *I Inherited from You Maqām al-Nahāwand* by the Late Great Poet Nazih Khair." [In Arabic.] Bukja, February 16, 2022. www.bukja.net/archives/1046494.

Jayyusi, Salma Khadra, ed. *The Legacy of Muslim Spain*. 2 vols. Leiden: Brill, 1992.

Jihād, Kāẓim. *Adūnīs muntaḥilan: dirāsah*. al-Dār al-Bayḍāʾ: Afrīqyā al-Sharq, 1991.

al-Jindī, Aḥmad Anwar. *al-Maʿārik al-adabiyyah*. Cairo: Anjilo-Miṣriyyah, 1982.

al-Jindī, Aḥmad Anwar. *al-Maʿārik al-adabiyyah fī al-shiʿr wa-l-thaqāfah wa-l-lughah wa-l-qawmiyyah al-ʿArabiyyah*. Cairo: Maṭbaʿat al-Risālah, 1961.

Jūdī, Wadād. "Aswāq al-warrāqīn fī Baghdād fī al-ʿaṣr al-ʿAbbāsī." MA thesis, University of Guelma, 2016–17.
al-Jurjānī, ʿAbd al-Qāhir. *Asrār al-balāghah*. Edited by Muḥammad Rashīd Riḍā. Beirut: Dār al-Maʿrifah, 2002.
al-Jurjānī, ʿAbd al-Qāhir. *Dalāʾil al-iʿjāz fī ʿilm al-maʿānī*. Beirut: al-Maktabah al-ʿAṣriyyah, 2002.
al-Jurjānī, Abū al-Ḥasan al-Qāḍī ʿAlī b. ʿAbd al-ʿAzīz. *al-Wasāṭah bayna al-Mutanabbī wa-khuṣūmihi*. Cairo: ʿĪsā al-Bābī al-Ḥalabī, 1900.
al-Jurjānī, Abū al-Ḥasan al-Qāḍī ʿAlī b. ʿAbd al-ʿAzīz. *al-Wasāṭah bayna al-Mutanabbī wa-khuṣūmihi*. Edited by Muḥammad Abū al-Faḍl Ibrāhīm and ʿAlī Bajāwī. Cairo: ʿĪsā al-Bābī al-Ḥalabī, 1966.
al-Jurjānī, Abū al-Ḥasan al-Qāḍī ʿAlī b. ʿAbd al-ʿAzīz. *al-Wasāṭah bayna al-Mutanabbī wa-khuṣūmihi*. Edited by Muḥammad Abū al-Faḍl Ibrāhīm and ʿAlī Bajāwī. Ṣaydā: al-Maktabah al-ʿAṣriyyah, 2006.
al-Kalāʿī, Abū al-Qāsim Muḥammad b. ʿAbd al-Ghafūr. *Iḥkām ṣanʿat al-kalām*. Edited by Muḥammad Raḍwān al-Dāyah. Beirut: Dār al-Thaqāfah, 1966.
Kantorowitz, Ernst H. *The King's Two Bodies: A Study in Medieval Political Theology*. Princeton, NJ: Princeton University Press, 1957.
al-Karwī, Ibrāhīm. *Ṭabaqāt mujtamaʿ Baghdād fī al-ʿaṣr al-ʿAbbāsī al-awwal*. Baghdad: Shabāb al-Jāmiʿah, 1989.
Katānī [or Kattānī], Jaʿfar. *Ḥilyat al-muḥāḍarah fī ṣināʿat al-shiʿr*. Baghdad: Wizārat al-Thaqāfah wa-l-Iʿlām Dār al-Rashīd li-l-Nashr, 1979.
Kermode, Frank. *Forms of Attention*. Chicago: University of Chicago Press, 1985.
Kermode, Frank. *The Sense of an Ending: Studies in the Theory of Fiction*. Oxford: Oxford University Press, 1967.
Khawājah, Ibrāhīm Shihādah. *Shiʿr al-ṣirāʿ al-siyāsī fī al-qarn al-thānī al-hijrī*. Kuwait: Sharikat Kāẓimah li-l-Nashr wa-l-Tarjamah wa-l-Tawzīʿ, 1984.
Khouri, Elias. *Awlād al-ghītū: ismī Ādām*. Beirut: Dār al-Ādāb, 2016.
Khouri, Elias. *Majmaʿ al-asrār*. Beirut: Dār al-Ādāb, 1994.
Khoury, Elias. *Children of the Ghetto: My Name Is Adam*. Translated by Humphrey Davies. Brooklyn: Archipelago Books, 2019.
al-Khwārizmī, Abū Bakr Muḥammad al-Baghdādī. *al-Amthāl al-muwalladah*. Abu Dhabi: al-Mujammaʿ al-Thaqāfī, 2003.
Kilito, Abdelfattah. *Anbiʾūnī bi-l-ruʾyā*. Beirut: Dār al-Ādāb, 2010.
Kilito, Abdelfattah. *The Author and His Doubles: Essays on Classical Arabic Culture*. Translated by Michael Cooperson. Syracuse, NY: Syracuse University Press, 2001.
Kilito, Abdelfattah. *al-Kitābah wa-l-tanāsukh*. Translated from the French by ʿAbd al-Salām Benʿabd al-ʿĀlī. Beirut: al-Tanwīr, 1985.
Kilito, Abdelfattah. *L'Auteur et ses doubles: Essai sur la culture arabe classique*. Paris: Éditions du Seuil, 1985.
Kilpatrick, Hilary. "Adab." In *Encyclopedia of Arabic Literature*, 2 vols., edited by Julie Scott Meisami and Paul Starkey, 1:54–56. London: Routledge, 1998.
Kristeva, Julia. *Sēmeiōtikē*. Paris: Seuil, 1969.
Kzārah, Ṣabāḥ. "Fī al-muʿjamiyyah al-ʿArabiyyah." *Majallat Majmaʿ al-Lughah al-ʿArabiyyah bi-Dimashq* 78, no. 4 (2003): 965–88.

Lacan, J. "Some Reflection on the Ego." *International Journal of Psycho-Analysis* 34 (1953): 11–17.

Ladha, Hassanaly. "Allegories of Ruin: Architecture and Knowledge in Early Arabic Poetry." *Journal of Arabic Literature* 50, no. 2 (2019): 89–122.

Lindey, Alexander. *Plagiarism and Originality*. Westport, CT: Greenwood Press, 1974. First published 1952.

Lyall, Charles James, ed. and trans. *The Mufaḍḍaliyyāt: An Anthology of Ancient Arabian Odes. Compiled by al-Mufaḍḍal, son of Muḥammad, according to the Recension and with the Commentary of Abū Muḥammad al-Anbārī*. Oxford: Clarendon Press, 1918–24.

Lyotard, Jean-François. *The Postmodern Condition: A Report on Knowledge*. Translated by Geoff Bennington and Brian Massumi. Minneapolis: University of Minnesota Press, 1984.

al-Maʿarrī, Abū al-ʿAlāʾ Aḥmad b. ʿAbdallāh. *al-Lāmiʿ al-ʿazīzī sharḥ Dīwān al-Mutanabbī*. Edited by Muḥammad Saʿīd al-Mawlawī. Riyadh: Markaz al-Malik Fayṣal li-l-Buḥūth wa-l-Dirāsāt al-Islāmiyyah, 2008.

Macherey, Pierre. *A Theory of Literary Production*. Translated by Geoffrey Wall. London: Routledge, 1978.

Majālī, Jihād. *Ṭabaqāt al-shuʿarāʾ fī al-naqd al-adabī ʿinda al-ʿArab ḥattā nihāyat al-qarn al-thālith al-hijrī*. Beirut: Dār al-Jīl, 1992.

al-Mālikī, Abū al-Ḥasan Muḥammad b. ʿAlī b. Naṣr. *Kitāb al-mufāwaḍah*. N.p., n.d.

Mallon, Thomas. *Stolen Words: Forays into the Origins and Ravages of Plagiarism*. New York: Ticknor and Fields, 1989.

Mandūr, Muḥammad. *al-Naqd al-manhajī ʿinda al-ʿArab*. Cairo: Nahḍat Miṣr, 1996.

al-Maqqarī, Shaykh Aḥmad b. Muḥammad. *Nafḥ al-ṭīb min ghuṣn al-Andalus al-raṭīb*. Edited by Iḥsān ʿAbbās. Beirut: Dār Ṣādir, 1968.

Margoliouth, D. S. "The Discussion between Abu Bishr Matta and Abu Saʿid al-Sirafi on the Merits of Logic and Grammar." *Journal of the Royal Asiatic Society of Great Britain & Ireland* 4 (1905): 79–129.

Margoliouth, D. S., ed. *Irshād al-arīb ilā maʿrifat al-adīb, or Dictionary of Learned Men of Yaqut*. London: Luzac, 1923–31.

Margoliouth, D. S. "The Origins of Arabic Poetry." *Journal of the Royal Asiatic Society* 57, no. 3 (1925): 417–49.

Marx, Karl. "Theories of Surplus Value." In *Das Capital*, 4 vols., translated by Emile Burns, 1:47–106. Moscow: Progress Publishers, 1975.

al-Marzubānī, Abū ʿAbdallāh b. Muḥammad b. ʿUmrān b. Mūsā. *al-Muwashshaḥ*. Edited by ʿAlī Muḥammad al-Bajāwī. Cairo: Nahḍat Miṣr, 1965.

al-Marzubānī, Abū ʿAbdallāh b. Muḥammad b. ʿUmrān b. Mūsā. *al-Muwashshaḥ*. Edited by Muḥammad Ḥusayn Shams al-Dīn. Beirut: Dār al-Kutub al-ʿIlmiyyah, 1995.

al-Marzubānī, Abū ʿAbdallāh b. Muḥammad b. ʿUmrān b. Mūsā. *al-Muwashshaḥ fī maʾākhidh al-ʿulamāʾ ʿalā al-shuʿarāʾ*. Edited by ʿAlī Muḥammad al-Bajāwī. Cairo: Dār al-Fikr al-ʿArabī, 1965.

al-Marzūqī, ʿAlī Aḥmad b. Muḥammad b. al-Ḥasan. *Sharḥ dīwān al-ḥamāsah*. Beirut: Dār al-Kutub al-ʿIlmiyyah, 2002.

Maʿtūq, Aḥmad Muḥammad. "Al-Sharīf al-Murtaḍā's Contribution to the Theory of Plagiarism in Arabic Poetry." PhD diss., University of Pennsylvania, 1987.

Mauss, Marcel. *The Gift: Forms and Functions of Exchange in Archaic Societies.* Translated by Ian Cunnison. New York: Norton, 1967.

Mauss, Marcel. *The Gift: The Form and Reason for Exchange in Archaic Societies.* Translated by W. D. Halls. London: Routledge, 1990.

McLarney, Ellen. "Freedom Justice and the Power of Adab." *International Journal of Middle East Studies* 48, no. 1 (2016): 25–46.

Mee, Jon, ed. *Institutions of Literature, 1700–1900.* Cambridge: Cambridge University Press, 2022.

Meisami, Julie Scott, and Paul Starkey, eds. *Encyclopedia of Arabic Literature.* 2 vols. London: Routledge, 1998.

Miṣfār, Maḥmūd. *al-Tanāṣṣ bayna al-ruʾyah wa-l-ijrāʾ fī al-naqd al-adabī: muqārabah muḥāyithah li-l-sariqāt al-adabiyyah ʿinda al-ʿArab.* Sfax, 2000.

Monroe, James T. *Hispano-Arabic Poetry: A Student Anthology.* Berkeley: University of California Press, 1974.

Monroe, James T. "*Zajal* and *Muwashshaḥa.*" In *The Legacy of Muslim Spain,* 2 vols., edited by Salma Khadra Jayyusi, 1:398–419. Leiden: Brill, 1992.

Moretti, Franco. *Graphs, Maps, Trees: Abstract Models for Literary History.* London: Verso, 2005.

Muḥammad, Saniyyah Aḥmad. *al-Naqd al-adabī fī al-qarn al-thānī al-hijrī.* Baghdad: Dār al-Risālah li-l-Ṭibāʿah, 1977.

Muhanna, Elias. *The World in a Book: Al-Nuwayri and the Islamic Encyclopedic Tradition.* Princeton, NJ: Princeton University Press, 2017.

al-Musawi, Muhsin J. "Abbasid Popular Narrative: The Formation of Readership and Cultural Production." *Journal of Arabic Literature* 38, no. 3 (2007): 261–92.

al-Musawi, Muhsin J. *Arabic Disclosures: The Postcolonial Autobiographical Atlas.* Notre Dame, IN: University of Notre Dame Press, 2022.

al-Musawi, Muhsin J., ed. *Arabic Literature for the Classroom: Teaching Methods, Theories, Themes and Texts.* London: Routledge, 2017.

al-Musawi, Muhsin J. *Arabic Poetry: Trajectories of Modernity and Tradition.* London: Routledge, 2006.

al-Musawi, Muhsin J. *Arabic Poetry: Trajectories of Modernity and Tradition.* New York: Routledge, 2009.

al-Musawi, Muhsin J. "Dedications as Poetic Intersections." *Journal of Arabic Literature* 31, no. 1 (2000): 1–37.

al-Musawi, Muhsin J. "The Iraqi Spectres of Marx." *Journal of Contemporary Iraq & the Arab World* 14, no. 3 (2020): 169–88.

al-Musawi, Muhsin J. *Islam on the Street.* Lanham, MD: Rowman and Littlefield, 2009.

al-Musawi, Muhsin J. *The Islamic Context of "The Thousand and One Nights."* New York: Columbia University Press, 2009.

al-Musawi, Muhsin J. *The Medieval Islamic Republic of Letters: Arabic Knowledge Construction.* Notre Dame, IN: University of Notre Dame Press, 2015.

al-Musawi, Muhsin J. "The Medieval Turn in Modern Arabic Narrative." In *The Oxford Handbook of Arab Novelistic Traditions*, edited by Wail Hassan, 67–88. Oxford: Oxford University Press, 2017.

al-Musawi, Muhsin J. *The Postcolonial Arabic Novel*. Leiden: Brill, 2003.

al-Musawi, Muhsin J. "Pre-modern Belletristic Prose." In *The Cambridge History of Arabic Literature*. Vol. 6, *Arabic Literature in the Post-classical Period*, edited by Roger Allen and D. S. Richards, 99–133. Cambridge: Cambridge University Press, 2006.

al-Musawi, Muhsin J. "The Prize-Winning Arabic Novel." *The Middle East in London* 15, no. 1 (2018–19): 16–17.

al-Musawi, Muhsin J. "Teaching the Modernist Arabic Poem in Translation." In *Arabic Literature for the Classroom: Teaching Methods, Theories, Themes and Texts*, edited by Muhsin J. al-Musawi, 189–210. London: Routledge, 2017.

al-Musawi, Muhsin J. "Vindicating a Profession or a Personal Career? Al-Qalqashandī's *Maqāmah* in Context." *Review of Mamluk Studies* 7 (2003): 111–35.

al-Mūsawī, Muḥsin Jāssim. "Taqallubāt al-usṭūrah wa-l-talmīḥ." In *al-Muʾaththirāt al-ajnabiyyah fī al-shiʿr al-ʿArabī al-muʿāṣir*, edited by Fakhrī Ṣāliḥ, 105–42. Amman: al-Muʾassasah al-ʿArabiyyah li-l-Dirāsāt, 1995.

al-Mūsawī, Muḥsin J. "al-Tarjīʿāt: naẓariyyat al-tafāʿul fī al-shiʿr al-ʿArabī." *ʿAlāmāt* 6, no. 24 (1997): 45–78.

al-Mutanabbī, Abū al-Ṭayyib Aḥmad b. al-Ḥusayn. *Amthāl Abī al-Ṭayyib al-Mutanabbī: allatī jamaʿahā al-Ṣāḥib b. ʿAbbād li-Fakhr al-Dawlah b. Būyah wa-maʿahā mā dhakarahu al-Thaʿālibī fī Yatīmat al-dahr min maḥāsin amthālihi wa-ḥikamihi wa-mā dhakarahu al-ʿUkbarī min aʿjāz abyātihi allatī dhahabat amthālan*. Edited by Muḥammad Ibrāhīm Salīm. Cairo: Dār al-Ṭalīʿah, 1993.

al-Mutanabbī, Abū al-Ṭayyib Aḥmad b. al-Ḥusayn. *Dīwān Abī al-Ṭayyib*. Edited by Frīdarikh Dītrīṣī. Berolini: Mittler, 1861.

al-Mutanabbī, Abū al-Ṭayyib Aḥmad b. al-Ḥusayn. *Dīwān bi-sharḥ al-Wāḥidī*. Edited by Muṣṭafā Rajab. Dasūq: Dār al-ʿIlm wa-l-Īmān li-l-Nashr wa-l-Tawzīʿ, 2019.

Naaman, Erez. "An Outline of a Plagiarism Controversy from the Abbasid Era: Al-Sarī l-Raffāʾ vs. the Khālidī Brothers." *Journal of Arabic Literature* 54 (2023): 51–72.

al-Nadīm, Abū al-Faraj Muḥammad b. Isḥāq. *The Fihrist: A 10th-Century AD Survey of Islamic Culture*. Edited and translated by Bayard Dodge. New York: Columbia University Press, 1988. First published 1970.

Nagel, Thomas. *The Possibility of Altruism*. Oxford: Oxford University Press, 1970.

al-Naḥwī, Ibn Bassām. *Sariqāt al-Mutanabbī wa-mushkil maʿānīhi*. Edited by Muḥammad al-Ṭāhir b. ʿĀshūr. Tunis: al-Dār al-Tūnisiyyah li-l-Nashr, 1970.

Nājī, Hilāl. *Aḥmad b. Abī Ṭāhir Ṭayfūr: ḥayātuhu, dīwānuhu, rasāʾiluhu*. Damascus: Tawzīʿ Dār al-Hilāl, 2008.

Nantij, Salah. "Le concept d'adab est-il dérivé du mot daʾb? Retour sur une hypothèse ancienne de Vollers et Nallino." *Journal of Arabic Literature* 50 (2019): 342–68.

al-Nawājī, Muḥammad b. Ḥasan. *Kitāb al-ḥujjah fī sariqāt Ibn Ḥijjah*. Undated MS Arab, 285 Houghton Library, Harvard University. http://nrs.harvard.edu/urn-3:FHCL.HOUGH:2600641.

Nicholson, Reynold A. *A Literary History of the Arabs*. Cambridge: Cambridge University Press, 1956. First published 1907 by Charles Scribner's Sons (New York).

al-Nuwayrī, Shihāb al-Dīn. *The Ultimate Ambition in the Arts of Erudition: A Compendium of Knowledge from the Classical Islamic World*. Edited and translated by Elias Muhanna. New York: Penguin, 2016.

Orfali, Bilal. *The Anthologist's Art: Abū Manṣur al-Thaʿālibī and His Yātimat al-dahr*. Leiden: Brill, 2016.

Orfali, Bilal. "A Sketch Map of Arabic Poetry Anthologies." *Journal of Arabic Literature* 43 (2012): 29–59.

Ouyang, Wen-Chin. *Ethical Living through Stories: Encounters with Adab*. London: I.B. Tauris, 2025.

Ouyang, Wen-Chin. *Literary Criticism in Medieval Arabic-Islamic Culture: The Making of a Tradition*. Edinburgh: Edinburgh University Press, 1997.

Őzkan, Hakan. "Donkey or Thief: Defamation or Well-Deserved Criticism? An-Nawāǧī and His Treatise *al-Ḥujjah fī sariqāt Ibn Ḥijjah*." In *The Racecourse of Literature: An-Nawāǧī and His Contemporaries*, edited by Alev Masarwa and Hakan Őzkan, 83–94. Baden-Baden: Ergon Verlag, 2020.

Paniconi, Maria Elena. "Reframing the Politics of Aesthetic Appropriation in the Late-Nahḍah Novel: The Case of 'Plagiarism' in Ibrāhīm al-Māzinī's *Ibrāhīm al-kātib*." *Journal of Arabic Literature* 50, no. 1 (2019): 56–80.

Peter, Hermann. *Wahrheit und Kunst Geschichtschreibung und Plagiat im klassischen Altertum*. Leipzig: B. G. Teubner, 1911.

Pomerantz, Maurice A. *Licit Magic: The Life of al-Ṣāḥib b. ʿAbbād*. Leiden: Brill, 2018.

Qalqīlah, ʿAbduh ʿAbd al-ʿAzīz. *Naqd al-naqd fī al-turāth al-ʿArabī*. Cairo: Maktabat al-Anjlū al-Miṣrīyah, 1975.

al-Qarṭājannī, Ḥāzim. *Minhāj al-bulaghāʾ wa-sirāj al-udabāʾ*. Edited by al-Ḥabīb b. Khujah. Tunis: al-Dār al-Tūnisiyyah, 1966.

al-Qayrawānī, al-Ḥuṣrī. *Zahr al-ādāb*. Edited by ʿAlī Muḥammad al-Bajāwī. Cairo: ʿĪsā al-Bābī al-Ḥalabī, 1953.

Qays, Shams-i. *al-Muʿjam fī maʿāyīr ashʿār al-ʿAjam*. London: Luzac & Co., 1909.

al-Qazwīnī, Ibn Fāris Aḥmad b. Zakariyyā. *Mutakhayyar al-alfāẓ*. Edited by Hilāl Nājī. Baghdad: Maṭbaʿat al-Maʿārif, 1970.

al-Qazwīnī, al-Khaṭīb. *al-Īḍāḥ fī ʿulūm al-balāghah*. 2 vols. Edited by ʿAbd al-Munʿim Khafājī. Beirut: Dār al-Jīl, n.d.

al-Qazwīnī, al-Khaṭīb. *Talkhīṣ al-Miftāḥ*. Karachi: Maktabat al-Bushrā, 2010.

al-Qifṭī, Jamāl al-Dīn. *Inbāʾ al-ruwāt ʿalā anbāʾ al-nuḥāt*. Edited by Muḥammad Abū al-Faḍl Ibrāhīm. Beirut: al-ʿAṣriyyah, 2003.

al-Rāfiʿī, Muḥammad Ṣādiq. *Tārīkh ādāb al-ʿArab*. Cairo: Maṭbaʿat al-Akhbār, 1911.

Reynolds, Dwight F. *Medieval Arab Music and Musicians: Three Translated Texts*. Leiden: Brill, 2022.

Riffaterre, Michael. *Fictional Truth*. Baltimore: Johns Hopkins University Press, 1993.
Riffaterre, Michael. "Intertextual Representation: On Mimesis as Interpretive Discourse." *Critical Inquiry* 11, no. 1 (1984): 141–62.
Saadawi, Ahmed. *Frankenstein in Baghdad: A Novel*. Translated by Jonathan Wright. New York: Penguin, 2018.
al-Sabtī, Abū al-Qāsim Muḥammad al-Sharīf. *Raf' al-ḥujub al-mastūrah*. Edited by Muḥammad al-Ḥajuwī. Rabat: Wizārat al-Awqāf wa-l-Shu'ūn al-Islāmiyyah, 1997.
Sa'danī, Muṣṭafā. *al-Tanāṣṣ al-shi'rī: qirā'ah ukhrā li-qaḍiyyat al-sariqāt*. Alexandria: Tawzī' Munsha'at al-Ma'ārif, 1991.
Sa'dāwī, Aḥmad. *Farānkashtāyn fī Baghdād*. Beirut: Dār al-Jamal, 2014.
al-Ṣafadī, Khalīl b. Aybak. *al-Wāfī bi-l-wafayāt*. Edited by Hilmut Ritter. Wiesbaden: Franz Steiner, 1962.
Sa'īd, Ḥamīd. *Dīwān: ulā'ika aṣḥābī*. Amman: Mirsāl, 2018.
Sa'īd, Jamīl, and Dā'ūd Sallūm, eds. *Nuṣūṣ al-naẓariyyah al-naqdiyyah*. Baghdad: Dār al-Shu'ūn al-Thaqāfiyyah al-'Āmmah, 1986.
al-Sakkākī, Abū Ya'qūb Yūsuf. *Miftāḥ al-'ulūm*. Edited by Na'īm Zurzūr. Beirut: Dār al-Kutub al-'Ilmiyyah, 2nd print, 1987.
Sallūm, Dā'ūd. *al-Sariqāt al-fanniyyah li-l-āthār al-adabiyyah: sariqāt al-Duktūr Muḥammad Nabīl Ṭarīfī anmūdhajan*. Baghdad, 2005.
Salvatore, Armando. "Secularity through a 'Soft Distinction' in the Islamic Ecumene? Adab as a Counterpoint to Shari'a." In "Islamicate Secularities in Past and Present." Special issue, *Historical Social Research* 44, no. 3 (2019): 35–51.
Sanni, Amidu. "Arabic Literary History and Theory in Muslim Spain." *Islamic Studies* 34, no. 1 (1995): 91–102.
Sanni, Amidu. *The Arabic Theory of Prosification and Versification: On Ḥall and Naẓm in Arabic Theoretical Discourse*. Beirut: Franz Steiner, 1998.
Sanni, Amidu. "Filiation: The Arabic Theorist's Prescription for Artistic Excellence." *Quaderni di Studi Arabi* 12 (1994): 3–14.
Sanni, Amidu. "The Historic Encounter between al-Mutanabbī and al-Ḥātimī: Its Contribution to the Discourse on *Ghuluww* (Hyperbole) in Arabic Literary Theory." *Journal of Arabic Literature* 35, no. 2 (2004): 159–74.
Sanni, Amidu. "Al-Marzubānī in the Context of Arabic Literary Theory: An Analytical Study of al-*Muwashshaḥ*." PhD diss., University of London, 1989.
Schrift, Alan D. *The Logic of the Gift*. London: Routledge, 1997.
Sells, Michael A., ed. and trans. *Early Islamic Mysticism: Sufi, Qur'an, Mi'raj, Poetic and Theological Writings*. New York: Paulist Press, 1996.
Shākir, Abū Fihr Maḥmūd Muḥammad. *Barnāmaj Ṭabaqāt fuhūl al-shu'arā'*. N. p., 1980.
Shākir, Abū Fihr Maḥmūd Muḥammad. *Ṭabaqāt fuḥūl al-shu'arā'*. Cairo: Maṭba'at al-Madanī, 1974.
al-Sharīshī, Abū al-'Abbās Aḥmad b. 'Abd al-Mu'min. *Sharḥ Maqāmāt al-Ḥarīrī*. Edited by Muḥammad 'Abd al-Mun'im Khafājī. Cairo: 'Abd al-Ḥamīd Aḥmad Ḥanafī, 1952.

Sharlet, Jocelyn. "Inside and Outside the Pleasure Scene in Poetry about Locations by al-Sarī al-Raffāʾ al-Mawṣilī." *Journal of Arabic Literature* 40, no. 2 (2009): 133–69.

Sharlet, Jocelyn. "The Thought That Counts: Gift Exchange Poetry by Kushājim al-Ṣanawbarī and al-Sarī al-Raffāʾ." *Middle Eastern Literatures* 14, no. 3 (2011): 235–70.

Shukrī, ʿAbd al-Raḥmān. *al-Muqtaṭaf*. January 1917.

Sperl, Stefan. "Man's 'Hollow Core': Ethics and Aesthetics in Ḥadīth Literature and Classical Arabic Adab." *Bulletin of the School of Oriental and African Studies* 70, no. 3 (2007): 459–86.

Stemplinger, Edward. *Das Plagiat in der griechischen Literatur*. Leipzig: B. G. Teubner, 1912.

Stetkevych, Jaroslav. *The Zephyrs of Najd: The Poetics of Nostalgia in the Classical Arabic Nasīb*. Chicago: University of Chicago Press, 1994.

Stetkevych, Suzanne P. *Abū Tammām and the Poetics of the ʿAbbāsid Age*. Leiden: Brill, 1991.

Stetkevych, Suzanne P. "From Jāhiliyya to Badīʿiyyah: Orality Literacy and the Transformations of Rhetoric in Arabic Poetry." *Oral Tradition* 25 (2010): 211–30.

Stetkevych, Suzanne P. "From Text to Talisman: Al-Būṣīrī's 'Qaṣīdat al-Burdah': Mantle Ode and the Supplicatory Ode." *Journal of Arabic Literature* 37, no. 2 (2006): 145–89.

Stetkevych, Suzanne P. *The Mantle Odes: Arabic Praise Poems to the Prophet Muhammad*. Bloomington, IN: Indiana University Press, 2010.

Stetkevych, Suzanne P. *The Poetics of Islamic Legitimacy: Myth Gender and Ceremony in the Classical Arabic Ode*. Bloomington, IN: Indian University Press, 2002.

Stetkevych, Suzanne P. "Toward a Redefinition of *Badīʿ* Poetry." *Journal of Arabic Literature* 12 (1981): 1–29.

al-Ṣūlī, Abū Bakr Muḥammad b. Yaḥyā. *Akhbār Abī Tammām*. Beirut: al-Tijāriyyah, n.d.

al-Ṣūlī, Abū Bakr Muḥammad b. Yaḥyā. *Akhbār Abī Tammām*. Beirut: Dār al-Āfāq al-Jadīdah, 1980.

al-Ṣūlī, Abū Bakr Muḥammad b. Yaḥyā. *The Life and Times of Abū Tammām*. Translated by Beatrice Gruendler. New York: New York University Press, 2018.

al-Ṣūlī, Abū Bakr Muḥammad b. Yaḥyā. "Muqaddimah." In *Dīwān Abī Nuwās bi-ruwāyat al-Ṣūlī*, edited by Bahjat ʿAbd al-Ghafūr al-Ḥadīthī, 31–48. Abu Dhabi: Hayʾat Abū Ẓabī li-l-Thaqāfah, 2010.

al-Ṣūlī, Abū Bakr Muḥammad b. Yaḥyā. *Sharḥ al-Ṣūlī li-Dīwān Abī Tammām*. Edited by Khalaf Rashīd Nuʿmān. Baghdad: Wizārat al-Thaqāfah wa-l-Iʿlām, 1978.

Sulṭān, Munīr. *Ibn Sallām wa-Ṭabaqāt al-shuʿarāʾ*. Alexandria: Manshaʾat al-Maʿārif, 1977.

Ṭabānah, Badawī Aḥmad. *al-Sariqāt al-adabiyyah: dirāsah fī ibtikār al-aʿmāl al-adabiyyah wa-taqlīdihā*. 2nd ed. Cairo: Maktabat al-Anjilū al-Miṣriyyah, 1969.

al-Taftazānī, Sa'd al-Dīn. *Mukhtaṣar al-Sa'd: sharḥ talkhīṣ kitāb Miftāḥ al-'ulūm.* Edited by 'Abd al-Ḥamīd Hindāwī. Ṣaydā: al-Maktabah al-'Aṣriyyah, 2010.

al-Taftazānī, Sa'd al-Dīn. *al-Muṭawwal: sharḥ Talkhīṣ al-miftāḥ.* Beirut: Dār Iḥyā' al-Turāth al-'Arabī, 2004.

Ṭāhā, Hind Ḥusayn. *al-Naẓariyyah al-naqdiyyah 'inda al-'Arab.* Baghdad: Dār al-Rashīd, 1981.

al-Ṭāhir, 'Alī Jawād. *Muḥammad b. Sallām wa-kitābuhu Ṭabaqāt al-shu'arā'.* Amman: Dār al-Fikr li-l-Nashr wa-l-Tawzī', 1995.

al-Ṭā'ī, 'Abd al-Laṭīf Ḥammūdī. *Ḥammād al-Rāwiyah: kabīr ruwāt al-shi'r al-'Arabī al-muftarā 'alayhi.* Damascus: Dār al-Hilāl li-l-Ṭibā'ah wa-l-Nashr wa-l-Tawzī', 2010.

Talib, Adam. *How Do You Say "Epigram" in Arabic? Literary History at the Limits of Comparison.* Leiden: Brill, 2018.

Ṭayfūr, Aḥmad b. Abī Ṭāhir. *Kitâb Baġdâd.* Leipzig: Harrassowitz, 1908.

al-Tha'ālibī, Abū Manṣūr. *al-Kināyah wa-l-ta'rīḍ.* Beirut: Dār Ṣa'b, n.d.

al-Tha'ālibī, Abū Manṣūr. *Kitāb khāṣṣ al-khāṣṣ.* Beirut: Dār al-Ḥayāt, n.d.

al-Tha'ālibī, Abū Manṣūr. *Yatīmat al-dahr.* Edited by Muḥammad Muḥyī al-Dīn 'Abd al-Ḥamīd. Cairo: al-Maktabah al-Tijāriyyah al-Kubrā, 1947.

al-Tha'ālibī, Abū Manṣūr. *Yatīmat al-dahr fī maḥāsin ahl al-'aṣr.* Edited by Mufīd Muḥammad Qumayḥah. Beirut: Dār al-Kutub al-'Ilmiyyah, 1983.

al-Tibrīzī, al-Khaṭīb. *Kanz al-ḥuffāẓ.* N.p., 1895–98.

Toorawa, Shawkat M. *Ibn Abī Ṭāhir Ṭayfūr and Arabic Writerly Culture: A Ninth-Century Bookman in Baghdad.* London: Routledge, 2010.

Trabulsi, Amjad. *La critique poétique des Arabes jusqu'au Ve siècle de l'Hégire.* Damascus: l'Institut Français de Damas, 1956.

Ṭūqān, Fadwā. "Lan Abkl." In *Dīwān Fadwā Ṭūqān,* 511–17. Beirut: Dār al-'Awdah, 2000.

al-Tuṭīlī, al-A'mā. *Dīwān.* Edited by Iḥsān 'Abbās. Beirut: Dār al-Thaqāfah, 1963.

al-'Ubaydī, Rashīd 'Abd al-Raḥmān. *Mushkilāt al-ta'līf al-lughawī fī al-qarn al-thānī al-hijrī.* Baghdad: Maṭba'at Dār al-Jāḥiẓ li-l-Ṭibā'ah wa-l-Nashr, 1980.

al-'Ukbarī, Abū al-Baqā 'Abdallāh b. al-Ḥusayn. *Dīwān Abī al-Ṭayyib al-Mutanabbī bi-sharḥ Abī al-Baqā' al-'Ukbarī al-musammā al-Tibyān fī sharḥ al-dīwān.* Edited by D. Kamāl Ṭālib. Qum, 2015.

al-'Ukbarī, Abū al-Baqā' 'Abdallāh b. al-Ḥusayn. *Dīwān al-Mutanabbī.* Beirut: Dār al-Ma'rifah, n.d.

al-'Ukbarī, Abū al-Baqā' 'Abdallāh b. al-Ḥusayn. *Sharḥ al-Tibyān li-l-'Ukbarī 'alā Dīwān Abī al-Ṭayyib Aḥmad b. al-Ḥusayn al-Mutanabbī.* Cairo: Dār al-Ṭibā'ah, 1870.

Ullmann, Manfred. *Wörterbuch der klassischen arabischen Sprache.* Wiesbaden: Harrassowitz, 1970.

Valery, Paul. *Oeuvres complés.* Vol. 2. Paris: Bibliotheque de la Pléïade, 1960.

van Gennep, Arnold. *The Rites of Passage.* 2nd ed. Chicago: University of Chicago Press, 2019. First published 1960.

von Grunebaum, Gustave. "Arabic Literary Criticism in the 10th Century A. D." *Journal of the American Oriental Society* 61, no. 1 (1941): 51–57.

Warren, James F., trans. *Al-Mutanabbi: The Complete Poems*. Vol. 3. Washington, DC: Cultural Books, 2022.

Wilk, Mateusz. "In Praise of al-Andalus: Andalusi Identity in Ibn Ḥazm and al-Shaqundī's Treatises." *Imago Temporis Medium Aevum* 4 (2010): 141–73.

Williams, Jeffrey J. *The Institution of Literature*. New York: State University of New York Press, 2002.

Witkam, Jan Just. "Ibn al-Akfānī (d. 749/1348) and His Bibliography of the Sciences." *Manuscripts of the Middle East* 2 (1987): 37–41.

Wormhoudt, Arthur, trans. *The Diwan of Abu Tayyib ibn al-Husayn al-Mutanabbi: Translated from the Text of Abu al-Hasan Ali ibn Ahmad al-Wahidi al-Naishaburi (d. 468/1075)*. Oskaloosa, IA: William Penn College, 1971.

Wormhoudt, Arthur, trans. *Poems from the Diwan of Abu Tayyib ibn al-Husain al-Mutanabbi*. Oxford: Shakespeare Head Press, 1968.

Wormhoudt, Arthur, trans. *The Revelations of the Plagiarisms of al-Mutanabbī*. Oskaloosa, IA: William Penn College, 1974.

Yāqūt al-Ḥamawī, Abū ʿAbdallāh al-Rūmī. *Muʿjam al-udabāʾ*. Vol. 8. Cairo: Dār al-Maʾmūn, n.d.

Yāqūt al-Ḥamawī, Abū ʿAbdallāh al-Rūmī. *Muʿjam al-udabāʾ aw Irshād al-arīb ilā maʿrifat al-adīb*. Beirut: Dār al-Kutub al-ʿIlmiyyah, 1991.

Yūsuf, Saʿdī. *al-Aʿmāl al-kāmilah*. Damascus: Dār al-Madā, 1995.

Zakī, Aḥmad Kamāl. *al-Ḥayāt al-adabiyyah fī al-Baṣrah ilā nihāyat al-qarn al-thānī al-hijrī*. Damascus: Dār al-Fikr, 1961.

Zarrūq, al-Ḥusayn. *Nuṣūṣ al-naqd al-adabī fī Ṭabaqāt fuḥūl al-shuʿarāʾ li-Ibn Sallām al-Jumaḥī*. Fes: Kulliyyat al-Ādāb wa-l-ʿUlūm al-Insāniyyah, 2019.

Zarrūq, al-Ḥusayn. *Nuṣūṣ al-naqd al-adabī ladā Ḥammād al-Rāwiyah*. Riyadh: al-Majallah al-ʿArabiyyah, 2015.

Zaydān, Jirjī. *al-Falsafah al-lughawiyyah wa-l-alfāẓ al-ʿArabiyyah*. 1886. Reprint. Cairo: al-Hilāl, 1904.

al-Zubaidi, A. M. K. "The Dīwān School." *Journal of Arabic Literature* 1 (1970): 36–48.

Index

ʿAbbās, Iḥsān, 40, 85, 87, 200, 216, 220, 221, 229
Abbasid court, 85, 159, 163, 172, 175
  anthologies, 77
  influence on literary standards, 122
  poets and patrons, 85
Abbasid cultural influence, 198–99
  Baghdad as a hub, 199
  dissemination of poetic works, 198
  travel and book transmission to Andalusia, 198
Abbasid empire, poetic ownership, 158
Abbasid era
  influence of cultural refinement, 18
  knowledge consortiums, 57
  permissions and intertextual practices, 10
  poetic arbitration, 2
  urban expansion of poetry, 18
Abū Ḥayyān, 56, 114, 224
Abū al-Mughīrah, 203–4
Abū Nuwās, 10, 28, 37, 65, 72–74, 82, 89, 98, 103–8, 111–17, 126, 130, 160, 192, 218
  influence on later poets, 72
  as influence on modern Arabic poetry, 113
  poetic innovations, 103
  relationship to predecessors, 103
Abū Tammām, 2, 7, 18–19, 44–50, 54, 65–66, 69, 71–74, 84–86, 90, 98–103, 107, 111, 113, 119, 122–28, 130, 153, 159–66, 168, 171, 178–79, 184–85, 192–95, 200–8, 216–29
  accusations of plagiarism, 119
  anthology compilation, 44
  al-Buḥturī and, 71, 90, 111, 123, 126, 168, 178, 185, 195
  comparison with al-Buḥturī, 44
  echoes and borrowings, 44
  influence al-Buḥturī, 125
  al-Mutanabbī and, 208, 216
  poetic originality, 119
adab, xix, 36, 41–43, 59, 70, 74–76, 90, 101, 106–10, 119, 240
adaptation
  distinction from theft and influence, 158
  vs. imitation, 18
  influence on literary innovation, 133
  lexical influences, 43
  modern adaptation of classical models, 2
  from Persian, Indic, or Greek, 51
  strategies in prose and poetry, 98
  structural adaptations, 6
  in Sufi poetry, 97
  thematic redirection (*naql*), 202
  theories of, 153
  transformative use of Eastern themes, 200
adīb (literary person)
  definitions of social roles, 107
  status and public recognition, 107
Adūnīs, 51, 102, 112–14
allusion(s)
  classical poetry examples, 105
  concept of coincidence, 65
  as a literary device, 62, 152
  techniques in Arabic poetics, 56
  theoretical discussions, 102
al-Āmidī, Abū al-Qāsim al-Ḥasan b. Bishr, x, xiii, xxi, 23, 44–50, 53–56, 61–70, 85–91, 99, 105, 109, 118–34, 140, 148, 156, 159–74, 181, 189–92, 206, 220
ʿamūd al-shiʿr, xxii, 18, 21, 46–48, 52, 98, 115, 128, 163
al-Andalus, 199, 201–2, 205, 216, 221, 223, 227, 230. *See also* Andalusia
Andalusia, 201, 208, 215, 230–32, 234–35
  legacy of, 234, 236
  literary assemblies and intellectual hubs, 198
  role of *al-Dhakhīrah fī maḥāsin ahl al-Jazīrah*, 202

Andalusians, xxii, 197, 201–2, 208, 219, 223, 228–29, 235
  contemporary, 205
anthologies
  influence on literary theory, 90
  as preservers of poetic legacy, 82
anxiety
  achieved, 22, 30
  of influence, xviii, 73, 141, 228
  poetic, 73, 213
Arabic literary
  history, 73, 76, 84
  production, 5
  tradition, xviii, 1, 11, 14, 75–76
al-Aṣghar, Abū Ḥafṣ b. Burd, 215, 246
al-ʿAskarī, Abū Hilāl, 62, 66–69, 101–5, 132
al-Aṣmaʿī, ʿAbd al-Malik, 28, 53, 61–66, 72, 78, 80, 86, 100–1, 106, 109–10, 119, 136
assemblies, literary
  Abū al-Qāsim ʿAlī b. Ḥamzah al-Baṣrī's, 177, 183
  and Arabic literary criticism, 127, 172
  flourishing in Andalusia, 205
  al-Muhallabī's, 178, 182, 185
  and plagiarism debates, 131
  Sayf al-Dawlah al-Ḥamdānī's, xiv, 175, 182, 185
assignment of verses (*inḥāl*), xviii, 76, 81, 89, 99–100, 109, 129, 136
  distinction from other forms of plagiarism, 130
authorities
  knowledgeable, 78, 80, 165
  poetic, 182, 210
authorship, ethics of
  evolving views, 127
  relationship to plagiarism accusations, 130

badīʿ, xxii, 18, 21, 45, 62, 83–84, 126–27, 144, 148–49, 152, 155, 162, 163–64, 168, 192, 195, 198, 203, 204
  as defined by Ibn al-Muʿtazz, 126
  as a literary device, 62
  movement, 163
  a new poetic meaning, 169
  praise and critique by jurists, 89
  rare, 221
  relation to originality and plagiarism, 148
  the science of inventiveness, 154
  tradition, 148, 164
al-Badīʿī, Yūsuf, 128, 169–72
Baghdad, 28, 79, 107, 153, 177, 183, 194, 201, 225
  as cultural epicenter, 158
Barthes, Roland, theory of intertextuality, 239
battle, literary, 12, 110
al-Bayātī, ʿAbd al-Wahhāb, xxi, 22, 66, 70, 74, 115, 120, 195, 239
belles lettres, 89, 148, 176–77, 189, 215–16
Bloom, Harold, xviii, 8, 22, 33, 57, 59, 69, 74–76, 140, 238
  poetic anxiety and canonization, 22
  six terms in influence theory, 60
  theory of misreading, 59
books
  Adab al-dunyā wa-l-dīn, 245
  Adab al-kātib. *See* Ibn Qutaybah
  al-Alfāẓ al-kitābiyyah, 23, 53, 62, 83, 104, 200
  al-Amthāl, 121
  al-ʿĀṭil al-ḥālī wa-l-murakhkhaṣ al-ghālī, 211
  Dalāʾil al-iʿjāz, 150
  Dār al-ṭirāz fī ʿamal al-muwashshaḥāt, 209, 212
  al-Dhakhīrah fī maḥāsin ahl al-Jazīrah, 201
  al-Durr al-farīd wa-bayt al-qaṣīd, 92
  Ḥalbat al-Kumayt, 21
  Ḥilyat al-muḥāḍarah fī ṣināʿat al-shiʿr, 61, 71, 103, 131, 133–48, 175, 179–83, 199
  al-Ibānah ʿan sariqāt al-Mutanabbī lafẓan wa-maʿnā, 166
  al-Īḍāḥ fī ʿulūm al-balāghah, 129
  Iḥkām ṣanʿat al-kalām, 204
  Ikhwān al-Ṣafāʾ, 50, 94, 132
  al-Intiṣār li-Abī al-Ṭayyib, 204
  Jamharat ansāb al-ʿArab, 199
  Jawāhir al-ādāb wa-dhakhāʾir al-shuʿarāʾ wa-l-kuttāb, 216
  Kitāb al-aghānī, 81, 94, 134
  Kitāb al-ʿayn, 76
  Kitāb Baghdād, 158
  Kitāb al-ḥayawān, 92, 110, 131, 158
  Kitāb al-lumaʿ, 132
  Kitāb al-manthūr wa-l-manẓūm, 91
  Kitāb al-sariqāt al-kabīr, 24
  Kitāb al-ṣināʿatayn, 103
  Kitāb tahdhīb al-alfāẓ, 53
  Mafātīḥ al-ʿulūm, 34
  Majmaʿ al-asrār, 28
  al-Mathal al-sāʾir fī adab al-kātib wa-l-shāʿir, 91
  Miftāḥ al-ʿulūm, 147, 154, 156

Mukhtaṣar al-Saʿd
Sharḥ talkhīṣ kitāb Miftāḥ al-ʿulūm, 154
al-Mumtiʿ, 143
al-Muwashshaḥ fī maʾākhidh al-ʿulamāʾ ʿalā al-shuʿarāʾ, 58
al-Muwāzanah, xiii, 46, 128
Nathr al-naẓm wa-ḥall al-ʿiqd, 20
Nihāyat al-arab fī funūn al-adab, 35
al-Qānūn fī al-ṭibb, 21
Qurāḍat al-dhahab fī naqd ashʿār al-ʿArab, 144–45, 148, 221–22
al-Risālah al-mūḍiḥah, 175–76
Risālah fī sariqāt Abī Tammām, 127
al-Risālah al-Saʿīdiyyah fī al-maʾākhidh al-Kindiyyah min al-maʿānī al-Ṭāʾiyyah, 166
Risālat al-tawābiʿ wa-l-zawābiʿ, 220
Samṭ al-laʾāliʾ fī sharḥ amālī al-Qālī, 199
Sariqāt al-Buḥturī min Abī Tammām, 24
Sariqāt al-Kumayt min al-Qurʾān, 91, 153
Sariqāt al-Mutanabbī wa-mushkil maʿānīhi, 216
Sharḥ al-mukhtār min shiʿr Abī al-Ṭayyib al-Mutanabbī, 215
Sharḥ shiʿr al-Mutanabbī, 223
al-Ṣiḥāḥ fī al-lughah, 36, 244
Sirr al-adab wa-sabk al-dhahab, 215, 246
Ṭabaqāt fuḥūl al-shuʿarāʾ, 76, 110
Ṭawq al-ḥamām, 26
al-ʿUmdah, 71, 91, 144–48, 199
Unique Necklace, The, 201, 210, 245
al-Wasāṭah, xxii, 58, 70, 145, 192, 224–25
al-Wasāṭah bayna al-Mutanabbī wa-khuṣūmihi, 174
Washī al-marqūm fī ḥall al-manẓūm, 20, 154
Yatīmat al-dahr fī maḥāsin ahl al-ʿaṣr, 128

borrowing
Andalusian leniency toward (*istiʿārah*), 203
categories of, 60
in classical Arabic literature, 54
classical debates, 4
comparison of *istiʿārah* and Eastern literary theft, 208
historical perspectives, 50
poetic gifts as obligation, 6
reinterpretations, 8–9
terminologies, 121

borrowing and theft in Arabic literature
debate on borrowing, 10
poetic hospitality, 6
sariqāt as a cultural practice, 5

al-Buḥturī, Abū ʿUbādah, xxi–xxii, 2, 7, 18, 45–47, 71, 74, 90, 101, 107, 111, 123–28, 160–61, 168, 178–85, 192, 195, 204, 207, 220–25, 246
accusations of theft from Abū Tammām, 160
criticism by al-Āmidī, 124
influence on modern Arabic poetry, 127
poetic style and influence, 160

Caesar, 28, 70

canonization
disruption of classical norms, 18
formation of canonical authority, 18
impact on originality, 8, 15, 56, 230
urbanized settings on canonical norms, 36

centers, cultural, 108, 208

classicists, Arab, 1, 3, 4, 5, 15, 17, 203, 238

colonialism, settler, 240–43

competitiveness, in Abbasid literary culture, 52, 106

confiscation (*ihtidām*), xviii, xxiii, 65, 90, 140, 202, 207, 217, 219

contamination, 15, 22–24, 56, 242–43

continuity, 31, 35, 40
and rupture, 2, 17, 35, 102

corpus
al-Buḥturī's, 161
al-Mutanabbī's, 170, 179, 191
of *sariqāt*, x, xviii, 7, 10, 15, 21, 38, 42, 59, 61, 69, 74, 82–83, 87–88, 129, 201, 206
of *wasāṭah*, 17

criticism, xii, 11, 27, 42, 49–50, 61, 68, 70, 73, 87, 110–11, 127, 144–45, 159–60, 190–91, 194, 204, 206, 226
accusations of poetic theft, 158
Andalusian poetic critiques, 208
cultural, 209
dialogic, 18, 233, 238
early, 23, 131, 229
harsh, 46, 196, 220
interplay of originality and borrowing, 206
literary, xix, 42, 73, 87, 120, 129, 131, 133, 145, 156, 159, 162, 169, 209
metacriticism, 42
partiality in, 90
systematic, 109
underpinnings of literary disputes, 159

critics, x, 12, 24, 36, 38, 40, 42, 84–85, 113, 125, 139–40, 156, 159–61, 165, 169, 175, 184–85, 199, 230
bitter, 225
conservative, 181
formidable, 125

critics (cont.)
illustrious, 12
prominent, 50, 101, 108, 168
sharp, 78
sober-minded, 51, 52
tenth-century, xix, 68, 118, 130
twentieth-century, 5, 11
Culler, Jonathan, theory of intertextual discourse, 4
cultural
dynamics, 59, 90, 140
dynamism, 34, 79
economies, 35
environment, 58, 130
exchange, 14, 140
market, xx, 35–37, 48, 62, 72, 90, 127, 130, 139, 170, 190, 200, 215, 220, 223, 227
market inspectors, xxi, 38
market of thefts, 219
market, poetic expressions as commodities, 163
phenomena, 35
pre-Islamic literary standards, 83
production, 15, 20, 35, 37, 110, 198, 208, 220
scene, 48, 101, 108, 204, 236
shared cultural script, xiv, 15, 45, 110, 118, 140, 154
shared cultural script and poetic property, 127
tribal influences, 45, 76, 80
cultural life, 120, 159
Andalusian, 198
eighth-century, 82
cultural tree, xx, 31, 78, 118–19, 128
cultures
Andalusian, 197, 202, 209, 227
Arab, 201, 234
contemporary, 2, 15
dynamic, 57, 63, 206
European (twentieth-century), 57

Darwīsh, Maḥmūd, xii–xiii, 27–36, 70, 230–35, 240–42
literary ancestry in poetry, 27
poems, 28, 231, 242
poetry, 30, 31, 233, 234
use of pre-Islamic themes, 18
Derrida, Jacques
theories on poetic exchange, 10
devices, rhetorical *See also sariqāt*
ijtilāb (procuring support), xviii, 77, 92, 131, 135–36, 139, 146, 222
distinction
battle for, 66, 119, 158, 194, 243
drive for poetic excellence, ix, xviii, 44, 57, 85, 125
and hiding replication, 147
in the marketplace, 109
Dīwān group, 10–11, 69, 112

emulation (*iḥtidhā'*), xx, 52, 54, 68, 80, 93, 126, 129, 150, 207, 224
epistemic shifts, 4, 19, 21, 53, 55, 101, 118, 122, 125, 131, 132, 156, 159
key periods and theorists, 121
from *qadīm* to *muḥdath* in Arabic poetry, 162
ethics, Islamic, 247
exchange, poetic
gift-giving, 7–9
theory of *murāfadah*, 6, 138
exchanges, geographical
Ibn Bassām's observations on cultural periphery, 201
movement of poets and texts between East and West, 201

al-Farazdaq, 58, 61, 86, 92, 103, 106, 137, 138, 223
al-Fārisī, Abū ʿAlī, x, 14, 44, 51, 135–36, 161, 165, 175, 181
flank, Eastern, xxii–xxiii, 197, 201, 209, 211, 215, 219, 220–21, 223, 226, 229, 230
flaying (*salkh*), technique of rewording, xviii, 54, 65, 92–93, 131, 133, 150, 152, 156, 226
as reprehensible plagiarism, 129
forgery (*waḍʿ*, *intiḥāl*)
detection by philologists, 76
in early Arabic poetry, 77
form, literary, integration of colloquial and Romance language, 210

Genette, Gérard
hypotext theory, 44, 85, 113, 235, 241
transtextuality in poetics, xviii, 7, 13, 116
genres, Arabic poetry
amatory prelude, 96–97
lampooning and satire, 120
panegyric(s), 10, 84, 98, 120, 153, 195, 224, 227
gifts, poetic, xvi–xvii, 6–10, 138–39

Habermas, Jürgen, 119
ḥadāthah movement, 163

al-Hamadhānī, ʿAbd al-Raḥmān, 23, 53–54, 62, 67–69, 83, 104, 121, 144, 150, 168, 200
al-Ḥamdānī, Abū Firās, xiv–xvi, 172–73, 174–75, 184
al-Ḥātimī, Abū al-Ḥasan, xxii–xxiii, 38, 44, 48, 91, 92, 99, 103, 118, 129, 131–32, 133–48, 156, 162, 164–67, 174–92, 199, 206–8, 211, 219, 227
  Ḥilyat al-muḥāḍarah fī ṣināʿat al-shiʿr. See books
  role in terminological classifications, 199
  role in the vilification of prominent poets, 179
ḥirfat al-adab, xxi, 119–20, 122
hypotext and hypertext, 2, 13, 113
  theory. *See* Genette, Gérard

Ibn ʿAbd Rabbihi, xxiii, 201, 206, 210, 215, 219, 224, 228, 245
Ibn al-ʿAmīd, 83, 183, 187
Ibn al-Aʿrābī, 45, 99
Ibn ʿĀshūr, 217
Ibn al-Athīr, Ḍiyāʾ al-Dīn, xxii, 20, 64, 91, 95, 111–12, 128–29, 148, 153–54, 156–57
Ibn Aydamir (Aydamur), Muḥammad al-Mustaʿṣimī, 91–92, 244
Ibn Baqī, 213–14, 246
Ibn Bassām al-Shantirīnī, xxii–xxiii, 201–10, 215–17, 221, 227, 229
  compilation of *al-Dhakhīrah*, 202
  criteria for poetic quality, 202
  notable quotes and applications, 206
  treatment of poetic theft and originality, 203
  The Unique Necklace. See books
  value as criterion in poetics, 203
Ibn al-Dahhān, Abū Muḥammad Saʿīd b. Mubārak, 166, 172, 196
Ibn al-Fāriḍ, ʿUmar, 96–97
Ibn Ḥabīb, Yūnus, 53, 78, 81, 92, 101
Ibn al-Ḥajjāj, 177
Ibn Harmah, 101, 108, 111
Ibn Ḥazm, Abū Muḥammad ʿAlī b. Aḥmad b. Saʿīd, 26, 199, 208, 228–29
Ibn al-Iflīlī, xxiii, 204–5, 220–27
Ibn Jaʿfar, Qudāmah, 159
Ibn Jinnī, Abū al-Fatḥ ʿUthmān, 189, 193, 217
Ibn Manẓūr, 56
Ibn al-Muʿtazz, 126–27, 149, 207, 212–13, 223
Ibn al-Qāriḥ, 188
Ibn Qutaybah, 66, 72–73, 83, 87–89, 91–94, 98, 102, 105, 119, 129–31, 150, 155, 163, 168, 244–45
  arguments on creativity and shared themes, 168
Ibn al-Rabīb, 228
Ibn Rashīq, xxii–xxiii, 14, 40, 50, 71, 88–92, 99, 129, 131, 134, 136, 148, 152, 156, 174, 188, 199–206, 216, 221–23, 236
  terminology on poetic theft, 200
Ibn al-Rūmī, 69, 202
Ibn Sanāʾ al-Mulk, 209–10, 214, 231, 246
Ibn Sharaf, 188, 199–200, 209, 219, 225
  comparison to Ibn Rashīq's theories, 199
  critique of plagiarism, 200
Ibn Shuhayd, Abū ʿĀmir Aḥmad b. ʿAbd al-Malik, 204–6, 220, 224, 227
Ibn Ṭabāṭabā al-ʿAlawī, xvi, 47, 59, 68, 74, 89, 98, 104, 118, 127, 145, 153, 159, 161, 163, 174, 190, 192
  on poetic themes and ownership, 161
Ibn Ṭayfūr, Ṭāhir, 44, 46, 67, 87, 91–92, 145, 162
Ibn Thābit, Ḥassān, 74, 93, 106
Ibn al-Walīd, Muslim, 48, 72, 94, 101, 111, 126, 134, 159
Ibn Wakīʿ, 49, 145, 164–65, 171, 174, 187–92, 197, 225–26
  and al-Ḥātimī, 191
Ibn Zaydūn, Abū al-Walīd Aḥmad, xxiii, 206–7
  borrowing from Abū al-ʿAlāʾ al-Ma ʿarrī, 207
  evaluation by Ibn Bassām, 207
influence, urban, canonical impact, 36
infringements, textual, 232, 233
intelligence, artificial, ix, xxiii, 197, 238–39
interaction, 57, 88, 113, 209
interrelations, 55, 57
intertexts, xix, 33, 231
  differentiation from intertextuality, 3
intertextuality, x, xxi–xxii, 2–5, 10, 12–14, 17, 24, 26, 33, 35–36, 40, 82, 105, 112, 162, 196, 203, 239–40, 243
  adab, economics of, 48
  in the economics of borrowing, 48
  historical context, 73
  historical implications, 5
  poetic discourse as a shared cultural space, 206, 233, 237
  and presence of prior texts on creativity, 169
  reader-author relationship, 4

intertextuality (cont.)
  textual borrowing techniques, 64, 105, 138
  theories and applications, 162
  theories on reading, 3
intervention, xiv, 14, 27, 49, 57, 111, 129–30, 134, 156, 170, 173, 188, 197, 206, 210, 212, 223
invented meanings, xi, 46, 68, 144–45, 169, 179–80
  and virgin meanings (*al-maʿānī al-ʿuqm*), 137
al-Iṣfahānī, Abū al-Faraj, 65, 81, 94, 132–34

al-Jāḥiẓ, Abū ʿUthmān ʿAmr b. Baḥr, poetic textual navigation in *Kitāb al-ḥayawān*, 110
al-Jawharī, Abū al-Naṣr Ismāʿīl b. Ḥammād, 36, 42, 121, 244
al-Jumaḥī, Ibn Sallām, xx–xxi, 51–54, 66, 71–89, 92, 98–101, 107, 111, 131, 136–37
  contributions to poetic theory, 79
  ranking of poets, 110
  Ṭabaqāt fuḥūl al-shuʿarāʾ. *See* books
al-Jurjānī, ʿAbd al-Qāhir, xxi, 23, 53–54, 83, 96, 112, 128, 131
  emphasis on *muḥādhāt*, 96
  impact on Arabic poetics, 150
  theory of *naẓm* (compositional structure), 70
al-Jurjānī, al-Qāḍī ʿAlī b. ʿAbd al-ʿAzīz, x–xi, xix, xxi–xxii, 36, 47–48, 56, 65, 70–72, 83–85, 90, 98, 99, 105, 117–18, 128, 131, 136, 142–52, 156, 159–61, 168, 174, 181, 190, 200, 203, 206, 221, 239
  contributions to poetic theory, 36–37
  critique of grammarians and linguists, 90, 131
  his *sariqāt* foundational remarks, x
  naẓm, 83
  theories on shared meanings vs. theft, 88, 159
  al-Wasāṭah. *See* books

kalām (discourse), 44, 121, 123, 143, 145, 147, 162
  in defining authorship, 121
  and shared use in poetic production, 136
kalām al-ʿArab
  Ibn Ṭayfūr, 44, 65
  as interfused space, 44
Khālidī Brothers, 193–94
  sariqāt controversy, 185
  and al-Sarī al-Raffāʾ, 193
kharjah as a defining feature of *muwashshaḥāt*, 210–15
  Dār al-ṭirāz fī ʿamal al-muwashshaḥāt. *See* books
  history, 210
  shaking up plagiarism paradigms, xxiii
Khouri, Elias, xiii, 33
  and the idea of poetic ancestry, 32
al-Khubzarzī, Abū al-Qāsim Naṣr b. Aḥmad, 199, 219
knowledge, tabulation of, 94, 140
  and Arabic literary theory, 51, 81
  epistemological shift, 109, 159
  notable contributors, 94, 99, 152
Kristeva, Julia, 16, 49, 239
  ethics of intertextuality, 4
  theory of intertextuality, 5

language
  Arabic, 25, 31, 189
  Turkish, 56
laṭīf al-saraq, x, 24, 60
literariness, 42–43, 101, 122, 167
al-Maʿarrī, Abū al-ʿAlāʾ, 27, 65, 179, 207, 209
  his superb *talfīq*, 221
  his writing on al-Mutanabbī, 193
  Ibn Rashīq's praise, 236

Margoliouth, David Samuel, xx, 51, 77–78, 93, 136
  debate with Charles Lyall, 81
  theories on pre-Islamic poetry, 77
marketplace
  competitive, 48, 105
  and literary patronage, 122
al-Marzubānī, 86, 91–92, 128
  and criticism, 86
  significant anthology, 58
Mauss, Marcel, xvi
  theory of reciprocity, 10
al-Māzinī, Ibrāhīm ʿAbd al-Qādir, 10–14, 39, 51, 57, 74, 112
  assimilation of romantic literature, 11
  literary memory and borrowing, 13
meaning, poetic (*maʿnā*), 5, 64, 67, 137, 150, 152, 157, 197
  shared and poetic meaning, 151
meanings, virgin. *See also maʿānī ʿuqm*
  and the concept of inventiveness, 137
misreading, as literary technique, 59
movement, free verse, 40

al-Mubarrad, Muḥammad b. Yazīd, 136, 244–45
  and his disciples, 229
al-Muhallabī, Abū Muḥammad, 176, 178, 182–85
  al-Ḥātimī's vainglory, 182
  debate, 176
  his court. *See* assemblies, literary
muḥdathūn (modernists)
  relationship to classical works, 85
  views on originality, 192
al-Mutanabbī, Abū al-Ṭayyib, x–xvi, xxii–xxiii, 7, 34, 39, 51, 65, 70–71, 74, 105, 114, 128–32, 136–38, 145, 156–57, 159, 162–97, 199, 202–9, 215–29, 234, 236
  accusation of poetic theft, 199
  allegations of plagiarism, 159
  attacks on, 145, 165
  criticism by Ibn Sharaf, 199
  defense strategy, 162
  detractors, 170, 172, 174, 193
  innovations in Arabic poetry, 169
  al-Qāḍī al-Fāḍil's explanation of his popularity, 157
  shurūḥ of his *dīwān*, xxiii, 223, 224, 227
  and stylistic expressiveness, 180
  and *talfīq*, 40
  al-Tha'ālibī's chapter on, 195
muwashshaḥ(āt), xxiii, 208–14, 215, 231–33, 235

al-Nahshalī, 'Abd al-Karīm, 143–45, 208
al-Naḥwī, Ibn al-Sarrāj al Shantarīnī, 216–19
al-Nāmī, Abū al-'Abbās, 48, 165, 171, 191
navigation, textual, 5, 91, 129, 158
nostalgia, poetic, xi, 33, 116, 242
novels
  Awlād al-Ghītū: ismī Ādām, 26–28
  Qindīl Umm Hāshim, 25

ode(s), pre-Islamic
  Abū Nuwās's departure, 117
  as the canon, 28
  changing applications, 97, 116, 242
  as a hypotext, 241
  Imru' al-Qays, 28, 30, 117
  originality, 96
  Sir Chalres Lyall's logical inference, 77
  Ṭāhā Ḥusayn's skepticism, 51

parody
  and intertextuality, 33
  use in Arabic literature, 114, 115

patronage
  and debates, 122
  examples from classical Arabic culture, 7, 19
  impact on creative freedom, 27
  al-Muhallabī's Ḥātimī, 167
  Sayf al-Dawlah's al-Mutanabbī, 165
patterns, compositional, 153, 184, 190
period, classical, 246–47
philologists
  in literary criticism, 46
  al-Qāḍī al-Jurjānī's critique, 48
  role in authentication, 81, 86
  tenth-century, 24
philology
  key figures, 14, 24, 36, 103
  presence in Arabic literary criticism, 73
plagiarism, 1, 4, 10, 15, 42, 45, 46, 49–51, 54, 59, 89, 101, 109–10, 111–14, 122–23, 128–29, 131, 134, 151, 153, 157–62, 167–68, 190–91, 192, 196, 198, 200, 216, 218, 223, 225–27
  accusations of major figures, xv, 21, 40, 167, 183
  classical debates on theft, 24, 38
  corpus of, 7, 192
  debates in Arabic criticism, 48, 69–70
  and intertextuality, 12, 15, 18, 40
  misapplication, 40, 47, 50, 92
  ownership, cultural and legal implications, 23, 107
  property and ownership, 20, 150
  rubric of, 17
  structuralist reinterpretations, 2
  types of accusations. *See sariqāt*
poetics, Arabic, 113, 200, 211
  borrowing classifications, 10
  classical originality and imitation, 5
  urban influence on poetic expression, 36
poetry. *See also adab*; *sariqāt*; theft
  amatory, 98, 153
  ancient, xx, 33, 52, 61, 78, 100, 126, 130, 136
  Andalusian, 220, 226, 230
  Arabic, xiii, 25, 39, 42, 69, 77–78, 112, 160, 195
  canons of, 46, 47
  classical Arabic, 210
  collections of, 50, 78
  contrafactional, 58
  craft of, 123, 135, 144, 172, 174, 189
  early Islamic, 84, 121, 244
  and feuds, 58
  issue of originality, 8

poetry (cont.)
modern, 236
modernist, 130
Palestinian, 231
popular, 21
pre-Islamic, xi–xii, 2, 77, 82, 85, 92, 100, 110, 111, 131
ṣa'ālīk (vagabond), 111
transmitters of, 81, 90, 205
twentieth century, 56, 82
poets, tenth-century, 65
prelude
amatory, 96
Birwah immortalized in Darwīsh's "The Birwah Prelude," 240–42
property, ix, xiii, xvii, xxi–xxii, 2, 6, 8, 15, 18, 20, 40, 61–68, 82, 88, 99–102, 107, 118–19, 127, 130, 144, 150, 160, 173, 194, 196–97, 209, 215, 238–40
prose
and navigation between poetry and prose, 20, 54, 67, 132, 153, 186, 190, 203
the rise of the chancery, 96, 157
publicity in literature, marketplaces for literary fame, 107

al-Qabrī, Muḥammad b. Maḥmūd, 210
al-Qāḍī al-Fāḍil, 62, 96, 156, 195
al-Qāḍī al-Jurjānī *see* al-Jurjānī, al-Qāḍī 'Alī b. 'Abd al-'Azīz
al-Qālī, Ismā'īl b. al-Qāsim Abū 'Alī, 201–2, 205, 223
al-Qarṭājannī, Ḥāzim, xxii, 200, 202, 222–23
transactional categories, 197
a turn in the plagiarism discussion, 222
value as an economic criterion, 163
al-Qays, Imru' (Imru' al-Qays), xi–xiii, 25, 27–30, 33, 36, 38, 65, 70, 71–77, 93, 101, 116–17, 138, 145, 180–81, 223, 241
initiating the convention of the nostalgic prelude, xiii
al-Qazwīnī, Jalāl al-Dīn Muḥammad (al-Khaṭīb al-Dimashqī), 91, 148
and the new line in *sariqāt* criticism, 151–54

al-Raffā', al-Sarī, 37, 171, 193–94
reception, in *adab*, 21, 52, 203
redirection (*naql*), xviii, 140, 147, 163, 202, 206
use in Arabic literary criticism, 163
refraction of theme (*naẓar*), 81, 137, 140, 143, 207, 217
repetitiveness, inevitability in poetics, 5, 44, 50
rhetoric, in classical poetry, 44
rhyming, internal, 209–10
Riffaterre, Michael, 15, 240
intertext vs intertextuality, 3
role of the reader, 13
Romanticism, European, 11, 76, 140, 238

Sābūr, Ḥammād b., 99, 110
al-Rāwiyah, 100
suspected of *inḥāl* and *intiḥāl*, 109, 136
al-Ṣafadī, Ibn Aybak, 56, 196
report on Ṣāḥib b. 'Abbād's *karārīs* (booklets), 185
al-Ṣāḥib, Ibn 'Abbād, 83–84, 166, 174, 186–87
criticism of al-Mutanabbī's poetry, 184
al-Sakkākī, Abū Ya'qūb Yūsuf. *See* books: *Miftāḥ al-'ulūm*
al-Samā', Abū Bakr 'Ubādah b. Mā', 208–9, 210
saraq, ix, xii, xviii–xxiii, 5–7, 10–11, 35, 44, 47, 49–51, 58, 61–62, 77, 82–92, 98, 100, 101–7, 112, 120–21, 124, 126, 129, 135–47, 148–52, 156–64, 173, 178, 181–82, 184–85, 188, 191–97, 199, 200, 205–12, 217–33, 237–40, *See also laṭīf al-saraq*
accusations of, 49, 50, 90, 136, 212
discreet, 98, 205
kathīr al-saraq (excessive plagiarism), 47
al-saraq al-ṣaḥīḥ, xiii, 123, 168, *See also* al-Āmidī
sariqah, 38, 52, 54, 59, 63, 66, 88, 90, 92–93, 128, 131, 149, 153, 173, 208
sariqāt
and *adab* theorizations, 51
centrality to poetic criticism, 130
in classical Arabic poetics, 58
critical responses, 175
definitions, 3, 10, 29, 58, 101, 222
key theorists and works, 128
lexicon, xiv, 11, 14, 113, 155, 207, 219
significance in literary criticism, 42
terminology, xviii, xx
theoretical foundations, 122
Sayf al-Dawlah, xiv, 135, 165, 171–79, 182–85, 190–93
assembly of. *See* assemblies, literary
role in fostering poetic debate, 175
script, shared, xiii–xv, xix, xxiii, 92–93, 121, 206, 229
self-aggrandizement
in poetic tradition, 111

response by critics, 112
Shakespeare, William, 1, 73
view of canonization, 35
Shukrī, ʿAbd al-Raḥmān, 10–14, 39, 112
al-Sīrāfī, Abū Saʿīd, 103, 165–66, 178
space
competitive, 7, 20, 49, 50, 53, 61
discursive, x, xix, xxii, 4, 121, 129, 221, 239
integrated, 221
intertextual, xii, 15–20, 35, 49, 68, 74, 163, 206, 208, 211, 235–39
textual, xi, 6, 19, 63, 65, 70, 115, 127, 135, 234, 235
speech, figures of, 84, 132, 135, 148, 149, 151, 152, 160
Sufism, and Arabic literary theory, 96
al-Ṣūlī, Abū Bakr, 98, 129–30, 141, 163, 192
Akhbār Abī Tammām, 19
Dīwān Abī Nuwās, 98
early contributions to *sariqāt* repository, 129

al-Ṭāʾī, Ḥabīb b. Aws. *See* Abū Tammām
talmīḥ (allusion), 152, 154
tawārud (coincidental correspondence), 61, 144, 152, 168, 193
Ṭayfūr, Ibn Abī al-Ṭāhir, xv, 5, 65, *See also* Ibn Ṭayfūr
accusations of Abū Tammām, 159
discursive space in classical poetics, 4
interfused discursivity, 44
al-Thaʿālibī, Abū Manṣūr, xxi, 95, 104, 120, 149, 153, 169, 177, 183, 187–90, 195
his chapter on al-Mutanabbī, 128, 172–73
theft
accusations of, xv, xvi, 12, 41, 58, 62, 74, 82, 107, 108, 206, 211, 215–16
allegations levied against al-Mutanabbī, 49, 166
al-Buḥturī's, 125
economies of, 88, 147, 152, 208, 210
indiscernible, 93, 133, 143, 153
as a literary marketplace dynamic, 52
poetic, 10, 154
theme
common, 149
poetic, 88, 137, 151, 163, 180, 192, 202, 235
thievery
literary, 5, 87, 197, 202
terminology, development and applications, 163, 182, 199
traditions
Arabic, 1, 51, 79, 230, 240
classical, xv, 2, 16, 24, 39, 70, 112, 235
poetic, x, xii, xiii–xv, 1, 78, 100, 140, 235
transactions, poetic, 7, 9, 36
transcendence, textual, 3
transference, 96, 98, 133, 148, 152, 155, 163, 182
transformations, cultural, 55, 94, 147
translation, 12, 13
cross-cultural influence in Arabic novels, 22
mistranslation, 113
from Turkish and Persian, 56
transmission, xx, 51, 79–82, 88, 92, 98–101, 108–10, 196, 201, 209, 223
role of *ruwāt* (transmitters), 15, 80, 81, 85, 100, 109
transmission, of texts
dissemination of poetic knowledge, 201
influence of Eastern poets in Andalusia, 199
role of Abū ʿAlī al-Qālī, 199
Ṭūqān, Fadwā, 115
adaptations of classical poetry, 116
Lan abkī, 116

ʿUlayyān, Muṣṭafā, 224
critiquing al-Iflīlī, 224

wording
as a domain for inventiveness, 66
and expressiveness, 5, 23

al-Yaman, Waḍḍāḥ, literary legacy, 28, 30, 110, 122

For EU product safety concerns, contact us at Calle de José Abascal, 56–1°, 28003 Madrid, Spain or eugpsr@cambridge.org.

www.ingramcontent.com/pod-product-compliance
Lightning Source LLC
LaVergne TN
LVHW011803060526
838200LV00053B/3663